JONATHAN SWIFT

A Collection of Critical Essays

Edited by
Claude Rawson

Prentice Hall, Englewood Cliffs, New Jersey 07632

Library of Congress Cataloging-in-Publication Data

Jonathan Swift : a collection of critical essays / edited by Claude
   Rawson.
      p.   cm. — (New century views)
      Includes bibliographical references.
      ISBN 0–13–091299–9
      1. Swift, Jonathan, 1667–1745—Criticism and interpretation.
   I. Rawson, Claude Julien.   II. Series.
   PR3727. J635   1995
   828′.509—dc20   94–4782
                                                         CIP

Acquisitions editor: Alison Reeves
Editorial assistant: Lee Mamunas
Editoral/production supervision and
   interior design: Joan Powers
Cover design: Karen Salzbach
Copy editor: Garland Scott Pass
Production coordinator: Tricia Kenny

Printed in the United States of America
10   9   8   7   6   5   4   3   2   1

ISBN 0-13-091299-9

Prentice-Hall International (UK) Limited, *London*
Prentice-Hall of Australia Pty. Limited, *Sydney*
Prentice-Hall Canada Inc., *Toronto*
Prentice-Hall Hispanoamericana, S.A., *Mexico*
Prentice-Hall of India Private Limited, *New Delhi*
Prentice-Hall of Japan, Inc., *Tokyo*
Simon & Schuster Asia Pte. Ltd., *Singapore*
Editora Prentice-Hall do Brasil, Ltda., *Rio de Janeiro*

Contents

NB

Introduction

Claude Rawson

Jonathan Swift was born in Dublin on 30 November 1667, of English parents. His father died before he was born and Swift was supported by relatives in Dublin. He attended Kilkenny School, the best school in Ireland, from about 1674 to 1682, and Trinity College, Ireland's only university institution at that time, from 1682 to 1686. In 1689 he went to live at Moor Park in Surrey, the household of Sir William Temple, a retired diplomat and author, serving as his secretary, with two long interruptions, until Temple's death in 1699. It was towards the end of this period that Swift probably wrote most of *A Tale of a Tub* (not published until 1704). Swift never publicly owned the *Tale*, perhaps his most brilliant and certainly his most difficult book. Though intended as a defense of the Anglican Church against its Roman Catholic and Dissenting enemies, it was perceived by some Anglicans as an irreligious and subversive work, and Swift believed that this reputation later blocked his preferment to high office in the Church.

Career disappointments were from the beginning an obsessive topic for Swift. Though he remained loyal to Temple, he was already embittered by his lack of advancement under Temple's patronage. In 1694, he left Moor Park for a time and took orders, acquiring his first parish at Kilroot, near Belfast, in 1695. He was unhappy in a largely Presbyterian district, and had an inconclusive attachment with Jane Waring, a young Belfast woman. The most important attachment of his life was with Esther Johnson (1681–1728), the daughter of Temple's housekeeper, whom he met at Moor Park when she was a young girl. Swift directed her reading, and there developed between them a close bond, the intimacy and depth of which are reflected in the playful letters we know as the *Journal to Stella* and the series of poems he later wrote on her birthdays and some other occasions. These expressions of tender friendship are the closest Swift ever came to writing love poems.

The name Stella was taken from Sidney's famous sequence, and the gruff compliments Swift paid to Stella's beauties of body and mind belong to a tradition of love-poetry which Swift generally derided in his other writings. The famous "excremental poems," with their jeering reminder that "Celia, Celia, Celia shits," may be seen as the parodic obverse of the poems to Stella: very different in tone, but sharing the same view that it is not on bodily beauty, which

1

soon fades, but on moral and intellectual qualities, that true and lasting friendships, between men and women as between men and men, are founded. The nature of Swift's friendship with Stella is not fully understood. Some have thought they were secretly married. The night she died, on 28 January 1728, Swift wrote a prose memorial to her which begins:

> This day, being Sunday, January 28th, 1727–8, about eight o'clock at night, a servant brought me a note, with an account of the death of the truest, most virtuous, and valuable friend, that I, or perhaps any other person ever was blessed with. She expired about six in the evening of this day; and, as soon as I am left alone, which is about eleven at night, I resolve, for my own satisfaction, to say something of her life and character.
>
> She was born at Richmond in Surrey on the thirteenth day of March, in the year 1681. Her father was a younger brother of a good family in Nottinghamshire, her mother of a lower degree; and indeed she had little to boast of her birth. I knew her from six years old, and had some share in her education, by directing what books she should read, and perpetually instructing her in the principles of honour and virtue; from which she never swerved in any one action or moment of her life. She was sickly from her childhood until about the age of fifteen: But then grew into perfect health, and was looked upon as one of the most beautiful, graceful, and agreeable young women in London, only a little too fat. Her hair was blacker than a raven, and every feature of her face in perfection . . . .
>
> (*Works*, V, 227)

This has a stunned factuality, heightened rather than diminished by the rueful jokeyness which, in the second paragraph, offers the traditional superlatives of love-poetry modified by a gentle corrective realism, as though the parodic impulse needed even here to be given its head. It is perhaps the most intimate and unguardedly broken-hearted statement he ever made.

The friendship with Stella followed a pattern which has been traced in Swift's other relations with women, especially that with Esther Vanhomrigh (Vanessa, a name Swift seems to have given to the language), in which a strong teacher–pupil element acted as a kind of catalyst for a sexual rapport full of mystification and teasing secrecy. As with Stella, Swift taught Vanessa the lesson that mind, not beauty, is the surest foundation of love, and expressed his dismay at social conventions which treated women alternately as goddesses and as decorative idiots. On this topic, Swift, commonly perceived as misogynistic, was ahead of his time in promulgating the notion that women deserved educating in the same way as men, and were capable (more or less) of the same intellectual attainments.

Vanessa fell violently in love with her tutor, and Swift wrote about this in *Cadenus and Vanessa* (Cadenus is an anagram for *decanus* or dean), in which an older man is taken aback by the love of a beautiful young woman, who learned from his own lessons to love those qualities of intellect which distinguished both her and him from the shallow lovers of social or poetic convention. It is a repellent poem, at once self-castigating and archly defensive, and unaccountably admired by some revisionist feminist ideologues. Swift is more often and more predictably denounced for his supposed disgust at the Celias, Chloes, and Corinnas whose bodily functions are a source of dismay to the brainless Strephons of his later poems. As with Stella, the full facts of the relationship are unknown. Swift and Vanessa met in 1707 or 1708. They probably broke in 1722, and Vanessa died the following year. *Cadenus and Vanessa* was probably written around 1713, but not published until 1726.

During the years 1699–1710 Swift held a series of appointments and livings in the Church of Ireland (i.e., the Anglican Church in Ireland). He traveled to England and wrote several pamphlets and essays on religious and ecclesiastical topics, concerned with the place of dissenting sects in the state, with Occasional Conformity and the Sacramental Test, and with the privileges and respect he considered the Church and its ministers to be entitled to. In all these, he showed himself a jealous guardian of the interests of the established national church, against both secular and doctrinal encroachments. His writings included *The Sentiments of a Church-of-England Man, With Respect to Religion and Government* (1704?, published 1711), perhaps the most comprehensive summary of his main tenets, the brilliant ironic fantasy *An Argument against Abolishing Christianity* (1708, published 1711), and *A Project for the Advancement of Religion* (1709), an important statement sometimes wishfully read as ironic. He became friendly with Addison and Steele, and helped the latter to start the *Tatler*, which printed two of Swift's best-known early poems, "A Description of the Morning" and "A Description of a City-Shower." Although Swift was early aligned with the Whig lords whom he defended in the *Contests and Dissensions in Athens and Rome* (1701; their leader Lord Somers was also a dedicatee of *A Tale of a Tub*, but was later to be attacked in Swift's Tory writings), his ecclesiastical allegiances were closer to a Tory view of the prerogatives of the Church, and in the period 1710–1714 he became identified with the moderate Tory-led government of Robert Harley, created Earl of Oxford in 1711.

The years 1710–1714 were the only period in Swift's entire career when he was close to the center of political power. He wrote tirelessly on behalf of the Harley ministry, becoming editor of the *Examiner* in 1710, and going on to write a series of important pamphlets defending the policy of peace with France, against opposition charges that the government was throwing away the victories of Marlborough and betraying Britain's allies in the War of Spanish Succession. Among the most important writings of this period were the *Short Character of Thomas Earl of Wharton* (1710), an exceptionally witty and vitriolic attack; *The Conduct of the Allies* (1711); two attacks on Steele, *The Importance of the Guardian Considered* (1713) and *The Publick Spirit of the Whigs* (1714), which ended a friendship and literary collaboration under pressure of divided loyalties and party-political hostility; and the parody *Mr. Collins's Discourse of Free-Thinking, Put into Plain English, by Way of Abstract, for the Use of the Poor* (1713), one of his lesser-known but highly accomplished ironic works.

The most substantial preferment Swift achieved in the Church came in 1713, when he was made Dean of St. Patrick's Cathedral in Dublin. He had hoped to be made a bishop, and in England rather than Ireland, and felt that this disappointing promotion was due to the Queen's hostility, and to influential disapproval of supposed irreligious tendencies in *A Tale of a Tub*. Queen Anne died in 1714, and with her death ended the Tory administration to which Swift's (and Pope's) political fortunes were closely tied. From then on, Swift was almost uninterruptedly in political opposition, living mostly in Ireland, with rare visits to England. His Irish writings mainly belong to the period after 1719, as do *Gulliver's Travels* and the bulk of his best poetry.

Swift was increasingly afflicted with what we now understand to have been Ménière's syndrome, a disease of the inner ear which causes dizziness. Swift did not understand the symptoms, feared madness and believed himself to be going mad. He was not. In his seventies, however, he became senile, and was declared of unsound mind in 1742. The mythology of his madness, partly self-generated, has sometimes been linked with a supposed "Juvenalian" intensity in his writings. Both terms of the connection derive from misunderstandings, and Samuel Johnson's statement, in the *Vanity of Human Wishes*, that Swift expired "a Driv'ler and a Show," is coloured by an antipathy which perhaps tells us more about some deep resemblances between these two pessimistic conservative temperaments than about the factual realities of Swift's case. Swift died on 19 October 1745.

A Tale of a Tub, with its two appendages, the *Battle of the Books* and the *Discourse Concerning the Mechanical Operation of the Spirit*, is Swift's first important prose work and perhaps his most brilliant. It appeared anonymously. Indeed, most of Swift's major prose writings, including the *Drapier's Letters*, *Gulliver's Travels*, and *A Modest Proposal*, appeared anonymously or pseudonymously. The reasons doubtless had to do with his temperamental guardedness, his penchant for mystification, and a residual sense that it was ungentlemanly to appear by name in the public prints. But there was also a well-founded anxiety over legal sanctions and career setbacks, since all his works contained elements that might seem politically subversive or personally offensive to powerful interests. But the *Tale* was never publicly acknowledged in any way, and did not in his lifetime appear in authorized editions of his collected works, as *Gulliver's Travels*, for example, did: indeed, the major 1735 edition of his *Works* was used by Swift to bring out a carefully revised and extended version of *Gulliver's Travels*, while retaining the formal pretense of pseudonymity.

The *Tale* was a special case. Swift was extremely proud of it, and jealously irritated when he saw it, or parts of it, ascribed to others. He is said later in life to have exclaimed: "Good God! what a genius I had when I wrote that book." It was composed mainly in the 1690s, when Swift lived in the household of Sir William Temple, although it did not appear until 1704. Its final form, in which it is now generally read, was not arrived at until the fifth edition of 1710.

The *Tale*, along with the *Battle of the Books*, was perhaps the most impressive English contribution to the so-called quarrel of the Ancients and Moderns. The history or prehistory of this *querelle* (it is most familiarly referred to in its

French form) can be traced back to the Renaissance. The sense of intellectual and cultural liberation generated by the rediscovery and publication of the philosophers and poets of Greece and Rome also engendered a questioning of assumptions about the value of the classical models which helped to bring it about. Were these to be thought of as unsurpassable masterpieces, which modern writers could only hope to imitate from a distance? Or were modern achievements capable of excelling them, if they hadn't excelled them already (perhaps by accepting the old models and improving on them, like dwarfs standing on the shoulders of giants, an image often used; or by striking out in new directions, for example, in experimental science)?

The debate may now seem dated, but it brought into relief many contested issues and unresolved tensions which have reappeared in other forms since that time: between science and religion (since scientific enquiry probed into aspects of nature that God chose to keep secret, and since the discourse of scientific causality might seem to challenge a belief in God as creator of all things); between science and poetry, with its traditional links with a humanistic culture steeped in the Graeco-Roman past; between poets whose work failed to live up to or repudiated these associations, and those who, like Swift and Pope, were profoundly attached to them; between "specialists," technicians, poets who wrote for gain or for party, scholars who delivered pedantic discourses or annotated ancient texts, and a classically schooled patrician élite, including writers who (again like Swift and Pope) did not belong to it by birth but were loyal to its values and aspirations. The gentlemanly tradition of the *honnête homme* prided itself especially on its civilized knowledge "both of *Books* and *Humankind*," and its freedom from the narrow specialist vision of a Bentley, as portrayed in the *Battle of the Books*. Bentley, one of the towering figures in the history of classical scholarship, might in real life know a great deal more about the classics than any gentleman preening himself on his classical taste, but he was a Modern by virtue of his professional expertise in textual criticism and in ancient history. (For the sake of clarity, I use "Ancient" and "Modern", with capital letters, to mean participants in the dispute, and the lowercased forms to indicate chronological difference: thus, in the *Battle of the Books*, Virgil is both an Ancient and an ancient, Temple an Ancient and a modern, and Bentley a Modern and a modern.)

The English "Battle of the Books" (Swift's phrase has been appropriated in an important book by Joseph M. Levine as well as in John F. Tinkler's essay in this volume) reorientated the debate into one more concerned with the antagonistic perspectives of the "professional scholar and . . . the occasional man of letters" than with "moderns and ancients" as such. When Swift's patron Temple initiated the English debate in his "Essay upon the Ancient and Modern Learning" (1690), claiming that the moral and literary superiority of the Ancients was evidenced by the *Epistles of Phalaris* and the *Fables* of Aesop, "the two most ancient that I know of in prose," Bentley was able to demonstrate that both works were spurious and of a later date. He didn't presume to enter into the debate on literary merits, though he opined in passing that the high place accorded to those two authors was "criticism of a peculiar complexion," which "must proceed from a singularity of palate and judgement."

Bentley's remark deftly imputes to his patrician opponents the kind of perverse oddity of judgment which the latter would more readily ascribe to him. The English "Battle" was indeed one which not only pitted literary taste against pedantic expertise but exploited a rhetoric of gentlemanly superiority against boorish positiveness and "singularity." On the main scholarly issues, the case of the Ancients was in tatters, but the argument came to be seen as one in which patrician wits, including non-patrician allies like Swift, exposed the vulgarity of low-bred pedants like Bentley and his ally, the Anglican clergyman William Wotton. In Swift's *Battle*, the scholar Scaliger (a modern Ancient) berates Bentley for his boorishness:

> "*Thy* Learning *makes thee more* Barbarous, *thy Study of* Humanity, *more* Inhuman; . . . *All Arts of* civilizing *others, render thee* rude *and* untractable; Courts *have taught thee* Ill Manners, *and* Polite Conversation *has finish'd thee a* Pedant."

The passage is modeled on Odysseus's speech to Thersites in Book II of the *Iliad*. In another epic passage, near the end, Wotton hurls a lance at Temple, which hits his belt: but Temple "neither felt the Weapon touch him, nor heard it fall," a lofty ignoring so absolute that it resolves itself into a withering ignorance, implicitly literalizing the phrase "people one does not know."

After the *Tale* appeared in 1704, Wotton published a *Defense of the Reflections upon Ancient and Modern Learning, . . . With Observations upon The Tale of a Tub* (1705). The "Observations" offered an explication of the story of the three brothers, in the course of arguing that the *Tale* was a work of radical impiety. Swift was sensitive to this charge, which he earnestly sought to rebut in the "Apology," prefixed for the first time to the fifth edition of 1710. But Swift also impishly took over the explanatory matter in Wotton's attack, printing it in the notes to his own text, turning the *Tale* into an edition of itself, in the guise of a classical text *cum notis variorum* (with the notes of various authorities). Wotton is thus absorbed into the chain of pedantry, as a laboured drudge heavily engaged in explaining the obvious. But he is simultaneously enlisted as an aid to understanding a work he was more concerned to attack than to explain, outwitted by having his aggression read as exegetically helpful, and pilloried afresh by mock-editorial amiability every time his name appears gratefully at the end of a note.

Even before this, though on a smaller scale, the *Tale* had announced itself as a parody of learned editions, with gaps in the manuscript indicated by Latin marginalia and other flippant editorial routines. It was also from the beginning an attack on subliterary or journalistic hack-writing—slipshod, evasive, ignorant, self-consciously digressive, concerned to be up-to-the-minute, fatuously spontaneous in recording the most trivial domestic circumstances of the "author" and everything that entered his head at the very moment when it did so, including his thoughts on the writing of his thoughts.

Swift purported to be mocking Dryden and other seventeenth-century writers. None of them show anything like the outrageous textual egotism he ascribes to them, and Swift's manner has much closer analogues in a later literature of self-conscious, self-ironic writing, from Sterne's *Tristram Shandy* to Mailer's *Advertisements for Myself*—works Swift would have detested, and the first of which was expressly composed in the teeth of his derision. This suggests that Swift detected in Dryden and some of his contemporaries incipient elements of a later modernism which do not seem to have been visible to other readers. The use of Swift as a model by Sterne, Joyce, and Beckett, all of whom knowingly incorporate his proleptic derision, is a token of his extraordinary prescience as a cultural analyst, as well as of his almost magical inventiveness as a mimic. Though Marcus Walsh shows that Swift's preoccupation with "textuality," nowadays much discussed, was more widely shared in his lifetime than we previously knew, it was Swift's extraordinary elaboration of a parodic style that paradoxically created new possibilities of self-expression for the very modernism he was resisting.

The *Tale* proceeds on two parallel or alternating tracks, the satire on abuses in religion and the "digressions" which form a satire on modern learning. Swift claimed in the Apology to have written in defence of the Anglican Church against its Papist and Puritan enemies. The satire on the latter is probably the most biting. It targets sectarian groups which exalt the individual worshipper or small congregation, with their inner light, private conscience and spontaneous accesses of devotion, unchecked by tradition and institutional authority. Corresponding to them on a secular plane are the journalists, hacks, and bad poets satirized in the "digressions," with their cult of the immediate moment and their sense of the primacy of ego and whim. Both groups are seen as surrendering to the flow of irrational feeling, and the favored term for this abandonment of rational control is "enthusiasm," the state described in the Digression on Madness, in which the imagination overwhelms reason, the senses, and the common forms of conduct and thought.

Enthusiastic worship, in this sense, is a principal preoccupation of the *Discourse Concerning the Mechanical Operation of the Spirit,* where it is shown as manipulated by unscrupulous preachers, fanning the devotional excitability of their flock into orgiastic states of sexual lewdness, a frequent accusation against the Puritan sects. The fact that this *Discourse* takes the form of a scientific communication to a member of the "*Academy of the* Beaux Esprits *in* New-Holland" intimates how closely intertwined the religious allegory is with the satire on "learning," including scientific pretensions. The location of the learned society in New-Holland suggests that modern science and the savages of the South Pacific are more or less on a par: the author's complaint a little later that he has not recently heard from "the *Literati* of *Topinambou*" is an irony of the same sort, invoking another *locus classicus* of barbaric savagery, the Amerindian tribe of cannibals in whose defense Montaigne had once written (the author also likes to stay in touch with the society of "*Iroquois Virtuosi*"). Scientists, literati, and cannibal savages are mad Moderns of the same essential stripe. Modernism is atavistic, perhaps older than the Ancients, as old as the unregulated self. It goes back to the beginning of time, like the Modern critics of the Digression Concerning Critics, who descend "in a direct line from a Celestial Stem, by *Momus* and *Hybris*, who begat *Zoilus*, who begat *Tigellius*, who begat *Etcaetera* the Elder, who begat *Bently*, and *Rymer*, and *Wotton*, and *Perrault*, and *Dennis*, who begat *Etcaetera* the Younger."

The account of this riff-raff, in both the *Tale* and the *Mechanical Operation* (which is an addendum to the *Tale's* religious satire as the *Battle of the Books* is to the satire on learning), is so inventive, versatile, and brilliantly unruly that it risks contaminating the positive values Swift insisted in the Apology that he had been upholding. The sensible, moderate, and ecumenical speech Martin makes in Section VI is the sanest thing anyone is allowed to say in the *Tale*, but it is deflated both in advance and immediately after by some disconcerting and unruly ridicule, whose exact focus is unclear. It is interesting that Martin, the only representative in the *Tale* of any point of view endorsable by Swift, is given very little to say throughout, presumably because the book's atmosphere of total tearaway irony posed an insoluble dilemma: presenting Martin with the seriousness his views deserve could only introduce an incongruous solemnity; allowing him to be playfully subverted, as in Section VI, risked the appearance of impiety which Wotton was in the event quick to seize on. The only way out was to give Martin a low profile. There is no extended treatment of Martin, as there is of Peter and Jack. The lack was noted, and someone tried to make it good by adding a "History of Martin" to a spurious edition of 1720.

Swift ascribed his failure to secure promotion in the Church to the *Tale's* reputation for impiety, as we have seen. He wanted to be an English bishop, and resented being only an Irish dean. He felt himself to be English rather than Irish, claimed merely to have been "dropped" in Ireland by an accident of birth, disliked living in Ireland and felt embittered by his failure to obtain an English preferment. He was nevertheless, as W. B. Yeats said memorably in the great debate on divorce in the Irish Senate, one of several Anglo-Irishmen who played a historic role in furthering Ireland's struggle against the English: the list includes Burke, Grattan, Emmet, Charles Stewart Parnell, and Yeats himself.

Swift's objective was not Irish independence, however. Or rather, his belief was that Ireland was already constitutionally independent, its relation to England being that of a separate country ruled by the same King through separate parliaments, rather than "a dependent Kingdom" subject ultimately to rule from London. This doctrine, whose most influential formulation was to be found in William Molyneux's *The Case of Ireland Stated* (1698), was not universally accepted, and the constitutional position was drastically changed in Swift's lifetime by a statute which abolished the appellate jurisdiction of the Irish House of Lords and made Irish affairs almost totally dependent on English rule. Swift's constitutional views should not be taken to imply championship of the rights of a vanquished population. He didn't believe there had been a conquest in the normal sense anyway, and his resentment at English rule was not that of an indigenous patriot against a foreign invader, but more like that of European *colons* in French North Africa or British Kenya in the present century. It combined a contempt for "the savage old Irish" with resentment towards the mother-country for its supposed indifference or hostility to its own colonial class rather than to the native victims of colonial rule.

Swift's contempt for the Irish natives was similar to that shown by most of the English writers who, since the sixteenth century, had written about Ireland with some degree of personal knowledge or official expertise. Like Spenser, Camden, Fynes Moryson, and his own patron's father, Sir John Temple, Swift spoke of the Irish as a barbaric and almost bestial species, corresponding closely to his own portrayal of the Yahoos. These humanoid creatures, whose features ("the Face . . . flat and broad, the Nose depressed, the Lips large") were of the kind "common to all Savage nations" (*Gulliver's Travels*, IV.ii), remind us of the extent to which the English regarded the Irish as part of an undifferentiated primitive race. English writers spoke of them in language borrowed from the Spanish accounts of Amerindians (Moryson said Ireland was an "Iland in the Virginian Sea"), a rhetoric supported by a Graeco-Roman tradition that held them to be cannibal, and, through a tendentious etymology that linked *Scythae* with *Scoti* (Scots), derived from the Scythians, a central Asian people who settled in what is now southern Russia and eastern Europe (Amerindians were sometimes said to be descended from the Scythians too). The Scythians were to the Greek imagination a defining type of the savage, and Herodotus describes them as practicing cannibalism and manufacturing consumer goods from human skin and bones: this is part of the background to Book IV of *Gulliver's Travels* and especially to *A Modest Proposal*.

A Modest Proposal is not mainly a tract against the English, as Oliver Ferguson points out. The portrait of the Irish as a beggarly, idle, thieving, and dissolute rabble, who can only be deterred from ill-treating their pregnant women or their infants by the prospect of a profitable trade in eatable one-year-old children, offers no flattering view of the social and domestic mores of the Irish poor. But it is equally directed against the Anglo-Irish group to which Swift himself belonged, for the self-destructive habits to which he pointed as a major cause of Ireland's economic ruin. The *Proposal* has sometimes been read as a satire of the social or economic tracts whose form it mimics, but such parody is as marginal to its real concerns as parody of travel-books had been in *Gulliver's Travels*. Swift had himself in any case written several pamphlets of the sort mimicked in the *Proposal*, advocating the changes of habit and policy summarized in the famous "other Expedients" passage near the end of that work. It is the failure of these, the Proposer argues, that led him to understand that no sane solution—indeed nothing short of national mass-cannibalism—was likely to commend itself to such an insane people.

The Proposer ends by assuming the role of the disillusioned satirist, denouncing an evil world as incorrigible and accepting that the satirist's erstwhile hopes of improving it are no more than "visionary Thoughts." Gulliver felt compelled to make a similar declaration. Both characters have in common the unusual feature that—unlike the more habitual figure of the virtuous satirist who has merely lost hope—they are, by any normal standard of behaviour Swift would be likely to uphold in "real life", visibly unbalanced. The Proposer goes beyond Gulliver's eccentrically unsocial behaviour to the advocacy of a monstrously *anti*-social project. Swift has to execute the delicate balancing act of suggesting in both cases not that the speaker is too mad to be trusted, but that his perceptions are essentially right and that the situation they reveal is so dreadful that it will naturally unhinge the mind of a decent man. Swift's achievement is to make the "madness" of his two spokesmen something which intensifies the rhetoric rather than undercutting it (though some critics, mainly in the case of *Gulliver's Travels*, argue otherwise). At the same time, the comedy of an excessive reaction or utterance in both works allows Swift to dissociate himself from Timon's manner, an intemperate rhetoric which might leave an author unduly exposed and which readers might be disposed to think over the top. Far from undermining the gist of the denunciation, this comedy acts (I believe) as an enabling agent for its release.

The attack on the Irish in *A Modest Proposal*, like the attack on mankind in *Gulliver's Travels*, is comprehensive: even good Yahoos, like the Portuguese Captain Don Pedro, are Yahoos. It is nowadays widely recognized that the Yahoos are portrayed in ways which identify them with the savage Irish, who become in a sense representative of a degenerate humanity. In *A Modest Proposal*, all Irish are included, the Anglo-Irish establishment of merchants, landlords, politicians, and expensively dressed women who buy English clothes, and the beggarly natives who are idle, thieving, promiscuous, and given to wife-beating and child-neglect. Swift didn't always think of the two groups as connected. The title of the fourth of the *Drapier's Letters*, "A Letter to the Whole People of Ireland," addresses only the Anglo-Irish, the phrase "whole people" excluding the natives as without legal rights or human standing, a usage not unknown in the seventeenth and eighteenth centuries in a sense which excluded the domestic poor as well as the foreign savage.

For all his dislike of Ireland, Swift exerted himself strongly in defense of Irish interests, and is still honored in Ireland as a great patriot. His most effective intervention occurred in 1724–1725 over the issue of Wood's halfpence. An English entrepreneur called William Wood had been granted a patent for producing Irish coinage. This was widely perceived as an intolerable English intrusion in Irish affairs, and (rightly or wrongly) as likely to be damaging to the Irish economy. Swift intervened in a series of pamphlets known as the *Drapier's Letters*, in which, in the character of a Dublin cloth merchant or draper, he mobilized opinion against the scheme with such effect that it had to be abandoned. In doing so, he had run serious risks, and his victory made him something of a popular hero. Though the real identity of the author was widely known, no one was found who would formally identify Swift, and his printer Harding was imprisoned for a time.

Swift was proud of his achievement and wrote about it in his poem about himself, *Verses on the Death of Dr. Swift* (1731):

> Fair LIBERTY was all his cry;
> For her he stood prepared to die;
> For her he boldly stood alone;
> For her he oft exposed his own.
> Two kingdoms, just as factions led,
> Had set a price upon his head;
> But, not a traitor could be found,
> To sell him for six hundred pound.
> (ll. 351–58)

These lines are supposed to be spoken by an impartial commentator, not Swift himself. Swift was not easily given to high styles, especially not in self-celebration, and the attribution of these words (which are entirely justified by the record) to a non-authorial speaker may be thought not entirely in good faith. When Pope wrote in defence of his record as a poet and satirist, he made no pretense of enlisting another speaker, and was content to rely on the sanctioned public persona of the *musarum sacerdos* (priest of the muses), whom most readers, whether learnedly or intuitively, do not mistake for the private autobiographical person in a crude sense.

Others have celebrated Swift in the terms he established for himself in the *Verses on the Death*. Yeats, a poet who thought of Swift as belonging like himself to the great Anglo-Irish tradition of Irish patriots, wrote in "Swift's Epitaph":

> Swift has sailed into his rest;
> Savage indignation there
> Cannot lacerate his breast.
> Imitate him if you dare,
> World-besotted traveller; he
> Served human liberty.

Yeats's poem is a translation of the Latin epitaph Swift composed for himself, which is now in St. Patrick's Cathedral in Dublin: a rare example of a high style used of himself, here protected by posthumous use, in the formal anonymity of a tombstone, and the marmoreal impersonality of the Latin language. Yeats, or rather a character in *The Words upon the Window-Pane*, his play about Swift, called it "the greatest epitaph in history."

The epitaph also speaks of his *saeva indignatio* (savage indignation), a phrase which has linked him with the irritable majesties of the Roman satirist Juvenal. With a few small exceptions, however, Swift never adopted accents of angry grandiloquence, preferring low-key styles closer to those of Horace. In "To a Lady," a poem of about the same date as the *Verses on the Death*, he expressly insisted that he avoided "lofty styles" and preferred an idiom of unsettling and flattening ridicule, though he did make clear that his feelings of anger and aggression were strong. Something like the same distinction appears to be in his mind in a famous letter to Pope (29 September 1725) about *Gulliver's Travels*, in which he speaks of having written on a great foundation of misanthropy, but not in Timon's manner. It is a paradox of the history of reputations, and of the fortunes of a poet's self-image, that the supposedly Juvenalian Swift was closer to Horace than Pope, the official imitator of Horace, in whose Horatian poems a strong Juvenalian majesty has frequently been detected.

Swift's avoidance of lofty styles extended to parodies of such styles, presumably on the assumption, formulated in John Dryden's "Discourse Concerning Satire," that in such cases "the majesty of the heroic," finely mixed with the venom of satire, would create a genre in which satire itself became a species of heroic poetry. In other words, Swift's fear was that heroic majesties might rub off on the mockery, as occurred with deliberate effect in Dryden's *Mac Flecknoe* or Pope's *Dunciad*. Swift hated Dryden, but he was Pope's close friend and admirer: indeed the *Dunciad* was dedicated to him. He regarded Pope as a poet capable of the highest poetic eloquence, and accepted his superiority to himself, claiming for his part only to be a man of rhymes, who never wrote "serious Couplets in my Life, though never any without a moral View." Swift used the Popeian heroic couplet very sparingly, preferring instead the rhyming tetrameter (four-foot, eight-syllable lines), which was more hospitable to levity and could be made to seem close to demotic balladry or doggerel. The idea that the high couplet was the quintessential idiom of eighteenth-century poetry is part of Pope's success in reputation-management. Swift himself was convinced of it. His own reputation as the greatest prose satirist in the language has also tended to obscure his achievement as a poet, though he wrote almost as much verse as Pope did (if one excludes Pope's Homer translations). Later poets have been readier than critics to recognize Swift's distinction as a poet: his admirers and imitators included Byron, Eliot, and Auden.

Swift's temperamental guardedness ensured that none of his important writings in either verse or prose lacked an element of parodic undercutting. He is probably the most consistently parodic of all eighteenth-century writers. His poems about women, for example, are unremittingly conscious of what he perceived as the routines of post-Petrarchan love-poetry, whether he is violently overturning these routines (as in the scatological poems or "A Beautiful Young Nymph Going to Bed") or paying deeply felt compliments to Stella. It is as though nothing seriously evocative of a "serious" style could be uttered without some parodic deflation of a "high" alternative. In the prose satires, *Gulliver's Travels* and *A Modest Proposal*, parody functions in a separate and marginal way, providing a vehicle, or an added level of bookish jokerie, in writings whose main satiric energies and concerns (the exposure of human turpitude in *Gulliver's Travels*, the condition of Ireland in *A Modest Proposal*) have little or nothing to do with travel-books or economic tracts.

In the poems, as in *Tale of a Tub*, the texts parodied are often primary embodiments or expressions of the things Swift is attacking (stupid attitudes to sexuality, various follies of the intellectual life). But it is striking that this most parodic of authors never attempted the quintessentially Augustan genre of mock-heroic, except in the *Battle of the Books*, where parody of epic styles is attenuated by a separate strand of mock-journalism and by the medium of prose. It seems likely that Swift's *pudeur* over mock-heroic involved more than the resistance to residual majesties I have already noted. Whereas Pope and some other contemporaries used mock-heroic as a tribute to epic rather than as a subversion of it, Swift's irony was perhaps too corrosive for him to risk deploying it in the vicinity of a genre still regarded in his time as the pinnacle of poetic achievement. As with the character of Martin, that embodiment of a sane Anglicanism, Swift chose the path of minimal exposure, probably for him the safest form of praise.

In all Swift's imaginative works, the narrative or argument is conducted by a speaker, usually derided, whose relationship to Swift is oblique and unstable, and whom (as in the case of the deranged Gulliver or Modest Proposer) it is perilous to separate too radically from the author. It was for a time a fashion in literary criticism, and especially in Swift studies, to discuss texts as though they were written or spoken by a clearly distinguishable "persona" or "mask." The impulse came from various sources: psychological theories of role-playing and defense-mechanisms, poetic doctrines derived from the use of masks in the theatre of ancient Greece or of Japan, and especially from a recognition that ever since classical times, poets have spoken in a formally sanctioned role, as priests of the muses, champions of virtue, courageous opponents of corrupt men in power, rather than in a mode of private disclosure, let alone autobiographical intimacy. In critical practice, persona-criticism was a valuable corrective to an opposite tendency to confuse an author's views with those of his fictive speakers or even his fictional characters.

What began as a valuable refinement soon turned into a mechanical routine as reductive as those it reversed. Painstaking studies identifying the personae of an author, defining the supposed characters of each, positing that an unnamed narrator like that of *A Tale of a Tub* was really a series of distinct characters whose different identities would be successfully charted from sentence to sentence, became commonplace. For a time, undergraduates discussing any first-person utterance in a poem by Pope or Wordsworth or Yeats would refer to "the persona of the poet," having been terrorized by the critical climate into believing that poets never said anything directly, or that intelligent readers would be unable to understand, in a phrase like "Wordsworth says such-and-such in *Tintern Abbey*," that the normal obliquities of poetic discourse were not necessarily being overlooked.

In the case of a highly self-conscious and defensive ironist like Swift, it seemed especially necessary to issue strenuous reminders that the author should not be mistaken for his speakers, as though that truth had been unavailable to intelligent readers before personae had been wheeled into the classroom. The habit of writing as though "persona" meant "person" rather than "mask" (or "role" or "projection") had the wholly inappropriate effect of treating such figures—whether named and formally identifiable, like Gulliver, or unnamed and too elusive even to characterize, like the "author" of the *Tale*—as if they were autonomous creations analogous to the characters of a novel or play, and of suggesting that because Gulliver evidently did not closely resemble Swift there must be a total disengagement of the one from the other. In reality it has always been important to understand that the two are neither the same nor separable, that the one is speaking through the other, sometimes directly, sometimes adversarially, and most often in complex and elusive combinations of the two; that an author who speaks through a mask has in all cases written the script and created the persona, and stands responsible for the result, including the persona's views and the exact attitude to them which may be inferred from the context; that, in other words, authors speak *through* their personae if not always with or in favor of them; and that in Swift, the sense of an aggressive and taunting authorial presence is unusually active. Kurt Vonnegut's remark that "we are what we pretend to be, so we must be careful about what we pretend to be" offers a salutary warning, provided it is taken to mean not that "author" equals "persona" but that authors stand responsible for their inventions in their totality. No criticism of Swift can function usefully without some sense of the complexities which the concept of the persona seeks to come to terms with, and perhaps the wisest and most subtle treatment of the question since Maynard Mack's "The Muse of Satire" (a famous essay of 1951, now reprinted in Mack's *Collected in Himself*, 1982) is to be found in Robert C. Elliott's posthumous book, *The Literary Persona*, whose chapter "Swift's Satire: Rules of the Game" is reprinted here alongside a statement of my own which Elliott was contesting.

A large number of "casebooks" on Swift are in existence, and some of the older classics of Swift criticism (Johnson's *Life*, the hostile discussions in Thackeray's *English Humourists* and in Leavis's profoundly acute essay, "The Irony of Swift") have not only been widely reprinted but are in any case easily accessible in other contexts. The same is true of some famous twentieth-century discussions, by Yeats, by Orwell and by some academic critics. For this reason, and because a good deal of excellent commentary, supported by recent scholarship, has appeared since 1960, I have generally restricted my selection to this period.

The one exception is the essay by John Lawlor, "Radical Satire and the Realistic Novel" (1955), a seminal discussion, unaccountably too little known. The relation (in many ways antithetical) of Swift to the genre of the novel is still insufficiently understood, though it is often alluded to superficially (Michael McKeon's discussion of *Gulliver's Travels*, reprinted as chapter 11, is another significant exception). The resemblances and differences between Swift and Flaubert, two deeply misanthropic writers whose superficial unlikeness disguises a kinship which throws light on both, have also not received the attention they deserve. Lawlor's essay is one of the few to bring Swift and Flaubert together in a serious attempt to define the nature and limits of both genres. Its observations won't command universal agreement. In particular, his notion that Swift brings satire to a point where human depravity is seen as so natural that the satirist must express himself as beyond anger, seems to me to read certain rhetorical gestures with an inappropriate literalness. Nevertheless, the quality and unusualness of Lawlor's insights, and the centrality of the issues he raises, give his essay an importance that deserves to be more widely acknowledged.

Another under-recognized topic is Swift's profound affinity with the great masters of Renaissance Humanism—Erasmus, More, Rabelais, Montaigne—an affinity all the deeper for being only infrequently acknowledged in explicit terms. Swift's debt to Rabelais is well-recognized, though little studied. And the kinship of the Scriblerus group (including Swift, Pope, and Gay) to the great Humanist coterie of Erasmus and More has still to be adequately understood, as has the importance of Montaigne to both Swift and Pope. The debt of *A Tale of a Tub* to Erasmus's *Praise of Folly*, or of *Gulliver's Travels* to More's *Utopia*, has received intermittent attention, notably from John Traugott and Brian Vickers, and most recently in several studies by Jenny Mezciems, whose essay on Book III of *Gulliver's Travels*, reprinted in this volume, is also one of the most interesting defenses of a relatively neglected part of that work.

A theme that has received attention in recent years, especially after the appearance of Hugh Kenner's *Stoic Comedians* (1962), is that of Swift's treatment, most notably in *A Tale of a Tub*, of the phenomenon of print culture, his consciousness of the book as a technology of communication rather than merely a tacit mode for the dissemination of his own words, his preoccupation with the book as book. There are perceptive discussions of this by Denis Donoghue, Gabriel Josipovici, Terry Castle, and others. I have chosen an essay by Marcus Walsh which suggests that a degree of awareness of this and related issues existed in Swift's own time.

Swift's writings have always been controversial among women. It is the poems which have elicited the most attention from women critics, as recent books, from a variety of perspectives, by Nora Jaffe, Louise Barnett, and Ellen Pollak testify. I have selected Penelope Wilson's "Feminism and the Augustans," which does not appear in a book and has not had wide exposure. Both it, and the essays by Rees, and Mezciems, have been chosen for their importance and excellence, without reference to gender. That they make up only twenty percent of the contents of this book is a reflection of cultural factors outside the scope of this introduction.

Part 1
SATIRE AND THE NOVEL

Radical Satire and the Realistic Novel

John Lawlor

Only you must be honest with yourselves; you are to live by the word, not content merely to listen to it. One who listens to the word without living by it is like a man who sees, in a mirror, the face he was born with; he looks at himself, and away he goes, never giving another thought to the man he saw there.

— The General Epistle of James, L 22–24 (KNOX)

Come, come, and sit you down; you shall not budge.
You go not till I set you up a glass
Where you may see the inmost part of you.
— *Hamlet,* III. 4.

I

The triumphs of Augustan verse-satire are of so distinctive a kind that we may tend to accept them as definitive. The brilliant exploitation of principles of "refinement" of language and metre can however prompt certain misunderstandings concerning the nature of English satirical writing in general. There is loss as well as profit in the general movement away from "grossly familiar" diction and "numbers purposely neglected". To be sure, Augustan critical theory can find a place for the low manner of the "Varronian" satire; and any account of Augustan satire may reasonably on these grounds give an honoured place to Butler. But it is doubtful whether Augustan taste, for all its theoretical approval of a style "constantly accommodated to the subject, either high or low", can ever unreservedly accept it in practice. The words of Dryden just cited are sometimes used to support a general contention that "the style of a poem was expected to suit the poet's subject and the kind which he was practising".[1] But we should not fail to notice that, as Dryden offers it, the statement applying an honoured critical principle lies between two particular reservations. Dryden is speaking of Horace, Persius, and Juvenal:

As for the subjects which they treated, it will appear hereafter that Horace writ not vulgarly on vulgar subjects, nor always chose them. His style is constantly accommodated to

From *Essays and Studies,* New Series, 8 (1955), 58–75. Reprinted by permission of the author and The English Association.

[1] *Augustine Satire,* by Ian Jack. Oxford, 1952, p. 6.

his subject, either high or low. If his fault be too much lowness, that of Persius is the fault of the hardness of his metaphors, and obscurity: and so they are equal in the failings of their style; where Juvenal manifestly triumphs over both of them.[2]

It is clear that the "accommodation" of style to subject has its limits: and it would be a work of some critical nicety to establish them. The satirist is not to write "vulgarly" if he chooses "vulgar subjects", and it will be as well for him not to choose them too frequently. "Lowness" is permitted: but there can be "too much lowness": and, characteristically, the palm is awarded to the satirist who is not guilty of "failings of style". For our present purpose it is sufficient to notice that "lowness" of style, however well founded as doctrine, in its particular instances offers difficulties to a sensibility that cherishes the ideal of "correctness".

Where Butler is concerned, the case is no better: and this time Dr. Johnson is present to examine the actual contradiction presented by modified approval. Johnson is a valuable witness: no friend to "low" language and negligent versification, and indeed painfully rigorous in his notion of metre, his good sense will yet not permit him to pass over in silence Dryden's treatment of *Hudibras*. Butler, says Dryden, "is above my censure"; and then proceeds to state his aversion to the essential characteristics of Butler's work:

> The choice of his numbers is suitable enough to his design, as he has managed it; but in any other hand, the shortness of his verse, and the quick returns of rhyme, had debased the dignity of style. And besides, the double rhyme (a necessary companion of burlesque writing) is not so proper for manly satire; for it turns earnest too much to jest, and gives us a boyish kind of pleasure. It tickles awkwardly with a kind of pain, to the best sort of readers: we are pleased ungratefully, and, if I may say so, against our liking. . . . 'Tis indeed below so great a master to make use of such a little instrument.[3]

Dryden assesses well enough the characteristic effects of Butler's chosen medium, but regards them as undignified: his preference, as his noble patron will already have understood, is for the heroic couplet. Johnson makes short work of this as criticism:

> To the critical sentence of Dryden the highest reverence would be due, were not his decisions often precipitate, and his opinions immature. When he wished to change the measure he probably would have been willing to change more. If he intended that, when the numbers were heroic, the diction should still remain vulgar, he planned a very heterogeneous and unnatural composition. If he preferred a general stateliness both of sound and words, he can be only understood to wish Butler had undertaken a different work.[4]

This goes to the heart of the matter. The judgement of "the best sort of readers", when confronted with an extended example of "low" style approaches the

[2] *A Discourse concerning the Original and Progress of Satire.* (Essays of John Dryden, ed. W. P. Ker. Oxford, 1900; Vol. I, p. 78.)
[3] *Discourse,* Ker, I. 105.
[4] Life of Butler, in *Lives of the Poets.*

absurdity of denying the essential qualities of the work under review. The root cause is plain when we consider Dryden's own expressed preferences in satire: the "best and finest" is "that sharp, well-mannered way of laughing a folly out of countenance"; "the most beautiful, and most noble" is "the majesty of the heroic, finely mixed with venom" as in Boileau's *Lutrin*.[5] "Fineness of raillery" and mock-heroic hold the field: preoccupation with a well-mannered style affords no good ground for appreciating the range of effects open to "grossly familiar" diction and "numbers purposely neglected". The truth is that the high spirits of the rougher (and older) tradition in English satire can at best secure an effect denied to polished expression. By the careful negligence of the unrefined epithet, the run-on line, and that most characteristic device, the double-rhyme, the folly under review can be reduced to absurdity by being denied even the dignity of measured statement. What is essential to this effect is what Augustanism does not readily tolerate in the poet. I would call it the poet's sense of predicament, his willingness to share the absurd situation with his reader, even to the point of mock-helpless involvement. An illustration is readily available if we turn to an Augustan at work polishing an older poet. Comparison of Donne's Fourth Satire with Pope's "versifying" of it will show us that indeed it is no base metal that Pope transmutes. But "the weighty bullion" is perhaps not entirely that which Pope assesses and in his own fashion appropriates. What we gain from Pope has to be paid for, in the loss of the whole comically dramatic situation where poet and reader are alike at the mercy of pedantry and affectation, and the madcap movement of the run-on lines perfectly parallels the hither-thithering of the trapped mind. To take but a fragment:

> He names me, and comes to me; I whisper, God
> How have I sinn'd, that thy wraths furious rod,
> This fellow, chuseth me!

This breathless recognition of the inevitable is not Pope's self-possession in the face of dullness:

> He spies me out. I whisper, gracious God!
> What Sin of mine cou'd merit such a Rod?
> That all the Shot of Dulness now must be
> From this thy Blunderbuss discharg'd on me!

Such satire as this of Pope's offers a humble instance of the great and specific delight of Augustanism—the cool excellence of the poet always in control of his theme, everywhere master of the comic predicament. Whether the satire is urbane or vehement, the satirist is a commanding figure, the champion of intelligence and good sense: and it is unthinkable that a champion should lose his footing. This is the real achievement of Augustanism in general; the imposition of order, the self-possession of the artist in face of apparent contradiction and complexity: for it is his task to show us the harmony and symmetry of design which

[5]*Discourse*, Ker, I. 105, 108.

too much attention to mere particulars will obscure. But in satire this is not achieved without loss. As the satirist becomes a champion, so there is the danger that his reader may become a spectator. The rigours of the struggle against folly or knavery are not so readily apparent: the blunderbuss is no match for the rapier in the most skilled hands. The odds are now delicately but decisively weighted against disturbers of the peace. The real change that requires our notice is in the standpoint of the satirist, his role as *censor morum*, and the implied appeal to all men of good sense to admire the skill with which he despatches the common foe. What is gained is abundantly evident: what is lost is not merely high spirits and amiable ridicule, but something of incalculable importance to the satirist who would seek to involve his reader in the figures of folly or knavery that are to be despatched. Dryden's highest aim was to win both approval of skill and self-recognition from the victim: "fineness of raillery" need not be offensive. "A witty man is tickled while he is hurt in this manner."[6] But even Dryden has to admit that "a fool feels it not". The continued practice of Augustan satire might lead to others besides fools becoming insensible to the satiric thrust. Indeed, satire might become "a sort of glass, wherein beholders do generally discover everybody's face but their own; which is the chief reason for that kind reception it meets with in the world, and that so very few are offended with it".[7]

A second misunderstanding which may be encouraged by Augustan achievement need not detain us long, though it introduces us to a widening of our inquiry. Dryden's enthusiastic advocacy of "fineness of raillery" presents us with a very clear conception of what "urbanity" might mean: and though urbane satire of this kind is but one facet of Augustan achievement, we may be tempted, in charting the large outlines of satiric practice, to feel that the great distinction to be observed is that between virulence and urbanity, uncontrolled vehemence and "fine raillery". Certainly the distinction is of primary importance for classification: but it does not take us as far into the nature of the satiric activity as we might suppose. If we take the satirist's primary field of activity as the observed discrepancy between what men are and what they ought to be, satire is "indignant" in proportion as the "ought" is felt to approach the status of final obligation, and the discrepancy therefore wide, extending it may be to inversion. "After all", observes Dryden when comparing Horace and Juvenal, "Horace had the disadvantage of the times in which he lived; they were better for the man, but worse for the satirist": Juvenal had "a larger field": and it needs no argument of Dryden's to show that "Little follies were out of doors when oppression was to be scourged instead of avarice."[8] Satire can be more urbane when the "ought" is felt to be self-evident to all men of good sense, its fulfilment demanding no excessive effort: discrepancy will not seem finally harmful, but will approach the merely eccentric or humorously self-contradictory. If, for example, we take the Langland of the *Visio* as representative of the first grouping, the Addison of the

[6]*Discourse*, Ker, I. 93.
[7]Swift, *The Battle of the Books*, The Preface of the Author,
[8]*Discourse*, Ker, I. 87.

Coverley papers will illustrate the second. Langland's passionate contempt is indeed a different thing from Addison's gentle sarcasm. Moderation could hardly go further than the mild reflection on the practical discomforts that follow from Sir Roger's method of selecting accommodation:

> we were not so inquisitive about the inn as the inn-keeper; and, provided our landlord's principles were sound, did not take any notice of the staleness of his provisions.[9]

We may be tempted to explain away this difference by calling Addison's the morality of prudence where Langland's is the morality of obedience to Right Reason, and to make the shift in satirical emphasis correspond with this difference of implied values. But the matter is not settled by easy reference to intellectual climate. One and the same period gives us the vehemence of Langland and the urbanity of Chaucer. It is sounder to ask, if we are to seek crucial distinctions, what is common to all the satirists we have named: and clearly it is the tacit assumption that man is a free and therefore responsible agent. Whether the satirist castigates or cajoles, the root assumption is that his reader can perceive folly or knavery, and perceiving it can, by an effort of will, in some degree amend his ways. Hence we have the standard defence of the satirist's vocation as salutary: "rough" or "smooth", "toothed" or "toothless", vehement or diffident, satire offers us the mirror in which we perceive our deformities or eccentricities. The lesson need not always be painful; the older association between the ridiculous and the contemptible reminds us that our teachers may vary their methods, so long as, seeing ourselves, we begin to be wise. Certainly, Augustan satirists will brilliantly run the gamut of satiric utterance. The very assumption that permits of "fineness of raillery" will also sanction fierceness of contempt. As Professor Pinto has recently reminded us, satire "realistic" in this way is possible only to poets who have "thoroughly absorbed" an aristocratic culture "and understood its excellencies as well as its weaknesses".[10] The distinction between virulence and urbanity is one of means to a common end. If we are to look for radical change in the satiric tradition, it is not to be found here.

II

If, however, Augustanism with its fundamental principles of order is approached without the preconceptions that it offers either unqualified advantage or cardinal development in the satiric tradition, the particular case of urbane "correction" is peculiarly worth examination, and may point us towards the decisive alterations in satiric presentation. Both Chaucer's Madame Eglentyne and Addison's Sir Roger succeed in their effect by the implied suggestion that, whatever may be the case with the reader, these persons cannot alter in their ways.

---

[9]*Spectator*, No. 126.
[10]"John Wilmot, Earl of Rochester, and the Right Veine of Satire," in *Essays and Studies of the English Association*, London, 1953.

Addison the cool Whig is brilliantly able to indulge Sir Roger's eccentricities; for there is no danger in this old Tory: his day is done. As Mr. C. S. Lewis has remarked, this is no fortress but a ruin.[11] So the inconsistencies in Sir Roger assume the quality of permanence: he is a figure of amiable humour for he would be the last to realize the eccentricities of his own behaviour. As for Chaucer, no one can fail to perceive that the strength of his General Prologue portrait of the Prioress lies in the fact that she represents an unwitting reconciliation of opposites—on the one hand the demands of her Order and her own place of authority within it, and on the other her unconscious desire to be the *grande dame*, to "countrefete cheere of court". So the charming irregularities of dress, the painstaking table-manners, the troop of hounds that substitute for a great lady's "brachet", and, over all, the pleasing ambiguity of *Amor vincit omnia*—all delight the eye of an observer who sees no reason why she should ever change. This quality of satiric description, urbanely refusing any concern with correction, is clearly of the most effective order. The distinctive effect that Sir Roger and Chaucer's Prioress secure is that they are totally unaware of their eccentricities. But to achieve this effect we have come perilously close to abandoning the whole basis of satire: for, grant that in some instances at least we do not know ourselves, what then becomes of our privileged position as spectators? Dryden's high aim, at all events, is placed out of reach: to make the victim both suffer and smile, it is first necessary to make him *see*.

Dryden had indeed touched upon the possibility that the victim might not perceive himself and had given it as an additional defence of "fine raillery": "A witty man is tickled while he is hurt in this manner, and a fool feels it not." Some indeed might hold, where the "fool" is concerned,

> that in effect this way does more mischief; that a man is secretly wounded, and though he be not sensible himself, yet the malicious world will find it out for him; yet there is still a vast difference betwixt the slovenly butchering of a man, and the fineness of a stroke that separates the head from the body, and leaves it standing in its place.[12]

"Secretly wounded"—Dryden's ratiocinative genius leads him to consider a possibility that he had brought in to adduce support for his main contention: and even in dismissing it from further consideration he has used the most telling phrase to describe it. The secret wound that urbane satire can give its insentient victim should remind us of the limits not only of urbanity but of the satiric activity itself. If we call "major" satire that which draws upon the field of discrepancy between what men are and what for the highest purposes they ought to be, we are committed to the notion of "minor" satire as treating the comic discrepancy between what we are and what we think we are, the amusing presentation of what we are happily unconscious of being. "Major" satire, thus understood, will deal with great obligations and our blameworthiness in respect of them: and the weakening of assumptions concerning universal obligation will seriously impair or

[11]*Essays on the Eighteenth Century presented to David Nichol Smith.* Oxford, 1945, p. 3.
[12]*Discourse*, Ker, I. 93.

render altogether invalid satire of this order. The "minor" satire of the incurably eccentric will not be so easily dislodged. But suppose the eccentric is taken not as the exceptional case but as the general rule, then we are all in danger of being "secretly wounded": and "minor" satire in fact offers us the major truth that the universal predicament is not to see ourselves.

The satiric intelligence, in proportion as it seeks a comprehensive effect, must often run the risk of being merely destructive—not by directly cutting away the premises of its argument, but by creating the uneasy suspicion that wisdom or right conduct are not to be expected of mankind. *A Tale of a Tub* may well be described as an attack upon "corruptions in religion and learning": but more than one reader may be excused if, after this devastating parade of theological absurdities, he can find no foothold for the dogmas of Christianity. The satiric attack is pressed home on three fronts: three kinds of self-deception and internal contradiction leave little encouragement for any supposition that there is a true religion of which these absurdities are proper corruptions. Sooner or later in the course of extended satire, if a sweeping effect is to be obtained, the satirist is likely to find himself on dangerous ground. It may be necessary to the satiric presentation to show all men gone astray: but it may undermine its final "truth" if the satirist leaves us with no understanding of why this should be so. He must then touch the frontier of satire: for if the satire is nourished in a world where all men are aware of the standards by which they fall short, and can thus be "corrected", with whatever degrees of vehemence or gentle admonition, the matter looks very different once we are brought to ask, "*Are* we to blame?" Dryden very properly insists on the relation between satire and the heroic, and from this point of view we can grant that by wholly contrasting methods each affirms the dignity of man, the responsible agent. But whereas in the heroic mode the values are triumphantly vindicated, the probing satiric intelligence can reveal a strange state of affairs. It is not only the ancient truth that everywhere we appear to know the good, and nowhere do we know ourselves. It is the strangeness of our approving what should condemn us, the satire that we gladly perceive to be true of others, never of ourselves.

The approach to this frontier may vary, in two main ways. A writer who, like Swift, comes to maturity in an age of copious and often brilliant satiric portrayal, may find his way forward in terms of the sheer necessity of bringing home his point to the individual reader. When satiric production is common, and it is, moreover, production of the Augustan kind, where the reader is a spectator of the satirist's skill, it may well be felt that the satirist's task of penetrating his reader is rendered peculiarly difficult. Immunity is readily gained where production is abundant: toleration and even approval of satire lead to the suspicion that "beholders do generally discover everybody's face but their own". The very defence of the satirist's vocation is itself absurd:

> I have observed some satirists to use the public much at the rate that pedants do a naughty boy, ready horsed for discipline: first, expostulate the case, then plead the necessity of the rod from great provocations, and conclude every period with a lash.

Now, if I know anything of mankind, these gentlemen might very well spare their reproof and correction: for there is not, through all nature, another so callous and insensible a member as the world's posteriors, whether you apply to it the toe or the birch.[13]

Swift is concerned with all the evidence of our self-contradictory nature, including the contradiction that the very fact of satire presents. Faithfully followed, the paradoxical situation can yield but one answer: man is not *animal rationale* but is *rationis capax*.[14] We have an explanation of our insensibility and incapacity to alter. It is an answer that takes us beyond correction. The satire becomes radical, for it brings into the light the comfortable assumption that we can see our folly, let alone amend it. The inquiry is now to ask what is man's nature, in the light of the evidence, including the evidence of satire itself? Is man's nature finally at odds with his intermittent notion of duty? In *Gulliver's Travels* Swift writes a satire that at once ensures that we shall inescapably see ourselves, and is at the same time a satire to end all notions of "correction". The means by which this is effected will concern us below.

The other main approach to what I have termed the "frontier" is to be met with in a philosophical poet, whose starting-point is in a world where all is for sale. The Langland of the *Visio* is the satirist of a world where all men know they do wrong: when Repentance calls, all obey. One good man is found to set society to rights; but he himself is not exempt from reproach. Langland calls in question the good man: for if the satire had portrayed a world of falling short, yet the standard by which this was readily measured is still beyond the one good man. So Piers the Ploughman must repent. As the poem develops in its B and C texts,[15] the issues this must have are hammered out in the poet's further reflections. There can be an end of satire, of correcting men, only on one condition—perfect fulfilment of the Moral Law. But who can fulfil it?—man's nature seems permanently opposed to the duty enjoined upon him. Yet in the Christian scheme of things this is ground at once for repentance and hope: the implacable Law has been fulfilled for man by Incarnate Deity. Langland crosses the frontier from satire when he asks the radical question—is not imperfection to be expected of us? So he moves on to the thinker's task of construction: satire has revealed the nature of man, and in revealing it has done its work. The Ploughman moves from active self-sufficiency to creaturely dependence upon a merciful God. Swift also, in *Gulliver's Travels*, asks the radical question: he, too, measures humanity by the standard of perfection: and the answer he gives makes an end of satire; we see that the satirist's habitual targets of folly and knavery are "all according to the due course of things".

[13]Preface to *A Tale of a Tub*.
[14]Letter of Swift to Pope, 29th September, 1725.
[15]There is nothing known to the writer in the present state of *Piers Plowman* studies to forbid the assumption that the three texts are the work of one poet. Indeed, the recent and substantial contribution of Dr. E. T. Donaldson (*Piers Plowman: The C-Text and its Poet,* Yale, 1949) reaffirms the view of R. W. Chambers that the onus of proof is all on the other side.

III

The master-stroke in the design of *Gulliver's Travels* is the characterization of Gulliver himself. If the satirist's problem, in Swift's conception, is to break down the defensive reaction of the reader, it is of the highest importance that Gulliver himself, the observer and reporter, shall win respect for his candour and objectivity. Once we have learnt to trust Gulliver the rest of the way to self-revelation will be made insensibly, even fatally, easy. It is therefore vital that Gulliver's qualifications for his task shall be carefully conveyed. Gulliver's education is happily rounded; he is versed in both arts and sciences, and yet without any suggestion of the paragon. He must be *l'homme moyen*—disinterestedness will win confidence. Secondly, the pattern of his voyaging must be so arranged as to bring about, albeit insensibly, development in his character. These fundamental considerations are well understood by Mr. A. E. Case in his notable treatment of "The Significance of *Gulliver's Travels*".[16] Swift's "intention to deepen the character of his principal figure" is "an integral part of his main design": and Mr. Case traces very well the development from "an amused and superior toleration" to the turning point, in the sixth chapter of the Voyage to Brobdingnag, where Gulliver is "really on the defensive for the first time".[17] Swift's artistry at this point is of the highest order, and it is perhaps doubtful whether Mr. Case does full justice to it. Gulliver begins the seventh chapter with a confession that he has not told the whole truth to the King of Brobdingnag—for the first time he takes the reader into his confidence: his report of European institutions has been edited, out of "that laudable Partiality to my own Country" which he knows the honest reader will share. Mr. Case appears to miss the force of this development in Gulliver, though he notes both the statement of "partiality" and the significant fact that Gulliver later exhibits "only a modified rapture upon his return to England". What has happened is that Swift, through the King of Brobdingnag, has fired his first broadside, the denunciation of the "most pernicious race of little odious vermin that nature ever suffered to crawl upon the surface of the earth". This Gulliver cannot accept: he is bound as the truthful narrator to record it, but the reader need not fear that so fantastic a charge is to be taken seriously. Not only does Gulliver share with the reader his "partiality" for our "noble and most beloved country", as Mr. Case notes, but he goes on to explain that the King's notions are part of "the miserable effects of a confined education". Gulliver the practical man is well to the fore here: the King's ideas are conceived in isolation from the real world—"the manners and customs that most prevail in other nations". The account of Brobdingnagian institutions that follows runs in the same vein: it is all too easy—for example, since in their army everyone serves under his own landlord or elected leader, the fact that they are "perfect enough in their exercises, and under very good discipline" is one "wherein I saw no great merit; for how should it be otherwise . . . ?" Mr. Case is right to speak of Gulliver "on the defensive"; contempt is a well-recognized form of defensive reac-

---

[16]The concluding essay in *Four Essays on "Gulliver's Travels."* Princeton, 1945.
[17]*ibid.*, pp. 105, 115 and 116.

tion. What has helped to bring about the change is the fact of size. Tolerance in Lilliput, where man is the giant, must give way to increased wariness where a man may be trodden underfoot. Johnson's comment on bigness and littleness is wide of the mark unless we underline "*Once you have thought*" of it. The decisive transition that Swift accomplishes at this point—the change from Gulliver the neutral observer to Gulliver the apologist for his own country—is prepared for in the commanding simplicity of the King, dwarfing his human interlocutor. So Gulliver is not harmed by the broadside. What was to devastate passes harmlessly over his head: in the "glass" the King holds up Gulliver disclaims any recognition of himself. The satiric train has been laid and fired—but to no effect: "narrow principles and short views" are all this outburst can illustrate. The King, from this point of view, is that fantastic idealist the satirist, who seeks to castigate our faults by clear appeals to reason: and Gulliver is his unscathed reader, refusing the appeal and explaining its laughable inappositeness.

So we can move on with Gulliver, who remains in this special sense *our* witness. In the celebrated third book, as Mr. Case observes, "he has now become the detached and half-cynical commentator on human life from without. In this voyage alone he is an observer and not an actor". This is the interval before he is drawn in again to active participation: and Mr. Case comments soundly on the opening paragraph of the last book where Gulliver speaks of his having remained at home "in a very happy condition". At the outset of his last voyage he is

> a man who has adjusted himself to a consciousness of the ordinary and even the extraordinary vices and follies of humanity. In this state he does not recognize that the Yahoos have any likeness to man. . . .[18]

It is of the highest importance to remember that Swift is faced with a distinct problem of contrivance. The worst that can be said about humanity has left Gulliver unconvinced. How then to bring home to Gulliver his true predicament? Mere pronouncement will have no decisive effect: that has been tried in Brobdingnag, where the King's implied appeal to Reason had left Gulliver unmoved but wary of fantastic idealism. This time, the assault is to come from within. The *tour de force* that Swift contrives is that Gulliver is drawn to love the Houyhnhnm race. Out of his own mouth is man condemned. No longer is it for the satirist to state the law and pronounce sentence for shortcomings. The method is precisely inverted—let man declare his "positives", and then he has involved his own law and judged himself. So it is fitting that the Gulliver who is at last brought to self-recognition is not the untried, superior traveller of the beginning of the work, but the experienced observer.

The point is deepened when we recall his first encounter with the Yahoos and with the Houyhnhnm. Each seems to this experienced traveller a kind of beast: and his aversion from the insufferable Yahoos is only paralleled by the condescension of his attempt to fondle the noble Houyhnhnm "using the common style and whistle of jockeys". The development of this book is Gulliver's deepening

[18]*op. cit.*, pp. 117–118.

awareness that the Yahoo-kind is his own species: and the pathos that accompanies this progressive realization proceeds all the way from that first act of unwitting effrontery, through the painful clinging to all that prevents complete identification with the Yahoos, his one suit of clothes, to the final realization that even as a servant and disciple there can be no place for him in the land of the Houyhnhnms. It is not always understood why Gulliver must go: his is a supreme loneliness, for, falling infinitely short of the perfection of his masters, he is yet differentiated from the " wild Yahoo" in possessing "some rudiments of reason". This is potentially dangerous, for when "added to the natural pravity of those animals", the consequences are impossible to contemplate. Gulliver's plight is indeed desperate. Swift's satiric genius has penetrated to the final truth that when man falls, he falls below the level of the brute creation. A wild Yahoo is one thing: a Yahoo with "some rudiments of reason" presents incalculable possibilities of harm. This time the mirror has been so contrived that we cannot choose but see ourselves, and turn revolted from what we are.

> When I happened to behold the reflection of my own form in a lake or fountain, I turned away my face in horror and detestation of myself, and could better endure the sight of a common Yahoo than of my own person.

Mr. Case's treatment fails at this most crucial moment of Gulliver's rejection. "In the end", he writes, "the master dismisses Gulliver with regret and shows no disinclination to his society. In other words, a somewhat above-average Englishman was not altogether unacceptable company for a perfect being".[19] This is at the furthest remove from Gulliver's leave-taking; for

> as I was going to prostrate myself to kiss his hoof, he did me the honour to raise it gently to my mouth. I am not ignorant how much I have been censured for mentioning this last particular. For my detractors are pleased to think it improbable that so illustrious a person should descend to give so great a mark of distinction to a creature so inferior as I.

We are a world away from that first attempted condescension of Gulliver "using the common style and whistle of jockeys" towards the Houyhnhnm. The reversal of roles perfectly exemplifies the truth towards which Swift has directed us through our guide. The conclusion of the whole endeavor is that pride is an absurdity. "I am not in the least provoked", says Gulliver in the close, "at the sight of a lawyer, a pickpocket, a colonel, a fool . . . this is all according to the due course of things." There is the vocation of the satirist at an end: how to blame men for what is "all according to the due course of things"? But there is still one task left for intelligence and imagination: let man realize that things *are* thus with him, so that he will refrain from pride, the crowning absurdity in "a lump of deformity and diseases both in body and mind". We have left the world of corrective satire: nothing is to be done. The citadel of the reader's insentience has been taken not by outward assault, but from within. The defensive blindness has been penetrated. If the beginning of wisdom is to know ourselves, how very far we are from wisdom when normal satire

[19]*op. cit.*, p. 119.

cannot bring us even to identify ourselves! So the radical question is asked and decisively answered. Swift has reached the frontier of satire: man is not to be blamed for what is his natural state. Only let him *see* himself for what he is.

IV

If there is no return to a world governed by the comfortable assumption that we can see our follies and by an effort of will amend them, where does the journey take us? Is the satiric intelligence from this point onwards disqualified from sustained inquiry? Dryden, as we have seen, had naturally linked satire with the heroic; each in its distinctive way vindicated that Right Reason to which all men must owe final allegiance. But it is not in a world of "heroic" dimensions that the inquiry is to be pursued. With an end of the assumption that man can identify his failings and redress his state, a new world is brought into being. The very failure becomes itself the centre of serious imaginative attention. If we are ever to know ourselves, we must examine more closely "this *bovarysme,* the human will to see things as they are not".[20] What blindly resists the assaults of corrective satire unfolds to the radical inquiry: and, if we pass beyond contempt into objective appraisal, a new territory is decisively entered. We move from satire to what may be called, with suitable qualifications, Realism.

The term "realism" has attracted to itself so many varying interpretations that it has become virtually meaningless. A serviceable distinction may however be suggested by the opposition of the terms "realism" and "naturalism", if "realism" is used to denote concentration upon the painful, the sordid, or the distressing within the whole field of "deeds and language such as men do use". One recalls Flaubert's anxiety when, during the writing of *Madame Bovary,* the school headed by Champfleury proclaimed itself "realist": but the reading of *Les Aventures de Mademoiselle Mariette* and *Madame d'Aigrizelles* removed any doubts. It is not merely "the choice of modern and popular subjects" (in Champfleury's definition) that makes for "realism" in the sense here proposed: what is directly involved at this level is concentration upon those particularities of experience which may be termed sordid or distressing. From this proceeds the positive achievement of "realism" in the only distinctive sense of the term—the presentation of character which, condemned by universal judgement, is yet immune to self-awareness, much less self-criticism. This of course is not incompatible with feelings of aversion or even contempt on the part of the artist. Flaubert's complaint that he had been generally misunderstood contains its own irony:

> On me croit épris du réel, tandis que je l'exècre; car c'est en haine du réalisme que j'ai entrepris ce roman. Mais je n'en déteste pas moins la fausse idéalité dont nous sommes bernés par le temps qui court.[21]

[20]T. S. Eliot, "Shakespeare and the Stoicism of Seneca" (*Selected Essays*, p. 131).
[21]Letter to Madame Roger Des Genettes (Oct.–Nov. 1856): *Correspondance*, Paris, 1927; Vol. IV, p. 134.

Flaubert's portrayal of Emma Bovary remains the decisive contribution to the modern art of fiction, for it builds a bridge between the world of satire and the extended portrayal of character. In Flaubert's presentation attitudes of irony and contempt are not precluded. With later interpretation, however, when conceptions of human status have undergone deterministic influence, his work is read as a penetrating study of the human condition, immune to praise or censure, the faithful portrayal of what we inescapably are. The predicament of Emma is one we have met before in urbane satire: she cannot be aware of what she is. She is incapable of doing other than dignifying her petty, provincial amours into *grandes passions*. But there is no urbanity in the feelings with which her creator regards her. The world of "heroic" pretension is consumed in the fire of his wrath against "la fausse idéalité"—"Haine au Almanzor comme au Jean Couteaudier! Fi des Auvergnats et des coiffeurs!" Flaubert's work is indeed a bridge, beginning well within the frontier of satire; but because the creature must be shown as immune to self-awareness, "realism" in this decisive sense is a final comment on the human capacity to grasp "reality". It is thus that the philosopher Jules de Gaultier apprehends Emma Bovary, and coins from her name the term which denotes in all seriousness one of the essential human faculties—"the power granted to man to conceive himself as other than he is." This is no longer material for satire, a tendency which we can finally correct: it is now a fundamental truth with which the serious portrayal of human nature must reckon. It was for satiric insight to identify this predicament and convey it, firstly with urbane amusement, and latterly with overtones of contempt and aversion. But once conveyed, altering conceptions of the nature of man will prepare for its reception as profound truth. Precisely because Emma is shown as incapable of self-recognition, the censure of her author affects neither her nor Flaubert's later readers. The insensibility of the reader to the portrayal of his own vice or folly can spur the satirist on to greater endeavours, provided only the condition is felt to be curable. When it is diagnosed as an unchanging condition, there is no room for satiric correction: we need not be "in the least provoked". As Swift observed to Pope, hatred or anger is for *"vous autres"*, who are disappointed when in fact there was no reason to hope.[22] There is, then, no room, once the frontier of radical satire is reached, for censure: but a new terrain for imaginative exploration lies in view. If Swift reaches "a point of no return" in the radical satire on which he embarks, the "Newfound land" towards which his course directs us is the realm of Realism: and the journey does not end there. The "minor" satire of the unchangeable eccentric in the long run leads to the major triumphs not only of Realism, where the frontier has been crossed, but of that developed art of the novel which is concerned with the shifting masks through which alone our complex and ambiguous nature makes itself known, to prompt all our investigation, provided only that we do not attempt to impose the order of law.

[22]Letter of 26th November, 1725.

Part 2

TWO VIEWS OF PERSONAE

Order and Cruelty

Claude Rawson

HAMM . . . you're on earth, there's no cure for that!

—Samuel Beckett, *Endgame*

Swift's satire often suggests an impasse, a blocking of escape routes and saving possibilities. This feeling presses on the reader for reasons which do not necessarily follow from the satiric topic as such, from the specific wickedness Swift is castigating, or any outright assertion that the wickedness is incurable. Incurability is certainly often implied, and the sense of an impasse is (by a paradox which is only apparent) related to a complementary vision of unending paths of vicious self-complication, bottomless spirals of human perversity. This is less a matter of Swift's official ideological views than of mental atmosphere and ironic manipulation: that is, of a more informal, yet very active, interplay between deliberate attacking purposes (and tactics), and certain tense spontaneities of self-expression. My concern is with the stylistic results of this interplay, though I do not pretend that the deliberate purposes can be clearly distinguished from the more shadowy ones. It may be that in Swift such dividing lines *need* to be unclear. I begin with Swift's most frequently discussed passage, the mock-argument[1]

> that in most Corporeal Beings, which have fallen under my Cognizance, the *Outside* hath been infinitely preferable to the *In*: Whereof I have been farther convinced from some late Experiments. Last Week I saw a Woman *flay'd*, and you will hardly believe, how much it altered her Person for the worse. Yesterday I ordered the Carcass of a *Beau* to be stript in my Presence; when we were all amazed to find so many unsuspected Faults under one Suit of Cloaths: Then I laid open his *Brain*, his *Heart*, and his *Spleen*; But, I plainly perceived at every Operation, that the farther we proceeded, we found the Defects encrease upon us in Number and Bulk: from all which, I justly formed this Conclusion to my self; That . . . He that can with *Epicurus* content his Ideas with the *Films* and *Images* that fly off upon his Senses from the *Superficies* of Things; Such a Man truly wise, creams off Nature, leaving the Sower and the Dregs, for Philosophy and Reason to lap up. This is the sublime and refined Point of Felicity, called, *the Possession of being well deceived*; The Serene Peaceful State of being a Fool among Knaves (*Tale*, IX).

From Claude Rawson, *Gulliver and The Gentle Reader* (London: Routledge, 1973, and London and New Jersey: Humanities Press, 1991), 33–59. (Earlier version originally published in *Essays in Criticism*, 20 (1970), 24–56.) Reprinted by permission of the author and the editors of *Essays in Criticism*.

[1]*Works*, I.109–10.

Here, the example of the flayed woman supports an argument similar to that of *A Beautiful Young Nymph Going to Bed*: whores can look horrible when their finery is stripped off, conventional celebrations of female beauty gloss over some ugly facts, the *Outside* looks better than the *In* and creates inappropriate complacencies. The flayed woman is portrayed in less detail, and seems physically less shocking, than the nymph of the poem, with her artificial hair, eyes and teeth, and her 'Shankers, Issues, running Sores'.[2] But she is, in a sense, more 'gratuitous'. In the poem, however horrible the details, the main proposition is sustained by them in a manner essentially straightforward, formulaic, and indeed conventional.[3] The account is a nightmare fantastication, but it is also simply a *donnée*: the poem asks us to imagine such a woman, and the point is made. The nymph is entirely subordinated to obvious formulaic purposes, even though 'subordination', in another sense, ill describes the vitality of the grotesquerie.

The flayed woman (and stripped beau), on the other hand, are momentary intensities which do not merely *serve* the argument they are meant to illustrate, but actually *spill over* it. They take us suddenly, and with devastating brevity, outside the expectations of the immediate logic, into a surprising and 'cruel' domain of fantasy. 'Cruel' is here used in something like Artaud's sense, as lying outside or beyond ordinary moral motivations, and Swift's brevity is essential to the effect. For this brevity, and the astringent blandness of the language, arrest the play of fantasy sufficiently to prevent it from developing into a moral allegory in its own right. The point is important, because brevity is not a necessary feature of what we nowadays think of as the literature of cruelty, that is, of such writers as Sade, Jarry, the followers of Artaud in the theatre, the authors included in Breton's *Anthologie de l'Humour Noir* and allied literary explorers of the black joke and the 'gratuitous' shock. When Breton placed Swift at the head of his anthology, as *véritable initiateur* of a black humour emancipated from the 'degrading influence' of satire and moralising,[4] he told a real truth, for Swift has (I believe) a temperamental tendency in this direction. But the tendency is powerfully held in check by conscious moral purposes which harness it to their own use. Hence his gratuitous cruelties are usually brief eruptions, only as long (so to speak) as the Super-Ego takes to catch up, and any extensive development of a grim joke normally dovetails into a fully-fledged moral demonstration or argument, as in the *Beautiful Young Nymph* or the *Modest Proposal*. Brief quasi-cannibalistic frissons in *Gulliver* (Gulliver using the skins of Yahoos for making clothes or sails, *G.T.*, IV.iii and x)[5] are more gratuitous than the *Modest Proposal*, as the flayed woman is more gratuitous than the *Beautiful Young Nymph*. The *Gulliver* passages are extremely minor comic

---

[2] *Poems*, II.581–3.
[3] See Irvin Ehrenpreis, *The Personality of Jonathan Swift* (London, 1958), pp.43 ff.
[4] André Breton, *Anthologie de l'Humour Noir*, new edn (Paris, 1966), pp.25, 17.
[5] *Works*, XI.236, 276, 281. Cf. the passage in the *Modest Proposal* about the use of the 'flayed' skins of the cannibalized children to 'make admirable *Gloves for Ladies*, and *Summer Boots for fine Gentlemen*' (*Works*, XII.112).

assaults on our 'healthy' sensibilities, lacking the intensity of the passage from the *Tale*; but in one paradoxical sense they also are more unsettling than the more extended use of the cannibal image, precisely because in the *Proposal* the image is the direct sustaining principle of a moral argument. To this extent Breton seems off the mark when he follows his Swift section (which includes a substantial portion of the *Proposal*) with an elaborate cannibal extravaganza from Sade.[6]

This is not to say that the briefer passages have no moral implication (nor that the extended ones lack the power to shock, or have no local and subsidiary intensities of their own). Presumably the clothes of Yahoo-skin are also a reminder of the animality of man, while the flayed woman purports to illustrate the notion that appearances are more agreeable than reality. But it would take a perverse reader to feel that these moral implications provide the dominant effect. The gruesomeness of the flayed woman is so shockingly and absurdly *over*-appropriate to the ostensible logic as to be, by any normal standards, inappropriate. Critics who recognize this sometimes sentimentalize the issue by arguing that the flayed woman overspills the immediate moral not into an amoral gratuitousness, but into a different and more powerful moral significance: that she represents, for example, Swift's pained protest at this treatment of whores.[7] This seems as wrong as William Burroughs's notion that the *Modest Proposal* is 'a tract against Capital Punishment'.[8] I doubt Swift's opposition to either oppression, and if anything the allusion to flaying invites comparison with this sudden *redirection* of the cannibal irony in the *Modest Proposal*:[9]

---

[6]For other collocations of Swift and Sade by Breton, see the passages from the Surrealist manifestos cited by Denis Donoghue, *Jonathan Swift: A Critical Anthology* (Harmondsworth, 1971), p.130. Swift has no elaborate cannibal extravaganzas in Sade's manner, but it is probable that Sade took some of his inspiration from Swift, whom, according to Simone de Beauvoir, Sade 'used and even copied' (*Must We Burn de Sade?* trs. A. Michelson (London and New York, 1953), p.62).

[7]See William Frost, 'The irony of Swift and Gibbon: a reply to F. R. Leavis', *Essays in Criticism*, xvii (1967), 44–5: 'Swift alludes . . . to a well-known public sight visible in his London, the bloody back of a prostitute whipped at the end of a cart on the way to the Fleet Prison . . . [and comments on] the widespread callousness to the sufferings of not very advantaged groups in Augustan England'. I agree that Swift is probably referring to a whore, or other malefactress, but believe that it is more correct to say, with E. W. Rosenheim, that she 'would, for eighteenth-century readers, be recognizable as someone who deserved flaying' (*Swift and the Satirist's Art* (Chicago, 1963), p.202), and that Swift himself thought so too. Swift was not notably soft-hearted in his ideas about the treatment of 'not very advantaged groups'. In his *Proposal for Giving Badges to the Beggars* and in several other writings, for example, he recommended the whipping of certain classes of beggars, drunkards, whoremongers and others, and did not think that 'those profligate, abandoned Women, who croud our Streets with their borrowed or spurious Issue' deserved any charity (*Works*, XIII.131–40; IX.202). For some disagreements between myself and others about the flayed woman, see *Essays in Criticism*, xx (1970), 496–7; xxi (1971), 115–16 and 417–18. The last of these discussions contains a suggestion by Mr Philip Drew 'that "a woman *flay'd*" may mean "a woman without her make–up on" ', which seems to me wholly improbable. It is partly based on a passage in *The Way of the World* where the use of the term to suggest lack of make-up is manifestly metaphorical and mock-violent.

[8]William S. Burroughs, *Naked Lunch* (New York, 1966), p.xliv. I find it difficult to accept suggestions that this is not what the passage means.

[9]*Works*, XII.114.

> Neither indeed can I deny, that if the same Use were made of several plump young girls in this Town, who, without one single Groat to their Fortunes, cannot stir Abroad without a Chair, and appear at the *Play-house,* and *Assemblies* in foreign Fineries, which they never will pay for; the Kingdom would not be the worse.

In both cases the black joke suggests, if not literal endorsement of the hideous punishment, a distinct animus against the victim. The presence of this animus indicates that the irony is not, after all, gratuitous in the strictest Gide-ian sense. No human act can be entirely gratuitous (that is, absolutely motiveless), as Gide himself admitted:[10] it can only be disconnected from its normal *external* functions, in this case the moral implications expected of the satire. If in both cases the animus is transferred suddenly away from the official paths of the formula (truth vs. delusion; eating people is wrong), yet still carries a redirected moral charge (against whores, or foolish girls whose vanity is crippling Ireland's economy), there is an explosive overplus in the sheer wilful suddenness of the act of redirection as such. A haze of *extra* hostility hangs in the air, unaccounted for, dissolving the satire's clean logic into murkier and more unpredictable precisions, spreading uneasiness into areas of feeling difficult to rationalize, and difficult for the reader to escape. Part of Swift's answer to the dilemma posed for the satirist by his own belief that '*Satyr is a sort of* Glass, *wherein Beholders do generally discover every body's Face but their own*' (*Battle of the Books,* Preface)[11] is thus to counter, by a strategy of unease, the reader's natural tendency to exclude himself from the explicit condemnation: his escape into 'Serene Peaceful States' is blocked off even when he is innocent of the specific charge.

Often in such cases, moreover, the irony is manipulated in such a way as to suggest that the reader cannot be wholly unimplicated even in the specific charge. It is not only through unexpectedness or diversionary violence that the flayed woman and stripped beau spill over the logical frame. They also have an absurd tendency to generalize or extend the guilt to the rest of mankind, through a tangle of implications which act in irrational defiance of any mere logic. If the argument had been overridingly concerned to demonstrate that appearances can be fraudulent, superficial views inadequate, and vanity misplaced, the notion that people look ugly when stripped of their clothes or cosmetics would have been a sufficient, and a logically disciplined, support to it. To specify whores and beaux would be a perfectly legitimate singling out of social types who trade disreputably on appearances, and are otherwise open to moral censure. These didactic reasonings, and the larger-scale exposure of mad 'moderns', obviously remain present. But, in the wording as it stands, they are also, characteristically, subverted; as though the several wires crossed, making an explosive short-circuit. Flayed or dissected bodies hardly produce the most morally persuasive evidence of the delusiveness of appearances; nor do they as such prove a moral turpitude. If a whore's body alters for the worse when flayed, or a beau's innards look unsavoury when laid open, so would anyone else's, and the fact does not obviously demonstrate

---

[10]See G. W. Ireland, *Gide* (Edinburgh and London, 1963), pp.46–50.
[11]*Works,* I.140.

anybody's wickedness. The images, which begin as specific tokens of guilt aimed at certain human types, teasingly turn into general signs of the human condition. The images' strong charge of undifferentiated blame is thus left to play over undefined turpitudes attributable to the whole of mankind. The beau's innards recall an earlier statement by the *Tale's* 'author', about having 'dissected the Carcass of *Humane Nature,* and read many useful Lectures upon the several Parts, both *Containing and Contained;* till at last it smelt so strong, I could preserve it no longer' (*Tale*, v).[12]

The passage parodies Wotton and others,[13] but, as often with Swiftian parody, transcends its immediate object. And the imagery's characteristic oscillation between moral turpitude and bodily corruption irrationally suggests a damaging equivalence between the two, placing on *Humane Nature* a freewheeling load of moral guilt which is inescapable and which yet attaches itself to faults outside the moral domain.

For if satire that is 'levelled at all' (i.e. 'general' rather than 'personal') 'is never resented for an offence by any, since every individual Person makes bold to understand it of others, and very wisely removes his particular Part of the Burthen upon the shoulders of the World, which are broad enough, and able to bear it' (*Tale,* Preface),[14] this is only likely to be true of a 'general' satire of *specific* vices. Where the aggression turns indistinct, and overspills the area of specifiable moral guilt, no opportunity is given for complacent self-exculpation on a specific front, and the reader becomes implicated. Instead of permitting the individual to shift his load on to the world's shoulders, Swift forces the reader to carry the world's load on *his*. The result, second time round, is that even the specific charges begin to stick: we become identified with whores, beaux, moderns. We cannot shrug this off by saying that it is Swift's 'author' who is speaking and not Swift. The intensities are Swift's, and depend on the blandness and even friendliness of the 'author'. The 'author' is saying in effect *hypocrite lecteur, mon semblable, mon frère,* and saying it kindly and welcomingly; but it is Swift who is making him say it, and the reader must decide whether he likes the thought of such a brother.

The cumulative sense of impasse (all mankind becoming implicated in the attack, the attack surviving any dismissal of specific charges, the curious revalidation of these charges by that fact, the miscellaneous blocking of the reader's escape-routes) depends, then, on energies which exceed the legitimate logical implications of the discourse. These energies cannot be accounted for by a mere retranslation of the mock-logic into its non-ironic 'equivalent', and part of their force depends on the violation of whatever consequential quality exists either in the hack's zany reasoning or its sober didactic counterpart. The carefully and extensively prepared polarity between the mad values of the modern

---

[12]Ibid., 77.
[13]*Tale of a Tub*, ed. A. C. Guthkelch and D. Nichol Smith, 2nd edn (Oxford, 1958), p.123n.; Ronald Paulson, *Theme and Structure in Swift's Tale of a Tub* (New Haven, 1960), pp.53 ff.
[14]*Works*, I.31.

hack, and the sanity of the non-singular, traditionalist, rational, unsuperficial man of sense, may seem for a while, in the Digression on Madness, solid and definite enough to provide at least limited reassurance against the more unsettling stylistic tremors. The reassurance is undermined but perhaps not eliminated by the flayed woman and stripped beau. But in the final sentence of the paragraph, the bad and good cease to function in lines that are parallel and opposite: the lines collapse, and cross. The comforting opposition is brought to a head, and then shattered, against the whole direction of the argument, by the suggestion that the alternative to being a fool is to be not a wise man but a knave.[15]

Critics often assume some form of 'diametrical opposition' between putative and real authors at this point. Either Swift's voice suddenly erupts, nakedly, from the other's vacuous chatter, or at best 'fools' and 'knaves' have simultaneously one clear value for Swift and an opposite one for his 'author'. I suggest that the relationship is at all times more elusive, and that the rigidities of mask-criticism (even in its more sophisticated forms) tend to compartmentalize what needs to remain a more fluid and indistinct interaction. (The theoretically clear opposition, in the preceding part of the Digression, between mad and sane, or bad and good, is a different thing: a temporary build-up, created for demolition.) The notion that in the 'Fool among Knaves' we suddenly hear Swift's own voice makes a kind of sense: but it runs the danger of suggesting quite improperly both that we have not actively been hearing this voice throughout, and that we now hear nothing else. In actual fact, the phrase trades simultaneously on our feeling that the sudden intensity comes straight from Swift, and on our reluctance to identify Swift even momentarily with an 'author' whom the work as a whole relentlessly ridicules. The paradox of that 'author' is that he has enormous vitality, a 'presence' almost as insistent as Swift's, without having much definable *identity* as a 'character'. He needs to be distinguished from Swift, but hardly as a separate and autonomous being. He is an ebullient embodiment of many of Swift's dislikes, but the ebullience is Swift's, and the 'author' remains an amorphous mass of disreputable energies, whose vitality belongs less to any independent status (whether as clear-cut allegory or full-fledged personality) than to an endlessly opportunistic subservience to the satirist's needs. Unduly simplifying or systematic speculation as to when Swift is talking and when his 'persona', or about their 'diametrically opposite' meanings if both are talking at once, often turns masks into persons, and induces in some critics the most absurd expectations of coherently developed characterization. Thus W. B. Ewald's classic work on Swift's 'masks' footnotes its discussion of the fools-knaves passage with the astonishing statement that 'The author's interest in observing and performing anatomical dissections is a characteristic which

---

[15]Something of the same shock may be felt in Blake's juxtaposition of these two aphorisms in the 'Proverbs of Hell', nos 18–19: 'If the fool would persist in his folly he would become wise. / Folly is the cloke of knavery.' Blake's first aphorism belongs straightforwardly to the traditional paradoxical exaltation of wise folly. Swift, too, as I shall argue, is invoking that tradition, although his relationship to it is even more elusive than Blake's.

remains undeveloped in the *Tale* and which does not fit very convincingly the sort of *persona* Swift has set up.'[16]

It is, of course, true that the 'author' uses 'fool' as a term of praise, as Cibber in the *Dunciad* praises Dulness. The Digression on Madness is a 'praise of folly', and the 'author' proudly declares himself 'a Person, whose Imaginations are hard-mouth'd, and exceedingly disposed to run away with his *Reason*'.[17] The *Tale* presents, in its way, quite as much of an upside-down world as Pope's poem, but relies much less systematically on any single or dominant *verbal* formula. I do not mean that the *Dunciad* lacks that rudimentary two-way traffic between terms of praise and blame which we see in the *Tale* when, for example, the 'author' praises his 'Fool' as 'a Man truly wise', although it may be true that even at this level the *Tale's* ironic postures are more teasingly unstable (indeed the 'author' seems not only to be scrambling simple valuations of wisdom and folly, but also perverting the 'true' paradox that 'folly is wisdom'). But the poem's mock-exaltation of fools rests essentially on a few strongly signposted terms (*dunce, dull,* etc.), which advertise the main ironic formula, and guarantee its fundamental predictability. When we feel uneasy or embarrassed in the *Dunciad,* it is because the main irony is *too* consistently sustained, rather than not enough. When Cibber praises Dulness ('whose good old cause I yet defend', 'O! ever gracious . . .', I. 165, 173, etc.), we may feel that Pope's blame-by-praise becomes awkward, not because the formula threatens to slip, but because it strains belief through overdoing. The implausibility may be no greater in itself than the hack's celebration of 'Serene Peaceful States'. But Cibber's praise has the slow unemphatic stateliness of a rooted conviction, while the hack's occurs in a context full of redirections, 'Fool' being disturbed by 'Knaves', as indeed the paragraph's happy style is disturbed throughout by alien intensities (flayed woman, beau's innards). Cibber at such moments fails to take off into the freer air of Pope's satiric fantasy, and solidifies instead into an improbably oversimplified 'character'. His heavy 'consistency' embarrasses differently from the 'inconsistencies' of Swift's hack, who, being in a sense no character at all, obeys no laws but those of his creator's anarchic inventiveness. The embarrassments in Pope are rare, but damaging. They are unintended, and disturb that poise and certainty of tone essential to Pope's verse. In Swift's satiric ambience, embarrassment is radical: it is a moral rather than an aesthetic thing, and is the due response to the rough edges and subversions of a style whose whole nature it is to undermine certainties, including the certainties it consciously proclaims.

Such blurred and shocking interchange (rather than sharp ironic opposition) between speaker and satirist is not confined to unruly works like the *Tale.* It occurs even in the *Modest Proposal,* that most astringent and tautly formulaic of Swift's writings. When the proposer uses the famous phrase, 'a Child, *just dropt*

---

[16]W. B. Ewald, *The Masks of Jonathan Swift* (Oxford [Blackwell], 1954), p.39, n.73. Actually, Ewald's remark is not only irrelevant to the real feeling of the passage, but also wrong on its own terms. There actually *is* 'consistency', if one wants it, in the fact that the 'author' is the sort of fool who performs experiments in order to discover the obvious.

[17]*Works,* I.114.

from its Dam',[18] a shock occurs because the style has hitherto given no unmistakable indication of its potential nastiness. Swift means the phrase to erupt in all its cruel violence, yet it is formally spoken by the proposer, and we are not to suppose *him* to be a violent, or an unkind man. Is the nasty phrase 'inconsistent' with his character? In a way, yes. On the other hand, part of Swift's irony is that prevailing values are so inhumane, that a gentle and moderate man will take all the horror for granted. If he can sincerely assert his humanity while advocating monstrous schemes, may he not also be expected to use a nasty phrase calmly and innocently? In which case, the usage might be 'consistent' with his character, thus indicating 'diametrical' opposition between him and Swift. But inhumane propaganda which claims, or believes itself, to be humane (say that of a 'sincere' defender of apartheid), does not use inhumane language; and we should have to imagine the speaker as incredibly insensitive to English usage, if he really wanted himself and his scheme to seem as humane as he believed they were. Such discussion of the 'character' and his 'consistency' leads to deserts of circularity. But the problem hardly poses itself in the reading (as it poses itself, down to the question of insensitivity to usage, over Cibber's praise of Dulness), and what becomes apparent is the irrelevance, rather than the truth or untruth, of the terms. The violent phrase is not an 'inconsistency' but a dislocation, among other dislocations. It has nothing to say about character, but breaks up a formula (the formula of a calm, kindly advocacy of horrible deeds), within a style which both includes such formulas and is given to breaking them up. Thus, when (in contrast to the *Dunciad's* blame-by-praise, where it is easy to translate one set of terms into its opposite) Swift's speakers praise fools, or proclaim their humanity in brutal language, our reaction is to oscillate nervously between speaker and satirist. If we bring this oscillation into the open by asking (as critics are always asking) whether a bad speaker is using bad terms in a good sense, or whether Swift himself is making some form of explosive intervention, we find no meaningful answer. But there is a sense in which it is a meaningful *question,* for it brings into the open an uncertainty which is essential to the style.

The uncertainty is most strikingly illustrated in the Digression's 'Knaves'. For it is this electrifying term, with all its appearance of simplifying finality, which most resists tidy-minded schematisms of parallel-and-opposite valuation and the rest. If 'Fool' was good to the 'author' and bad to Swift, are 'Knaves' bad to the 'author' and good to Swift? Does the sentence's impact really reside in our feeling that 'Knave' is the fool's word for a quality Swift would name more pleasantly? If so, which quality? The answer is deliberately indistinct. Perhaps the 'Knaves' are those 'Betters' who, in the Preface to the *Battle of the Books,* are said to threaten the serenity of fools (the Preface too is 'of the Author', though an 'author' at that moment more similar than opposite to Swift).[19] But if this points to a partial explanation, it does so *ex post facto,* and is not experi-

[18]Ibid., XII.110.
[19]Ibid., I.140.

enced in the reading. To the extent that we are, in context, permitted to escape the suggestion that the world is absolutely divided into fools and knaves, we confront alternatives that are elusive, unclear. If we do not take 'Knaves' as Swift's word, literally meant, we cannot simply dismiss it as coming from the 'author' and being therefore translatable into something less damaging. We cannot be sure of the nature of any saving alternative, and may even uneasily suspect that we are in a fool's 'Serene Peaceful State' for imagining that such alternatives exist. The style's aggressive indistinctness thus leaves damaging possibilities in the air, without pinning Swift down to an assertion definite enough to be open to rebuttal. And so it seems more appropriate to note the imprisoning rhetorical effect of 'Fool among Knaves' than to determine too precisely who means what by those words. A rhetorical turn which wittily blocks off any respectable alternative to being a fool, is reinforced by those either-way uncertainties which the whole style induces in the reader. The reader is thus poised between the guilt of being merely human, and an exculpation which is as doubtful as the charges are unclear. The apparent definiteness of the epigram, and the reader's cloudy insecurity, mirror and complete each other in an over-riding effect of impasse.

Fools and knaves go proverbially together, balancing one another in a variety of traditional sayings, a familiar source of more or less ready ironies for the witty phrase-maker. Swift's mot tends towards the most universalizing of fool-knave proverbs ('Knaves and fools divide the world'). But part of its flavour lies outside the grimmer implications, in the stylistic bravura which makes an established phrase complete itself in defiance of contextual expectations. The sudden appearance of 'Knaves' at the end of the sentence has a delighted rightness. It is a witty and exhilarating idiomatic homecoming. The wit gives pleasure in itself, and playfully suggests the survival of linguistic order within a certain mental anarchy.

Wit (in the high as well as the restricted sense) knows its enemies well: 'By *Fools* 'tis *hated,* and by *Knaves undone*',[20] and the erection of symmetries of style as a means of maintaining order among life's unruly energies is a familiar function of Augustan wit. Such symmetries have their effect more as acts of authorial presence, authorial defiances of chaos, than necessarily as embodiments of a widespread or active faith in stability or harmony. If the witty completeness of Swift's 'Fool among Knaves' holds together a world of unruly energies, the joke is also, by its qualities of surprise and shock, an unruly energy in its own right. The idiomatic homecoming is achieved with such tear-away unpredictability, that it leaves equally open the possibility of a fresh engulfment in the hack author's chaos, or of further victorious but unexpected versatilities from the satirist. The sudden poise seems more like a tense individual triumph, uncertain to be repeated and wholly dependent on our momentarily vivid sense of the satirist's mastery, than like the revelation of a serenely ordered structure on which we may henceforth depend.

[20]Pope, *Essay on Criticism*, l.507.

Even the more predictable symmetries of Augustan style, the parallelism, antithesis, balance, the patternings which complete a formula or satisfy an expectation (idiomatic, syntactical, metrical, or logical), do not always evoke harmonious parterres of order, stability and ease. Pope's couplets are full of the kind of symmetry in which damaging alternatives are so starkly paired as to suggest not the comforting boundaries of a fixed and ordered world, but closed systems of vice or unhappiness from which there is no apparent release. Many thumbnail characterizations in the *Epistle to a Lady*, for example, contain such imprisoning paradoxes as 'A fool to Pleasure, and a slave to Fame', 'The Pleasure miss'd her, and the Scandal hit', 'Young without Lovers, old without a Friend' (ll. 62, 128, 246). These perhaps have a brevity of the ready-made, and certainly an external quality. Pope's concern is psychological, to define character, but his subjects here are either placed in predicaments mainly circumstantial ('Young without Lovers'), or described in very generalized psychological terms ('A fool to Pleasure') which suggest rapid and sketchy inference from outward behaviour. If the stylistic patterns evoke certain forms of impasse, rather than an easy sense of order, the impasse hardly becomes total or absolute. One is free to feel that circumstances might change or behaviour improve, whereas prisons of the mind will seem correspondingly inescapable because (as Milton's Satan discovered when he saw that hell was partly a mental state)[21] they are carried everywhere within us. The typical impasse in Swift rests on a psychological factor, a perpetual perverse restlessness (madness close to badness) similar to what Johnson more compassionately saw as 'that hunger of imagination which preys incessantly upon life'.[22] . . .

But Pope's usual way with damaging generalizations is to turn quickly to particulars, which are more amenable to the sort of enclosed definition which lets the rest of humanity out. 'Characters' overwhelm their universalizing contexts. In the *Epistle to Cobham*, the generalizing lip-service to human nature's 'puzzling Contraries' (l. 124) is even greater than in *To a Lady*: 'Our depths who fathoms, or our shallows finds,/Quick whirls, and shifting eddies, of our minds?' (ll. 29–30). The corresponding stress on triumphs of individual categorization is also greater. The 'ruling passion' seems a convenient formula less because it is a particularly good means to psychological insights than because of the pleasures of conclusive definition which it yields:

> Search then the Ruling Passion: There, alone,
> The Wild are constant, and the Cunning known.
> (ll. 174ff.)

The satisfactions are largely aesthetic. The lengthy portrait of Wharton which follows this couplet is full of vivid debating triumphs:

---

[21]*Paradise Lost*, I.254–5; IV.20–3, 75 ff. For the literary and theological background, see Helen Gardner, 'Milton's "Satan" and the theme of damnation in Elizabethan tragedy', *Essays and Studies*, N.S., i (1948), 58 & n.; and Merrit Y. Hughes, ' "Myself am Hell" ', *Modern Philology*, liv (1956), 80–94.

[22]*Rasselas*, ch. xxxi[i].

> This clue once found, unravels all the rest,
> The prospect clears, and Wharton stands confest. . . .
>
> Ask you why Wharton broke thro' ev'ry rule?
> 'Twas all for fear the Knaves should call him Fool.
>   Nature well known, no prodigies remain,
> Comets are regular, and Wharton plain.

If the concept of a 'ruling passion' is something whose ramifying completeness imprisons the satiric victim, and if Pope's play of paradox and antithesis reinforces this imprisonment, there is nevertheless in the poem a feeling not of imprisonment but of release. 'The prospect clears': such manifest delights of the controlling intellect have at least as much vitality as the turpitudes of Wharton and the rest. Contrast the very different finality of Swift's famous mot about Wharton's father, where the witty energy is entirely devoted to closing-in on the victim, and where the astringency of the prose-rhythms makes Pope's verse seem almost jaunty: 'He is a Presbyterian in Politics, and an Atheist in Religion; but he chuseth at present to whore with a Papist'.[23]

This astringency is revealing. It is often found where Swift practises what we may call couplet-rhetoric, that style in both verse and prose whose qualities of balance, antithesis, and pointedness mirror (ironically or not) Augustan ideals of coherence, regularity and decorous interchange, as well as paradoxes of enclosed self-contradiction.[24] He seldom wrote heroic couplets, perhaps resisting the almost institutionalized sense of order which the form seemingly aspires to proclaim, and preferring more informal verse styles. His more exuberant effects, unlike Pope's, occur in more open-ended or unpredictable styles, and the patternings of a pointed or epigrammatic manner frequently freeze in his hands to a slow harsh deliberateness. The fact that such patternings occur mostly in his prose may have something to do with the greater amplitude of the prose medium, which makes possible longer, slower units of sense. But there is no Popeian buoyancy in Johnson's verse, and plenty in Fielding's prose, as the following passage shows: [25]

> Master Blifil fell very short of his companion in the amiable quality of mercy; but he as greatly exceeded him in one of a much higher kind, namely, in justice: in which he followed both the precepts and example of Thwackum and Square; for tho' they would both make frequent use of the word *mercy*, yet it was plain, that in reality Square held it to be inconsistent with the rule of right; and Thwackum was for doing justice, and leaving mercy to Heaven. The two gentlemen did indeed somewhat differ in opinion concerning the objects of this sublime virtue; by which Thwackum would probably have destroyed one half of mankind, and Square the other half.

[23]*A Short Character of . . . Thomas Earl of Wharton* (*Works*, III.179).
[24]Aspects of Augustan couplet-rhetoric are further discussed in my *Henry Fielding and the Augustan Ideal Under Stress* (London, 1972), chs ii and iii. For a good account of the range and variety of Pope's couplet styles, see John A. Jones, *Pope's Couplet Art* (Athens, Ohio, 1969). William Bowman Piper, *The Heroic Couplet* (Cleveland and London, 1969) is a very full historical and analytical study of the couplet, from the beginnings to Pope and after, and contains much that is pertinent to my discussion.
[25]*Tom Jones*, III.X.

This may recall some of the passages from Pope's *Epistle to a Lady*: balance, contrast, a tremendous display of powers of summation, an obvious delight in the feats of style which so memorably and satisfyingly categorize some unsavoury facts. There is, too, the confident authorial presence, a decorous and gentlemanly self-projection, simplified but enormously alive, free of the vulnerabilities of undue intimacy with the reader or undue closeness to the material, yet proclaiming an assured and reassuring moral control. The categorizations point to a kind of vicious closed system, but unlike Swift's imprisoning paradoxes and like those of Pope, they deal with single persons or types, rather than with mankind at large or with wide and damagingly undefined portions of it. Moreover, the kind of exuberance found in Fielding as in Pope turns the closed systems into authorial triumphs of definition, instead of allowing them to generate an oppressive feeling of impasse. When Swift is exuberant on Fielding's or Pope's scale, he does not produce a finality towards which the preceding rhetoric has been visibly tending, but assaults us with sudden shocks of *re*definition, turning us into knaves if we refuse to be fools. Fielding, like Pope, rounds his paradoxes to a conclusiveness which, being both prepared-for and specific, limits their applicability and creates a feeling of release. If the buoyant brevities of Pope's couplets are absent in Fielding's passage, the amplitude of the prose medium in his case permits versatilities of elaboration, of weaving and interweaving, which are their counterpart in exuberant definition.

Prose, then, does not in itself make couplet-rhetoric astringent. Here, however, is Gulliver on prime ministers:[26]

> he never tells a *Truth*, but with an Intent that you should take it for a *Lye*; nor a *Lye*, but with a Design that you should take it for a *Truth* . . .;

—(IV.vi)

and on the causes of war:[27]

> Sometimes one Prince quarrelleth with another, for fear the other should quarrel with him. Sometimes a War is entered upon, because the Enemy is too *strong*, and sometimes because he is too *weak*. Sometimes our Neighbours *want* the *Things* which we *have*, or *have* the Things which we want . . .

—(IV.v)

These passages create little 'anti-systems', absurdly self-consistent worlds of perverse motivation, whose complete disconnection from humane and rational purposes gives them an air of unreality, of disembodied vacancy. (The vision is partly a satiric counterpart to Johnson's tragic sense of man, shunning 'fancied ills' and chasing 'airy good'.) Such satiric systematizations are not uncommon in Augustan literature, and Pope's *Moral Essays* also occasionally turn excesses of vice and irrationality into paradoxical pseudo-systems. Pope does not, however, allow them to

---

[26]*Works*, XI.255.
[27]Ibid., 246. This and the preceding passage are also discussed in *Henry Fielding and the Augustan Ideal Under Stress*, pp.46–7.

take on so much crazy autonomy, but often refers them to an all-explaining ruling passion. Because Swift deliberately withholds explanations at this level, we have to fall back on some absolute notion of the ingrained perversity of the human species, which alone can account for such ghoulishly self-sustaining perversity.

Above all, where the epigrammatic summations of Pope or Fielding suggest that vicious matters have been 'placed' or disposed of, there is here a sense of being weighed down. The categorizations are witty and precise, but the voice is flat and rasping, not buoyant with those righteous energies with which Pope and Fielding can outmatch the most viciously animated turpitudes. I suggest that this astringency is Swift's rather than Gulliver's, so far as we bother to disentangle them. This is not (once again) to say that Gulliver and Swift are identical, but that the feeling seems to come from behind the Gulliver who is speaking. Within a page of the last passage, in the same conversation or series of conversations, Gulliver gives this, not astringent but high-spirited, account of human war (which has already been discussed from another point of view):[28]

> I could not forbear shaking my Head and smiling a little at his Ignorance. And, being no Stranger to the Art of War, I gave him a Description of Cannons, Culverins, Muskets, Carabines, Pistols, Bullets, Powder, Swords, Bayonets, Sieges, Retreats, Attacks, Undermines, Countermines, Bombardments, Sea-fights; Ships sunk with a Thousand Men; twenty Thousand killed on each Side; dying Groans, Limbs flying in the Air: Smoak, Noise, Confusion, trampling to Death under Horses Feet: Flight, Pursuit, Victory; Fields strewed with Carcases left for Food to Dogs, and Wolves, and Birds of Prey; Plundering, Stripping, Ravishing, Burning and Destroying. And, to set forth the Valour of my own dear Countrymen, I assured him, that I had seen them blow up a Hundred Enemies at once in a Siege, and as many in a Ship; and beheld the dead Bodies drop down in Pieces from the Clouds, to the great Diversion of all the Spectators.[29]

—(IV.v)

The note of animated pleasure is at odds with the preceding astringency, and with the notion (see especially the *later* stress on this, IV.vii)[30] that he was in these conversations already disenchanted with humanity: but there is a very similar, complacently delighted, account of war given to the King of Brobdingnag before Gulliver's disenchantment (II.vii).[31] The method of the *Travels*, putatively written after the disenchantment, is often to have Gulliver present himself partly as he was at the relevant moment in the past, and not merely as he might now see himself, so that in both chapters (II.vii and IV.v) twin-notes of affection and dislike might be felt to mingle or alternate. Unless we are prepared to regard Gulliver as a very sophisticated ironist or rhetorician (let alone a highly-developed Jamesian consciousness)—and some readers are—we must feel that the alternations are modulations of Swift's ironic voice. Even if we deny Gulliver's pleasure in the list about war, we cannot deny the list's comic exuberance, and

[28]*Gulliver and the Gentle Reader*, pp.15–17.
[29]*Works*, XI.247.
[30]Ibid., 258 ff.
[31]Ibid., 134.

its difference from the dry epigrams of a moment before. However we describe Gulliver's attitude at this time, the shift cannot be attributed to any significant variation in his feelings, just as the inordinate and chaotic cataloguing cannot be accounted for as a subtly motivated departure from Gulliver's earlier announcement in IV.v that he is only reporting 'the Substance' (and an ordered summary at that) of these conversations.[32] The modulations in the *actual* atmosphere as we read emphasize again the abstractness of any separation of Swift from his speaker (even where that speaker, unlike the *Tale's*, has a name, wife, family and other tokens of identity). Swift's most expansive satiric energies kindle not at those sharp and witty summations which would have delighted Fielding or Pope, but at the humour of Gulliver's anarchic submission to an evil whose chaotic vitality has not been subdued to epigrammatic definition. At the mental level at which we, as readers, respond to such transitions, we are face to face with Swift's inner fluctuations, without intermediaries. Big men, little men, Gulliver and the rational horses, become so many circus animals, deserting. The encounter is, of course, unofficial: we do not admit it to ourselves, as distinct from experiencing it, and no suggestion arises of Swift's conscious design. When Swift participates harshly in Gulliver's tart epigrams there is no formal difficulty in imagining that the two converge, almost *officially*. But when the tartness unpredictably gives way to Gulliver's unruly exuberance (whether Gulliver is felt *at that instant* to hate war or to relish it is not a problem which occurs to us in the reading, as distinct from knowing Swift hates it, and sensing the exuberance), Swift's participation is unofficial and closer, a variant form of that mirror-relationship I have already suggested between an unruly and right-minded Swift who wrote the *Tale*, and the *Tale's* unruly but mad and wicked 'author'.

These identities establish themselves in that very charged penumbra where the satirist's personality overwhelms his own fictions, in a huge self-consciousness. It is no coincidence, from this point of view, that Swift's *Tale* is both a preenactment and an advance parody of Sterne; nor that the self-irony, at once selfmocking and self-displaying, of Sterne, or Byron, or Norman Mailer (whose *Advertisements for Myself*, for example, use every trick that the *Tale* satirically *ab*used, digressions, self-interruptions and solipsisms, solipsistic reminders of digression or solipsism, etc.) sometimes develops from Swift or shares formal elements with his work. The major formal difference is that Swift's 'authors' (the hack, the proposer, Gulliver) are predominantly satirized figures, officially Swift's complete antithesis most of the time, whereas the speakers or narrators of the later writers are either identical with their creators (as in many of Mailer's *Advertisements*), or projections and facets, hardly massively dissociated. The satiric plots and formulae which guarantee this dissociation in Swift may be thought of as immense protective assertions of the Super-Ego, part of the same process which sees to it that potentially 'gratuitous' effects of any length are in fact more or less subdued within frameworks of moral allegory. Because Swift's person is not *openly* permitted to take the slightest part in the affair, his self-

[32]Ibid., 245.

mockery (for example) is denied all the luxuries of coy self-analysis available to the later writers. (Where he does, however, speak through voices which are direct self-projections, as in *Cadenus and Vanessa* or the *Verses on the Death,* a tendency to such luxuries becomes evident.) The fact that Swift's presence remains felt despite the formal self-dissociation creates between the reader and Swift an either/or relation whose very indefiniteness entails more, not less, intimacy. In that whirlpool of indefiniteness, where any tendency to categorize is arrested, individual characters become fluid and indefinite, as in Sterne, despite the unSternelike (but rather nominal and cardboard) firmness of 'characters' like the modest proposer, or like Gulliver in his more self-consistent interludes. There is a relation between this and Swift's readiness in some moods to think of the human mind as prone to bottomless spirals of self-complication. An implication that hovers over both is that human behaviour is too unpredictable to be usefully classified in rounded conceptions of 'personality', as 'in (or out of) character'. . . .

A reflection of this on a more or less conscious, or 'rhetorical', plane are those familiar fluidities of style: the irony seldom docile to any simple (upside-down or other) scheme; 'masks' and allegories seldom operating in an unruffled point-by-point correspondence with their straight nonfictional message, or with sustained consistency to their own fictional selves; stylistic procedures at odds with one another, or deliberately out of focus with the main feeling of the narrative; contradictory implications on matters of substance. The effect is to preclude the comforts of definiteness, while blocking off retreats into woolly evasion, so that both the pleasures of knowing where one stands, and those of a vagueness which might tell us that we need not know, are denied.

Pope's writing, by contrast, depends on a decorous clarity of relationship (with the reader and subject) without the active and radical ambiguity we find in Swift. Pope's speakers (outside the *Dunciad*) are usually not enemies, from whom he must signpost his dissociation, but rhetorically simplified projections of himself (as urbane Horatian commentator, righteously angry satirist, proud priest of the muses). The somewhat depersonalized postures are traditional and 'public', secure within their rhetorical traditions (and so not subject to unpredictable immediacies), and they permit certain grandeurs of self-expression precisely because the more intimate self recedes from view. Urbane or passionate hauteurs ('Scriblers or Peers, alike are *Mob* to me', 'I must be proud to see/Men not afraid of God, afraid of me')[33] can then occur without opening the poet to easy charges of crude vanity. The 'masks' of Pope may thus be thought of as melting the poet's personality in a conventional or public role, but also as a release for certain acts of authorial presence. The finalities of the couplet form serve Pope in a similar way. They formally sanction a degree of definiteness which might otherwise seem open to charges of arrogance or glibness. The clearly patterned artifice hardly engulfs Pope. He moves within it with so much

---

[33]Pope, *The First Satire of the Second Book of Horace Imitated,* l.140; *Epilogue to the Satires,* II.208–9.

vitality and such an assurance of colloquial rhythm, that a powerfully dominating presence is always felt. But it remains a simplified presence, and Swift is in many ways paradoxically closer to his parodied enemies than is Pope to his own rhetorical selves.

But if couplets help Pope to formalize his presence, and to free it from certain inhibiting vulnerabilities, the effect is largely personal to Pope, and not primarily a cultural property of the form. Couplets do not, in Johnson, guarantee to suppress vulnerability, nor create triumphs of self-confidence; and their prose-counterparts do not in Swift (as they do in Fielding) attenuate the close intimacy of the satirist's presence. The balanced orderliness of couplet-rhetoric need not, even in Pope, reflect a serenity of outlook, nor a civilization which is confident, stable and in harmony with itself. The *Dunciad*, like the *Tale* and *Gulliver*, envisages cherished ideals not only under threat, but actually collapsing. The absurd moral universes which are locked away in the neat satiric patternings of both Swift and Pope often show 'order' parodying itself in its nasty uncreative antithesis. Each vicious 'anti-system' seems the ironic expression not of an Augustan order, but of a 'rage for order' gone sour. Pope's later style (at least) suggests no easy dependence on stabilities visibly and publicly achieved, but (like Swift's) highly personal encroachments on chaos.

Pope's way with chaos, however, is to keep his distance. He is temperamentally one of those for whom categorization and wit offer satisfactions which as such reduce chaos, or keep it at bay: not only aesthetic satisfactions as, once labelled by 'ruling passions', 'the prospect clears', but the comforting moral solidity of a decisive summation, however damaging or pessimistic. A style had to be forged for this, since the hostile realities to be mastered were pressing and vivid enough to expose the smallest verbal evasion or complacency. Pope's rhetoric suggests not denial but *containment* of powerful and subtle forces, and thrives on an excited decisiveness. If his lapses lead to complacency and patness, his strengths are those of a thrilling and masterful vision, in which delicate perceptions and massive urgencies of feeling marvellously cohere. Swift's rhetoric is no less masterful, but its whole nature is to suggest forces which cannot be contained, thus tending away from categorization. This is often evident at moments of clinching finality, and nowhere more clearly than in the phrase about the 'Fool among Knaves'. The clear and uncompromising lines of the completed epigram imply, as we saw, that 'knaves and fools divide the world'. But the surprise of this implication, its violation of the general run of the preceding argument, and our impulse to discount something (we do not know what, nor how much) because the words are formally spoken by the mad 'author' cause a blur of uncertainty to play over the cheeky patness of the phraseology. Categorization yields to unresolved doubts. The clinching phrase, subverting its own finality, becomes disorderly and inconclusive. If it is also a self-assertion, buoyant with the satirist's masterful grasp over his material, it is not, in Pope's manner, part of a steady rhetoric of definition, but seems a dazzling momentary victory wrested from chaos. Of course, the playing for sudden dazzling victories, and to some extent the chaos itself, are also a rhetoric, though not (like Pope's) self-announced and openly visible as such.[34] It is important to Pope's manner that he should seem to stand clear-sightedly on top of his material; and essential to Swift's to appear, as the phrase from *Lord Jim* puts it, in the destructive element immersed.

This is evident not merely in the mechanics of verbal style, narrowly conceived. Whole allegorical sequences, whose straightforward message has Swift's full endorsement, dissolve in a self-undercutting inconsistency, or explode in violence. The most unsettling thing about the Academy of Lagado in *Gulliver's Travels*, III.v–vi, and especially its School of Political Projectors, is not the allegorical *substance*, but the Swiftian manoeuvres which force changes of focus in the midst of an apparent moral certainty. The projectors are associated not only with predictably silly and repugnant programmes, but, by an astonishing redirection in III.vi, also with 'good' schemes ('of teaching Ministers to consult the publick Good', etc.). These 'good' programmes in turn dissolve into a 'cruel' Ubu-like absurdity, as in the crazily beneficent proposal to eliminate political dissension by sawing off the occiputs of 'each Couple' of opponents, and interchanging them 'in such a Manner that the Brain may be equally divided' between both men in a new balanced mixture of 'two half Brains'. After this beneficent 'cruelty', the redirections continue, by way of further 'good' proposals reminiscent of the *Project for the Advancement of Religion,* intermixed with some silly nastiness, until we arrive at crude totalitarian horrors.[35]

Or consider this initially straightforward allegory from section IV of the *Tale*:

> whoever went to take him by the Hand in the way of Salutation, *Peter* with much Grace, like a well educated Spaniel, would present them with his *Foot* . . .

This is one of several Swiftian jokes about the papal ceremony, and the passage so far is adequately accounted for in Wotton's gloss, which Swift prints in a note: *'Neither does his arrogant way of requiring men to kiss his Slipper, escape Reflexion'.* The passage then continues:[36]

> and if they refused his Civility, then he would raise it as high as their Chops, and give them a damn'd Kick on the Mouth, which hath ever since been call'd a *Salute.*

This development is outside the scope of Wotton's comment, outside the clean outlines of the allegory. It is not, as with the school of projectors, a redirection of the allegory, but an overspilling. One may argue it into the allegorical scheme by saying (accurately enough) that it represents the authoritarian brutality of the Roman Church. But the real force of the passage is to explode the emphasis away from the domain of allegorical correspondence as such.

---

[34] A suggestive recent comment by W. B. Carnochan is apt in this connection: 'irony, Swift's especially, is the satirist's rhetorical victory in the presence of self-defeat' ('Swift's *Tale*. On satire, negation, and the uses of irony', *Eighteenth-Century Studies*, v (1971), 124).

[35] *Works*, XI.187–92. See *Gulliver and the Gentle Reader*, pp.21, 144.

[36] Ibid., I.71.

The sudden violence is only one of several means of subversion, capping other subversions inherent in the context. Swift's appropriation, here and throughout the *Tale*, of Wotton's hostile exegesis, is not merely a means of explaining the allegory. Various piquancies of attack and of mocking self-exhibition, which lie outside the mere purposes of allegorical translation, are at work: the bravura of exploiting an enemy's attack for the serious illumination of one's own work; the tendency of this trick, while explaining the text, to mock it as requiring such solemn annotation, and from such a source; all the conventional seasoning of mock-scholarship, and so on. These effects combine with the fact that the allegory, like everything else, is spoken by the crazy 'author', and that it is an allegory which parodies allegories. The straightforward import of the story of the three brothers is thus not only undercut, but fragmented by a host of competing energies. Swift's real commitment to the direct import or core (the potted history of the Church) and to the primary satiric implications (the 'Abuses in Religion') becomes complicated by huge and distracting pressures: of self-mockery, of self-concealment, of tortuous and exuberant self-display. To say that this self-mockery simply subverts the allegory, or satirizes allegories in general, would be too crude, not only because part of the allegory somehow survives straight, but also because that diffusive spikiness injected by Swift is an attacking thing, *adding* to the satire's total fund of aggression and reinforcing the allegory's attack by that fact. But there is certainly, in practice, an exposure of the limits of the allegory to express all that Swift wants, to a degree which far exceeds the superficial and routine self-deflations of 'self-conscious narrative'.

The centre cannot hold. These unharnessed centrifugal energies of the form, its huge disruptive egotism, mirror the satirist's conscious vision of man's self-absorbed mental restlessness endlessly spiralling away from the rule of sense and virtue. The satirist is reflected in that mirror, 'satirized' beyond all his rhetorical reaches, yet *aptly* implicated, since his attack, so deeply rooted (as we saw) in a *psychological* diagnosis, extends to all mankind. The violence which Swift deplores is mirrored by the violence with which he charges his own style, just as, in the *Modest Proposal* and elsewhere, the murderous projects he satirizes in others are paralleled by aggressive velleities of his own, like the half-ironic desire to include in the cannibal project those Irish girls who wear foreign fineries.[37] The authoritarianism and the extremism which he exposes in others correspond to powerful authoritarian and extremist elements in himself, while his professed admiration for compromise, moderation and the common forms is balanced by moods or by contexts of suspicion or dislike for these very things, or things for which he uses uncannily similar language.[38] He is temperamentally given to subverting his own positives, as the treatment of Martin in the

---

[37]See *Gulliver and the Gentle Reader*, pp.13–14, 35–6.

[38]A more fully documented discussion of this point is given in *Focus: Swift*, ed. Claude Rawson, London, 1971, pp.43, 47 ff., and *Henry Fielding and the Augustan Ideal Under Stress*, pp.44 ff.

Tale tends to show.[39] He is quick to see in himself, as in all men, those anarchic proclivities of the inner man which may emerge in a hypertrophied and institutionalized form in sectarians, free thinkers and similar factious or individualistic groups. The controls which he requires that the law should place upon dissenters, free thinkers and proponents of 'innovations in government' closely resemble the controls which he expects himself and others to impose upon their own spontaneously subversive impulses and thoughts.[40] The King of Brobdingnag's comment upon 'the several Sects among us in Religion and Politicks', that there was 'no Reason, why those who entertain Opinions prejudicial to the Publick, should be obliged to change, or should not be obliged to conceal them' (*G.T.*, II.vi)[41] closely parallels Swift's own views in 'Some Thoughts on Free-Thinking':[42]

> I cannot imagine what is meant by the mighty zeal in some people, for asserting the freedom of thinking: Because, if such thinkers keep their thoughts within their own breasts, they can be of no consequence, further than to themselves. If they publish them to the world, they ought to be answerable for the effects their thoughts produce upon others.

The passage occurs in work in which (as we shall see) Swift is deliberately blurring the distinction between 'free thinking' in the technical or religious sense, and the looser etymological sense of 'unrestricted flow of thought', arguing that the sanity of every man depends on his ability to control his own internal 'free thinking'. And it is not surprising therefore that the passage is very similar not only to the King of Brobdingnag's views about the control of public free thinkers, but also to Swift's own statements about the limits of his answerability for his inner subversive doubts, provided he took care to conceal these doubts, tried to subdue them, and prevented their visible influence on his conduct of life ('Thoughts on Religion').[43]

These introspective statements are very close to Johnson's mode of thinking, and the whole Swiftian vision of the psychologically rooted restlessness of human nature, including that of the satirist himself, is one which Johnson shared very deeply (it may be that Johnson's dislike of Swift was indeed partly motivated by an unconscious sense of likeness). Johnson was to take that vision a step away from moral censure, but largely by means of compassion and a rueful self-tolerance rather than by any radical reappraisal of moral standards. It is only much later that one hears of a 'human condition', psychologically determined, but without God

---

[39]See *Focus: Swift*, pp.50–7. Many of the points in this paragraph are considered in greater detail in the essay on 'The character of Swift's satire' in *Focus: Swift*.

[40]See *Focus: Swift*, pp.18 ff. Swift's sense of his own turbulent restlessness of spirit comes out very strongly in a famous passage of his letter to the Rev. John Kendall, 11 February 1692, in which he cites the comment of a distinguished man who 'us'd to tell me, that my mind was like a conjur'd spirit, that would do mischief if I would not give it employment . . .' (*Correspondence*, 1.4).

[41]*Works*, XI.131.

[42]Ibid., IV.49.

[43]Ibid., IX.261–2.

and without attribution of sin.[44] Nevertheless, the vicious spirals, and those related energies (of sudden violence, or of deliquescence) which overspill their official (didactic or discursive) purposes, have the further point in common with black humour and the cult of the 'gratuitous' that their world is no longer secure in its values. When straightforward categorizable vice has dissolved into the unpredictabilities of the *Tale's* freewheeling madness (the vice/madness equation is commonplace, but the *Tale* is surely something special), the most cherished finalities no longer seem to solve anything. A conclusiveness where, 'Nature well known, no prodigies remain, / Comets are regular, and Wharton plain', yields to conclusions in which 'nothing is concluded'.[45] Swift and Johnson clung, of course, with an urgency often authoritarian and sometimes close to despair, to their faith in a traditional morality, to their Anglican piety and Augustan ideals of order. They had no consciously formulated sense that traditional values cannot any longer apply. This partly explains the tendency of Swift's 'gratuitous' effects to dovetail into a moral argument, especially if they are protracted; and it doubtless has something to do with Swift's and Johnson's stylistic attachment to the perspicuous finalities of couplet-rhetoric, Swift's in some of his prose, Johnson's in prose and verse. But Johnson's laboured, eloquent sadness in this mode, and Swift's imprisoning harshness, also tell their story. So, I believe, does the corresponding tendency of Swift's prose to kindle to a fero-

[44]The phrase 'human condition', in various senses, had long been in common use, and I note here what seem to me the three best-known examples of the usage most closely pertinent to the present discussion. Pascal's '*Condition de l'homme:* inconstance, ennui, inquiétude' is no atheistic void, but the reflexion of a man who, like Swift and Johnson (with both of whom he has from time to time been interestingly compared), is convinced of the 'Misère de l'homme sans Dieu' and of the corresponding 'Félicité de l'homme avec Dieu' (*Pensées*, nos. 61, 29; ed. Louis Lafuma (Paris, 1960), pp.122, 117). See Chester F. Chapin's brief recent rebuttal of the notion of an 'existentialist' Pascal, depicting 'the human condition as absurd' ('Johnson and Pascal', in *English Writers of the Eighteenth Century*, ed. John H. Middendorf (New York and London, 1971), pp.7–8; and see the whole essay, pp.3–16, for a valuable discussion of Pascal and Johnson on the subject of human 'restlessness'). The well-known lines about the 'wearisome Condition of Humanity' in the Chorus at the end of Fulke Greville's *Mustapha*, according to Geoffrey Bullough, should be read as meaning that peace is to be found neither in Nature, nor in ritual and dogma, but in 'the knowledge of God within the heart' (Fulke Greville, *Poems and Dramas*, ed. Bullough (Edinburgh and London, n.d.), II.136–7, 251). For a more recent discussion of the play, and its religious orientation, see Joan Rees, *Fulke Greville* (London, 1971), pp.139–81, esp. 169, 171, 181. Mrs Rees, p.181, notes the ironic fact that Archbishop Tillotson felt obliged to refute the opening lines of Greville's Chorus, which were 'so frequently in the mouths of many who are thought to have no good will to Religion' (John Tillotson, *Works*, 1704, p.329). C. S. Lewis, citing the lines from *Mustapha*, compares Greville to Pascal (*English Literature in the Sixteenth Century* (Oxford, 1968), pp.524–5).

Hobbes presents a somewhat different picture. Religion is prominent in his system, but primarily in its functional, i.e. psychological and political, aspects; and God's nature and existence are much more problematic in him than in Fulke Greville or Pascal. But even Hobbes's 'Natural Condition of Mankind' is defined as a condition of war only so long as it is understood that man is placed in it by 'mere nature': the condition is remediable by government ('a common power to keep them all in awe'), by various operations of the passions and the reason, etc. (*Leviathan*, I.xiii, ed. Michael Oakeshott (Oxford [Blackwell], n.d.), pp. 80–4). The actual state of social man in an adequately organized society is by definition different from the state of nature, and does not seem to be open to the kind of radically absurdist view of the 'human condition', whatever the social arrangements, which is frequently met in thinkers of more recent times.

[45]Pope, *Epistle to Cobham*, ll.208–9; Johnson, *Rasselas, ad fin.*

cious vitality in proportion as (in much of the *Tale*, and in Gulliver's list about war) its subject grows anarchic. The radical difference from Pope lies here, for all Swift's conscious closeness to Pope's outlook, and for all the likelihood that he would have given Breton and the other modern theorists a most comfortless home in his *Tale*. The matter transcends official themes, and outward feelings, as it transcends mere couplets. Cultural disorder for cultural disorder, the Academy of Lagado's relatively lighthearted or low-pitched inconsequence (not to mention the *Tale's* hectic craziness) seems more disturbing than the *Dunciad's* Fourth Book, Miltonic Darkness and all. This is perhaps part of what Leavis meant about Pope being more 'positive' than Swift, and if so it leads me to an exactly opposite valuation of the two men. For if Pope's positives, even in defeat (when the massive heroic ruin of the *Dunciad* proclaims the world that has been lost), are vividly adequate to the crisis as Pope so brilliantly recreates it, they do not measure up to the evoked quality of deepest malaise with which Swift *relives* that crisis. Swift's writing exists at a level where no act of containment, however complete and resourceful, can in the end be validated, its subject being, not Augustan culture, but the nature of man. And the matter of Swift's vitality in anarchic contexts is not wholly accounted for by Leavis's notion (in what is, despite its hostility, the most acute general discussion of Swift ever written) that Swift is most creatively alive in 'rejection and negation'.[46] The slow harsh epigrams negate and reject just as much, and when it comes to the Yahoos having 'all the life',[47] we may wonder whether (as in the *Tale*) Swift is not most profoundly in his element not merely as a scourge of anarchy, but as its *mimic*; participating inwardly, as well as protesting at those limitless escalations of folly and vice, those feverish spirals of self-complication. As the satire finally devolves from the third on to the first person, from world to gentle reader and back to the satirist, we could do worse than entertain the thought that Swift, in that place where all the ladders (and the spirals) start, was and sensed that he was, in all rebellious recalcitrance, himself Yahoo.

---

[46]F. R. Leavis, 'The irony of Swift', *The Common Pursuit* (Harmondsworth, 1962), pp.79, 86, etc.
[47]Ibid., p.84.

Swift's Satire: *Rules of the Game*

Robert C. Elliott

Claude Rawson says in his splendid essay "Order and Cruelty" that the discussion of character in Swift's satires leads to deserts of circularity. This is true
if we approach character in the usual novelistic sense, explaining specific utter-
ances by reference to personality or cultural traits of the speaker, matching
word and deed to motive within a frame of psychological consistency, and so on.
On the other hand, to dismiss the question of character in Swift's works—to go
along with Denis Donoghue, for example, who, as we have seen, recommends
that we think of the language of *A Tale of a Tub* as sourceless, ignoring the character of the speaker entirely—won't do, if only because that would be to dismiss
the fundamental fictive postulate on which the satirist bases his work. When in
any work of the imagination the author creates a spokesman, tells the reader (as
Swift does in the *Tale*) who the spokesman is, why he is writing, what his qualifications are, something of the kind of person he is (no matter in how mocking a
way), all this has both purpose and function. A major function of Swift's impersonations—as a mad Modern, an Irish projector, as Gulliver—is that they
allowed him to think himself into the heart of evil, to traffic with the impermis-
sible; and if we are ever to understand the results of those encounters, it will
have to be by way of the creatures under whose protection he ventured.[1]

Swift's feats of impersonation operate according to rules which every reader
senses but which no critic I know of has been able to specify very precisely. The
game is this: Swift must express himself through a zany alter ego, say truth by
means of a lie, speak sense through a madman's lips. He must manipulate a persona whose utterance simultaneously expresses and unwittingly condemns the
folly Swift is pursuing. As for the reader, his part in the game is to follow the
complex maneuvers as closely as possible, recreating them in his own mind as he
is flung wildly about, from rides on broomsticks and flying islands to plunges into
Bedlamite horrors. Curiosity—that "Spur in the Side, that Bridle in the Mouth,
that Ring in the Nose of a lazy, impatient, and a grunting Reader"—keeps him
going through *A Tale of a Tub*: curiosity to know where the ideas lead, of course,

From Robert C. Elliott, *The Literary Persona* (Chicago: University of Chicago Press, 1982), 124–43.
The article originally appeared in *ELH*, 41 (1974), 413–28. Reprinted by permission of the Johns
Hopkins University Press and the University of Chicago Press.

[1]C. J. Rawson, "Order and Cruelty," *Essays in Criticism* 20 (1970): 24–56; reprinted in *Gulliver
and the Gentle Reader* (London: Routledge and Kegan Paul, 1973), 33–59; Donoghue, *Swift*, 5–9.

but in an important sense, curiosity to know whether Swift in the crazy guise he has assumed can keep his footing in the perilously intricate dance he has set in motion. To keep footing means to follow the rules of the game.

The most important rules governing *A Tale of a Tub* as well as the other satires have to do with the functioning of Swift's fictional spokesmen, with (in some sense) character, for although these spokesmen are not refugees from the novel or from drama and cannot be expected to follow the conventions of those very different games, there are unmistakable "family resemblances" between them and the personages of better-understood literary forms. Perhaps these can best be seen from a negative perspective. In the novel a writer's initial commitment to a tone, a style, a mode of being for his spokesman limits drastically the possibilities for development in the ensuing work. After the opening pages of their respective novels Fielding could not have married Sophia to Blifil, Jane Austen could not have allowed Elizabeth Bennet to catch a fever and die. As the information theorists say, the early paragraphs of these novels contain a significant element of redundancy, as do most literary works. Think of the immense ranges of experience the first lines of *Paradise Lost* rule out for Milton.

The principle operates in a similar (although less exclusive) way even in a maverick work like *A Tale of a Tub*. As we have it now, the *Tale* opens with an Apology, which is extrinsic to the *Tale* proper, and with some pleasant mystifications from the bookseller; the first words spoken by the Tale-teller who is the source of all that follows are these in the Dedication to Prince Posterity:

> *Sir,*
> I here present *Your Highness* with the Fruits of a very few leisure Hours, stollen from the short Intervals of a World of Business, and of an Employment quite alien from such Amusements as this: The poor Production of that Refuse of Time which has lain heavy upon my Hands, during a long Prorogation of Parliament, a great Dearth of Forein News, and a tedious Fit of rainy Weather.

The self-characterization in this utterance is enough to trigger an elaborate scanning process on the part of the reader—a process that, negatively, allows him to rule out many possibilities in the way the *Tale* might develop; one that, positively, gives him clues enabling him to guess at what kind of game he is entering on. From our initial impression of any work we intuit a sense of the whole, without which, as E. D. Hirsch says, any individual trait of the work would be rootless and without meaning. As we read further, of course, we refine our sense of the whole accommodating new details, adjusting our expectations, ruling out what had once seemed possibilities until, firmly involved in the hermeneutic circle, we approximate a grasp of the appropriate rules. But from the beginning our sense of the whole is grounded in our reading of the source of all our information: in *A Tale of a Tub* it is the crack-brained Modern whose genius lies, as he tells us, in devising tubs for the amusement of leviathanic wits.[2]

---

[2]E. D. Hirsch, *Validity in Interpretation* (New Haven: Yale University Press, 1967), 71ff.

Doubtless "character" is an inadequate word here: we are not speaking of a coherent personality or intellectual position. Rawson, who has a splendid way with language, speaks of the Tale-teller as "an amorphous mass of disreputable energies." Nevertheless, because those energies are associated with a designated speaker, certain renunciations that we normally associate with "character" as understood in other genres necessarily are involved. For example, amorphous as he is, the Tale-teller cannot be wholly inconsistent; that is, he cannot at one moment espouse the cause of the Moderns, at the next that of the Ancients. A position and a point of view fairly steadily grounded are a necessary condition for the satire to operate intelligibly. (When in book three of the *Travels* Gulliver expresses contempt for the Laputans, then immediately praises them warmly, we are confused, and not in an artistic way: I would say Swift here has momentarily lost his footing.) Again, the Tale-teller cannot (except in parody, which makes it a different thing) deliver Swift's sermon on the Trinity or even the one on sleeping in church; he cannot compose *A Project for the Advancement of Religion and Reformation of Morals.* These would be gross violations of the rules because of their inappropriateness in the mouth of a maker of tubs. As soon as the Tale-teller utters his effusion to Prince Posterity, a horizon of appropriate styles and meanings is established, a system of reasonable expectations, reasonable probabilities. The horizon is wide but its exclusions are fairly clear. Among them, fundamentally, is the possibility that the Tale-teller should without warning become a non-ironical Swift—a Swift who writes straight from his convictions. The rules of the genre allow this persona occasionally to speak Swift's sentiments but only after formal provision for the shift in point of view has been made. In the midst of the Digression on Madness, for example, the Tale-teller utters the purest kind of Swiftian doctrine: "For, the Brain, in its natural Position and State of Serenity, disposeth its Owner to pass his Life in the common Forms, without any Thought of subduing Multitudes to his own *Power,* his *Reasons* or his *Visions;* and the more he shapes his Understanding by the pattern of Human Learning, the less he is inclined to form Parties after his particular Notions." The Tale-teller can legitimately speak in this way because immediately before he has made it clear that he himself is a partisan of the vapor which the world calls madness, without which we would be deprived of "those two great Blessings, *Conquests* and *Systems,*" and consequently he has no love for the "common Forms." Thus the Tale-teller can utter Swift's sentiments without speaking in Swift's unmediated accents. The basic rule is that although the persona need not be a consistent character, the personation must be consistently maintained.

At a certain memorable point in the *Tale,* Swift (I think) deliberately violates the rules. The Digression on Madness divides the world in two and demands that the reader choose between them. Unlike the knight in the Wife of Bath's tale, the reader cannot refuse choice itself but must align himself with one of two intellectual-moral positions: either with happiness, delusion, credulity, the surface of things (as these are defined in the Digression), or with curiosity and officious reason which cuts and pierces and anatomizes in order to demonstrate the ugliness beneath the skin. The argument coils to its bitter climax:

> whatever Philosopher or Projector can find out an Art to sodder and patch up the Flaws and Imperfections of Nature, will deserve much better of Mankind, and teach us a more useful Science, than that so much in present Esteem, of widening and exposing them (like him who held *Anatomy* to be the ultimate End of *Physick*.) And he, whose Fortunes and Dispositions have placed him in a convenient Station to enjoy the Fruits of this noble Art; He that can with *Epicurus* content his Ideas with the *Films* and *Images* that fly off upon his Senses from the *Superficies* of Things; Such a Man truly wise, creams off Nature, leaving the Sower and the Dregs, for Philosophy and Reason to lap up. This is the sublime and refined Point of Felicity, called, *the Possession of being well deceived*; The Serene Peaceful State of being a Fool among Knaves.

The shock to the reader is traumatic as he suddenly finds himself trapped in an intolerable dilemma: if he has chosen happiness and the surface of things he is a fool; if he has chosen reason he is a knave. There is no way out. No wonder he is shaken. But beyond that I think the reader has a strong sense that he has been not only trapped but booby-trapped. It is not part of the game that the Tale-teller should be able to speak in the savagely hostile accents which end the paragraph; they violate his mode of being, amorphous as it is. Instead, Swift has momentarily tossed the Tale-teller aside, speaking out in his own voice, breaking his own rules. It is as though one's chess partner suddenly reached across the board and hit one in the head with one's queen.[3]

In the passage in question the Tale-teller argues consistently for the value of happiness (*"a perpetual possession of being well deceived"*) of fantasy, imagination, the surface of things. "Such a man, truly wise, creams off nature." In my view it makes no sense to say that it is the Tale-teller who in the next sentence identifies the happiness he has been praising with being "a Fool among Knaves." To be sure, throughout the *Tale* he can and does praise folly and madness—they are "good" words for him—but only in suitable contexts and with the appropriate formal insulation of meaning; here he cannot possibly be giving a favorable sense to *Fool* and *Knaves*. This would be simple incoherence, not irony; it would have the Tale-teller maintaining that true wisdom is to be a fool. There are contexts, of course, in which such a paradoxical assertion makes very good sense indeed—the wisdom of the holy fool, for example—but those contexts are not invoked here. It is as though Gulliver should say, "the Houyhnhnms are wise and just creatures and should be despised." If the "Fool among Knaves" is the Tale-teller's phrase, the customary transvaluation of

---

[3]This momentary violation of the rules is comparable to a similar violation in the last book of *A la recherche du temps perdu*, discussed in chapter five, where Proust, not Marcel, practically shouts the name of Françoise's cousins, who live in the real world.

terms does not work; if it is Swift's phrase, however, it enacts even as it expresses his sense of the human entrapment.

That Swift should be caught in his own trap was entirely appropriate as he doubtless knew. Assuredly no fool, he was snagged by the nether jaw of the device he had set. Swift's imagery shouts his awareness of the knavish character of his own satiric procedures. Throughout the Madness section it is Reason that cuts and mangles and pierces; it is Reason that explores weak sides and publishes infirmities, that unmasks what is hidden, that exposes the flaws of Nature, that flays women and anatomizes beaux. All this bloody work is knavery, but necessary knavery; for the exercise of reason as a scalpel, with all the moral ambiguity associated with the procedure, is precisely the satirist's function. Knavery of this anatomizing kind is Swift's métier.[4]

Rawson thinks it a mistake to try to make schematic the relation between Swift and his persona, and certainly no neat system of invariant opposition will do. He thinks that despite the crushing finality of the "Fool among Knaves" the sense of the passage is left deliberately indistinct because we cannot be certain how Swift and his speaker relate. On the contrary, I think Swift's violation of the rules makes the schematism of the passage inexorable: the rhythms of the prose enforce it as does the sense. Swift imposes upon us choices ("happiness" vs. anatomizing) that are matched symmetrically by the two terms with which he springs the trap. The system is closed and out of its closure shattering energies erupt. Oddly, not all those energies are destructive. If, as Rawson says, the passage affirms an ancient proverb: "Knaves and fools divide the world," its brilliance is such as to assert its own kind of order in defiance of its literal message. Just as a physicist interferes with the "state of the system" when he undertakes a quantum description of a light beam, so Swift (or Pope in *The Dunciad*) alters the system of folly he is examining by giving form to his conception of it. "The wit gives pleasure in itself," says Rawson, "and playfully suggests the survival of linguistic order within a certain mental anarchy."

The issue of character arises again in a work like *A Modest Proposal*. No one would claim that the figure Swift creates to put forward the proposal is a consistent or complex or interesting person in his own fictional right. In a way the whole notion of character as applied to him seems irrelevant. In another sense, however, it is precisely our *idea* of character, and how that idea functions with respect to the projector, that controls our response to the work. Consider:

> It is a melancholly Object to those, who walk through this great Town, or travel in the Country; when they see the *Streets,* the *Roads,* and *Cabbin-doors* crowded with *Beggars* of the Female Sex, followed by three, four, or six Children, *all in Rags,* and importuning every Passenger for an Alms. These *Mothers,* instead of being able to work for their honest Livelyhood, are forced to employ all their Time in stroling to beg Sustenance for their *helpless Infants;* who, as they grow up, either turn *Thieves* for want of Work; or

---

*The dissection metaphor is common in Swift. See the Drapier's characterization of William Wood's defense of his coinage as nothing more than "the last Howls of a Dog dissected alive, as I hope he hath sufficiently been." "Letter IV. To the Whole People of Ireland," *The Drapier's Letters,* in *Prose Works,* ed. Herbert Davis (Oxford: Basil Blackwell, 1941), 10:54.

leave their *dear Native Country, to fight for the Pretender in* Spain, or sell themselves to the *Barbadoes.*

Swift plays upon what he knows will be the reader's assumptions about the kind of man who can speak so sympathetically of the Irish condition. Given the conventions of character depiction, only that slight intimation is necessary to establish in the reader's mind a formidable set of expectations about what can and cannot follow from such an introduction. These are the expectations that Swift manipulates with such extraordinary results.

Although a tool of the satiric fiction, the persona of *A Modest Proposal* is bound by the same minimal generic rules that govern the spokesman of *A Tale of a Tub*; that is, he cannot contradict himself haphazardly, he cannot speak in Swift's unmediated voice. Nevertheless. that voice comes through once or twice in defiance of the rules. One advantage the projector sees in his cannibalistic proposal is that it will not disoblige England: "For, this Kind of Commodity will not bear Exportation; the Flesh being of too tender a Consistence, to admit a long Continuance in Salt; *although, perhaps, I could name a Country, which would be glad to eat up our whole Nation without it.*" The last part of the sentence is unmistakably not the projector but Swift himself. Whereas in *A Tale of a Tub* Swift's intervention produces a shattering experience for the reader, here the unsignaled shift in tone disturbs him momentarily if at all. An English reader in Swift's day would doubtless have responded to the intrusion much more intensely. It all depends on who the victim is.

The identification of victims of Swift's satire is no longer as simple as once it was, the catalogue having been expanded by recent criticism far beyond obvious targets to include the reader—all readers—and, as we saw in chapter six, Swift himself. On the face of it, such identifications are startling, for they radically violate received notions about satire's aims and function, matters on which Swift's official ideas at least, are as conventional as his ideas on religion. "There are two Ends that Men propose in writing Satyr; one of them less noble than the other, as regarding nothing further than the private Satisfaction, and Pleasure of the Writer; but without any View towards *personal Malice:* The other is a *publick Spirit,* prompting Men of *Genius* and Virtue, to mend the World as far as they are able." The satirist effects this noble end by laughing men out of their follies and vices. It is one of the pattest formulas of self-justification in the lexicon and one of the least examined. Swift puts the formula under some pressure, as we shall see, but never, I think, to the point where his own role as satirist is seriously in question. His aligning himself in the passage above with men of "*Genius* and Virtue" hardly shows him as a conscious victim of his own ridicule. As for the generality of readers as victims, the discussion of the range and effect of satire in the Preface to the *Tale of a Tub* shows Swift acutely aware of the weakness in indiscriminate attack: "Satyr being levelled at all, is never resented for an offense by any, since every individual Person makes bold to understand it of others, and very wisely removes his particular Part of the Burthen upon the shoulders of the World, which are broad enough, and able to bear it." The argument for individual, local satire, as opposed to that which inveighs against mankind, is explicit and pointed: the satirist's proper target is *"such a one* [who] starved half the Fleet,"* not "People in general." Obviously, Swift does not stick to his own prescription: he attacks individuals, professions, institutions, creeds—in the Digression on Madness he involves the world. Our question is whether (except in the last instance and perhaps one or two others) the reader, however remote he may be from the obvious targets, is himself victimized by the satire— whether, as Rawson puts it, his escape routes are closed. And then, to what degree is Swift himself, rather than his persona, involved.[5]

Satire is purportedly written to two audiences: in one are the guilty and those most likely to be infected by the guilty, in the other "all right-thinking men," or, as Swift says, *"a great majority among the Men of Tast,"* who share the author's view and values. This latter group, although sometimes in danger of ricochets, is unlikely to be brought under direct fire, most obviously because it forms a friendly camp and is presumably untainted by the vice or folly under examination. The satirist normally arranges things so that the object of his attack is definable against the background of what that object is not: Wotton is defined by contrast with Sir William Temple (clearly a Man of Tast), dissenting Jack by contrast with Martin, who, we are told, represents the *"most perfect"* of all churches in *"Discipline and Doctrine."* A Tale of a Tub provides a surprising number of such positives for the reader to cling to: the coats, of course (i.e., *"the Doctrine and Faith of Christianity by the Wisdom of the Divine Founder fitted to all Times, Places and Circumstances"*) and Martin, but positives also in the Digressions. Those of us who write on Swift doubtless take heart from the knowledge that at one happy time in the world's history there were critics other than that formidable race descended from the union of Momus and Hybris, who begat Zoilus. One group of critics used to restore ancient learning from the ravages of time and neglect; another group "invented or drew up rules for themselves and the World, by observing which, a careful Reader might be able to pronounce upon the productions of the *Learned,* form his Taste to a true Relish of the *Sublime* and the *Admirable,* and divide every Beauty of Matter or Style from the Corruption that Apes it." Although these critics have long been extinct, we are told, each of us must feel that somehow we are the true heirs. How else could we write?

Even in fiercer passages of the satires—those that seem to be torn from the nightmares that tormented Swift—there is likely to be formal provision for a way out. One of his worst fears was certainly, as Empson says, that religion may be no more than a perversion of sexuality, a thesis propounded in great detail by Swift's spokesman in the *Mechanical Operation of the Spirit.* So brilliant and so shocking is this exposition that one forgets the ways to transcendence, other than the mechanical way, mentioned in the text: inspiration from God, possession by the devil, natural causes such as imagination, grief, pain. Swift has no more interest in discussing these legitimate ways of transporting the soul beyond mat-

---

[5]Swift's characterization of satire is in *Prose Works,* 12:34.

ter than, as a clergyman, he has in discussing the doctrine of the Trinity; but their presence in his text is a necessary element freeing his subversive imagination to show how the spirit may be improved by belching or by prudent management of syphilitic infection, giving him and us, at least in formal terms, a way out.[6]

This is a characteristic mark of Swift; it is his way of exercising what Murray Krieger calls the classic vision. Swift entertains the possibility that the structures which order reality, whether those of reason or religion, may be mere projections of our minds, desperate but factitious attempts to impose order on what is ineluctably chaos. He fantasizes himself into the skins of those who represent horror to him most fully—a Lord Wharton, a madman—or of those who must face head-on what he fears—a Gulliver. Through their eyes and in their voices he confronts the extreme: confronts but does not embrace. The extreme is there, invoked by the violence of thought and metaphor, but rejected at the same time by the formal ordering of his work, by the paths he leaves open.[7]

Many readers, to be sure, find that *Gulliver's Travels* blocks all escape routes; and, clearly, if Gulliver's "All men are yahoos" is Swift's last word, then the closure of the system is complete. To read the *Travels* this way, however, is to conclude that in Swift's view no moral distinction can be made between Dr. Arbuthnot and Lord Wharton, between Sir Thomas More and Henry VIII, between Stella and Mrs. Manley. All are equally loathsome brutes, and Swift is brutish among them. I find the reading incredible, ignoring as it does the possibilities of a reasonable society adumbrated in Brobdingnag, of a decent life shown in Don Pedro. In literature Don Pedro serves Swift as an escape from Yahoodom, just as in life John, Peter, Thomas, and Councillor Such-a-One (whom Swift told Pope he dearly loved) served as an escape from total misanthropy. Don Pedro provides a way out.[8]

Thus I think it a mistake to read Swift's satire as though it were all one vast "Fool among Knaves" trap into which reader and author fall together. It is glib to say that we are all involved in all the vices that satire attacks—that we are all Lord Whartons or John Duntons or whatever, and it is a flaccid morality that refuses to discriminate. On the other hand, the escape routes which make discrimination possible are ill-marked in Swift's work, obscure and easy to overlook altogether—a very different situation from that in Pope, who emphatically draws the distinction between the righteous and the wicked. Swift's assaults generate such an overplus of energy, they come from so many directions with such unexpected vehemence and wit that ways out are likely to he forgotten as the reader is enveloped by the storm. Rawson is splendid on this. He speaks of how the sudden intensity of a sentence like "Last Week I saw a Woman *flay'd,* and you will hardly believe, how much it altered her Person for the worse," not only serves the argument it illustrates but spills over the surrounding context: the energies

[6]See his sermon on the Trinity, in *Prose Works,* 11:159–68.
[7]Murray Krieger, *The Classic Vision* (Baltimore: Johns Hopkins University Press, 1971), 255–69.
[8]Swift, *Correspondence,* ed. Harold Williams, 5 vols. (Oxford: Clarendon Press, 1963–65), 3:103.

of the sentence are in excess of the demands of the logic. This spill-over phenomenon, Rawson says, is characteristic of Swift's style; it contributes to the
reader's sense of impasse, of unease, to the feeling that he is somehow catching
the hostility meant for someone else.[9]

This seems to me an important insight into the way Swift's prose works. At
one point or another in his satire we all recognize aspects of ourselves in the
object of ridicule; if we don't we are either hypocrites or poor readers. On the
other hand, we are also conscious of being battered even when free of guilt;
attacks on abuses in which we as individuals can have no conceivable part hurt,
not because of our complicity, but simply as a result of the overplus of hostility in
the air. Normal identification with the satirist and its attendant invulnerability,
although possible at a formal, rational level, is hopelessly disturbed by the dangerous charges of animus flying about. My impression is, however, that in these
instances the reader feels attacked—as though someone has hit him from a dark
corner—rather than made to feel guilty. Rawson writes: "Where the aggression
turns indistinct, and overspills the area of specifiable moral guilt, no opportunity
is given for complacent self-exculpation on a specific front, and the reader
becomes implicated. Instead of permitting the individual to shift his load onto
the world's shoulders, Swift forces the reader to carry the world's load on *his*."
But I doubt that it is *guilt* the reader feels about the woman flayed; he is not in
fact guilty of the flaying, nor is he likely to feel the same equanimity before the
image of horror that Swift's spokesman exhibits—surely a matter for guilt. If the
reader recognizes that, like the Tale-teller, he sometimes treats people as things,
or that he lives complacently in a society that endorses unspeakable cruelties,
the vaguely guilty twinges accompanying these reflections are low-order
responses compared to the shock he gets from the sentence, the battering he
undergoes from the spill-over of negative emotion. At the same time, as Irvin
Ehrenpreis points out, the reader may experience an illicit joy (for which he may
feel guilt) that a man could write such a "beautiful" sentence.[10]

In analyzing the overspill phenomenon, Rawson is pointing to real effects in
Swift's satire that run counter to the formal ordering of things. These are subjective matters, impossible to specify precisely or measure accurately; but I think
the analysis goes a long way toward accounting for the feelings of unjustified vic-
timization likely to result from a bout with Swift. The danger of concentrating
too exclusively on these effects is that we may be led to read all Swift's satire as
though it were the climactic passage of the Digression on Madness. Not even
Swift's work can live consistently at that heat.

In the preceding chapter I tried to define my sense of the degree to which
Swift, through his persona, expresses his own complicity in the madness and the
badness that he exposes; here I want to explore self-reflexive implications of
Swift's frequently expressed distrust of his own medium. In the Apology to *A
Tale of a Tub* Swift, speaking in his own person, affirms and reaffirms the tradi-

[9]Rawson, *Gulliver and the Gentle Reader*, 33ff (above, pp. 29ff).
[10]Ehrenpreis, "Swift and the Comedy of Evil," 213–19.

tional justifications of satire: gross corruptions in religion and learning can best be eliminated by satire's cleansing action. On the other hand, in the Preface to the same work, he (or, as I prefer, his persona) launches a brilliantly destructive foray—a satirical foray—against the practice of satire itself. Satirists lash vices, says the Tale-teller, but with pathetic futility; for "there is not, through all Nature, another so callous and insensible a Member as the *World's Posteriors.*" Satirists' attacks on avarice and hypocrisy are meaningless: " 'Tis but a *Ball* bandied to and fro, and every Man carries a *Racket* about Him to strike it from himself among the rest of the Company." If satirists dare to expose the villainy of individual persons, they only invite persecution. This attack on satire is managed with a great flurry of denigratory imagery, in one paragraph satirists being compared with flogging pedants, nettles, weeds, thistles, their wit with dull razors and rotten teeth. The "Satyrical Itch" is a disease.

In an interesting analysis of these matters, Gardner Stout, Jr., reads the relevant passages of *A Tale of a Tub* as Swift's own admission that satire serves no useful purpose. "Though he finds Alecto's whip a congenial instrument for scourging fools, he recognizes that, in lashing the world with wit and humor to mend it, his satire is impotent, partly because those it strikes are temperamentally disqualified from feeling it by the very vices for which they are satirized." Stout finds Swift condemning his own motives and procedures: like the True Critic, the Satirist—Swift included—is a collector of mankind's faults, which become distilled into his own person. The satirist messes about in the ordure of human nature, as much a part of the Bedlamite world he describes as any committed lunatic. According to this reading, Swift sees himself as implicated in all that he attacks even as he recognizes that the attack itself is impotent. Here, from some cosmic perspective, the satirist is indeed satirized.[11]

But is it so? The expressed distrust of satire is unmistakable, the only question being whether Swift's own satire comes within the orbit of critique. The whole passage in the Preface is framed by an elaborate disclaimer from the Tale-teller: " 'Tis a great Ease to my Conscience that I have writ so elaborate and useful a Discourse without one grain of Satyr intermixt; which is the sole point wherein I have taken leave to dissent from the famous Originals of our Age and Country." If the Tale-teller dissents from the Originals, then Swift, following the rules of the rhetorical game, can legitimately attack them through the mouth of his persona: hence the denigratory images. The sentence about the world's posteriors sounds like Swift, but the sentiments are those of a hundred earlier satirists, who have rarely had many illusions about their real power to effect reform. Besides, Swift's target here is the spate of satire in the 1690s which so offended Sir William Temple, the satire to which Aesop refers when, speaking with Swift's authority in the *Battle of the Books*, he asserts that the only genuine production of the Moderns is "*a large Vein of Wrangling and Satyr, much of a Nature and Substance with the* Spider's *Poison.*" To attack *that* satire is by no means the same as attacking satire itself.

[11]Stout, "Speaker and Satiric Vision in Swift's *Tale of a Tub*," *ECS*, 2 (1969): 186.

Furthermore, an odd paradox obtains whereby to admit that satire has little or no effect on a guilty audience is to reinforce the satirical attack. Yeats once thought that Wyndham Lewis's *Apes of God* would shake up London literary society. But Lewis disagreed: "Nothing could change the kind of people of whom I wrote—they had not the necessary vitality for that." The confession of futility turns into the ultimate put-down. Whether that, in turn, has effect is, of course, open to the same doubt as before. Swift's best-known statement questioning the efficacy of satire is in the Preface to the *Battle of the Books*. Here he speaks in his own person, as the author, not in the guise of a muddle-headed modern: "*Satyr is a sort of Glass, wherein Beholders do generally discover every body's Face but their Own; which is the chief Reason for that kind Reception it meets in the World and that so very few are offended with it.*" Although this wryly admits that most satire does not get home to those for whom it is intended, that fact itself condemns those who look in the glass: they wilfully refuse to see their own images and either stupidly or hypocritically welcome what exposes their folly. An admission of satiric futility here is overborn by the attack, which in the following sentences escalates into a most unpleasant threat that the wit of the satirist's opponent will end up as something fit only to be thrown to the hogs. The truculence of this satirist has nothing to do with impotence: these teeth can bite.[12]

Interesting logical issues arise when, as in the Preface to *A Tale of a Tub*, a satirist satirizes satire. Wyndham Lewis involves himself in this situation in a very Swiftian way in his novel *Apes of God*. Horace Zagreus, who speaks for Lewis, uses Swift's imagery: "'How is it that no one ever sees *himself* in the public mirror?'" The world, he concludes, is hopelessly past mending:

> "People feel themselves under the special protection of the author when they read a satire on their circle—am I right! . . . . It is always the *other fellows* (never them) that their accredited romancer is depicting, for their sport. . . . At all events nothing happens. It would seem that it is impossible to devise anything sufficiently cruel for the rhinoceros hides grown by a civilized man and a civilized woman . . . . It is almost as if, when they saw him approaching, they exclaimed: '*Here comes a good satirist! We'll give him some sport. We are just the sort of animals he loves.*' Then the official satirist fills his pages with monsters and a sprinkling of rather sentimental 'personnages sympathiques,' and everybody is perfectly happy. The satirist is, of course, quite as insensitive as his subjects, as a rule. Nothing really disgusts him."

This satirical denigration of both the function of satire and the character of the satirist comes in the midst of one of the fiercest satirical novels ever written. Is Lewis victimized by his own attack? Only in the most remote way, I should think. Satire about satire is like thinking about thought, or communication about communication: as Bertrand Russell made clear, in his theory of logical types, different logical orders are involved and should not be confused. The satirical attacks on satire of both Lewis and Swift are launched from levels

---

[12]Wyndham Lewis, *Rude Assignment* (London: Hutchinson, 1950), 201.

higher than their object. This is metasatire, and according to the rules of this game the position of the authors is privileged. Except for nonlogical effects of the kind Rawson discusses, they escape their own critique.[13]

On January 11, 1710–11, Swift recorded in the *Journal to Stella* that he was setting up his protégé, "little" Harrison, as the new Tatler, Richard Steele having given up the journal. On March 14 he writes: "little Harrison the Tatler came to me, and begged me to dictate a paper to him, which I was forced in charity to do." Next day the *Tatler* appeared, lauding old times when men of wit had power: "The Hopes of being celebrated, or the Dread of being stigmatized, procured an universal Respect and Awe" for the poets. Swift's bias is revealed when he cites Aretino as the great example: all the princes of Europe trembled lest they be pilloried in his satire. A week later in another paper (also attributed to Swift) Isaac Bickerstaff playfully identifies himself as one who, in accordance with Pythagorean doctrine, was born centuries ago and has lived through many incarnations. At one time, Bickerstaff says in this metempsychic version of persona theory, he was the leading wit of France, at another time had a statue erected to him in Italy; and when he came to England at the end of the seventeenth century he entered the body of the most talented man of letters there—a man easily identified as Jonathan Swift. The common element in Isaac Bickerstaff's incarnations, he tells us, is that "I have in every one of them opposed my self with the utmost Resolution to the Follies and Vices of the several Ages I have been acquainted with, that I have often rallied the World into good Manners, and kept the greatest Princes in Awe of my Satyr."[14]

The battered reader of his work finds it pleasant to see Swift relaxing into fantasy, playing the role of satirist-hero: slaying dragons, rescuing princesses, laughing the world into civility. It is one of many images of the satirist in his work, from the rotten-toothed mumbler of the Tale, through the bloody anatomist and the culture hero to the derisive Jove of the poem "The Day of Judgment." In that nightmare vision Jove lays bare hypocrisy, exposes secret pride and mean motives—acts, in short, as a satirist: acts, as Lord Chesterfield said, like Voltaire:

With a Whirl of Thought oppress'd,
I sink from Reverie to Rest.
An horrid Vision seiz'd my Head,

---

[13]Wyndham Lewis, *Apes of God* (Baltimore: Penguin, 1965), 268. As for the paradox of the satirist satirizing satire, it is of the order of the ancient "liar"paradox: Epimenides the Cretan said that all Cretans are liars, or of Bertrand Russell's paradox of the class of all classes not belonging to themselves. For Russell's solution—or as W. V. Quine puts it, his parrying of the paradoxes by way of his theory of a hierarchical order of logical types—see *Principia Mathematica*, with Alfred North Whitehead, 3 vols., 2d ed. (Cambridge: Cambridge University Press, 1935), 1:60ff. Quine's characterization is in "Russell's Ontological Development," *Bertrand Russell: Philosopher of the Century* (London: George Allen and Unwin, 1967), 307. An excellent discussion of some of these matters appears in the chapter "Paradoxical Communication" in Paul Watzlawick and others, *Pragmatics of Human Communication* (New York: W. W. Norton, 1967), 187–229.

[14]Swift, *Prose Works*, 2:257–63. For the attribution, see Herbert Davis's Introduction to the volume, xxxv–xxxvi.

I saw the Graves give up their Dead.
Jove, arm'd with Terrors, burst the Skies,
And Thunder roars, and Light'ning flies!
Amaz'd, confus'd, its Fate unknown,
The World stands trembling at his Throne.
While each pale Sinner hangs his Head,
Jove, nodding, shook the Heav'ns, and said,
"Offending Race of Human Kind,
By Nature, Reason, Learning, blind;
You who thro' Frailty step'd aside,
And you who never fell—*thro' Pride;*
You who in different Sects have shamm'd,
And come to see each other damn'd;
(So some Folks told you, but they knew
No more of Jove's Designs than you)
The World's mad Business now is o'er,
And I resent these Pranks no more.
I to such Blockheads set my Wit!
I damn such Fools!—Go, go, you're bit."[15]

As part of the "Offending Race of Human Kind" Swift is damned with the rest, but his major identification is clearly with the satirist-god of the vision. In public apologiae Swift asserted the conventional moral justification of the satirist; in private he battled the doubts that assailed him, expressing some of those doubts indirectly by way of the Tale-teller and others of his erratic personae; but in the compensatory mode of fantasy, and speaking through the most congenial persona of all, Swift lays claim to mythical powers.

"My Lord," wrote Swift in *A Letter Concerning the Weavers*, "I freely own it a wild Imagination that any words will cure the sottishness of men or the vanity of women . . . ," but the confession of futility becomes the springboard of attack as he pushes forward his argument with a caustic jibe. Whatever doubts Swift entertained about satire, he never allowed them to interfere with his métier. That he explored to the limit.

---

[15]*The Poems of Jonathan Swift*, ed. Harold Williams, 3 vols. (Oxford: Clarendon Press, 1958), 2:578–79.

Fathers and Sons: Swift's
A Tale of a Tub

Michael Seidel

"Know," says King Lear, "that we have divided / In three our kingdom; and 'tis our fast intent / To shake all cares and business from our age, / Conferring them on younger strengths, while we / Unburthen'd crawl toward death" (I, i, 36–40). Of the partible estate, Cordelia has nothing to say. "Nothing?" asks Lear, "Nothing will come of nothing" (I, i, 89). *A Tale of A Tub* accommodates Lear's paradox—it follows the partible estate through to its natural end. Nothing comes in complicated ways. The allegory of the *Tale* is a fable of misinheritance; the legacy conveyed by the allegory reveals the diminished mental integrity of the allegorist. In all respects, the *Tale* is about satirically weakened lines of descent: fathers to sons, ancients to moderns. The *Tale* is dedicated to a Prince of Posterity who never escapes a kind of infantile status because his minions die hard upon their births. The inheritors of the modern spirit in the *Tale* "spend their judgment as they do their estate, before it comes into their hands," and it is tempting to suspect a last satiric joke here, an onanistic ritual at the expense of wasted spirit.

The putative subject of the *Tale* is the inability to transmit donated value across historical and generational boundaries. And as is usually the case in satire, the satirist's thematic subject is objectified—even overcompensated—in the satire's form. To complete or satisfy the narrative is to enervate its subject. At the end of the *Tale*, its exhausted author, having forgotten what he is doing and not possessing the memory to remember just what he has done, contemplates writing on nothing, recognizing insofar as his powers allow him exactly what is left him, that is, what he has inherited and what he still controls.

The narrative strategy of *A Tale of A Tub* is subversive. To comment authoritatively upon Swift's meaning or, more suggestively, upon his "positioning" within the *Tale* risks a kind of aimless vertical bobbing against the line of the narrative horizon—like a tub itself in satirically fickle waters. The personated,

From Michael Seidel, *Satiric Inheritance: Rabelais to Sterne* (Princeton: Princeton University Press, 1979), 169–200. Copyright © 1979 by Princeton University Press. Reprinted by permission of the author and the Princeton University Press.

[1]For a full-length study of the *Tale* from this perspective, see John R. Clark's *Form and Frenzy in Swift's A Tale of A Tub* (Ithaca, 1970). My discussion is also greatly indebted to Frank Palmeri's work in progress on short satiric narratives (a Columbia University dissertation).

benighted, once-and-future Bedlamite of Swift's concoction makes a special point of complaining that he can hardly bear the mode that accommodates him—his overstrained sensibilities resist "the Satyrical Itch" that so irritates "this part of our Island" (pp. 48–49).[2] The "Apology" affixed to the 1710 edition of the *Tale* admits the parodic and satiric thread of irony running through the piece, but the represented author has "neither a Talent nor an Inclination for Satyr" (p. 53). Rather, he is in a hurry to judge the world all too well; but partly for intellectual and partly for domestic reasons (perhaps recommitment to Bedlam), he judges it not at all.

> On the other side, I am so entirely satisfied with the whole present Procedure of human Things, that I have been for some Years preparing Materials towards *A Panegyrick upon the World*; to which I intended to add a Second Part, entituled, *A Modest Defence of the Proceedings of the Rabble in all Ages*. Both these I had Thoughts to publish by way of Appendix to the following Treatise; but finding my Common-Place-Book fill much slower than I had reason to expect, I have chosen to defer them to another Occasion. Besides, I have been unhappily prevented in that Design, by a certain Domestick Misfortune, in the Particulars whereof, tho' it would be very seasonable, and much in the *Modern* way, to inform the *gentle Reader*, and would also be of great Assistance towards extending this Preface into the Size now in Vogue, which by Rule ought to be *large* in proportion as the subsequent Volume is *small*; Yet I shall now dismiss our impatient Reader from any farther Attendance at the *Porch*; and having duly prepared his Mind by a preliminary Discourse, shall gladly introduce him to the sublime Mysteries that ensue. (Pp. 53–54)

In rejecting satire for panegyric, Swift's author performs neither but is victimized by both. The process is complicated by the author's dismissal of satire as a peculiarly modern pursuit—a mode that followed the Stuarts out of Scotland to England ("first brought among us from beyond the *Tweed*," p. 49). Even though a nominal modern, he rests uncomfortably with those modern arts that could (and probably were) turned against him and his like. He goes on to observe that the Stuarts replaced the Tudor rose with the Scottish thistle, a progress from sweetness to blight.[3] It may be that the thistle replacing the rose

---

[2] All citations from the *Tale* and from the *Mechanical Operation of the Spirit* will be from *A Tale of A Tub, To which is added The Battle of the Books and the Mechanical Operation of the Spirit*, ed. A. C. Guthkelch and D. Nichol Smith (Oxford, 1958). Swift borrows the phrase, satirical "itch," from Sir William Temple's "Of Ancient and Modern Learning," in *The Works of Sir William Temple* (London, 1814), 3:486: "I wish the vein of ridiculing all that is serious and good, all honour and virtue, as well as learning and piety, may have no worse effects on any other State: it is the itch of our age and climate, and has over-run both the Court and the Stage; enters a house of Lords and Commons as boldly as a coffee-house, debates of Council as well as private conversation."

[3] In *The Formation of English Neo-Classical Thought* (Princeton, 1967), James William Johnson points out that the parallel of English and Roman history that occasioned the name the "Augustan Age" could well identify the height of English civilization, not in the time of the Restoration but in the Elizabethan "Golden Age." Johnson ponders the implications: "But if the classicist accepted the idea of the Elizabethan Age as the culmination of English history, and if he also believed that a nation followed a 'life' cycle like that of Rome, he was forced to some disturbing conclusions. From the 'high instances of power and sovereignty,' the 'happy times,' and the *imperium et libertas* of the Age of Elizabeth, said Clarendon in his *History of the Rebellion*, there was no way for England to go but downward into strife and corruption" (p. 60).

wittily confuses satire's cause with its effect,[4] but whatever the emblematic joke, the author blames his times for the itch he refuses to scratch. Swift, of course, insists we recognize that the author *is* the itch that the ironist who conceived of the *Tale* feels compelled to scratch.

Recent critics have become increasingly wary of trying to pin Swift down as the man behind the voices in the *Tale*, a man standing firm as a principle of reason like Mr. Ramsay in Virginia Woolf's *To the Lighthouse* who "as a stake driven into the bed of a channel upon which the gulls perch and the waves beat inspires in merry boat-loads a feeling of gratitude for the duty it is taking upon itself of marking the channel out there in the floods alone." John Traugott, for example, has put aside what to earlier commentators was the most important question of all: How far does Swift stand apart from the represented author, the Hack, in the comprehensive pattern of "authorship" that controls the *Tale*? Rather, Traugott assumes that anyone who would produce such a "thing" is himself deeply recessed in its structure, and the paramount question to ask is, what could so plague and unsettle a young man to make him write it?[5]

Traugott's partial answer is that Swift was strikingly unsure about the nature of his relationship to his pseudo or surrogate father, Sir William Temple, and to the values in whose "ancient" cause Swift undertook to defend Temple. Another critic, Gardner Stout, argues that satire is unsure and protean by the dictates of its modal nature and that Swift's position in the *Tale* is inevitably inconsistent.[6] *A Tale of A*

---

[4]Pope sees satire rising at about the same period, but for different reasons. At the end of Elizabeth's reign Archbishop Whitgift decreed a censorship proclamation (1599) because of what the government deemed an unwholesome spate of scurrilous satiric productions in the older invective vein. Satirists such as Marston, Guilpin, and Marlowe were interdicted. Pope argues that the 1599 edict forced the tone of satire to change and encouraged a more sophisticated, indirect satiric strategy. He writes in his ironic *Epistle to Augustus*.

> But Times corrupt, and Nature, ill-inclin'd,
> Produc'd the point that left a sting behind;
> Till friend with friend, and families at strife,
> Triumphant Malice rag'd thro' private life.
> Who felt the wrong, or fear'd it, took th' alarm,
> Appeal'd to Law, and Justice lent her arm.
> At length, by wholesom dread of statutes bound,
> The Poets learn'd to please, and not to wound:
> Most warp'd to Flatt'ry's side; but some, more nice,
> Preserv'd the freedom, and forbore the vice.
> Hence Satire rose, that just the medium hit,
> And heals with Morals what it hurts with Wit.
>   (Ll. 251–262)

[5]See John Traugott, "A Tale of A Tub," in *Focus: Swift*, ed. C. J. Rawson (London, 1971). Rawson himself has touched on these matters in an essay, "Order and Cruelty: A Reading of Swift (with some Comments on Pope and Johnson)," *Essays in Criticism* 20 (1970): 24–56 (above, pp. 29ff), as has Gardner Stout, Jr. in two important essays, "Speaker and Satiric Vision in Swift's *Tale of a Tub*," *Eighteenth-Century Studies* 2 (1969): 175–199 and "Satire and Self-expression in Swift's 'A Tale of A Tub,' " in *Studies in the Eighteenth Century*, ed. R. F. Brissenden (Canberra, Australia, 1973), pp. 323–39.

[6]In "Speaker and Satiric Vision," Stout writes: "[Swift's] vivid personations express essential aspects of his own personality—they embody his radical, antagonistic kinship with his satiric butts and his complicity in their extravagance, aggressive pride, and subversiveness" (p. 184). Stout, Rawson, and Traugott recognize Swift's stated Anglican rationalism and moderation in all this, but they choose to concentrate on some of the potentially deeper implications of psychological strategies in Swift's satiric works.

Tub may well be the product of Swift's psychic and generic dilemma. To represent anything seems to subvert it in some shape or form. It may be that the mind behind such a satiric extravagance knows as little security as the mind represented in it, but there is at least one notion we can entertain about the *Tale* and that, characteristically, is a notion eschewed in it. From its staggered beginning(s) to its exhausted ending, the *Tale* disinherits itself. Its author claims he has no truck with satirists, that "large eminent Sect of our *British* Writers" (p. 49), but the very mode of the work is given over to the thing its author (in one of his avatars) protests it is not. Swift will return to this satiric problem later in his career with Gulliver, a born-again satirist who wishes he were the thing he can never be, a horse.

That Swift should speak of the satiric art as practiced by a "sect" calls to mind the sectarian spirit of the times and its radical and "enthusiast" manifestations. Besides the satiric sect, the only significant sect mentioned in the *Tale* are the Aeolists, the winded-spirit (or exhaust) of factional lunacy. Because it is characteristic of satiric fiction to take on the nature of what it represents, the Aeolist beliefs become a version of satiric strategy. The impulse to radical inversion is common to both of Swift's "sects." The Aeolists are not alone in believing

> that, as the most unciviliz'd Parts of Mankind, have some way or other, climbed up into the Conception of a *God,* or Supream Power, so they have seldom forgot to provide their Fears with certain ghastly Notions, which instead of better, have served them pretty tolerably for a *Devil.* And this Proceeding seems to be natural enough; For it is with Men, whose Imaginations are lifted up very high, after the same Rate, as with those, whose Bodies are so; that, as they are delighted with the Advantage of a nearer Contemplation upwards, so they are equally terrified with the dismal Prospect of the Precipice below.[7] (P. 158)

There is a kind of universality in the revelation of an extravagant state of mind, and in the *Tale* Swift's procedure as satirist relies on the "Aeolist" imagination, which is akin to that presented in the *Mechanical Operation of the Spirit*: *"the Corruption of the Senses is the Generation of the Spirit"* (p. 269). Such a connection or satiric crossover is obvious to Swift's critics, but what is perhaps less obvious is the full implication of what his scheme means for satire. It would appear that only the satiric subject is elevated by corruption, thus inverting normative hierarchies of order and worth. But the real question is how can anyone escape from the descendent intellection produced by ascendant bodily pressures?[8] Two hundred years after Swift, Nietzsche posed the same question: "Tell

---

[7] In his *Language as Symbolic Action: Essays on Life, Literature, and Method* (Berkeley, 1966), Kenneth Burke offers a few remarks on appropriate literary modes that bear indirectly on the content of Swift's analysis of the general Aeolian mind: "Insofar as language is intrinsically hortatory (a medium by which men can obtain the cooperation of one another), God perfectly embodies the petition. Similarly, insofar as vituperation is a 'natural' resource of speech, the Devil provides a perfect butt for invective" (p. 20).

[8] This is the subject of Norman O. Brown's discussion of Swift and the excremental vision in *Life Against Death: The Psychoanalytic Meaning of History* (Middletown, Conn., 1959). See also, Michael V. Deporte's fascinating book, *Nightmares and Hobbyhorses: Swift, Sterne, and Augustan Ideas of Madness* (San Marino, Calif., 1974).

me, my brothers: what do we consider bad and worst of all? Is it not *degenera-tion*? . . . Upward goes our way, from genus to overgenus. But we shudder at the degenerate sense which says, 'Everything for me.' Upward flies our sense: thus it is a parable of our body, a parable of elevation. Parables of such elevations are the names of the virtues."[9] For Nietzsche and perhaps for Swift, elevation of the human spirit into that which breathes virtue is a saving fiction. The truth is closer to the satiric spirit—the fear that remains when the promise of regenera-tion becomes a natural and opposing fiction, when the contemplation upwards determines the plunge below. For Swift, the mind and body in perpetual vertical motion is madness, and in the *Tale's* elaborate "Digression on Madness" we see pathology in action.

As "modern" commentators are insistent in pointing out, when Swift presents or parodies the processes of modern thought and apprehension he does not absolve himself as victim of these processes. Curiously, neither does Sir William Temple, who supposedly stands behind the *Tale's* indictment of modern values. In his writings, Temple confirms a universal insecurity of human character. What follows could well serve as a strategic program for Swift's author—a sym-pathetic, if extreme, representative of the generic human mind. Temple writes that there is

> a certain restlessness of mind and thought, which seems universally and inseparably annexed to our very natures and constitutions, unsatisfied with what we are, or what we at present possess and enjoy, still raving after something past or to come, and by griefs, regrets, desires, or fears, ever troubling and corrupting the pleasures of our senses and of our imaginations, the enjoyments of our fortunes, or the best production of our reasons, and thereby the content and happiness of our lives.[10]

Thus an "ancient" voice in the modern controversy. And if Temple is privi-leged to say what he says, Swift ought to be privileged to represent in the condi-tion of authorship not merely the elevated values of the reasoning writer but the descendent insecurities of a complex and often troubled satiric impersonator. In the *Tale*, Swift plays off both ancients and moderns as Laurence Sterne will later do in *Tristram Shandy*. In addressing his readers, Tristram seems to remember Swift's author.

---

[9]Nietzsche, *Thus Spoke Zarathustra*, in *The Portable Nietzsche*, trans. Walter Kaufmann (New York, 1976), p. 187.

[10]Sir William Temple, "Of Popular Discontents," *Works*, 3:32. Temple goes on to write of the nat-ural instability of the entire body politique:

> This is the true, natural, and common source of such personal dissatisfactions, such domestic complaints, and such popular discontents, as afflict not only our private lives, conditions, and for-tunes, but even our civil states and governments, and thereby consummate the particular and general infelicty of mankind: which is enough complained of by all that consider it in the common actions and passions of life, but much more in the factions, seditions, convulsions, and fatal revo-lutions that have so frequently, and in all ages, attended all or most of the governments in the world. (P. 32)

Temple's remarks read like a version of Swift's "Digression on Madness."

Thus,——thus my fellow labourers and associates in this great harvest of our learning, now ripening before our eyes; thus it is, by slow steps of casual increase, that our knowledge physical, metaphysical, physiological, polemical, nautical, mathematical, ænigmatical, technical, biographical, romantical, chemical, and obstetrical, with fifty other branches of it, (most of 'em ending, as these do, in *ical*) have, for these two last centuries and more, gradually been creeping upwards towards that Ακμή of their perfections, from which, if we may form a conjecture from the advances of these seven years, we cannot possibly be far off.

When that happens, it is to be hoped, it will put an end to all kind of writings whatsoever;—the want of all kind of writing will put an end to all kind of reading;—and that in time, *As war begets poverty, poverty peace,*—must, in course, put an end to all kind of knowledge,—and then—we shall have all to begin over again; or, in other words, be exactly where we started. (Vol. I, ch. 21)

In his commentary on the caves of the nymphs in the *Odyssey*, Porphyry has occasion to allude to a Platonic metaphor from the *Gorgias* (493) where Socrates describes the desiring soul as a vessel or a jar because it can be so easily swayed. Porphyry explains: "Souls, however, are tubs, because they contain in themselves energies and habits, as in a vessel."[11] In similar fashion, Swift's *Tale of A Tub* contains the energies and habits of its teller. The teller is the "tale"—the allegory (the narrative of the tailored coats) is but a thread in the larger fabric of the satiric whole. Like Socrates' vessel, the teller *as* tub is allegorical in a comprehensive sense. He is the *one* who represents the variable *other*.

Although the whole of *A Tale of A Tub* is a representation of the momentary mind and the time it takes to express its phenomenal profusions, the allegorical line, *sub specie aeternitatis,* is reconstructable. The tale within the tale has folk roots in the partible succession. Inheritance is tripartite and usually competitive. In many of the examples collected by the Grimms of the inheriting brothers (or sisters) tale, each child possesses a special talent and employs that talent in competing for paternal favor or wealth (most often land).[12] In comic forms of the structure, talents may be negative and the person with the least claim of worthiness inherits. One of Grimms' *Tales* depicts three sluggard brothers in a laziness contest. Life's "loser" is declared the winner by proving, when provided with a sword, that he lacks the energy to sever the rope that will hang him. In another Grimms story, the brother who has learned his occupation as fencing master so well that he can slice raindrops as they fall inherits over two brothers, one who can shave the whiskers off a hare running at full speed and the other who can shoe a horse in full gallop.

---

[11]"On the Cave of the Nymphs," 13, trans. Thomas Taylor, in *Select Works of Porphyry* (London, 1823), pp. 194f. I am indebted to James Nohrnberg's study, *The Analogy of the Faerie Queene* (Princeton, 1976), p. 16, for this reference.

[12]For a review of the structure of many of these inheritance tales, see Vladimir Propp, *Morphology of the Folk Tale,* trans. Lawrence Scott; revised Louis A. Wagner; introduction Alan Dundes (Austin, 1975). Propp speaks of departure and marriage as the flanking structures of the folk tale, but in between he marks various stages of familial competition, lack, or desire. The three-brother and three-sister variety partakes of all structural stages, depending upon the narrative sequences unfolded in the specific tale.

In the folk tale the ritual of transference may or may not have anything to do with laws of inheritance or with relevant qualifications for succession. A contest seems an arbitrary way to avoid rivalry or to concentrate rivalry in the hopes of settling it at once. Of course, the tragic dimensions of such a scheme are present in a play such as *King Lear,* where the old man demands more than equally divided loyalties for a share he tells his youngest daughter is "more opulent" than those he has already doled out in a self-flattering competition. The folk motif appears with even more sinister motives in Shakespeare's *The Merchant of Venice,* when the three-siblings story is replaced by a tale in which there is a choice of three objects. In his analysis of the three-casket tale, Freud discovers an inversion of the three-children inheritance myth or perhaps a revulsion toward what the inheritance motif represents. The choice is no longer one that allows the line to continue whole; rather, it becomes a suppressed wish for extinction. Tired of life's rivalries, the blind choice is a choice for death.

Although it is not so dark, the allegoric fable of the three brothers in *A Tale of A Tub* has its mysterious devolutions. Possibly recognizing the unstable, frenetic quality of all transmitted things, Swift understands that the father's will (literally a "will" to inertia) stands scant chance of having its stipulations fulfilled. The brothers are obligated to do nothing (a task more appropriate to the *Tale's* author). Their inheritance comes to them unadorned—it is their legal and organic portion.

> ONCE upon a Time, there was a Man who had Three Sons by one Wife, and all at a Birth, neither could the Mid-Wife tell certainly which was the Eldest. Their Father died while they were young, and upon his Death-Bed, calling the Lads to him, spoke thus,
>
> SONS, *because I have purchased no Estate, nor was born to any, I have long considered some good Legacies to bequeath You; And at last, with much Care as well as Expence, have provided each of you* (here they are) *a new Coat. Now, you are to understand, that these Coats have two Virtues contained in them: One is, that with good wearing, they will last you fresh and sound as long as you live: The other is, that they will grow in the same proportion with your Bodies, lengthning and widening of themselves, so as to be always fit.* (P. 73)

We learn from the *Tale* that the accomplishment of nothing is an elaborate procedure. Inevitably, the brothers overcompensate—they adorn their inherited coats. The outline of the fable as representative of the history of Christianity assumes the nonpartible nature of truth: "Their Father having left them equal Heirs, and strictly commanded, that whatever they got, should lye in common among them all" (p. 121). The Romish Peter, however, reinstitutes rivalry by arguing for primogeniture: "HE told his Brothers, he would have them to know, that he was their Elder, and consequently his Father's sole Heir" (p. 105). The argument is not only for ascendancy but for "title" and authority: "Nay, a while after, he would not allow them to call Him, *Brother,* but Mr. *PETER*; and then he must be styl'd, *Father PETER,* and sometimes, *My Lord PETER*" (p. 105). Later he signs pardons, which do no good, as "Emperor Peter" (p. 113). Our "generous Author" follows the progress; he "finds his Hero on the Dunghil, from thence by gradual Steps, raises Him to a Throne, and then immediately withdraws, expecting not so much as Thanks for his Pains: in imitation of which Example, I have placed *Lord Peter* in a Noble House, given Him a Title to wear, and Money to spend" (p. 133).

Lord Peter is too big for his britches and too good for his allegorical coat. Not only does he usurp the entire inheritance but he further inflates his image by beginning to call himself "*God Almighty,* and sometimes *Monarch of the Universe*" (p. 115). The act of usurpation is given its emblematic image with Peter's three-tiered hat, a parody of papal bearing and an alternative to the three coats. It is as if Peter has taken all the family onto his head. He locks up the original will of the father, and he allows doctrines to be pronounced "*ex Cathedra*" with "*Points* [that] were absolutely *Jure Paterno*" (p. 90). He absorbs even secular space, robbing a Lord of his estates by "the way of contriving a *Deed of Conveyance* of that House to Himself and his Heirs" (p. 91).[13]

Inheritance becomes usurpation. Peter begins dividing a house against itself, and nothing divided against itself (even Satan, as Christ points out in the *Gospels*) can stand. Martin remembers what everyone else seems to forget: "*the Testament of their good Father was very exact in what related to the wearing of their Coats; yet was it no less penal and strict in prescribing Agreement, and Friendship, and Affection between them. And therefore, if straining a Point were at all dispensable, it would certainly be so, rather to the Advance of Unity, than Increase of Contradiction*" (p. 139). But we see very little of Martin in the *Tale*: he represents unity and satire treats of contradiction. Rather, we see too much of Peter and Jack, both alike in their extremity. Trying to abrogate the terms of their father's will by avoiding each other, they meet—like the extremes of the imagination—by coming full circle:"Yet after all this, it was their perpetual Fortune to meet. The Reason of which, is easy enough to apprehend: For, the Phrenzy and the Spleen of both, having the same Foundation, we may look upon them as two Pair of Compasses, equally extended, and the fixed Foot of each, remaining in the same Center; which, tho' moving contrary Ways at first, will be sure to encounter somewhere or other in the Circumference" (pp. 198–199). The allegory is similar to the *Tale's* general theory of momentous expression. Swift's compass extends far and wide, and it would be risky to assume that anyone's energies and habits are fully or even partially exempted from patterned extravagancies.

> AND, whereas the mind of Man, when he gives the Spur and Bridle to his Thoughts, doth never stop, but naturally sallies out into both extreams of High and Low, of Good and Evil; His first Flight of Fancy, commonly transports Him to Idea's of what is most Perfect, finished, and exalted; till having soared out of his own Reach and Sight, not well perceiving how near the Frontiers of Height and Depth, border

---

[13]Wotton's note on this passage explains the historical significance of the allegory: "Thus the Pope, upon the decease of the duke of Ferrara without lawful issue, seized the dutchy, as falling to the holy see, *jure divino*" (p. 91).

upon each other; With the same Course and Wing, he falls down plum into the lowest Bottom of Things; like one who travels the *East* into the *West*; or like a strait Line drawn by its own Length into a Circle.[14] (Pp. 157–158)

The mind is allegorically quixotic, and for every upward venture there is a bottoming out. When the Father dies early his sons are set in contradictory motion; when the authorizing mind gives vent it turns round upon itself. In the *Tale* Swift sets out not merely to catalogue abuses in religion and learning (thus joining the allegorical narrative with the digressive one) but to reveal the underlying structure of satiric succession. Fathers, no matter what they "will," generate multiplicity. In this sense, the testamentary father of the allegory stands in the same relation to the corruption of his will as a figure such as Sir William Temple stands in relation to Swift's personated digressiveness in the *Tale*. After all, the controversy that the *Tale* inherits and carries on—a local skirmish in the perpetual crusade of ancients against moderns—has essentially the same structure as the allegory of the one coat and the many.

Inheritance is dwindled substance. Writing "In Praise of Digressions," the *Tale's* author takes stock of the modern estate: "For this great Blessing we are wholly indebted to *Systems* and *Abstracts,* in which the *Modern* Fathers of Learning, like prudent Usurers, spent their Sweat for the Ease of Us their Children. For *Labor* is the Seed of *Idleness,* and it is the peculiar Happiness of our Noble Age to gather the *Fruit"* (pp. 145–146). Fruit-gathering suggests a patrimonial inheritance that may not exist. In fact, as in Pope's *Dunciad,* the modern inheritance is maternal and reversionary, especially for the *Tale's* "*dark* Authors" who have "found out this excellent Expedient of *Dying"* (p. 186). Modern progeny are the seeds of chaos.

> For, *Night* being the universal Mother of Things, wise Philosophers hold all Writings to be *fruitful* in the Proportion they are *dark*; And therefore, the *true illuminated* (that is to say, the *Darkest* of all) have met with such numberless Commentators, whose *Scholiastick* Midwifry hath deliver'd them of Meanings, that the Authors themselves, perhaps, never conceived, and yet may very justly be allowed the Lawful Parents of them: The Words of such Writers being like Seed, which, however scattered at random,

---

[14]Freud has some intriguing things to say on the process of reversal in dreams that bears on this famous passage from the *Tale*.

> Incidentally, reversal, or turning a thing into its opposite, is one of the means of representation most favoured by the dream-work and one which is capable of employment in the most diverse directions. It serves in the first place to give expression to the fulfillment of a wish in reference to some particular element of the dream-thoughts. 'If only it had been the other way round!' This is often the best way of expressing the ego's reaction to a disagreeable fragment of memory. Again, reversal is of quite special use as a help to the censorship, for it produces a mass of distortion in the material which is to be represented, and this has a positively paralysing effect, to begin with, on any attempt at understanding the dream. For that reason, if a dream obstinately declines to reveal its meaning, it is always worth while to see the effect of reversing some particular elements in its manifest content, after which the whole situation often becomes immediately clear.

See *The Interpretation of Dreams,* trans. James Strachey (London, 1953), 4:327.

when they light upon a fruitful Ground, will multiply far beyond either the Hopes or Imagination of the Sower. (P. 186)

Some books are freaks of nature. Modern fathers have already defrauded nature by turning the process of transmission around and trying to produce unity from multiplicity: "And indeed, it seems not unreasonable, that Books, the Children of the Brain, should have the Honor to be Christned with variety of Names, as well as other Infants of Quality. Our famous *Dryden* has ventured to proceed a Point farther, endeavouring to introduce also a Multiplicity of *Godfathers*; which is an Improvement of much more Advantage, upon a very obvious Account" (pp. 71–72). With Dryden as a model, the modern author (father of his *Tale*) divides his progeny only to find himself entirely disinherited: "having employ'd a World of Thoughts and Pains, to split my Treatise into forty Sections, and having entreated forty Lords of my Acquaintance, that they would do me the Honor to stand, they all made it a Matter of Conscience, and sent me their Excuses" (p. 72). The author's progeny is satirically cut out of an inheritance because modern progenitors spread their seed too thin. As in the violation of the allegorical will of the father, contradiction (or division) weakens unity.

Sons and "moderns" in the *Tale*, therefore, take on analogous roles. And where, one wonders, does the author of the whole enterprise fit in? One answer is that as an "extreme" mind he circulates as both progenitor and progeny, ancient and modern, father and son. His commission to write the *Tale* makes him modernity's putative enemy, and in the *Apology* we learn that the author writes in support of the Ancient's cause and waves the paternal banner of one *Sir W.T.*, "*a certain great Man then alive, and universally reverenced for every good Quality that could possibly enter into the Composition of the most accomplish'd Person*" (p. 11). Furthermore, the volume is dedicated to Lord Somers, who as a father has title to the first place if only because the modern brood keep naming him second: "For, I have somewhere heard, it is a Maxim, that those, to whom every Body allows the second Place, have an undoubted Title to the First" (p. 24).

But "*there generally runs an Irony through the Thread of the whole Book*" (p. 8), and father-Swift engenders a son-author who is liege slave to modernism. "I have profess'd to be a most devoted Servant of all *Modern* Forms" (p. 45), he writes, and a bit later he refers with reverence to one of the works at the source of arguments "bandied about both in *France* and *England*, for a just Defence of the *Modern* Learning and Wit, against the Presumption, the Pride, and the Ignorance of the *Antients*" (p. 69). The work is titled THE *Wise Men* of Gotham, and it parodies Wotton's attack on Temple by perverting one fable (the approach of three kings to one holy source) while echoing another (the three-brothers tale of the allegory of the coats). It is not surprising that the *Tale*'s author should represent inconsistent positions. Such is precisely his impulse. He counts himself a deep writer but advises that surfaces are preferable to depths (that is, if one wishes to remain sane, and the author may not wish to do so). Writing seems deepest for the author when, like a well, it contains no contents (that is, when it aims at shallowness by design).

The author's only inspiration is likely to come from a deficient muse. The son seeks the status of father and in so doing betrays the integrity of line. For example, the author follows "the Examples of our illustrious *Moderns*" (p. 92) in discovering from "*Antient Books and Pamphlets*" (p. 92) "the proper Employment of a *True Antient and Genuine Critick*" (p. 95). To do so, he reveals the counterfeit inheritance.

> THE Third, and Noblest Sort, is that of the *TRUE CRITICK*, whose Original is the most Antient of all. Every *True Critick* is a Hero born, descending in a direct Line from a Celestial Stem, by *Momus* and *Hybris* who begat *Zoilus*, who begat *Tigellius*, who begat *Etcætera* the Elder, who begat *B—tly*, and *Rym—r*, and *W—tton*, and *Perrault*, and *Dennis*, who begat *Etcætera* the Younger. (Pp. 93–94)

The generational status of the true critic is parodically testamentary: "their Admirers placed their Origine in Heaven, among those of *Hercules, Theseus,* and *Perseus,* and other great Deservers of Mankind" (p. 94). Such a descent is counterheroic and proliferate at the same time, connecting the deeper structure of the allegory (a descent by threes from a heavenly original) and the parodic state of modernity, an overelaborated contribution of one or another "Etcætera." When the true (modern) critic, "*a Discoverer and Collector of Writers Faults*" (p. 95), accommodates his descent, he does what the brothers do to their inherited coats: he corrupts tradition. The author of the *Tale* feels an obligation to take up his pen against a true literary source, the Homeric father: "IT was to supply such momentous Defects, that I have been prevailed on after long Sollicitation, to take Pen in Hand" (p. 129) against Homer.[15]

No fathers in the *Tale*—from the father of poetry, to the allegorical father of three brothers, to Sir William Temple—shall escape whipping from some of their sons. Even the epigraph parodies the father as source: "Basima eacabasa eanaa irraurista, diarba da caeotaba sobor camelanthi." Wotton identifies this seeming gibberish (for which Swift heaps some added abuse at his feet) as a transcription from the original Syriac of an initiation form used by the heretic gnostic sect, the Marcosians: "*I call upon this, which is above all the Power of the Father, which is called Light, and Spirit, and Life, because thou hast reigned in the Body*" (p. 323).[16] The epigraph is from Irenaeus, a Church Father, who stands in relation to the self-sufficient content of the citation in the same man-

---

[15]Sir William Temple, of course, sees Homer as "the most universal genius that has been known in the world." See "Of Poetry," in *Works*, 3:415. He continues: "there cannot be a greater testimony given, than what has been by some observed, that not only the greatest masters have found in his works the best and truest principles of all their sciences or arts, but that the noblest nations have derived from them the original of their several races, though it be hardly yet agreed, whether his story be true or a fiction" (p. 416).

[16]Wotton's notes to the epigraph appear on p. 187 and p. 323 of the Guthkelch and Smith edition of the *Tale*. The editors also reprint the response to Wotton included in *A Complete Key to the Tale of a Tub* (1710) where an appendage to a note records: "*Irenæus* corrected by Mr. *Wotton*: O! the depth of Modern Learning" (p. 348). For a discussion of gnosticism in *A Tale of A Tub*, see Ronald Paulson's chapter, "The Gnostic View of Man," in *Theme and Structure in Swift's A Tale of A Tub* (New Haven, 1960), pp. 87–144.

ner as the *Tale*'s father to the sons' coats or as Temple to the parodic impersonations of his modern "son" Swift.

As its epigraph says, the *Tale* is sufficient unto itself, but perhaps for different reasons. A mind that is "en-tubbed" drifts or bobs on its own—it has no connections with a past and can barely anticipate the future. Modernity knows only its own moment, and moderns tend to forget memorable transmission because their entire being is momentous. It is as Paul de Man says in describing Nietzsche's position on modernity: "Modernity invests its thrust in the power of the present moment as origin, but discovers that, in severing itself from the past, it has at the same time severed itself from the present."[17] Memory is an ancient enemy to modern being, or as the author of the *Tale* puts it: "*Memory* being an Employment of the Mind upon things past, is a Faculty, for which the Learned, in our Illustrious Age, have no manner of Occasion, who deal entirely with *Invention*, and strike all Things out of themselves, or at least, by Collision, from each other" (p. 135). Always complaining of an "unhappy shortness of my Memory" (p. 92), the author dips into his well and comes up dry: "Thrice have I forced my Imagination to make the *Tour* of my Invention, and thrice it has returned empty; the latter having been wholly drained by the following Treatise" (p. 42). This is another of many instances in which the author fulfills his plans to write upon nothing before having announced that such is precisely his plan: "I am now trying an Experiment very frequent among Modern Authors; which is, to *write upon Nothing*" (p. 208). With no memory, the subject is well chosen. Nothing is held, therefore nothing is produced. Laurence Sterne sums up the modern dilemma when in *Tristram Shandy* he writes about the failure of Lockean human memory: "Dull organs, dear Sir, in the first place. Secondly, slight and transient impressions made by objects when the said organs are not dull. And, thirdly, a memory like unto a sieve, not able to retain what it has received" (vol. II, ch. 2).

Like the gnosticism of the epigraph, modernity is almost pathological. Our author is a mad scribbler—some of his visits to Bedlam are homecomings. And in the "Digression on Madness" we learn the symptoms of self-conceived and self-extinguished imaginings. A madman, knowing little of things outside himself, "did ever conceive it in his Power, to reduce the Notions of all Mankind, exactly to the same Length, and Breadth, and Height of his own" (p. 166). Swift's scheme for madness is a kind of bodily sabotage: madmen finally consume their own excrement, eat their words, and whisper nothing. We learn to admire the manifestations of nothing because, in effect, we will learn nothing else. In the midst of the most crucial explanation in the *Tale*—the "knotty Point" of why forms of madness proliferate and vary—there is a hiatus in the text. The author has again written upon nothing, and "this I take to be a clear Solution of the Matter" (p. 170). To explain madness is to explain modernity,

---

[17]Paul de Man, "Literary History and Literary Modernity," in *Blindness and Insight: Essays in the Rhetoric of Contemporary Criticism* (New York, 1971), p. 149.

and such an explanation is too much to expect from a book with gaps for a memory.

The appropriate figure for modernity in the *Tale* is, naturally enough, the infant. Infants are brand new—they have nothing to remember. At the same time, to be an infant is to have just entered the scene, to be last: "But I here think fit to lay hold on that great and honourable Privilege of being the *Last Writer;* I claim an absolute Authority in Right, as the *freshest Modern,* which gives me a Despotick Power over all Authors before me" (p. 130). The author claims his inheritance or his birthright without waiting for either his talent or his estate to mature. In coming last, moderns come too fast—they spend themselves. Later in the *Tale* we learn that delusions of authority, "any Thought of subduing Multitudes to his own *Power*" (p. 171), are a symptom of madness. To be born a modern is to be born mad.

In terms of the structure of the *Tale,* picturing modernity as an infant has the advantage of connecting the fable of allegorical inheritance with the greater theme of cultural inheritance. In both cases past time is forgotten. The author dedicates his *Tale* to Prince Posterity, partly because his memory may fail him at any moment and partly because the future needs all the help it can get. Posterity's children—the works of his authors—rarely last until the next revolution of the sun: "Unhappy Infants, many of them barbarously destroyed, before they have so much as learnt their *Mother-Tongue* to beg for Pity" (p. 33). These infants, tainted by time's breath, "die of a languishing Consumption" (p. 33). The labors of Grub-Street are reminiscent of the perpetual labor of Sin in *Paradise Lost*: "These yelling Monsters that with ceaseless cry / Surround me, as thou saw'st, hourly conceiv'd / And hourly born, with sorrow infinite / To me. . . (II, 795–798). The *Tale*'s momentary productions are unluckier—they are not only hourly born but they hourly die. Swift may have remembered Sir William Temple's essay "Of Ancient and Modern Learning": "For the scribblers are infinite, that, like mushrooms or flies, are born and die in small circles of time; whereas books, like proverbs, receive their chief value from the stamp and esteem of ages through which they have passed."[18]

In the dedication to Prince Posterity Swift continues to ponder the problem of infant mortality by having the author put in a plea for "our Corporation of *Poets,*" whose "*never-dying* Works" time has committed to "unavoidable Death" (p. 33). Such a corporation is the organic body of poetry that cannot hold to form. Its proliferated "beings" escape "our Memory, and delude our Sight" (p. 34) like Hamlet's protean clouds.

> If I should venture in a windy Day, to affirm to *Your Highness,* that there is a large Cloud near the *Horizon* in the Form of a *Bear,* another in the *Zenith* with the Head of an *Ass,* a third to the Westward with Claws like a *Dragon*; and *Your Highness* should in a few Minutes think fit to examine the Truth,'tis certain, they would all be changed in Figure and Position, new ones would arise, and all we could agree upon would be,

---

[18]Sir William Temple, "Of Ancient and Modern Learning," *Works,* 3:446.

that Clouds there were, but that I was grossly mistaken in the *Zoography* and *Topography* of them. (P. 35)

In a sense, books are free form; their modern authors inherit no models and thus produce nothing but monstrosities. A monster is *sui generis*—its only property or possession is itself. What is come is done: "Books, like Men their Authors, have no more than one Way of coming into the World, but there are ten Thousand to go out of it, and return no more" (p. 36). In the "Digression on Madness," the conceit of the quick birth and perpetual death is picked up in the Lockean discourse on imaginary birth versus memorial death, fiction versus truth.

> If we consider that the Debate meerly lies between *Things past,* and *Things conceived*; and so the Question is only this; Whether Things that have Place in the *Imagination,* may not as properly be said to *Exist,* as those that are seated in the *Memory*; which may be justly held in the Affirmative, and very much to the Advantage of the former, since This is acknowledged to be the *Womb* of Things, and the other allowed to be no more than the *Grave.* (P. 172)

Since the works of the modern imagination are conceived and extinguished in virtually the same short breath, the womb *is* the grave. The author of the *Tale* has "a strong Inclination, before I leave the World, to taste a Blessing, which we *mysterious* Writers can seldom reach, till we have got into our Graves" (p. 185). There fame's "Trumpet sounds best and farthest, when she stands on a *Tomb*, by the Advantage of a rising Ground, and the Echo of a hollow Vault" (p. 186). Once again the author comes up empty. In this case monuments are not exactly memories. Since memory is not an issue of the modern imagination, it is not *even* the record of the imagination laid to rest. If we return to the dedication to Prince Posterity, we learn that the infants of the pen are buried in thin air; they come so fast from the womb that they earn no fixed grave: "the *Memorial of them was lost among Men, their Place was no more to be found*" (pp. 34–35).

Part of the design of *A Tale of A Tub* proclaims that a kind of zero-narrative time takes over from a more primitive concept of narrative advance. The very title of the work is digressive or diversionary, and the author announces that his commission is to decoy the modern destroyer, Hobbes's *Leviathan*, from imperiling the state. The author writes in a conservative cause as the defender of "Religion and Government" (p. 39). Of course, he is the perfect choice because his *Tale* is the perfect tub: "That Sea-men have a Custom when they meet a *Whale*, to fling him out an empty *Tub*, by way of Amusement, to divert him from laying violent Hands upon the Ship. This Parable was immediately mythologiz'd: The *Whale* was interpreted to be *Hobs's Leviathan*, which tosses and plays with all other Schemes of Religion and Government, whereof a great many are hollow, and dry, and empty, and noisy, and wooden, and given to Rotation" (p. 40).[19]

---

[19]The suggestion of rotation recalls the schemes for government around the time of the *Leviathan* and the English Civil Wars and Interregnum, specifically James Harrington's Republican Rota Club. Like Butler and Dryden, Swift seems to set the satiric principle of diversionary necessity in literature back to the internecine romance. From revolution (or rotation) comes the need for ironic countersub-

The whale and the tub are versions of each other and, just as in the allegory of the coats, moderation is not part of this satiric spectacle. We see nothing of sound government and little of sound religion (with the exception of Martin) in the *Tale's* allegory and digressions because satiric mimicry is itself extreme. What we do see are extremes coming "around." Section VIII is nominally distinguished as part of the allegory, but in actuality the discourse on the Aeolists *becomes* a digression. For the allegorical relation, time ought to be diachronic; for the digressions, time is inevitably synchronic. But Swift collapses allegorical time, first into the history of one family, then into local episodes, then into the synchronic state of religious faction—the perpetual Aeolian moment. The *Tale* reaches a point of narrative stasis when its author confuses progress and regress, when the diversion (or tub) takes over the tale. This happens quite literally in the Aeolist section when the allusionary tub materializes as a wind-container whose original was Odyssean.

> It was an Invention ascribed to *Æolus* himself, from whom this Sect is denominated, and who in Honour of their Founder's Memory, have to this Day preserved great Numbers of those *Barrels,* whereof they fix one in each of their Temples, first beating out the Top; into this *Barrel,* upon Solemn Days, the Priest enters; where, having before duly prepared himself by the methods already described, a secret Funnel is also convey'd from his Posteriors, to the Bottom of the Barrel, which admits new Supplies of Inspiration from a *Northern* Chink or Crany. Whereupon, you behold him swell immediately to the Shape and Size of his *Vessel.* (Pp. 155–156)

The tub is a mechanism for the compression and forcing of air, an operation that, when it occurs naturally, produces insanity (as we learn later from the "Digression on Madness"). But more important for the design of the *Tale,* the tub becomes an aid to organic self-sufficiency. With such a "digression" surrounding one's being, there are no sequences outside of one's self. The very idea of narrative sequence, then, is subsumed by digressive usurpation; "*Digressions* in a Book, are like *Forein Troops* in a *State,* which argue the Nation to want a *Heart* and *Hands* of its own, and often, either *subdue* the *Natives,* or drive them into the most *unfruitful Corners*" (p. 144). Earlier, in his "Digression in the Modern Kind," the author had distinguished between his tale and its digressions (later indistinguishable) on the basis of the Horatian formula of instruction and diversion.

> That the Publick Good of Mankind is performed by two Ways, *Instruction,* and *Diversion.* And I have farther proved in my said several Readings, (which, perhaps, the World may one day see, if I can prevail on any Friend to steal a Copy, or on certain Gentlemen of my Admirers, to be very Importunate) that, as Mankind is now disposed, he receives much greater Advantage by being *Diverted* than *Instructed*; His Epidemical

---

version, a need that produced elaborate satiric structures. In this sense, it is interesting that another tale of a tub crops up in the context of wartime in Rabelais when we hear of Diogenes' diversionary attempt to avoid enlistment in Philip of Macedon's campaign against the Corinthians. Rabelais writes of Diogenes: "he was giving his tub a thrashing in order not to seem the one lazy idler among a people so feverishly busy" *Gargantua and Pantagruel,* trans. J. M. Cohen (Harmondsworth, 1955), p. 283.

Diseases being *Fastidiosity*, *Amorphy*, and *Oscitation*; whereas in the present universal Empire of Wit and Learning, there seems but little Matter left for *Instruction*. (P. 124)

Like moderation and stability, instruction is not particularly fertile ground for the extremes of modernity or satire, and the author accurately describes the plan of the *Tale* in presenting "throughout this Divine Treatise" a "*Layer* of *Utile* and a *Layer of Dulce*" (p. 124). If usefulness is the measure of instruction and diversion the measure of sweetness, one concludes that the *Tale*'s digressions are pretty well useless. But as satiric mimicry they are delightful. They are such effective parodies of a world not in love with the productions of time that they have done exactly what Swift's perverse imitative genius represented them as not being able to do: they have lasted. This is satire's parodoxical testament. The "transitory State of all sublunary Things" (p. 66)—things on earth and under the moon (thus lunatic)— are given a permanent space in time by the power of satiric representation. Because the represented author is not capable of grasping time, the *Tale*'s digressive time becomes most memorable in the genius of a real author able to transcend it. Swift's author is similar to the increasingly schizoid lunatic in Dostoevsky's *Notes from Underground*, whose best sense of time is digressive but whose mental fabrications hold a more secure literary place than the sequential goings-on above ground from which he isolates himself. We are told in the *Tale* that "there is no inventing Terms of Art beyond our Idea's; and when Idea's are exhausted, Terms of Art must be so too" (p. 50). The writer *in* the *Tale* is a figure of exhaustion: he was sick when he wrote it; he cannot finish it; he can barely remember it. But the parody and energy of the effort is inexhaustible. Swift was amazed at his own genius when he "writ it," and in terms of its art the *Tale* creates and lives in its own satiric culture.

Much of the anxiety created by the subject of *A Tale of A Tub*, by Swift's place in it and by the reader's reading it, has to do with the temporal and spatial insecurities of its satiric vision. To represent a world of compressed time where it seems there is not enough time to get anything done is to distort the rhythms of life. In the *Tale*, Swift's spatial sense is constructed on the same axis as his temporal sense. All goes up and down in the same place; nothing seems to extend very far backward or forward. Metaphor is what fits in a tight place—a kind of materialized psychology of vapors, spirits, bulges, and barrels. From the great movements in history to the freaks of individual and sect behavior, accountability derives from the crowding of objects, temperaments, and ideas. Satire is that proliferate number from which it is impossible to "get quit." The incontinent, the mad, the shapeless, and the shiftless cram into every available space. We are given only the option of the vertical line, and comprehension itself becomes an imitation of descendent moments in time.

However, being extreamly sollicitous, that every accomplished Person who has got into the Taste of Wit, calculated for this present Month of *August*, 1697, should descend to the very *bottom* of all the *Sublime* throughout this Treatise; I hold fit to lay down this general Maxim. Whatever Reader desires to have a thorow

Comprehension of an Author's Thoughts, cannot take a better Method, than by putting himself into Circumstances and Postures of Life, that the Writer was in, upon every important Passage as it flow'd from his Pen; For this will introduce a Parity and strict Correspondence of Idea's between the Reader and the Author. (P. 44)

In the "Digression on Madness" we are warned to shy away from depths, but here we are asked to mimic profundity. And when we descend to the bottom of the sublime, we become vertically ambiguous. The sublime—the *sub limit* or the "tops"—ought to have nothing to do with the bottom. Of course, the spatial scheme is a scatological metaphor, and it is precisely the bottom's influence on the top (head; mind) that drives men mad. The "Digression on Madness" is the same spatial nightmare that appeared earlier in the section on Aeolists, but the directions are reversed. In the Aeolist discourse all things bottom out ("the imagination of what is Highest and Best, becomes overshot, and spent, and weary, and suddenly falls like a dead Bird of Paradise, to the Ground," p. 158); in the "Digression on Madness" a "*Phœnomenon* of *Vapours,* ascending from the lower Faculties to over-shadow the Brain" distills "into Conceptions, for which the Narrowness of our Mother-Tongue has not yet assigned any other Name, besides that of *Madness* or *Phrenzy*" (p. 167). Down or up, sexual or scatological, bodily inclinations are compressed anxieties.

The vertical line in the *Tale* is the line of satire, the line of digression, the line of compression. Elevation and debasement do not allow advance or transmission, merely mechanical operation. The directional scheme insures against the extension of the individual's properties in a beneficial line. In his *Mechanical Operation of the Spirit,* Swift borrows the Hobbist conceit of the artificial man at the beginning of the *Leviathan* and makes him into the natural man of satire: "Besides, there is many an Operation, which in its Original, was purely an Artifice, but through a long Succession of Ages, hath grown to be a natural" (pp. 267–268). Here the satiric inheritance is the result of material compressibility. Bound and squeezed heads of infant Scythians produced a sugar-loaf protrusion above the compressed area, a protrusion later passed on naturally as a deformation. A similar artificial production of natural monsters occurred during England's Civil War period. History's forms are materially shaped:

For, in the Age of our Fathers, there arose a Generation of Men in this Island call'd *Round-heads,* whose Race is now spread over three Kingdoms, yet in its Beginning, was meerly an Operation of Art, produced by a pair of Cizars, a Squeeze of the Face, and a black Cap. These Heads, thus formed into a perfect Sphere in all Assemblies, were most exposed to the view of the Female Sort, which did influence their Conceptions so effectually, that Nature, at last, took the Hint, and did it of her self; so that a *Round-head* has been ever since as familiar a Sight among Us, as a *Long-head* among the *Scythians.*[20] (Pp. 268–269).

[20]In the *Tale,* Swift makes a similar point about deformed Puritan ears: "And how can it be otherwise, when in these latter Centuries, the very Species is not only diminished to a very lamentable Degree, but the poor Remainder is also degenerated so far, as to mock our skillfullest *Tenure?* For, if the only slitting of one *Ear* in a Stag, hath been found sufficient to propagate the Defect thro' a whole Forest; Why should we wonder at the greatest Consequences, from so many Loppings and Mutilations, to which the *Ears* of our Fathers and our own, have been of late so much exposed" (p. 201).

Bodily pressures (up and down) in Swift's material satire produce the distortions that make life a history of natural opinions. A man like Jack in *A Tale of A Tub*, tongue up nose, braying like an ass, ears erect, dog-mad at the sound of music is subject to carnal forces that cannot help but produce monstrous human expressions of behavior and opinion. Whomever the satirist would destroy he first drives mad. Naturally, the scheme of the *Tale*'s material line appears most naturally in the "Digression on Madness."

> For, if we take a Survey of the greatest Actions that have been performed in the World under the Influence of Single Men; which are, *The Establishment of New Empires by Conquest: The Advance and Progress of New Schemes in Philosophy; and the contriving, as well as the propagating of New Religions:* We shall find the Authors of them all, to have been Persons, whose natural Reason hath admitted great Revolutions from their Dyet, their Education, the Prevalency of some certain Temper, together with the particular Influence of Air and Climate. Besides, there is something Individual in human Minds, that easily kindles at the accidental Approach and Collision of certain Circumstances, which tho' of paltry and mean Appearance, do often flame out into the greatest Emergencies of Life. (P. 162)

All that is "individual" is potentially mad. And the greatest of individuals in the *Tale* represents the greatest expression of modernity. Modernity sustains madness, the pretense that ascendancy, however insecure, is permanent. And all engines of the satirically spirited mechanical system are geared for the purpose of sustaining the higher or superior fiction. The author speaks of three necessary "Oratorial Machines" at the beginning of the *Tale*: "These are, the *Pulpit*, the *Ladder*, and the *Stage-Itinerant*" (p. 56). He rejects the Bar, for "tho' it be compounded of the same Matter, and designed for the same Use, it cannot however be well allowed the Honor of a fourth, by reason of its level or inferior Situation, exposing it to perpetual Interruption from Collaterals" (p. 56).[21] Engines of public performance are as principles of psychological elevation—they move toward sublime manifestations: "FROM this accurate Deduction it is manifest, that for obtaining Attention in Publick, there is of necessity required a *superiour Position of Place*" (p. 60).

Power is also a question of superior dimension. In the preface to the Tale Swift's author had spoken of a mountebank addressing a crowd in Leicester Fields. Here dominance becomes a metaphorical need to take in and control compressed space.

> *A Mountebank in* Leicester-Fields, *had drawn a huge Assembly about him. Among the rest, a fat unweildy Fellow, half stifled in the Press, would be every fit crying out, Lord!*

---

[21]The rejection of the fourth engine is commensurate with everything else in the *Tale* that seems to go by threes. Three is a parody of the mystical number, but it is also an exclusion of the middle by the extremes. The brothers of the *Tale* and the engines are not the only threesomes: "Now among all the rest, the profound Number *THREE* is that which hath most employ'd my sublimest Speculations, nor ever without wonderful Delight" (p. 57). Three is the subject of a planned panegyrical essay: there are three parts to the *Tale* (prefatory material, allegory, digressions), three critics, three winds, three London societies, three madmen, three types of readers. Three is both the odd number and extreme thought.

what a filthy Crowd is here; Pray, good People, give way a little, Bless me! what a Devil has rak'd this Rabble together: Z—ds, what squeezing is this! Honest Friend, remove your Elbow. At last, a Weaver *that stood next him could hold no longer: A Plague confound you* (said he) *for an overgrown Sloven; and who (in the Devil's Name) I wonder, helps to make up the Crowd half so much as your self? Don't you consider (with a Pox) that you take up more room with that Carkass than any five here? Is not the Place as free for us as for you? Bring your own Guts to a reasonable Compass (and be d—n'd) and then I'll engage we shall have room enough for all.* (P. 46)

The desire to subdue multitudes is a characteristic of madness, and physical displacement is the quest for power—what Hobbes has called a "general inclination of all mankind, a perpetual and restless desire of power after power, that ceaseth only in death" (*Leviathan*, pt. 1, ch. 11). Swift presents the Engines of his tale as power machines and then converts the press of the crowd into the satirically vertical line.

AND I am the readier to favour this Conjecture, from a common Observation; that in the several Assemblies of these Orators, Nature it self hath instructed the Hearers, to stand with their Mouths open, and erected parallel to the Horizon, so as they may be intersected by a perpendicular Line from the Zenith to the Center of the Earth. In which Position, if the Audience be well compact, every one carries home a Share, and little or nothing is lost. (Pp. 60–61)

Head back, mouth open, comprehension vertical: the share carried home by such an audience is little or nothing indeed, but the image is memorable. The "Physico-logical Scheme of Oratorial Receptacles or Machines" (p. 61) in action is both the subject and the strategy of *A Tale of A Tub*. And in satire the scheme for transmission is violated by the substance transmitted: in religion the audience carries home an embellished suit of clothes and a bag of wind; in poetry its reward is an earful of impropriety and a confusion of property ("a confounding of *Meum* and *Tuum*," p. 63); in learning its recompense is a mirror of brass "without any Assistance of *Mercury* from behind" (p. 103). The *Tale* ends with its author's finger on his own and his world's pulse. It is difficult to determine whether he plans to renew his efforts when the pulse beats again or when it stops beating forever.

Text, "Text," and Swift's
A Tale of a Tub

Marcus Walsh

Few printed texts make so apparent, or are so ingenious about, their textual nature and status as Swift's *A Tale of a Tub*, and few have given rise to so much interpretative controversy. The *Tale* has been a focus of some of the key disagreements in modern critical theory.

It has been possible to think of the *Tale* as embodying, as the Apology of 1710 so repeatedly suggests, 'the Author's Intention', its satiric purpose being 'to expose the Abuses and Corruptions in Learning and Religion'.[1] Readings of the *Tale* which explain that Swift uses the *persona* of a mad modern writer to exemplify and satirize scholastic and modern incoherence in learning and belief, and readings of the *Tale* (notably Ehrenpreis's) which deny the use of a persona and invite us to seek 'the direct sense implied by the irony',[2] have this in common: that they insist the *Tale* has an originating author, that this author's meaning intention is there to be found, and that, despite all of the *Tale*'s evident complexity, a valid interpretation of its essential message can be offered. In particular such readings tend to argue that Swift sets up standards of plain, comprehensible expression, against which the vacancy and chaos of the Modern's own writing, and interpretative principles, are found wanting.

More recently, however, the discussion of *A Tale of a Tub* has been dominated by a very different argument: that, far from satirizing expressive and interpretative incoherence, the *Tale* is a narrative without an authoritative voice, which sets out to exemplify the inevitable polysemy of writing, and, more especially, of print. In this view, it would be deluded to see *A Tale of a Tub* as even potentially stable, authoritative, bounded. The *Tale* is, in Barthesian terms, not a 'work' but a 'text,' which 'goes to the limit of the rules of enunciation (rationality, readability, etc.)'.[3] Textualizing studies have explored a number of the implications of this. In a recent essay Clive Probyn argues that, far

From *Modern Language Review*, 85 (1990), 290–303. Reprinted by permission of the author, the editors and the Modern Humanities Research Association.

[1] *A Tale of a Tub*, edited by A. C. Guthkelch and D. Nichol Smith (Oxford, 1958), pp. 7, 12. All quotations from the *Tale* are from this edition.

[2] Irvin Ehrenpreis, *Literary Meaning and Augustan Values* (Charlottesville, Virginia, 1974), pp. 49–60 (p. 54).

[3] Roland Barthes, 'From Work to Text', in *Roland Barthes: Image, Music, Text*, selected and translated by Stephen Heath (London, 1977), p. 157.

from implicitly confirming by its satiric negatives a confident humanist belief
in the comprehensibility and permanence of good writing and good printing,
the *Tale*, as well as *Gulliver's Travels*, reveals and explores Swift's most fundamental fears about the transience of all printed texts: 'a fear of supersession,
the prospect of literary obsolescence, the anxiety of loss, the horror of obscurity, and the cancellation of history'.[4] Nigel Wood has claimed that a key problem for the 'Modern' narrator of the *Tale* is 'how to maintain one's authority
over the *printed* word . . . . The mediation of the printing-press did not necessarily ensure clarity or even a desirable measure of survival for one's thoughts'.[5]
Other textualist critics suggest that Swift himself experienced and viewed this
dilemma much as his modern persona did. Thomas Docherty takes the hack's
invitation to 'every Prince in Christendom' to appoint commentators on his
Tale as evidence that Swift believed 'a multiplicity of readings are sanctioned
by the words of the text, independently of a supposedly pre-linguistic authorial
intention or psychology'.[6] In an essay which argues, or assumes, that Swift
thought of writing as dangerous supplement, Terry Castle describes the *Tale* as
part of a 'Swiftian critique of Text', which takes in all writing, including the
Bible:

> Every writing is a source of corruption, no matter what authority—natural, divine, or
> archetypal—we may wishfully invest in it. Because they constitute an earthly text, the
> Scriptures themselves pathetically and paradoxically make up part of the fallen world of
> writing . . . . Swift does not state . . . baldly that God's text itself is corrupt, but . . . the
> possibility is implicit everywhere in his satire.[7]

Such recent readings of the *Tale* arise not only from the presumed difficulty
or impossibility of identifying a securely present voice but also from the difficulties of establishing a context which might validate any voice. As Wood puts it, 'as
interpretation of the basic satiric context is problematic (such as, what is being
attacked and on what authority), most textual critics have concluded that the
main point of the *Tale* is to demonstrate the extreme difficulty of interpreting
anything without a divine yardstick' (p. 47). I would like to offer some qualifications of the textualist position by beginning to set *A Tale of a Tub* in a context
which has been surprisingly little discussed, and which seems to me to have an
immediate intellectual bearing on Swift's discussion of Scripture, text, and
meaning: that is, the argument between the Roman Church and the Anglican
Church through much of the seventeenth century concerning Scripture as a rule
of faith.

This polemic in very large part concerned itself, inevitably, with fundamental

---

[4] 'Haranguing upon Texts: Swift and the Idea of the Book', in *Proceedings of the First Munster Symposium on Jonathan Swift*, edited by Herman J. Real and Heinz J. Vienken (Munich, 1985), pp. 187–97 (p. 188).

[5] *Swift* (Brighton, 1986), p. 38.

[6] *On Modern Authority* (Brighton, 1987), pp. 246, 247.

[7] 'Why the Houyhnhnms Don't Write: Swift, Satire and the Fear of the Text', *Essays in Literature*, 7 (1980), 31–44 (p. 37).

problems about the nature, determinacy, stability, and comprehensibility of the printed book. Questions of text and hermeneutics were obsessively debated, notably in William Chillingworth's *Religion of Protestants* (1638), in the *Dialogues* (1640) of the exiled Romanist William Rushworth (and Chillingworth's *Answer*),[8] in John Sergeant's *Sure-Footing in Christianity* (1665) and in Tillotson's reply *The Rule of Faith* (1666),[9] in Bossuet's *Exposition de la doctrine de l'Église Catholique* (Paris, 1671) and its numerous English defenders and opponents, in Père Richard Simon's magisterial *Critical Histories* of the Old and New Testaments (1678, 1689),[10] and, most voluminously and passionately, in the debate of the 1680s between Anglican Churchmen (Tillotson, Sherlock, Stillingfleet, and others) and their Romanist adversaries led by John Gother. This was in no sense a set of peripheral pamphlet skirmishes, but a major war in the history of ideas, in which big guns on both sides were employed. The chief polemicists of the reign of James II engaged as officially-sanctioned public representatives rather than private individuals, the works of Gother and many of the other Roman Catholic writers being regularly published by Henry Hills, 'Printer to the King's Most Excellent Majesty', and those of their opponents commonly appearing under the imprimatur of the English Church. The arguments employed in these debates have significant resonances for modern textual and hermeneutic theory, and for the assessment of Swift's textual and hermeneutic position in the *Tale*. In this essay I shall address myself chiefly to issues of textual theory.

'Of Wills', as the Peter of the *Tale* remarks, '*duo sunt genera*, Nuncupatory and scriptory' (p. 85). Peter's preference for oral over written tradition is of course distinctly Roman, and as certainly not Swift's. The written Testament consists of 'certain plain, easy Directions' (p. 190) and says nothing about gold lace; but oral tradition will allow, for Peter, a desirable extension of its license: 'For Brothers, if you remember, we heard a Fellow say when we were Boys, that he heard my Father's Man say, that he heard my Father say, that he would advise his Sons to get *Gold Lace* on their Coats, as soon as ever they could procure Money to buy it' (p. 86). The official Roman position, from the Counter-Reformation onwards, was that truth was to be found equally in the written Scriptures and in unwritten tradition.[11] In their continuing polemic against Protestants, and against the inevitable Protestant dependence on Scripture as a rule of faith, however, Romanist writers repeatedly stressed what they thought to be the stability and continuity of oral tradition as preserved in the Church, the uncertainty of textual transmission and intrinsic textual interpretation, and the necessity of tradition to any safe understanding of Holy Scripture. Bossuet, in his

---

[8]*The Dialogues of William Rushworth or the Judgment of Common Sense in the Choise of Religion* (Paris, 1640); *An Answer to Some Passages in Rushworth's Dialogues*, printed in Chillingworth's *Works*, ninth edition (1719).

[9]*The Rule of Faith; Or, An Answer to the Treatise of Mr. J. S. Entituled, Sure-Footing, & c* (1666). All quotations from Tillotson in this article are from the *Works*, third edition (1701).

[10]Quotations in this article from Père Simon are from A *Critical History of the Old Testament. Written Originally in French by Father Simon . . . Translated into English by a Person of Quality* (London, 1682).

[11]See, for example, Paolo Sarpi, *Histoire du Concile de Trente*, 2 vols (London, 1736), I, 242, 254.

Exposition, regarded by many as an official account of belief, insists that the Church is founded on an original spoken word: 'JÉSUS-CHRIST ayant fondé son Église sur la prédication, la parole non écrite a esté la première regle du Christianisme; et lors que les Écritures du Nouveau Testament y ont esté jointes, cette parole n'a pas perdu pour cela son autorité' (pp. 158–59). Similarly, John Gother, the leading, most 'official', and certainly the wittiest polemicist on the Catholic side of this debate in the reign of James II, insisted that Christ's teaching was by word of mouth, and that the Apostles' '*Writing* was only *Accidental,* occasion'd by reason of their Absence from those they would teach'.[12] So the oral discourse takes precedence over the written text. The word of truth has been passed down from Christ to his Apostles, and thence through the agency of the Church to the modern believer. It is precisely the long, unbroken series of transmission, so much a joke to the Anglican Swift ('we heard a Fellow say . . ., that he heard my Father's Man say, that he heard my Father say . . .') which for an orthodox Roman Catholic validated oral tradition: 'n'étant pas possible de croire qu'une doctrine receûë dès le commencement de l'Église vienne d'une autre source que des Apôtres' (Bossuet, *Exposition,* p. 160). By contrast with the institutionalized certainty of the chain of oral tradition, Scripture was characterized by Roman polemicists as inadequate, on its own, as a rule of faith: uncertain in its transmission, dubious in its translation, and dangerously ambiguous in its sense. 'If we join not Tradition with the Scripture we can hardly affirm any thing for certain in Religion.'[13]

Anglicans resisted this privileging of the spoken word. Writing is neither an accident nor a substitute, but original, apostolic, fully equal to speech. If speech may be plain and comprehensible, so, argues Chillingworth, may writing. If the preaching of Christ and the Apostles could be understood by those who heard it, 'why may we not be as well assured, that we understand sufficiently what we conceive plaine in their writings?' (*Religion of Protestants* (1638), p. 111). Similarly, John Tillotson insisted that the Scriptures, not the oral tradition preserved in Peter's Church, 'are the means whereby the Christian Doctrine hath been brought down to us'. Like many of his Anglican contemporaries Tillotson understood that the defence of the Scriptures as a rule of faith inevitably depended on a defence of all writing and of all printed text as a determinate and reliable vehicle for the communication of meaning, fully equivalent to speech: 'Whatever can be spoken in plain and intelligible words, and such as have a certain sense, may be written in the same words . . . words are as intelligible when they are written as when they are spoken.'[14] In principle books may be written 'in plain and intelligible words', just as the Father's Will in *A Tale of a Tub* consists of 'certain plain, easy Directions', and just as the unambiguously comprehensible laws of Brobdingnag 'are expressed in the most plain and simple Terms'.[15]

[12]*The Catholick Representer,* Second Part (1687), p. 45.
[13]Simon, *Critical History of the Old Testament,* Author's Preface b1r.
[14]*Rule of Faith, Works,* pp. 658, 659, 674.
[15]*The Prose Writings of Jonathan Swift,* edited by Herbert Davis and others, 14 vols (Oxford, 1939–68), XI (1959), 136.

Clearly, a crucial difference between oral and written (or printed) tradition is the presence or absence of the speaking subject. Nigel Wood, in his discussion of the Modern's problem of control and authority over his published words in *A Tale of a Tub,* sums up a modern 'textualist' view of the uncertainties of writing and print consequent upon the disappearance of voice: 'The printed word may bear the same marks [as "living" speech] of the author's possession, but these are nominal compared with the speaker's power to retract, qualify and employ physical indicators (facial expression, posture of the body or gestures)' (pp. 38–39). The same argument was well known to Roman apologists. To have set down in writing even *exactly* the words Christ used in his spoken preaching could not have been enough, argues William Rushworth for example, to communicate Christ's meaning:

> Let him have written in the same language, and let him have set downe everie word and sillable, yet men conversant in noting the changes of meanings in words, will tell you, that divers accents in the pronunciation of them, the turning of the speakers head or bodie this way or that way, . . . may so change the sense of the words that they will seeme quite different in writing from what they were in speaking. (*Dialogues* (1640), pp. 275–76)

For Tillotson, however, the Scriptures are a fully adequate replacement for the presence of the speaking subject. In *The Rule of Faith* he quotes Eusebius to the effect that Matthew 'by the diligence and pains of Writing, did abundantly supply the want of his presence to those whom he left' (*Works,* p. 751). Tillotson quotes Rushworth's words on 'divers accents' and 'the turning of the speaker's head', and comments with a fine ironic anxiety for the necessary preservation of the gestural machinery:

> I hope that Oral and practical Tradition hath been careful to preserve all these circumstances, and hath deliver'd down Christ's Doctrine with all the right *Traditionary Accents, Nods* and *Gestures,* necessary to the understanding of it; otherwise the omission of these may have so altered the sense of it, that it may be now quite different from what it was at first. (*Works,* p. 696)

Oral tradition is reduced by Tillotson to an actor's inherited repertoire of poses. It is perhaps a disappointment not to find such a traditionary pantomime portrayed in *A Tale of a Tub.*

Modern accounts of the status and independence of text cover the spectrum, from the view that texts not only have an objective existence but contain meaning, to the view that texts are mere constructs, without physical existence. In *Objective Knowledge* Karl Popper argues that printed texts belong to the 'third world' of '*objective contents of thought,* especially of scientific and poetic thoughts and works of art'. A book, and its inherent meaning, have an objective existence, whether or not they are perceived by a knowing subject.[16] Perhaps the

---

[16]See *Objective Knowledge* (Oxford, 1979), pp. 106, 115.

closest to Popper's view amongst modern literary theorists is E. D. Hirsch, who, though he accepts that 'meaning is an affair of consciousness' and that 'the text does not exist even as a sequence of words until it is construed', none the less insists that an author's text embodies a determinate, self-identical, bounded meaning.[17] On the whole, however, recent theorists of text have not been willing to accept Popper's invitation to consider 'the objects of our understanding' in the humanities as 'third-world' objects, rather than as objects belonging to the 'second world' of mental states (pp. 106, 160–62). In particular, Derrida offers a 'graphocentric' model in which the text, shorn of the delusory presence of the speaking voice, becomes marks on paper, 'noir sur blanc', signifying only through difference. 'Text' has become open, destabilized, indeterminate, subject to interpretation, and indeed already multiply-interpreted.

Forms of the argument that truth and life inhere in spoken language, whereas writing is necessarily dead and incapable of explaining itself, go back to Plato's *Phaedrus*. Here Socrates denies that 'one can transmit or acquire clear and certain knowledge of an art through the medium of writing'. Written discourses, consisting merely of ink marks, are no more than the 'shadow' of 'the living and animate speech of a man with knowledge'.[18] St Paul platonizes, influentially, in II Corinthians 3.6: 'The letter killeth, but the spirit [*pneuma*] giveth life.' A similar emphasis is offered by the cabalistic tradition that 'the written Torah can take on corporeal form only through the power of the oral Torah'. The 'ink on parchment' of the written Torah cannot be understood, *does not exist,* except through the oral Torah, the interpretation which realizes it, which gives it sense. (My reference here, traditionally, is to Harold Bloom, quoting Scholem, quoting Rabbi Isaac the Blind.)[19]

As far as questions of the relative status of speech and writing were concerned, Romanist apologists in the century before Swift were the heirs of Plato and of the cabalists, insisting on the certainty and life of speech, against what they considered the dangerous indeterminacy, the deadness, of the written or printed text. The theme appears explicitly and repeatedly in the writings of French and English Romanists. John Sergeant's *Sure-Footing* insists, typically, on the difference between the living truth of Christ's words, and the 'dead Letters' or 'dead Characters' of the Scripture (pp. 127, 194).[20] Sense is not inherent in the 'Scripture', by which word Protestants can mean only 'that Book not yet senc't or interpreted, but as *yet to be senc't*' (p. 13). Worse, the black marks of Scripture are 'waxen-natur'd' characters, dangerously polysemous, 'fit to be plaid upon diversly by quirks of wit' (p. 68). Sergeant is one of those who take what Popper calls the 'mistaken subjective approach to knowledge', believing that 'a book is nothing without a reader: . . . otherwise it is just paper with black

---

[17]*Validity in Interpretation* (New Haven, Connecticut, 1967), pp. 4, 13.

[18]*Phaedrus*, translated by Walter Hamilton (Harmondsworth, 1973), pp. 97–99.

[19]'The Breaking of Form', in Harold Bloom and others, *Deconstruction and Criticism* (New York, 1979), pp. 7–8.

[20]See Rushworth, *Dialogues*, pp. 276–77.

spots on it' (*Objective Knowledge*, p. 115). For Sergeant, as for other Romanist apologists, it is Tradition which provides the text with a reader, giving determinate and living sense to the inert and mouldable words of the Holy Book: 'Tradition is to sence Scripture's Letter; and so that Letter no Rule but by virtue of Tradition . . . . Tradition gives us *Christ's Sence,* that is, the *Life* of the Letter ascertain'd to our hands' (pp. 130, 149).[21] Similarly, Richard Simon argues that 'the Church . . . alone is possess'd of the Scripture, because she possesses the true sence thereof'. Even if 'there were no Copies of the Bible in the World, Religion would be preserv'd, because the Church would always subsist' (III. 160). Religion and civilization are preserved not in the physical Bible (or in a complete set of Everyman's Library floating on the waters) but in the continuing mind of the living Church. The contrast between such a textual scepticism and the objectivism of Popper could scarcely be clearer: one of Popper's most dramatic knock-down arguments is the proposal of a 'thought experiment' in which all 'our subjective learning' (tradition, in fact) is destroyed, but *libraries and our capacity to learn from them* survive' (*Objective Knowledge*, pp. 107–08), enabling the continuation of our world.

Seventeenth-century Anglican apologists were conscious of the need to argue that the sense of Scripture, in essential points, is inherent in the words of Scripture, and may be understood without tradition's explication. William Chillingworth cast his *Answer to some Passages in Rushworth's Dialogues* in the form of a dialogue between 'Uncle' and 'Nephew'. The Roman Catholic Uncle is made to assert that the sense of Scripture is 'a distinct thing from the naked Letter', belonging 'to Tradition rather than Express Text of Scripture'. The Protestant Nephew replies that, in all those parts of Scripture which belong 'to faith and good manners' the sense is inherent and clear; such passages 'carry their meaning in their foreheads' (*Works* p. 58). Later in the century Tillotson similarly rejected Sergeant's premise 'that [Protestants] cannot by the Scriptures mean the Sense of them but the book'. Just as books of statute law can sufficiently convey knowledge to men, so Scripture can sufficiently convey Christ's doctrine; sense is inherent in both. Protestants 'mean by the Scriptures, Books written in such words as do sufficiently express the sense and meaning of Christ's Doctrine' (*Rule of Faith,* pp. 672, 673).

Ultimately the Protestant belief, that the Scriptures have an inherent and determinate sense, validly interpretable, required justification by a developed hermeneutic theory, including especially questions of authorial intention and historical context.[22] John Wilson argued that the Scriptures 'have a true Sense *Originally* and *Essentially* in themselves, given them by their Author when they were first indited'; that 'the Sense of Scripture is fixt and immutable, not varying with the times, . . . no other than what it always had, and ever will have to the Worlds end'; that 'the Rule of Interpretation is that which gives us the objective Evidence by which the true Sense of Scripture is discern'd' (*The Scripture's*

---

[21]See Bossuet, *Exposition,* p. 162.
[22]I discuss the hermeneutic arguments of Anglican writers at greater length in a forthcoming article.

Genuine Interpreter Asserted (1678), pp. 5–6). Such a hermeneutic was essential to a sophisticated defence of the Anglican view of the status of the Holy Scripture in particular, and of the book in general. It is also strikingly, and unsurprisingly, close to the position of such a modern objectivist as Hirsch.

The Roman argument for oral tradition shifts meaning, and authority, away from the text itself, and places both in the hands of Rome, the divinely-authorized interpreter. The argument is, explicitly, not confined to the Bible, but applicable, in principle, to any book. John Sergeant argues that if we read Aristotle (an author who was to become the standard example for this area of the debate), we cannot be sure of his 'Certain Sence' unless

> the Point he writes on be first clear'd to us through a Scientifical discourse by word of mouth, made by some Interpreter vers'd in his Doctrin and perfectly acquainted with his meaning .... Now what a well-skill'd and insighted Interpreter or scientifical Explicator... is to such an Author, the same is *Tradition* to Scripture. (*Sure-Footing*, pp. 146–47)

In his reply to Sergeant, Tillotson concentrated on questions of the relative status of text and traditional commentary:

> Suppose there were a controversie now on foot, how Men might come to know what was the true *Art* of *Logick* which *Aristotle* taught his Scholars; and some should be of opinion, that the only way to know this would be by Oral Tradition from his Scholars; which he might easily understand by consulting those of the present Age, who learned it from those who received it from them, who at last had it from *Aristotle* himself: But others should think it the surest way to study his *Organon,* a Book acknowledged by all his Scholars, to have been written by himself, and to obtain that Doctrine which he taught them. (*Works,* p. 668)

Tillotson does not attempt to prohibit commentary, or to deny the possible value of tradition: 'These have been of good helps.' To argue for the possibility of valid interpretation does not logically presage an end to all commentary, the mere reproduction of a supposedly pristine text, untainted by explication. But Tillotson does insist on the central status of the text as the 'measure and standard' of the author's doctrine, communicated in 'the obvious sense of his words'. There is a clear parallel with the Father's Will in the *Tale*: known to have been written by its author, consisting of 'certain plain easy directions', the repository of truth to which Martin and Jack have eventually to appeal if they are to challenge Peter's forced and forcing commentary. Peter is 'the Scholastick Brother' (p. 89), not merely because he applies perverse ingenuity to particular interpretative *cruces* but because he is characteristically a scholastic commentator, heir to a tradition which decentralizes and destabilizes Scripture. For Peter, his *scholia* replace the text itself; he allows no appeal beyond his subjective interpretations to any objective, publicly accessible truth.

Swift's examination of the relation of text and commentary is not confined to Peter's interpretation of the Father's Will. At one point the hack is confident that the '*Learned* among Posterity' 'will appoint ... Commentators upon this elaborate Treatise' (p. 114); at another, that 'sublime Spirits . . . shall be appointed to labor in a universal Comment upon this wonderful Discourse' (p. 186). He proposes that each Prince of Christendom might 'take seven of the *deepest Scholars* in his Dominions, and shut them up close for *seven* Years, in *seven* Chambers, with a Command to write *seven* ample Commentaries on this comprehensive Discourse' (p. 185). The text indeed already presents itself as overwhelmed by commentary. The kernel tale is introduced by a hack whose digressions, from the start lengthy, become less and less discrete, and at last force the 'text' out of sight altogether. The hack's account is reached only through a maze of prefatory materials attributed to a variety of voices. Wotton's notes are hoisted in, only to become themselves the subject of further commentary: for example, to call the coats given to each of the three sons 'the Garments of the *Israelites*' is 'an Error (with Submission) of the learned Commentator; for by the Coats are meant the Doctrine and Faith of *Christianity*' (p. 73). Clearly, the 'text' is becoming replaced by, is *becoming*, its commentaries. The principle that *A Tale of a Tub* exemplifies is stated clearly by the hack. Arguing as a Modern, he insists that, 'tho' Authors need be little consulted, yet *Criticks*, and *Commentators*, and *Lexicons* carefully must' (p. 148).

Formal parody of the gloss-making excesses of dull scholastic pedantry was of course to become a familiar method of Augustan humanist satire, reaching its apogee no doubt in the *Dunciad Variorum*. There are, however, some theoretical and historical implications of Swift's use of the form in *A Tale of a Tub* which need further exploration. A recent article by Louis Hay discusses the history of 'text' as term and concept. Hay points out that for a long time an important sense of 'text' was 'les propres paroles d'un auteur, considérées par rapport aux notes, aux commentaires, aux gloses'.[23] These are the words of the French Academy Dictionary of 1786. Hay's further citations make it clear that this sense of 'text' as something specifically distinct from gloss or commentary was pervasive. The examples in the *Oxford English Dictionary* ('text' sense 2) show that this sense operated in England at least as early as the fourteenth century. *OED*'s definition reads thus: '**text**: The very words and sentences as originally written, . . . in the original form and order, as distinguished from a commentary . . . or from annotations. Hence, in later use, the body of any treatise, the authoritative or formal part as distinguished from notes, appendices, introduction, and other explanatory or supplementary matter'. The last sentence of *OED*'s definition is obviously pertinent to the *Tale*, where distinction between text and 'notes, appendices, introduction, and other explanatory or supplementary matter' collapses.

Such a definition of 'text' is of course tendentious. The text may be thought of as pure, formal, original, authorial, canonical. Its commentary may be thought of as unauthorized, derivative, distorted, corrupt, apocryphal. As Hay points out, 'what is implied in such an arrangement is a distinction between the sacred and the profane' (p. 65). To make the distinction so as to privilege the text, to give it

[23]'Does "Text" Exist?', *Studies in Bibliography*, 41 (1988), 64–75 (p. 64).

canonic status and accept it as the determinate statement of an identifiable voice, is the Anglican position, the position of Martin and, I think, of Swift. Anglicans regarded the text of the Bible as, to use Barthes's changed terminology, a 'work'; 'the author is reputed the father and the owner of his work: literary science therefore teaches *respect* for the manuscript and the author's declared intentions' ('From Work to Text', p. 160). Martin attempts to reform his religion by 'serving the true Intent and Meaning of his Father's *Will*' (*Tale*, pp. 136–37). To collapse the distinction between text and gloss, to allow the original text to become subordinate to and lost in a controlling critical apparatus, is the position of Peter and the Modern writer. Both are scholiasts, writers of *scholia*. Both operate with a 'modern', scholastic view of textuality. In Barthes's words, 'no vital "respect" is due to the Text: it can be *broken* (which is just what the Middle Ages did with two nevertheless authoritative texts—Holy Scripture and Aristotle); it can be read without the guarantee of its father' ('From Work to Text', p. 161). The difference is that Peter and the Modern know that a text need not be 'broken' if it can be submerged or displaced by commentary.

The discussion of 'text' and Swift's *Tale* needs also to include another specific sense of the word: the material form of what we read, and its transmission. For most of this century, academic editing has worked on the assumption that it is the editor's task to recover the text intended by an author. The genealogy of this assumption may be traced back to the Renaissance humanists, who attempted to establish reliable texts of classical authors and, more especially, to go beyond the corrupted Vulgate and recover God's pristine Word. For the last two decades, however, debates about scholarly editing have increasingly had to address problems of textual ontology as well as technical problems of transmission. Is there an 'author'? What can 'intended' mean? What sense does it make to speak of 'the text', to entertain the belief that there is an original text to recover, or that confident reconstruction is possible? The posing of such questions acquired a special impetus from Roland Barthes's essay 'From Work to Text', and has grown stronger in the post-structuralist years. As early as 1971 Morse Peckham insisted, in an article entitled 'Reflections on the Foundations of Modern Textual Editing', that the textual editor works not with 'printed artifacts as physical objects' but with 'human behaviour in the past, human behaviour that no longer exists and cannot now be examined'. Inevitably, the editor's text is not a recovered original but a 'construct'. For Peckham, analytical bibliography, like historiography, cannot be 'scientific'; 'It is not talking about anything which is empirically, phenomenally, observable *now*, about anything which lies outside discourse.'[24] The Popperian answer is that discourse itself belongs to 'the world of intelligibles, or of *ideas in the objective sense*' (*Objective Knowledge*, p. 154), and is as much a real object for 'scientific' enquiry as nuclear physics. Popper makes the point explicitly in reference to textual editing. The 'method of problem solving, the method of conjecture and refutation', is common to science and

---

[24] *Proof*, I (1971), 122–55 (pp. 127–28, 131, 132–33).

the humanities; 'it is practised in reconstructing a damaged text as well as in constructing a theory of radioactivity' (p. 185). Deconstruction, however, has continued to mount a theoretical challenge to the notion that there is an 'ideal' text to reconstruct. Lee Patterson's words, in an essay on the iconoclastic Kane/ Donaldson *Piers Plowman*, may be taken as a representative application of Derridean concepts to the theoretical field of editing: 'For the postmodern critic, the text is a *bricolage* . . . insofar as the subject is constituted by its enunciation rather than vice versa, the very concept of a holograph as a text inscribed by its author becomes problematic.'[25]

There is no disputing that *A Tale of a Tub* 'as a text inscribed by its author' is 'problematic'. The work does not bear Swift's name, and the Apology intimates, with what credibility it is hard to establish, that 'in the Authors Original Copy there were not so many Chasms as appear in the Book' (p. 17). The words of the 'modern' author come to us, sometimes for the modern's own tactical reasons, with the signal losses of faulty transmission: here there is a '*Hiatus in MS.*' (p. 62), there '*multa desiderantur*' (p. 170), in another place '*desunt nonnulla*' (p. 200). The modern's whispered explanation concerning one of the students of Bedlam evaporates into the safety of blanks (p. 179), and the note emphasizes that such chasms invite 'conjecture', and 'more than one interpretation'.

Such textual absences and polysemy seem certainly attributable to the Modern, but may not be so safely attributable to Swift. Whatever accidents the 'Original Copy' referred to in the Apology may have met with, it is at least clear that a concept of original copy exists. There is a stable text in the *Tale*, though the Modern author (understanding that to offer quotation as evidence is a deluded humanist empiricism) naturally does not attempt substantially to reproduce it. Swift himself, however, might be thought to have been so convinced of the effectiveness and value of humanist textual scholarship that he could think the project of textual reconstruction credible, if not unproblematic. Martin and Jack are able, once they have found the Father's Will, to make a '*Copia vera*' without apparent difficulty (p. 121). For Swift a true humanist textual criticism, whose business is to recover the lost original, is possible: 'By the Word *Critick*, have been meant, the Restorers of Antient Learning from the Worms, and Graves, and Dust of Manuscripts' (p. 93). This is the Modern's second kind of 'false' critic, by clear implication for the intelligent reader therefore not a Grubean pedant but a humanist scholar. Guthkelch and Nichol Smith's note here makes the appropriate comparison with Temple's praise of those editors who have 'restored' old copies, and 'recovered' the jewels of ancient learning from the dust and rubbish. Also possible, however, to those of less pure motive and more duncely skills, has been the perversion and distortion of the text. The 'main Precept' of the Father's Will is that the sons must not add to, or diminish, their religion without a 'positive Command in the Will' (p. 81). Where a com-

---

[25]'The Logic of Textual Criticism and the Way of Genius: The Kane–Donaldson *Piers Plowman* in Historical Perspective', in *Textual Criticism and Literary Interpretation*, edited by Jerome J. McGann (Chicago, 1985), pp. 55–91 (p. 89).

mand does not exist, commentary may supply it. Here, as elsewhere, the Modern does not quote from the Will, but the note of 1734 makes the obviously germane reference to the anathema in Revelations 22.18,19, against *textual* omissions and additions: 'If any man shall add unto these things, God shall add unto him the plagues that are written in this book: And if any man shall take away the words of the book of this prophecy, God shall take away his part out of the book of life.' Both Peter and Jack invite the curse. Peter justifies the addition to their coats of *'flame Coloured Sattin* for Linings' (the addition to religion of the doctrine of purgatory) by arguing the desirability of appending to the Will a new-fangled (in fact an Apocryphal) 'Codicil' (pp. 86–87). Jack uses pieces and scrapings and inches of the Will on every occasion of his life (p. 190). Taken short, he remains filthy because of his application of a 'Passage' (Revelations 22.11) which may have been 'foisted in by the transcriber' (p. 191).

The *Tale* arguably presents a contrast, then, between a stated humanist belief in the possibility of recovery and transmission of a true copy, and that modern scepticism which displays the incoherence of textual transmission and allows subjective application of the text. In this the *Tale* echoes, once more, a characterizing disagreement between Roman and Anglican polemicists in the later seventeenth century. Romanists argued that all textual transmission is inescapably subject to error and corruption, whether accidental or malicious, and that the *Copia vera* is an impossible dream. Anglicans had to defend the Scripture as a rule of faith by arguing that true texts could indeed, given scholarly effort, good will, and God's help, be recovered from the dust and worms.

Rushworth sets out the normal Roman arguments particularly fully and clearly. Salvation or damnation is at issue; if Scripture is to be a judge of controversies, 'everie word, everie letter, and everie tit[t]le must be admitted of absolute and uncontrolable certaintie' (*Dialogues,* pp. 244–45). Scripture, however, is inevitably faulty, because of 'the multitudes of nations and languages' and the 'mutabilitie of the world, ever subject to a thousand accidents' (pp. 247, 248). Familiarly, to a modern editor of secular texts, the process of transcription introduces errors 'by the negligence of Servants, which copied the Bible', who may have been mercenary, or 'witlesse,' or 'weary' (pp. 250–52, 253). For John Sergeant, similarly, the 'material characters' of Scripture are as liable to destruction, to be 'burnt, torn, blotted, worn out', as any other object in this fallen world. Its transmission has inevitably been subject to the weakness of mortal behaviour, and the many diverse readings of the numerous surviving copies show that 'Scripture's Letter may be uncertain in every tittle'.[26] For Romans, so long as textual transmission is a human activity, the certainty essential to faith is impossible. Just as meaning can be guaranteed only by the divine presence (immediately in God's own spoken words, mediately in the Church), so textual accuracy can be guaranteed only by divine providence. Just as Scripture's 'sense' is located not in the Scripture itself but in the Church, so the accuracy of a text

[26]See *Sure-Footing,* pp. 37–38.

of Scripture cannot be established by textual criticism, and may be validated only by the conformity of its readings with Church doctrine.[27]

In this debate the Romans had some inevitable laws of information transmission on their side. Human transcription must produce error. The attempt to bypass the series of transmission and return to a now-lost original is bound to involve some degree of editorial construction. In their replies Protestant apologists argued that reliable transmission of the Holy Scripture, as of other books, was in principle possible. Tillotson's words in *The Rule of Faith* are typical: 'The Books of Scripture are conveyed down to us, without any material corruption or alteration. And he that denies this, must . . . reject the authority of all Books, because we cannot be certain whether they be the same now as they were at first' (*Works*, pp. 660–61). Absolute textual accuracy, the 'tittles' on which Rushworth and Sergeant had insisted, was not essential, provided that those passages which communicate truths necessary to faith were not substantially faulty. Arthur Bury, Rector of Exeter College, insisted that:

> *The Scriptures cannot be denied to be sufficient,* though they may have suffered the common Fate of all long-lived Books, by Carelessness of Copiers, Fraud of Hereticks, or Dust of Time . . . if all the rest of the Scripture were lost, but only those Texts which proclaim those Truths, to the Belief whereof eternal Life is promised; those few texts would be sufficient. (*The Naked Gospel* (1690) p. 43)[28]

However much of a concession this may seem, there lies behind it a confident assumption that the Scripture, like other texts, like 'all long-lived Books', contains an essential message, and continues adequately to communicate even where noise intrudes. The evident contingency of transmission is not allowed to lead to a despairing scepticism. For Swift and his Anglican contemporaries, that scepticism was familiar both as a Romanist and as a deist position. John Sergeant had warned his Protestant opponents that to make Scripture, with its 'almost innumerable *Variae Lectiones*', a sole rule of faith was to leave themselves without an answer to a deist's challenge, which Sergeant imagined posed in these terms: 'All depends on the Truth of the Copies immediately taken from the Original, or the very next to them; which, what they were, by whom taken, where and how preserved from time to time, how narrowly examined when they were first transcribed . . . is buried in obscurity and oblivion' (*Sure-Footing*, pp. 31–32). Sergeant was prophetic: precisely such a charge would be made by the deist Anthony Collins in his *Discourse of Free-Thinking* (1713). Understanding his position in the history of this idea, Collins pointed out that 'the *Priests* of all Christian Churches differ among themselves' about the copies, readings, and senses of Scripture, and reminded his readers that 'the Popish Priests contend that the Text of Scripture is so corrupted, precarious, and unintelligible, that we are to depend on the Authority of the Church' (pp. 54,55). Worse, the chaos of text undercuts all books. Collins quotes (translating from the original Latin)

---

[27] See Simon, *Critical History of the Old Testament*, III, 166.
[28] See Tillotson, *Works*, p. 678.

Whitby's apocalyptic response to John Mills's listing of some thirty thousand textual variants in the Greek New Testament: 'Nothing certain can be expected from Books, where there are various Readings in every Verse' (p. 89). Swift's parodic 'abstract' of Collins's, and Whitby's, words on the textual unreliability of the Bible clearly implies Swift's understanding that to attack scriptural authority is inevitably (and in Swift's view absurdly) to question the book itself, to deny the possibility of the transmission of doctrine and information in any book at all:

> All *Christian* Priests differ so much about the Copies of [their Scriptures], and about the various Readings of the several Manuscripts, which quite destroys the Authority of the Bible: For what Authority can a Book pretend to, where there are various Readings? And for this reason, it is manifest that no Man can know the Opinions of *Aristotle* or *Plato,* or believe the Facts related by *Thucydides* or *Livy,* or be pleased with the Poetry of *Homer* and *Virgil,* all which Books are utterly useless, upon account of their various Readings.[29]

Richard Bentley's devastating demolition of Collins (*Remarks upon a Late Discourse of Freethinking* (1719)) insists, just as Swift does here, that the textual case of Scripture is the same as that of other books. Mills's listing of the Greek Testament's numerous variants did not, as Whitby had feared and Collins had claimed, 'prove the Text of Scripture precarious'; such variants, Bentley insists, 'must necessarily have happened from *the Nature of Things,* and what are common and in equal proportion in all Classicks whatever'. The Scriptures are no less, and no more, subject to textual variation than other books. Like Swift, Bentley can afford to be relaxed about textual variance in Scripture, not because (with Père Simon, or modern textualists) he believes all text vulnerable and corrupt but because he is convinced the message an author intends can be adequately transmitted in a written text despite the inevitable accumulation of (generally minor) error. The ocean of meaning cannot be swallowed by one, or thirty thousand, soiled fish of the textual sea. Of ancient writers, such as Cicero and Plutarch, the 'Remains are sufficiently pure and genuine, to make us sure of the Writer's design'; the presence of 'a corrupt line or dubious reading' need not be thought 'to darken the whole Context'. Just as secular texts sufficiently communicate the author's intended meaning, so, despite all its textual changes, Scripture 'is perfect and sufficient to all the great ends and purposes of its first Writing'.[30]

This contextual evidence leads me to venture qualifications of some common assumptions in recent textualizing criticism of *A Tale of a Tub*. I am not convinced that the *Tale* is 'the most devastating onslaught on the authenticity of The Book in literary history to date' (Probyn, p. 189). Attacking the Book was a Roman Catholic activity: Anglicans tended to avoid sawing off the branch they sat on. It is reading particularly sharply against the grain to impute to Swift a

---

[29]*Mr. C—ns's Discourse of Free-Thinking, Put into Plain English, by Way of Abstract, for the Use of the Poor* (1713), *Prose Writings,* IV (1957), 33.

[30]*Remarks upon a Late Discourse of Freethinking,* in *Enchiridion Theologicum,* edited by John Randolph, 5 vols (1792), V, 156, 160, 163, 173–74.

radical textual scepticism which was evidently associated in his mind with the scholiasts, medieval and contemporary (and both 'modern') that he mocks, and with controvertists whose concern, for many decades before the *Tale*, had been to attack the Anglican Church and the assumptions about the nature and status of text upon which the Anglican Church indispensably and explicitly founded itself. The 'Apology' claims that the *Tale* 'celebrates the Church of *England* as the most perfect of all others in Discipline and Doctrine, it advances no Opinion they reject, nor condemns any they receive' (p. 5). Unless we are prepared to think this claim wholly disingenuous, or by reason of lapse of time or otherwise a wholly inaccurate account of Swift's intentions, we might do well to be cautious about reading into *A Tale of a Tub* attitudes to text radically opposite to fundamental Anglican positions.

Clive Probyn argues, in the context of the later debate with Collins, that for Swift the Bible was a special case; precisely because 'all language and therefore all texts are prone to deconstruct themselves', the anarchy of individualist reading must be corrected, must, 'in the single case of the Bible', be controlled by expert interpretation (p. 193). For Swift the Scriptures, for political as well as for religious reasons, needed to be vested with a distinguishing authority and respect. He knew that in a mortal world language and text are prone to be corrupted and forced (not, however, 'to deconstruct themselves'), and he had no naive misconception that the text of Scripture was angel-guarded. None the less, he did not consider Scripture a 'single case', and did not give up all the rest of written discourse as inevitably indeterminate, unstable, or opaque. Earlier Anglican writers, as I have said, in defending the text of Scripture as a rule of faith, explicitly and repeatedly defended the Bible on the grounds that, *like any other printed book*, it is determinable and comprehensible, an adequate means of conveying meaning. Any writing, in principle, may be good writing; though it may very well also be possible to write on nothing, to write darkly, deliberately to solicit misleading commentary.

We have learnt to collapse distinctions between primary and secondary texts, between author and critic. 'A strong reading is the only text', as Bloom puts it. Recent comment on *A Tale of a Tub* has therefore been less concerned with the possible difference between text and commentary. Probyn, for example, writes that '*self*-assertion as author *or* textual commentator is the sure Swiftian sign of amor sui' (p. 190). Authorship as the 'modern' conceives it, no doubt, for Swift is mere self-love. *A Tale of a Tub*, however, exemplifies throughout the essential Anglican (and humanist) distinction between a present real author and a parasitic commentator, between sacred original text and corrupt gloss. In *Gulliver's Travels* Swift uses Aristotle, as earlier Anglican apologists had done, as his exemplary case in the argument against self-serving commentary and its distortions of authorial meaning; Gulliver summons Aristotle, and Homer, to Glubbdubdrib, and learns that their commentators keep their distance in the lower world, shamed 'because they had so horribly misrepresented the Meaning of those Authors to Posterity' (*Prose Writings*, XI, 197).

Is it safe to assume Swift finds text problematic and speech divine and safe? Terry Castle argues that Swift's model of speech and writing is Platonic: 'The written object is a material rendering of something ideal, the pure world of speech' (p. 34). This does not in fact seem very convincingly supported by Castle's references to Swift's text itself, either to the fourth Voyage of *Gulliver's Travels* (in which the Houyhnhnms' purely oral traditions lead them to debate repeatedly the single proposition, 'whether the *Yahoos* should be exterminated from the Face of the Earth'),[31] or to the *Tale*, which includes a lengthy satire on aeolist oral preaching. (The aeolists should perhaps put us in mind of the Platonic view of good, 'pneumatological', 'natural writing', 'immediately united to the voice and to breath'.)[32] According to Castle, the account in the 'Apology' of the imperfect transmission of the text of the *Tale* 'hints' that all texts are 'impure in regard to the world of spoken discourse, which maintains here an assumed priority' (p. 34). This assumption of the priority of the voice seems to me nowhere stated or implied in the 'Apology' or in the *Tale* itself. Such an accommodation of Swift's writing as Castle makes to an originally Platonic, and wholly alien, textual value-system, seems to me possible only as a consequence of seeking what meanings the *Tale* may have through its absences, and, more especially, by operating without reference to contexts of textual theory in the years immediately before Swift wrote the *Tale*, contexts which at least define the terms of debate and at most delimit the lines of textual argument open to Swift.

Criticism of *A Tale of a Tub* used to assume that Swift made a distinction between competent and incompetent writing. The Hack writes badly, and invites indulgent interpretation, but there is a plain and meaningful text, the Will, whose interpretation is possible and necessary. Castle, however, denies that it is possible to 'separate good texts from bad texts'; 'No text is privileged in regard to truth; no text is scriptural' (Castle, p. 37). The Will is not only corrupted and distorted but also, in itself, 'a deathly, parasitic, artefact' (p. 35), feeding off the speech that gave it birth. These conclusions do not follow logically from the *Tale*. The aim of the *Tale* is 'to expose the Abuses and Corruptions in Learning and Religion' ('Apology', p. 12). To attack abuses and corruptions is not, as the 'Apology' insists, necessarily to attack learning or religion themselves, nor does such an attack logically deny the possibility of a genuine learning or a true religion. Many of the abuses and corruptions are, certainly, textual. The existence of corrupt texts is not, however, proof that all texts are, because of the nature of textuality itself, corrupt. More especially, the practice of abusive methods of interpretation of the Will is not proof either of the Will's inherent corruption or of the impossibility of believing in good interpretation. There is no disputing that Swift's satire reflects 'upon the problematic status of the written word' (Castle, p. 33), its vulnerability to mistransmission and misinterpretation. It is natural that a modern textual scepticism would wish to appropriate this cen-

---

[31]*Prose Writings*, XI, 271.

[32]See Jacques Derrida, *Of Grammatology*, translated by Gayatri Spivak (Baltimore, Maryland, 1976), p. 17.

tral concern and energy in the *Tale* in support of the much more radical proposition that *all* text is fundamentally and inevitably 'compromised, de-natured,
separated from truth at its moment of origin' (Castle, p. 35). Nothing in the *Tale*,
however, gives clear indication that Swift held this much more extreme position,
and the powerful and immediately relevant intellectual context I have outlined
makes it very unlikely that he could possibly have done so.

I do not wish to simplify. Clearly the meaning or meanings of *A Tale of a Tub*
are not straightforwardly given by, or in any simple way controlled by, the context of intellectual debate I have outlined. Recent textualizing critics have indispensably focused attention on Swift's obsessive concern with the nature, status,
and stability of writing itself. I do, however, wish to argue that we now too readily impute to Swift a notion of text to which he simply cannot have subscribed.
Of course, Swift is not Chillingworth, or Tillotson, or Ehrenpreis. But he is not
Rabbi Isaac, or Bossuet, or Derrida, either.

The Splitting of Humanism:
Bentley, Swift, and the English
Battle of the Books

John F. Tinkler

It was argued some years ago that the English "Battle of the Books" of the late seventeenth century was just another phase in a long Renaissance humanist *querelle des anciens et des modernes*.[1] The English Battle was thus another, and essentially repetitive, reworking of a theme that had become a commonplace. More recently, however, Joseph M. Levine has argued that an essential ingredient in the English Battle was "the bitter contest that resulted between the 'wits' and the scholars, rhetoric and philology, 'polite' learning and erudition. . . . It was, therefore, the argument between literature and learning that alone could be said to be new."[2] Levine's essay completely reorients the terms of the English Battle and locates it in a potentially more revealing and significant humanist controversy. Anthony Grafton has argued of the Renaissance that there were two tendencies in humanism: "One set of humanists seeks to make the ancient world live again, assuming its undimmed relevance and unproblematic accessibility; another set seeks to put the ancient world back into its own time, admitting that its reconstruction is a difficult enterprise and that success may reveal the irrelevance of ancient experience and precept to modern problems."[3] In this context Bentley belongs to the latter strand in humanism, while Swift belongs to the former. What is thus striking about their debate is the extent to which they fail to engage each other—the extent to which Bentley ignores the literary debate between ancients and moderns, and the extent to which Swift ridicules and rejects Bentley's scholarly enterprise. Swift, the man of letters, and Bentley, the scholar, belong to different discourses.

From *Journal of the History of Ideas*, 49 (1988), 453–72. Reprinted by permission of the author and the Johns Hopkins University Press.

[1] See Hans Baron, "The *Querelle* of the Ancients and the Moderns as a Problem for Renaissance Scholarship," *Renaissance Essays from the Journal of the History of Ideas*, ed. Paul O. Kristeller and Philip P. Wiener (New York, 1968), 95–114. An excellent recent study of the *querelle* in the Renaissance is Robert Black, "Ancients and Moderns in the Renaissance: Rhetoric and History in Accolti's *Dialogue on the Preeminence of Men of His Own Time*," *JHI*, 43 (1982), 3–32.

[2] "Ancients and Moderns Reconsidered," *Eighteenth-Century Studies*, 15 (1981–82), 83, 88. Levine's essay includes a good survey of scholarship concerning the Battle.

[3] "Renaissance Readers and Ancient Texts: Comments on Some Commentaries," *Renaissance Quarterly*, 38 (1985), 620.

The union of literature and learning had been a humanist ideal throughout the Renaissance: the English Battle seems to partake of a historic dissolution of this union. In relation to the Italian seventeenth century, Eric Cochrane has argued that "Baroque historiography split history as literature and history as research—which had been united in practice if not always in theory throughout the Renaissance—into two separate genres of historical writing."[4] The argument of the present paper is that Bentley's and Swift's contributions to the English Battle of the Books are more comprehensible in the context of this splitting of humanist scholarship and humanist literature into separate literary genres than in the context of the commonplace debate between ancients and moderns.

Rhetoric is currently understood to be one of the keys to understanding humanism.[5] Though Levine describes the English Battle in terms of a debate between rhetoric and philology, I shall argue that Bentley, like his Renaissance humanist precursors, derived his philological approach from rhetorical strategies of proof no less than Swift. The difference is that Swift and Bentley employed different rhetorical *genera* in a way that made the two sides of the debate incommensurable: each elaborated different, ultimately incompatible aspects of the humanists' rhetorical affiliation. My argument thus seeks to contribute to a reinterpretation of humanism that is less concerned with classicism (an affiliation to the ancients) than with the argument advanced by George M. Logan that "the development of humanism is to a considerable extent a dialectical exploration of tensions."[6]

My paper is divided into four sections. In the first I shall describe in more detail the two "sets" or tendencies within Renaissance humanism that are identified by Grafton. In the second I shall show that Bentley's scholarship was incommensurable with the other humanist literature of the debate because each was modelled on a fundamentally different rhetorical *genus*. I shall not be concerned with the rhetorical category of style (*elocutio*) but with the rhetorical strategies of argument and the differentiation among *genera* that relate to rhetorical invention (*inventio*). In the third section I shall briefly consider Swift's and Bentley's

---

[4]"The Transition from Renaissance to Baroque: The Case of Italian Historiography," *History and Theory*, 19 (1980), 34. See also the stimulating study by William J. Bouwsma, "Three Types of Historiography in Post-Renaissance Italy," *History and Theory*, 4 (1964–65), 303–14. For a similar development in England, see Denys Hay, *Annalists and Historians: Western Historiography From the Eighth to the Eighteenth Centuries* (London, 1977), 133–68.

[5]Classic studies on the place of rhetoric in humanism are by Paul Oskar Kristeller, many of them now collected in his *Renaissance Thought and Its Sources*, ed. Michael Mooney (New York, 1979). See also Hanna H. Gray, "Renaissance Humanism: The Pursuit of Eloquence," *Renaissance Essays from the Journal of the History of Ideas*, 199–216; Jerrold E. Seigel, *Rhetoric and Philosophy in Renaissance Humanism: The Union of Eloquence and Wisdom, Petrarch to Valla* (Princeton, 1968); Nancy S. Struever, *The Language of History in the Renaissance: Rhetoric and Historical Consciousness in Florentine Humanism* (Princeton, 1970); Bouwsma, *The Culture of Renaissance Humanism*, American Historical Association Pamphlets. No. 401 (Washington, 1973).

[6]"Substance and Form in Renaissance Humanism," *Journal of Medieval and Renaissance Studies*, 7 (1977), 32; cf. Bouwsma, "Changing Assumptions in Later Renaissance Culture," *Viator*, 7 (1976), 421–40. A classic and subtle study of Renaissance classicism is Erwin Panofsky's *Renaissance and Renascences in Western Art* (Stockholm, 1960).

careers for one explanation of why the two writers, who could both be considered successors to the humanists, went different ways. In the fourth section I shall argue that the debate between Swift and Bentley was not between moderns and ancients, but between two different approaches to texts—that of the professional scholar and that of the occasional man of letters. I shall conclude by arguing for the appropriateness of Swift's phrase "Battle of the Books" to describe the English debate, which was ultimately about texts and their status rather than about ancient and modern literature.

I

Sir William Temple, an elder statesman in his sixties, initiated the Battle in 1690 with his essay *Of Ancient and Modern Learning*, which praised ancient learning at the expense of modern and particularly commended the *Epistles of Phalaris* and *Aesop's Fables* as among the oldest and best literature. In 1694 the brilliant young William Wotton, not yet thirty, responded with his *Reflections upon Ancient and Modern Learning*, which defended the modern arts and sciences. At the beginning of 1695 a new edition of the *Epistles of Phalaris* appeared, undoubtedly in the wake of Temple's commendatory review, under the name of the Hon. Charles Boyle, a young undergraduate, though it was probably prepared as much by his academic seniors as by himself. The edition contained an accusation that Bentley, newly installed Keeper of the King's Libraries, had put difficulties in the way of making a necessary text of the *Epistles* available for collation.

Bentley, then in his mid-thirties, entered the Battle with his *Dissertation upon the Epistles of Phalaris, Themistocles, Socrates, Euripides and the Fables of Aesop*, appended to the second edition of Wotton's *Reflections* in 1697 and demonstrating that the works in question were spurious. It appears to have been at this stage that Swift, then about thirty, wrote his *Full and True Account of the Battel Fought last Friday, Between the Antient and the Modern Books in St. James's Library*—a title that focussed attention specifically on Bentley rather than Wotton—though it did not appear in print until 1704, after Temple's death. Meanwhile, in 1698, a vicious collaborative response to Bentley appeared under Boyle's name, *Dr. Bentley's Dissertations . . . Examin'd*; and Bentley responded in 1699 with a vastly expanded and monumentally erudite *Dissertation*, focussed entirely on the *Epistles of Phalaris*.[7]

---

[7]References to Bentley in this essay are to *The Works of Richard Bentley*, ed. Alexander Dyce (2 vols; London, 1836). References to Swift are to *A Tale of a Tub With Other Early Writings 1696–1707*, ed. Herbert Davis (Vol. I of *The Prose Writings*) (Oxford, 1957). Standard biographies of Bentley are by James Henry Monk, *The Life of Richard Bentley, D. D.* (2 vols.; London, 1833), and R. C. Jebb, *Bentley*, English Men of Letters (London, 1882), both of which are better than R. J. White, *Dr. Bentley: A Study in Academic Scarlet* (London, 1965); and of Swift by Irvin Ehrenpreis, *Swift: The Man, His Works, and the Age* (3 vols.; London, 1962–83). A close study of the relevant years of Swift's life is by A. C. Elias, Jr., *Swift at Moor Park: Problems in Biography and Criticism* (Philadelphia, 1982).

The role of Bentley's *Dissertation* in the Battle was to destroy the basis for Temple's argument that "the oldest books we have are still in their kind the best" by demonstrating that the *Epistles* and *Fables*, claimed by Temple as "the two most ancient that I know of in prose," were spurious forgeries (quoted Bentley, II, 133). Bentley's contribution to the Battle, then, was to reduce Temple's argument to absurdity by demonstrating that the writings which Temple praised as oldest and best were not in fact the oldest.

The detection of forgeries had been a characteristic enterprise of Renaissance humanists since Petrarch in the fourteenth century. In a letter to the Emperor Charles IV of 1355, Petrarch demonstrated that a document known as the Austrian Exemption, which was purported to have been granted by Julius Caesar, could not have been written either by him or in his time. Petrarch's letter has been claimed by Peter Burke as an early monument of the Renaissance "sense of the past."[8] It was in turn a precursor to Lorenzo Valla's celebrated exposure of the *Donation of Constantine* in the fifteenth century, a work that has been claimed by Donald R. Kelley as one of the foundations of modern critical method.[9]

For various reasons the detection of forgeries appears characteristic of the humanists. First, such detection requires the kind of extensive reading of ancient texts and the *auctores* that is typical of the humanists. Second, one of the humanists' defining characteristics was their concern to read complete texts, rather than excerpts in *florilegia*, and to read them as far as possible in the state in which they had been written. The humanists thus launched a massive project of collecting, editing, and emending ancient texts, to which Bentley, as a classical scholar, was a direct successor.

Nevertheless, the detection of forgeries had been practised before the Renaissance. Kelley observes that the rules and techniques for detecting forgeries had been developed by medieval canon lawyers, especially in the twelfth century.[10] Before the Middle Ages, ancient rhetorical textbooks gave directions about the detection of forged documents that must have been part of the stock-in-trade of ancient lawyers.[11] The walls of an ancient Egyptian tomb reveal, according to Jack Goody, that a legal case was won "on the grounds that not only were. . . title-deeds forged but there had been falsification of the land register at the time of the former trial."[12]

The detection of forgeries, then, has been a recurrently important judicial strategy. It is therefore significant that Petrarch's exposure of the Austrian

---

[8]Burke discusses and translates the letter in his *The Renaissance Sense of the Past* (London, 1969), 50–54.

[9]*Foundations of Modern Historical Scholarship: Language, Law, and History in the French Renaissance* (New York, 1970), 19–50.

[10]"Clio and the Lawyers: Forms of Historical Consciousness in Medieval Jurisprudence," *Medievalia et Humanistica*, New Series, No. 5 (1974) , 38.

[11]See, for instance, Quintilian, *Institutio oratoria,* ed. and tr. H. E. Butler (4 vols.; Cambridge, Mass., 1920–22), V. v.

[12]*The Logic of Writing and the Organization of Society* (Cambridge, 1986), 168.

Exemption also takes place in a judicial context. Though Petrarch leaves questions of law to Charles's *iurisconsulti*, his advice has obviously been sought in a judicial context, and he uses a judicial technique that we have seen to have been familiar to both ancient and medieval lawyers. Discussing the issue of a disputed document, Cicero recommended the argument that "it is inconsistent with the rest of the writings either of other persons or most preferably, if it be possible to say so, of the same person."[13] This may have been one of the sources for Petrarch's method, for he compares the Exemption with other writings of Caesar that were known to be authentic, as well as with the writings of other ancient authors, and demonstrates on substantive and stylistic grounds that Caesar could not have been the author.

Valla's exposure of the *Donation* is much more elaborate than Petrarch's letter, but it too is judicial. As Vincenzo de Caprio has shown, it follows the model of a full judicial oration.[14] Like Petrarch, Valla is concerned with authorship: he does not locate the true author of the text nor date its composition, but he does convincingly demonstrate that it could not have been written by Constantine nor in his time.

Two points are of importance. First, the detection of forgeries was a distinctively legal technique. It is no accident that the critical historiography that was developed at the end of the Renaissance was developed by "legal humanists" and relied, according to George Huppert, on "the jurists' approach to the detection of facts."[15] François Baudouin provided a theory for authenticating historical facts and documents on the basis of courtroom practice.[16] Accordingly, a judicial language and judicial concepts pervaded the method of textual criticism, and these essentially legal terms persist today in the language of "evidence," "witnesses," and "testimony" that is also to be found in the critical scholarship of the Renaissance.

Second, critical method was centered especially in the question of authorship. Both the ancient rhetors and the Renaissance humanists focus on the issue whether the purported author of a text was the true author. This question gave scholars a particular purchase on their enquiries. They could compare a text with other authenticated writings of the author or with information about the author contained in the writings of others.

The focus of critics on the identity of the author returns us to the humanist

---

[13]*De partitione oratoria*, ed. and tr. H. Rackham (Cambridge, Mass., 1942), 132.

[14]"Retorica e ideologia nella *Declamatio* di Lorenzo Valla sulla donazione di Costantino," *Paragone*, 29, no. 338 (1978), 36–56.

[15]*The Idea of Perfect History: Historical Erudition and Historical Philosophy in Renaissance Florence* (Urbana, 1970), 24. See also J. G. A. Pocock, *The Ancient Constitution and the Feudal Law* (Cambridge, 1957).

[16]See Julian H. Franklin, *Jean Bodin and the Sixteenth-Century Revolution in the Methodology of Law and History* (New York, 1963), 127–30. John Selden is a good English example of the "legal philologist": see *The Historie of Tithes* (1618; rpt. New York, 1969), Preface. On the political, argumentative motivation of Selden's scholarship, see Paul Christianson, "Young John Selden and the Ancient Constitution, ca. 1610–1618." *Proceedings of the American Philosophical Society*, 128 (1984), 271–315.

quality of critical scholarship. It is a truism of modern scholarship that the identity of the authors of texts was of relatively little importance in the Middle Ages. According to R. Howard Bloch, "few texts are ascribable to an author invested with more personality than a mere name."[17] By contrast Petrarch gave immense importance to authorship both as a reader and as a writer. As a reader, he insisted in a well-known passage that "philosophers must not be judged from isolated words but from their uninterrupted coherence and consistency. . . . He who wants to be safe in praising the entire man must see, examine, and estimate the entire man."[18] As a writer, he was especially concerned to present his own personality so that, as Kristeller observes, Petrarch "talks about a variety of things and ideas but essentially he always talks about himself."[19]

Nevertheless, the critical method of the humanists was in potentially uneasy alliance with the very interest in authors that encouraged it. When Petrarch sought to understand Cicero the man as author, he did so in order to converse with him. His familiar letters to ancient authors are one manifestation of a convivial attitude that led him to remark of Cicero and Vergil that "my admiration for and intimacy with their genius achieved through lengthy study led me to such love that you would think this kind of affection scarcely possible toward living men."[20]

The idea of a conversation with the men of the ancient world persisted to the time of Machiavelli and on to that of Montaigne, who remarked that "in this association with men I mean to include, and foremost, those who live only in the memory of books," and who, like Petrarch, had "a singular curiosity . . . to know the soul and the natural judgements of my authors."[21] When Petrarch could say that "if Cicero was a man, it follows that in some things, I do not say in many things, he will have erred" (*si homo fuit Cicero, consequens esse ut in quibusdam, ne dicam multis, erraverit*), he was able to regard Cicero not as a kind of disembodied, text-bound authority (*auctoritas*) but as a fallible *homo* just like himself—a mere mortal with whom he could hope to converse as an equal, and whom he could thus also hope to imitate as an equal.[22] The humanistic approach to texts made their authors more human, more approachable, more familiar. By contrast the method of humanist textual criticism eventually questioned this familiarity. As Mark Hulliung observes, "following every victory of the humanists in restoring a classical text to its context, there was that

[17]*Etymologies and Genealogies: A Literary Anthropology of the French Middle Ages* (Chicago, 1983), 16.

[18]*On His Own Ignorance and That of Many Others*, tr. Hans Nachod, *The Renaissance Philosophy of Man*, ed. Ernst Cassirer, Paul Oskar Kristeller, and John Herman Randall, Jr. (Chicago, 1948), 87.

[19]*Eight Philosophers of the Italian Renaissance* (Stanford, 1964), 13.

[20]*Letters on Familiar Matters: Rerum familiarum libri*, tr. Aldo S. Bernardo (3 vols; Albany, 1975, and Baltimore, 1982–85), III, 232.

[21]*The Complete Works of Montaigne*, tr. Donald M. Frame (Stanford, 1957), 115, 302.

[22]*Le familiari*, ed. Vittorio Rossi and Umberto Bosco, (4 vols.; Florence, 1933–42), XXIV.ii.13 (IV, 224). On Petrarch's new emphasis on familiarity, see A. J. Minnis, *Medieval Theory of Authorship: Scholastic Literary Attitudes in the Later Middle Ages* (London, 1984), 211–17.

much additional evidence of the absence of a common denominator between ancient and modern ways of life."[23] Humanism as a movement appears to hover between the two poles of a wholesale identification with antiquity and a critical distance from it.[24]

In the Renaissance the humanistic ideal remained that of a union of learning and eloquence. It was in the seventeenth century, according to Barbara J. Shapiro, that "English historical thought first reached its modern state of methodological ambivalence, poised between the competing claims of literature and science."[25] But the two "sets" of humanists identified by Grafton were potentially at odds. Grafton observes of the "tensions and contradictions" in humanism that "if we treat humanist readers as practitioners of a form of rhetoric, some difficulties vanish," since "most humanists interpreted—like good rhetoricians—for a specific purpose and a particular audience."[26] The different kinds or *genera* of rhetoric had since Aristotle been associated with different audiences and purposes. It is significant that the method of textual criticism was typically judicial because in other respects humanistic literature does not appear to have been of the judicial *genus*.[27]

There were three recognized *genera* or kinds of rhetoric: the judicial, the deliberative (political and moral), and the demonstrative or epideictic (the ceremonial art of praise and blame). Kristeller observes that "unlike ancient rhetoric, Renaissance rhetoric was not primarily concerned with the political and even less with the judiciary speech."[28] John M. McManamon argues that from the beginning of the fifteenth century "epideictic continued to enjoy preeminence among the *genera causarum* throughout the Italian Renaissance."[29] The importance of the demonstrative *genus* for the humanists was not restricted to oratory proper. The prominent humanist enterprise of history-writing, for instance, was basically demonstrative in kind—even though elements of the other *genera* might appear in humanist histories.[30] Demonstrative history was concerned with praise and blame and with providing useful moral lessons to the reader or hearer. Thus, as Felix Gilbert observes, "not factual

---

[23]*Citizen Machiavelli* (Princeton, 1983), 156.

[24]See especially Logan, "The Relation of Montaigne to Renaissance Humanism," *JHI*, 36 (1975), 613–32; and *The Meaning of More's "Utopia"* (Princeton, 1983).

[25]*Probability and Certainty in Seventeenth-Century England: A Study of the Relationships Between Natural Science, Religion, History, Law, and Literature* (Princeton, 1983), 119. A classic study of the seventeenth-century "crisis of the European consciousness" is Paul Hazard, *The European Mind 1680–1715*, tr. J. Lewis May (1953; rpt. Harmondsworth, 1964).

[26]"Renaissance Readers and Ancient Texts," 642.

[27]The different *genera* in Renaissance humanist literature are discussed in more detail by Tinkler, "Renaissance Humanism and the *genera eloquentiae*," *Rhetorica*, 5 (1987), 279–309.

[28]*Renaissance Thought and Its Sources*, 242.

[29]"Innovation in Early Humanist Rhetoric: The Oratory of Pier Paulo Vergerio the Elder," *Rinascimento*, 22 (1982), 9. On humanists' use of both the demonstrative and deliberative *genera*, see Tinkler, "Praise and Advice: Rhetorical Approaches in More's *Utopia* and Machiavelli's *Prince*," *The Sixteenth Century Journal*, 19 (1988), 187–207.

[30]See Tinkler, "The Rhetorical Method of Francis Bacon's *History of the Reign of King Henry VII*," *History and Theory*, 26 (1987), 32–52.

completeness and accuracy, but moral guidance was expected from the true historian."[31]

By contrast a judicial attitude toward the past had quite different aims, emphases and strategies. Aristotle observed that "to each of these [*genera*] a special time is appropriate: to the deliberative the future; . . . to the forensic the past, for it is always in reference to things done; . . . to the epideictic most appropriately the present. . . . It is not uncommon, however, for epideictic speakers to avail themselves of the past by way of recalling it."[32] The judicial approach to history was concerned with the past alone, and the more reliance it placed on inartificial evidence, "such as witnesses, tortures, contracts, and the like," the more it was concerned with precisely that factual accuracy that was of relatively little importance to the demonstrative historian.[33] In brief the judicial and demonstrative approaches to history were divergent and, if pushed to extremes, incommensurable.

Demonstrative history, as Quintilian observed, "has a certain affinity to poetry and may be regarded as a kind of prose poem."[34] Sir Philip Sidney argued that "the best of the historian is subject to the poet."[35] But in a judicial context the *inventio* of the demonstrative historian or the fictions of the poet create distortions. With the peculiar emphasis on the authenticity and authority of the written record that developed in European society from the twelfth century, the forgery was a particularly unacceptable fiction, even when documents were forged in order to lend written legitimacy to what had earlier been oral traditions.[36] Both forgery and the detection of forgery were brought into being by a judicial emphasis on documentary evidence.[37] But in this context there is also a sense in which the demonstrative historian "forged" the past, a practice particularly evident in the rhetorical historian's convention of inventing the speeches purportedly delivered by historical figures. The judicial critic had a commitment to expose such forgeries and to rely only on written records that could be authenticated. The judicial and critical approach to the past, then, always had the potential to invalidate the more inventive and imaginative demonstrative approach, especially in institutional or legalistic contexts that place a high value on verifiability and documentary authenticity.

[31]*Machiavelli and Guicciardini: Politics and History in Sixteenth-Century Florence* (Princeton, 1965), 225.

[32]*The "Art" of Rhetoric*, ed. and tr. John Henry Freese (Cambridge, Mass., 1926), I.iii.4.

[33]*Rh.* I.ii.2. The relationship between judicial and demonstrative historiography is discussed in more detail by Tinkler, "Humanist History and the English Novel in the Eighteenth Century," *Studies in Philology*, 85 (1988), 510–37.

[34]*Inst.* III.vii.28.

[35]*A Defence of Poesy*, ed. Jan van Dorsten (London, 1966), 37.

[36]Brian Stock observes that "the rise of forgery rather than its detection is about as good a witness as we have to the growth of general legal expertise": *The Implications of Literacy: Written Language and Models of Interpretation in the Eleventh and Twelfth Centuries* (Princeton, 1983), 60.

[37]M. T. Clanchy argues that "forged documents were often based on earlier authentic documents or on good oral traditions. The purpose of forgery was to produce a record in a form which was acceptable, particularly in courts of law, at the time it was made": *From Memory to Written Record: England 1066–1307* (London, 1979), 249. See also the "Introduction" by Eleanor Searle (ed.), *The Chronicle of Battle Abbey* (Oxford, 1980).

II

The foregoing discussion of rhetorical *genera* provides a necessary background for understanding the tensions involved in the English Battle of the Books. Because Bentley has an important place in the development of modern philology, modern commentators tend to ignore the rhetorical manner and approach of his *Dissertation* and *Phalaris*.[38] Yet both works were not only written in the context of controversy, they were also designed in their context to cause the maximum of embarrassment.[39] It is significant that the *Dissertation* has precisely the judicial character that we have seen to have been associated with critical scholarship. Bentley himself makes his judicial approach quite explicit. Alluding to Temple's acknowledgment that earlier scholars have questioned the authenticity of Phalaris's *Epistles* (guessing their author to be Lucian), Bentley begins by declaring that "I shall not go to dispossess him [i.e., Phalaris], as those have done before me, by an arbitrary sentence in his own tyranical way; but proceed with him upon lawful evidence, and a fair, impartial trial" (II, 139–40). As Bentley proceeds to make clear, his method is to adduce other writings that are "preserved to be a witness against him," as well as to examine anachronisms and inconsistencies in the text itself which he calls "confessions" (II, 141; 149). In brief Bentley's entire approach is quite explicitly conceived as a judicial examination of witnesses and comparison of testimony.

Bentley's forensic allusions are no mere ornamental flourish: rhetorical strategies of judicial proof led textual critics to ask what we can recognize as sound scholarly questions. They led Valla to treat the *Donation* not as a received text the terms of which should be debated but as an historical event that could be questioned according to the interrogative *topoi* used to examine a criminal accusation. Similarly, they led Baudouin to distinguish between the reliability of original and of secondary documents.[40] There is more scholarly validity in rhetorical argumentation and more argumentative rhetoric in scholarship than many positivist historians care to admit.[41]

Like Petrarch and Valla, Bentley bases his examination on the issue of authorship, demonstrating that the *Epistles* could not consistently have been written either by Phalaris or in his time. His method of procedure is exemplified in his

---

[38]C. O. Brink has recently examined Bentley's role in "the emergence of true scholarship" in a very insular context: *English Classical Scholarship: Historical Reflections on Bentley, Porson and Housman* (Cambridge, 1986). Less encomiastic and more persuasive is E. J. Kenney, *The Classical Text: Aspects of Editing in the Age of the Printed Book* (Berkeley, 1974), 71–74. Jebb discusses Bentley's debating tactics revealingly: *Bentley*, 68 ff.

[39]See Monk, *Bentley*, I, 91–92.

[40]See Franklin, *Jean Bodin*, 130.

[41]See Tinkler, "The Rhetorical Method of Bacon's *Henry*"; and "Humanism as Discourse: Studies in the Rhetorical Culture of Renaissance Humanism, Petrarch to Bacon" (Diss. Queen's, 1983), 79–99. It should be added that judicial rhetoric had long been applied to fields that were not strictly forensic: see, for instance, Robert Dick Sider, *Ancient Rhetoric and the Art of Tertullian* (London, 1971). On the (neglected) importance of lawyers in intellectual history, see Bouwsma, "Lawyers and Early Modern Culture," *American Historical Review*, 78 (1973), 303–27.

response, in the Preface of his *Phalaris,* to an accusation in Boyle's *Examination,* "*That Dr. B[entley] cannot be the Author of the Dissertation*" (quoted Bentley, I, lxx). Alluding to the fact that Boyle was not the main author, Bentley replies that "if another should answer him in his own way, and pretend to prove, *that Mr. B[oyle] cannot be the Author of the Examination* from the variety of styles in't, from its contradictions to his edition of Phalaris, from its contradictions to itself, from its contradictions to Mr. B.'s character and to his title of Honourable, and from several other topics; it would be taken perhaps for no raillery, but too serious a repartee" (I, lxx). Bentley is here drawing from the judicial "topics" (*loci* or *topoi*) that were recommended by ancient rhetors for questioning documents, and he displays a characteristic critical focus on the identity and character of the author.

In the context of the Battle, what is significant about Bentley's judicial approach is that it fails to interact with the conventional rhetorical assumptions of the long-standing *querelle des anciens et des modernes.* Black has shown that the debate between ancients and moderns was conventionally demonstrative in rhetorical approach.[42] The debate was geared to the topics of praise and blame: its intention was to praise either ancients or moderns by comparison, and it relied on such standard classical demonstrative strategies as "the celebration of deeds which our hero was the first or only man or at any rate one of the very few to perform," and the selection of "achievements that are of outstanding importance or unprecedented or unparalleled in their actual character."[43] Aristotle recommended amplification by comparison, which allows the orator to impute superiority to his subject, as especially suitable to demonstrative praise.[44] It was just such a comparison between ancients and moderns and a praise of the superior literary merits of the ancients, that provided the point of Temple's original essay.

Bentley does not hesitate to dissociate himself from the contest over praise and blame of relative literary merits. In the *Dissertation* he insists bluntly that "I write without any view or regard to your controversy, which I do not make my own, nor presume to interpose in it" (II, 136). He appears perfectly well aware of the conventional terms of the debate and acknowledges "that *some of the oldest books are the best in their kinds,* the same person having the double glory of invention and perfection, is a thing observed even by some of the ancients," adding drily that "the authors they gave this honour to are Homer and Archilochus. . . . The choice of Phalaris and Aesop, as they are now extant, for the two great inimitable originals, is a piece of criticism of a peculiar complexion, and must proceed from a singularity of palate and judgement" (II, 136). But Bentley dissociates himself from the demonstrative comparison of ancient and modern authors because, as we have seen, he is engaged on a different, judicial project.

[42]"Ancients and Moderns in the Renaissance."
[43]*Inst.* III.vii.16; Cicero, *De oratore,* ed. and tr. E. W. Sutton and H. Rackham (Cambridge, Mass., 1942), II.347.
[44]*Rh.* I.ix.38–40.

Marjorie O'Rourke Boyle has demonstrated that, in the debate between Erasmus and Luther, Erasmus's *De libero arbitrio* is deliberative in form and strategy, while Luther's *De servo arbitrio* is judicial. The result of this discrepancy of rhetorical *genera* was that the two writers' arguments failed to connect, and "fundamentally, each accused the other of speaking off the subject."[45] By choosing to respond judicially to Erasmus's deliberative *diatribe,* Luther did not grapple with Erasmus's arguments on equal terms but struck at the roots of his epistemology. Much the same can be said of Bentley's contribution to the Battle: by employing the judicial *genus,* he removes himself from the terms of the humanists' debate, using incommensurable argumentative strategies in pursuit of an entirely different kind of goal. Thus, he neither affirms nor denies that the oldest books are the best but proves that the *Epistles of Phalaris* and *Aesop's Fables* are not the oldest texts, while expressing surprise, as an aside, that anyone should think them on their own merits superior to Homer. Like critical historians who went about invalidating the fictions of demonstrative historians with their insistence on the evidence of written records, Bentley subverts the terms and assumptions of the humanists' conventional debate between ancients and moderns.

Bentley's judicial scholarship was an ingeniously disruptive rhetorical strategy, sweeping the ground from under Temple's arguments rather than engaging them on their own terms. But the current of feeling in the Battle ran deeper than such a strategy deserved. That there was something more fundamental at stake is suggested by the extent to which Bentley and Swift each regarded the other's kind of exercise as useless or irrelevant. Bentley refused to engage in the literary controversy that later engaged Swift's attention, while Swift, by imitating an Aesopian fable in his response, was making the point that Bentley's scholarship was valueless for the business of effective writing.

The deeper controversy was over the nature of humanism itself. The writing of humanists from Petrarch to Montaigne had been inspired by their understanding of ancient literature: classical scholarship assisted literary practice. But by Bentley's time, classical scholarship had become an end in itself, divorced from and even antagonistic to literary creativity. In the Battle literature and scholarship no longer recognized each other except as quite divergent enterprises or—worse—as enemies.

Swift made the battle over humanism clear. In Boyle's edition of Phalaris it was claimed that Bentley, as librarian, "*out of his singular humanity,* denied them [i.e. the editors] the further use" of a manuscript of Phalaris (quoted

[45]*Rhetoric and Reform: Erasmus' Civil Dispute with Luther,* Harvard Historical Monographs, Vol. LXXI (Cambridge, Mass., 1983), 94. Boyle further links Luther's rhetorical stance to a Stoic epistemology and Erasmus's to a Skeptical epistemology. On the relationship between formal rhetorical *genus* and substantive content, see the classic study by Hans Baron, "Imitation, Rhetoric, and Quattrocento Thought in Bruni's *Laudatio," From Petrarch to Leonardo Bruni: Studies in Humanistic and Political Literature* (Chicago, 1968), 151–71; John W. O'Malley, "Content and Rhetorical Forms in Sixteenth-Century Treatises on Preaching," *Renaissance Eloquence: Studies in the Theory and Practice of Renaissance Rhetoric,* ed. James J. Murphy (Berkeley, 1983), 238–52; and Tinkler, "Praise and Advice."

Bentley, II, 173). Bentley responded with familiar scholar's pique (and a revealingly legalistic tone): "*Pro singulari sua humanitate*! I could produce several letters from learned professors abroad, whose books our Editors may in time be fit to read, wherein these very same words are said to me candidly and seriously" (II, 175). When Swift wrote his *Battel*, the term "humanity" was particularly resonant in the debate. Swift picked up these resonances and made their implications clear. By the seventeenth century "humanity" not only had familiar modern meanings but also referred to the study of the ancient authors—the disciplines of the "Humanities." "Humanity" was an English derivation from the family of terms—*studia humanitatis, humanista*—that were the Renaissance precursors to the nineteenth-century term "humanism." A *humanista* was a "humanist," a teacher or scholar of "humanity," the *studia humanitatis*.[46] Swift, catching up Bentley's claim, has Scaliger remark to Bentley that "*Thy* Learning *makes thee more* Barbarous, *thy* Study of Humanity, *more* Inhuman" (161).

As a classical scholar, fluent in Greek and Latin and dauntingly erudite, Bentley had impeccable humanist qualifications. But for Swift, Bentley's "Study of Humanity" had made him "Inhuman"; his humanistic "Learning" had made him "Barbarous"—a label that humanists in the Renaissance regularly applied to the Latin of scholastics and other intellectual opponents. In Swift's Aesopian fable Bentley's humanistic studies have turned him into the reverse of a humanist, a scholastic spider in his web who is contrasted with that favorite metaphoric self-image of the humanists, the bee.[47] Swift, as a classicist rhetorical writer, also had excellent title to be thought a humanist—but the rhetorical, literary humanist is now opposed to the scholarly humanist.[48] Swift summarizes the paradox that had emerged by the late seventeenth century in the history of humanism: humanism was turned against itself, scholarship against literature.

III

Swift provides one explanation for why these two aspects of humanism should have come adrift in his fable of the spider and the bee. In Swift's fiction the humanist scholar has become a merely bookish spider, locked in the library; while the humanist orator is a bee, ranging at large, reading and gathering experience for the active life. The careers of the two men reinforce the point. Starting as a private tutor, Bentley rose to the position of keeper of all the king's libraries in England and thence to the Mastership of Trinity College, Cambridge, and a prominent, if turbulent, academic career. In brief Bentley's

---

[46]*Oxford English Dictionary*, s.v. "Humanity"; and Kristeller, *Renaissance Thought and Its Sources*, 21–22.

[47]On the apian metaphor see G. W. Pigman III, "Versions of Imitation in the Renaissance," *Renaissance Quarterly*, 33 (1980), esp. 2–9.

[48]On Swift's classicist rhetoric see Charles Allen Beaumont, *Swift's Classical Rhetoric* (Athens, Geo., 1961), and more recently, Thomas R. Thornburg, *Swift and the Ciceronian Tradition* (Muncie, Ind., 1980).

was the career of a professional scholar, a kind of career that only began to be opened up to humanists toward the end of the Renaissance: Grafton observes that "both classical philology and historical chronology became disciplines during the sixteenth century."[49] It is a function of the professionalization of scholarship to monopolize competence, withdrawing legitimacy from those non-professional scholars, as Petrarch was, who are henceforth known as "amateurs."

Like Bentley, Swift had a university training, and both men gloried in the title of Doctor of Divinity. But Swift's career was less straightforward than Bentley's and he resented more thoroughly the need to court patronage. "Climbing is performed in the same Posture with Creeping," he observed bitterly, presumably from galling personal experience (245). If Bentley's scholarship is in line of inheritance from the humanists, so are Swift's bitterness about the needs of patronage, and his relentless search for an independent income, personal literary fame and political involvement. In the Renaissance Petrarch was vitriolic about the papal court at Avignon, Machiavelli resentfully chose as dedicatees for his *Discourses* "not those who are princes, but those who because of their good qualities deserve to be," and More's character Hythloday in *Utopia* presents a scathing critique of the dishonesty required of councillors at court.[50]

Gilbert observes of Renaissance humanists that "they hardly ever took part at a policymaking level. . . .There remained a gap between the humanists and the ruling classes of their time."[51] The same could be said of Swift: obviously brilliant, he knew all too well that he was underemployed for his talents, kept at a distance from the center of activity in London, and unable to channel his skills as completely into his professional career as Bentley. Bentley's scholarship led him straight toward an academic career, backed by the consciousness that "learned professors abroad" highly approved his work. Swift's literary and political writings lacked the kind of institutional validity that Bentley could claim: he turned to rhetoric, the art of persuasion, as a way of calling attention to opinions (and talents) that he could not express through normal institutional channels. Thus, while Bentley as a scholar exposed the true author of the *Epistles of Phalaris* as a forging "Sophist" addicted to rhetorical fictions, Swift entered on an ambiguous literary program that was full of fictions and forgeries. In fact one of Swift's major literary models was Lucian, who had been claimed as the possible forger of Phalaris's *Epistles*. In J. S. Mill's terms, Swift was a characteristic "eccentric," an intellectual fulminating brilliantly from the margins of power, while Bentley, if he too was an intellectual *novus homo,* setting a cat among academic pigeons,

---

[49]*Joseph Scaliger: A Study in the History of Classical Scholarship*, I, *Textual Criticism and Exegesis* (Oxford, 1983), 3. See also Kelley, "History as a Calling: The Case of La Popelinière," *Renaissance Studies in Honor of Hans Baron*, ed. Anthony Molho and John A. Tedeschi (Dekalb, Ill., 1971), 771–89.

[50]*Discourses on the First Decade of Titus Livius*, in *The Chief Works and Others*, tr. Allan Gilbert, (3 vols.; Durham, N. C., 1965), I, 188–89; see also *Petrarch's Book Without a Name: A Translation of the Liber sine nomine*, by Norman P. Zacour (Toronto, 1973).

[51]"Bernardo Rucellai and the Orti Oricellari: A Study on the Origin of Modern Political Thought," *History: Choice and Commitment* (Cambridge, Mass., 1977), 242.

was nevertheless able to tailor his capacities more successfully to his professional career.

In this contrast between the two men, Bentley was closer by far than Swift to Kristeller's definition of the humanists as intellectuals who "established the humanities. . . . As teachers of the humanities, as writers and scholars in the literary and historical disciplines, we have every reason to look upon the Renaissance humanists as our predecessors and professional ancestors."[52] Yet Swift was closer to those humanists, from Petrarch to Montaigne, whose writings emerged not from their professional careers but on the contrary from the *otium* that they were able to cultivate outside their work. Bentley became a professional scholar: Swift became a churchman who incidentally wrote satires and pamphlets. John O. Ward has argued in the context of twelfth-century humanism that " 'humanist' literature is primarily the expression of social marginality; its authors operate on the margins of the established world of their day."[53] Swift was just such another marginal figure, overtrained and underemployed, and one who suffered the charge of insanity that always threatens such intellectuals, as Shakespeare saw in his portrait of Hamlet.

IV

The contrast between Bentley's and Swift's careers may elucidate a further, fundamental divide between the two writers' contributions to the Battle. I have argued that Petrarch was interested in Cicero as the author of texts because he wanted to understand Cicero as a fallible *homo,* a man just like himself, rather than be constrained to see him only as an *auctoritas,* an authority, a canonical text. Only in this way, by understanding Cicero as a man, could Petrarch make the orator's writings live again, comprehensible as the thoughts of a man with whom he could identify and whom he could thus also imitate. Petrarch wanted to see Cicero not as a book but as a man, not as a text but as a speaking human being. To understand Cicero as a mere man was, for Petrarch, to enable himself to write: "I shall for the most part follow the example of Cicero . . . in these letters. . . . Cicero restricted his philosophical concerns to his books and included in his letters accounts of the highly personal, unusual and varied goings-on of his time."[54] If Petrarch's understanding of Cicero was gained at the cost of copious reading and scholarship, it was a scholarship that assisted rather than hindered his own creative writing.

[52]"Studies on Renaissance Humanism during the Last Twenty Years," *Studies in the Renaissance,* 9 (1962), 23.

[53]"Gothic Architecture, Universities and the Decline of the Humanities in Twelfth Century Europe," *Principalities, Powers and Estates: Studies in Medieval and Early Modern Government and Society,* ed. L. O. Frappell (Adelaide, S. A., 1979), 68; cf. Stephen C. Ferruolo, *The Origins of the University: The Schools of Paris and their Critics, 1100–1215* (Stanford, 1985), 131–83. On the role of *otium* and marginality in Renaissance humanist culture, see Tinkler, "Renaissance Humanism and the *genera eloquentiae.*"

[54]*Letters,* I, 10.

Nevertheless, it is rarely remarked how thoroughly paradoxical Petrarch's think-ing—and that of humanists in general—was. Professionally, the humanists were defined by their sophisticated and elite literacy. The humanists of the Renaissance were the intellectual and literary cream that floated to the surface of a rapidly grow-ing pool of literate professionals—a pool created by the revolution in literacy that is associated especially with the administrative and legal reforms of the twelfth cen-tury and with what J. K. Hyde calls the "veritable explosion in higher education" in thirteenth-century Italy.[55] The immediate effect of this revolution of literacy was to produce an exaggerated respect for the written word.

What is paradoxical is that the humanists, elite successors to this revolution in literacy, were in some respects in rebellion against it. They turned to rhetoric, the art of speech, for their models, and as Gray has shown, "most frequently, . . . they called themselves 'orators.'"[56] In a letter to the grammarian Donato, accom-panying his *On His Own Ignorance*, Petrarch insisted that "you shall read this book, as you are in the habit of listening to me when I tell tales at the fireside on winter nights, rambling along wherever the impulse takes me. I have called it a book, but it is a talk."[57]

It is yet to be explained why the humanists turned from the book-oriented culture of scholasticism to the oratorical culture of the ancients. But it is prob-ably significant that, as Lauro Martines argues, "humanism . . . won the atten-tion of men not by going through the established bulwarks of higher learning first, the universities, but by moving around and outside them."[58] The culture of the book is associated with stable and legitimated institutions such as monaster-ies and universities—institutions that were themselves controlled by written regulations and codes. At the core of the culture of the book and at the heart of the medieval revolution in literacy was the written culture of the law, with its characteristic reliance on authenticated and authoritative documents—sur-rounded by a welter of glosses, commentaries, and attempted resolutions of contradictions.[59]

In an established discipline, its canonical texts readily become its law, whether the *corpus iuris,* the works of Aristotle, the *corpus Hippocraticum* or

---

[55]*Society and Politics in Medieval Italy: The Evolution of Civil Life, 1000–1350* (London, 1973), 167. An excellent study of the growth in importance of writing in medieval England is Clanchy, *From Memory to Written Record*. On the growing importance of intellectuals before the Renaissance, see Alexander Murray, *Reason and Society in the Middle Ages* (1978; rpt. Oxford, 1985).

[56]"Renaissance Humanism," 202.

[57]"On His Own Ignorance," 47.

[58]*Power and Imagination: City-States in Renaissance Italy* (New York, 1979), 277–78; cf. Gene A. Brucker, "Florence and Its University, 1348–1434," *Action and Conviction in Early Modern Europe: Essays in Memory of E. H. Harbison,* ed. Theodore K. Rabb and Jerrold E. Seigel (Princeton, 1969), 220–36—although see also the cautionary remarks of Peter Denley, "Recent Studies on Italian Universities of the Middle Ages and Renaissance," *History of Universities,* 1 (1981), 193–205.

[59]Murray observes of medieval universities that "at the top of the lucrative sciences stood law": *Reason and Society,* 224. For a stimulating argument about the relationship between legal and scholas-tic technique, see George Makdisi, "The Scholastic Method in Medieval Education: An Inquiry into Its Origins in Law and Theology," *Speculum,* 49 (1974), 640–61.

Scripture.[60] Competitive debate within such a discipline thus tends to take a legalistic course. Bentley advanced the cause of pure scholarship, but his motives and strategy were intensely competitive: by exposing forgeries, correcting his opponents and establishing texts, he undercut Temple's and the wits' scholarly authority (whatever their popular appeal) and established his own professional reputation as an expert in the canon.[61] Ironically, this competitive rhetorical strategy led away from rhetoric. Like Valla before him, Bentley's judicial approach led him to "inartificial" evidence—that which does not belong to the "art" of rhetoric. At its broadest, Bentley's is a grand attempt to describe the culture of ancient Greece. Cicero recommended this kind of project to the student of law who "has throughout the common law, and in the priestly books and Twelve Tables, a complete picture of the olden time, since a primitive antiquity of language can be studied there, and certain forms of pleading reveal the manners and the way of life of our forerunners."[62] Though Cicero argued that this study was valuable for the public orator, it could also contract into its own specialist legal expertise—that of the *iurisperitus*. Similarly, Bentley advanced a contraction of humanist learning into specialist philology.

By contrast the humanists initially won attention not only by going around the universities but also by cultivating a more persuasive and flexible, less legalistic and formulaic, writing.[63] They operated as men who needed to validate themselves and draw attention to themselves by rhetorical rather than institutional means. It is in this sense that Swift is a true successor of the humanists of the Renaissance. Like theirs, his writing is rhetorical, as spectacular and deliberately shocking as that other marginal attention-seeker, Machiavelli.

The contrast with Bentley is acute. Bentley focusses his attention on the authorship of Phalaris's *Epistles,* but he is not concerned to understand the human author of a text as Petrarch was: his concern is above all to authenticate a document. Bentley's is a book-oriented and legalistic mental culture. Bentley himself made his own legalism entirely clear. It was Swift who put his finger on the extent to which Bentley was embedded in the scholastic culture of the book, sharing the exaggerated respect for authenticated documents that is characteristic of institutionalized literates. Swift sees Bentley, the librarian, as a spider in a web of books who kills the past and gloats over the textual bodies

---

[60]On the role of an authoritative "paradigm" in institutionalized disciplines, see Thomas S. Kuhn, *The Structure of Scientific Revolutions,* International Encyclopedia of Unified Science, Vol. II, No. 1, 2nd ed. (Chicago, 1970). Galen can be seen advancing his own authority by claiming possession of the authentic interpretation of Hippocrates in the study by Wesley D. Smith, *The Hippocratic Tradition* (Ithaca, N. Y., 1979). Sider observes that "Tertullian was quick to see that the written documents of the advocate's world invited a ready comparison with the biblical documents of the church, and that the rules provided by rhetoric for controversies over the former might well work for struggles arising out of the latter": *Art of Tertullian,* 85.

[61]On the role of competitiveness in philological scholarship, see Grafton, *Scaliger,* I, 9–44.

[62]*De or.* I.193.

[63]See John F. McGovern, "The Documentary Language of Mediaeval Business, A. D. 1150–1250," *The Classical Journal,* 67 (1971–72), 227–39.

of dead authors.[64] By contrast the satirist's own humanist bee ranges over the open, if less secure, fields that lie outside the world of the book.

Swift's satire is, far more deeply than is usually recognized, a rejection of Bentley's judicial culture of the book. The critic exposes forgeries: Swift published his *Battel* as part of an elaborate fiction of forged authorship.[65] The critical historian will admit only authenticated documents as evidence: Swift wrote his pamphlet as a history, *A Full and True Account,* of events that are not only incredible but entirely fabulous. Bentley's *Dissertation* is redolent with complaints about late Antique Sophists: Swift's satire recalls the fabulous *Verae historiae* of one such rhetorician, Lucian, who had been credited by some scholars with writing the *Epistles of Phalaris,* and it includes a "forged" Aesopian fable for good measure. The spider-librarian kills ancient authors: Swift's fantasy brings them all to life. Bentley is concerned with which book belongs where in an accurate chronology: Swift has them all alive, talking, and acting at the same time. From top to bottom Swift's fantasy is Bentley's facts turned upside-down. If, as Swift says in his *Preface,* "Satyr is a sort of Glass," then it is Lewis Carroll's sort of glass which reverses what it mirrors (140).

In describing Bentley's and Swift's controversy, I have borrowed Swift's own title of a "Battle" rather than adopt the more conventional label of a *querelle.* I have done so because I believe Swift understood that the controversy involved was not the conventional *querelle des anciens et des modernes.* It was, as he claimed, a Battle of the Books. It was a battle between two approaches to writing and texts—between a judicial respect for the authenticated book or document, and a humanist commitment to the creative activity of writing.

Swift made no mistake that he was writing a book. On the contrary he called attention to the physical presence and limitations of the page by incorporating footnotes and obtrusive asterisks marking parts of his document that had supposedly been lost— *"hic pauca desunt."* But Swift is concerned with the creative possibilities—the subversions, parodies, reversals and games—that can be played with books. Swift is as much concerned with breaking the rules of books as Bentley is presented as being concerned to chain them down or file them away. His asterisks, for instance, draw attention to gaps in the reliability and completeness of the printed book. Swift yearns, along with his humanist bee, for the open fields outside the rule of the book, as surely as Bentley is concerned to classify and to authenticate.

Neither Bentley nor Swift belonged to the Establishment. Bentley was a *novus homo,* and he used his judicial technique as a weapon against entrenched interests. When Swift's "Bookseller" tells us that "the Town highly resented to

---

[64]The great Hellenist Ulrich von Wilamowitz-Moellendorff does not entirely disagree, observing that Bentley's *Dissertation* "establishes the facts, but that is only a means to an end. Scholarship of this kind can purify an author's text . . . but it cannot bring his work to life": *The History of Classical Scholarship,* tr. Alan Harris (London, 1982), 82.

[65]It should be added by way of qualification that serious forgery is in its way as scholarly an enterprise as its detection: Swift's "forgery" is parodic, tending to confuse and deflate the importance of questions of authenticity and forgery.

see a person of Sir *William Temple's* Character and Merits, roughly used by the two Reverend Gentlemen aforesaid" (i.e., Wotton and Bentley), he tells us a great deal about the oppressive pressure of the unwritten code of class and status against which Bentley fought with legalistic determination (139). Bentley's legalism, which he applied not only to Phalaris but also to his aristocratic detractors, was itself a rhetorical strategy in the battle for recognition. But Bentley's was the rhetoric of professional institutional legitimacy, and he reaped its rewards of place.

Swift, aspiring to an aristocratic independence that he could not attain, tended to fall between stools: he supported the Establishment, but he did so for the most part as a Tory in opposition. Bentley, aggressive and touchy a new man as he was, spoke the language of professional legitimacy; Swift, no less touchy but less legalistic, yearned for open fields that were sealed in written contract to other owners. He was a brilliant manipulator of the word and parodist of the text, but he could not challenge the power of the mundane, notarized, and authenticated document. By contrast, Bentley, the supporter of the Moderns, was a professional man who understood the legitimacy of the authenticated document very well and successfully pursued the route of professionalism toward social mobility.[66]

In the struggle for power Swift was on the losing side. In history he stands as a conservative opponent to a triumphant Whiggism. This is not to say, however, that his writing has lost either its vitality or its relevance. Ironically (but appropriately), it is Bentley who has been consumed in the inexorable turnover of scholarly progress. Swift, the "eccentric" and outsider, the rhetorical and humanist opponent to the rule of the book, continues to speak to the children of Mill as a living literary and intellectual force.

---

[66]On the legal and political uses of antiquarian scholarship, see Kevin Sharpe, *Sir Robert Cotton 1586–1631: History and Politics in Early Modern England* (Oxford, 1979). On the symbiosis between the landed elite and the professions (especially public officials and lawyers) in the eighteenth century, see Lawrence and Jeanne C. Fawtier Stone, *An Open Elite? England 1540–1880*, abridged ed. (Oxford, 1986), 283. The Stones also point out the growing enthusiasm of some members of the elite for collecting and antiquarian studies (220–23). Monk estimates the income from Bentley's several preferments at 1300–1400 pounds a year: *Bentley*, II, 414. For Swift, the Deanery of St. Patrick's was a financially valuable preferment, but it was isolated from his friends and from the center of power.

Gay, Swift, and the Nymphs
of Drury-Lane

Christine Rees

'TRUE Poets', wrote Swift in one of his admirable, casually analytic poems to Stella, 'can depress and raise; / Are Lords of Infamy and Praise'.[1] For Augustan poets like himself and Gay, it is not an inflated claim: nor indeed would it have seemed so to earlier generations of poets apropos the subject of woman, which Swift has just been considering. But after implying that poetry begins with an act of judgment, he outlines the manner of its execution, by which the poet himself is judged:

> They are not scurrilous in Satire,
> Nor will in Panygyrick flatter.
> Unjustly Poets we asperse;
> Truth shines the brighter, clad in Verse;
> And all the Fictions they pursue
> Do but insinuate what is true.
>
> (55–60)

Coming from Swift in particular, that final couplet arrests our attention. In practice, surely Swift's use of lyric conventions—his 'fictions'—diverges sharply from what he suggests here? If his fictions insinuate truth, it is not through expressing the truth of the imagination, but because he destroys their credibility and concedes nothing to suspended disbelief—at least according to the critical view of his verse as in some sense anti-poetic.[2] So these lines defining 'True Poets' are either ironic, or present a deliberate serious contrast. If we extend the definition to John Gay, we may feel that he eludes it for another reason: his charm of manner insinuates the fiction rather than the truth. But however unlike Swift in this respect, Gay often chooses similar subjects and bases his treatment on broadly similar assumptions. Instead of setting up tensions within an image, both poets concentrate on the tension existing between literary image and literal fact, which results in an interesting and complex relation of truth and fiction in their work. I

From *Essays in Criticism*, 23 (1973), 1–21. Reprinted by permission of the author and editors.

[1]'To Stella, Who Collected and Transcribed his Poems', 53–4. All quotations from Swift's poetry are from *Poetical Works*, ed. Herbert Davis, 1967.

[2]v. H. Davis, 'Swift's View of Poetry' (*Jonathan Swift: Essays on his Satire, and Other Studies*, 1964).

want to examine one particular fiction used by Gay and Swift, since it allows us to appreciate their distinctive characteristics on common ground, and to measure their verse against Swift's theoretic standard. The fiction in question is that of the 'nymph' whose beauty is satirically defined by the conflicting principles of art and nature. Traditionally, this conflict links the fiction to moral judgment; it commonly occurs in poems where infamy is disguised as praise.

The literary antecedents for the nymphs of early eighteenth-century poetry are extensive, and more than one tradition is involved. It would be superfluous to trace in detail one prominent line of descent, that of conventionally grotesque satire directed against female use of cosmetic arts, since several scholars have already fully established this line.[3] But one general point is worth noting: although, in its narrowest form, this type of satire throws up remarkably similar versions in different periods (for instance, Turberville's sixteenth-century lyric 'To An Olde Gentlewoman, That Painted Hir Face' meets an eighteenth-century reflection in Thomas Parnell's 'Elegy, to an Old Beauty'), yet when writers interpret it in depth they almost inevitably combine the simple motif with the larger literary themes which dominate a given period. And so the woman who paints to allure men and defy age becomes an imaginative focal point for contemporary attitudes to sexuality and death. To prove the point, we have only to remember the anti-cosmetic satire in Jacobean drama, where it manifests the all-pervading theme of human mortality (Tourneur, for example, in *The Revenger's Tragedy* imagines 'false forms' as bone-deep so that not only paint but flesh itself is an obscene and delusive mask). Normally, however, paint is the emblem of art, flesh the emblem of natural beauty; and this kind of distinction crosses over from satire to pastoral.

As her name suggests, the nymph is also entitled to a pastoral pedigree, a literary line of descent even more important than the one derived from pure satire. For whereas the cosmetic motif represents one specific variation on the nature / art antithesis, the fundamental relation between nature and art is one of the most serious moral and philosophical issues that pastoral is designed to express. Indeed E. W. Tayler describes the pastoral genre as the analogue in literature of the debate in philosophy.[4] Also, although the most obvious relation between nature and art in pastoral is the antithetical one, several of the poets writing in this essentially sophisticated genre are drawn further to explore the range and complications, the possible harmonies as well as conflicts, which the dual concept involves. In spite of this, it remains true that where woman is concerned the theme is too easily and too often coarsened into cliché. When the nymph migrates to the town, uniting, so to speak, with her satiric image, she then creates a new image with paint and mannerisms instead of being content that the poet should do it for her with words. In pastoral language, she becomes seductive and evil, the profane counterpart of the innocent country nymph: they per-

[3]For a convenient summary v. *The World of Jonathan Swift*, ed. B. Vickers, 1968, pp. 23–4, footnote 10.

[4]*Nature and Art in Renaissance Literature*, 1964, pp. 4–6.

sonify art and nature as morally antagonistic principles. The street ballads (an influence on both Gay's and Swift's verse) popularize this simple formula, and a ballad such as 'The Innocent Country-Maid's Delight' adds the toilette motif for good measure: the London lasses paint and powder themselves for their lovers—

> But every morning,
> Before their adorning,
> They're far unfit for Sale;
> *But 'tis not so, with we that go,*
> *Through frost and snow, when winds do blow,*
> *To carry the milking-payl.*
> > (*The Common Muse*, ed. V. de S. Pinto
> > and A. E. Rodway, 1965, p. 200)

Predictably, in poetry of more pretensions, the theme connects with primitivist ideals of paradise or a golden age, also deep-rooted in pastoral and satire (the *locus classicus* in the latter case being Juvenal's *Satire* VI). With varying skill, minor eighteenth-century poets lament the decline from pure womanhood which the nymph represents. Anne Finch, Countess of Winchilsea, furnishes a curiosity in this line, entitled 'Adam Posed':

> Could our first father, at his toilsome plough,
> Thorns in his path and labour on his brow,
> Cloth'd only in a rude, unpolish'd skin,
> Could he a vain fantastic nymph have seen,
> In all her airs, in all her antic graces,
> Her various fashions, and more various faces,
> How had it pos'd that skill, which late assign'd
> Just appellations to each several kind,
> A right idea of the sight to frame!
> T' have guessed from what new element she came,
> To have hit the wav'ring form, or giv'n this thing a
> > name![5]

If she weakens the poem's logic by an evidently post-lapsarian Adam, she strengthens its pastoralism by the contrast between rustic labourer and frivolous city nymph. Matthew Green's later version of the topic lacks this slight eccentricity: he compares the Creator's original intention with the modern female corrupted by social arts, and declares unequivocally

> Rather than by your culture spoiled,
> Desist, and give us nature wild.
> > (*The Spleen*, 248–9)

In spite of the official policy of disapproval however, it is clear (especially from the better poetry on the subject) that it is the sophisticated nymph and not

---

[5] *Minor Poets of the Eighteenth Century*, ed. H. I'a. Fausset, 1930, p. 71. The germ of this poem was presumably Donne's line describing a courtier, 'A thing, which would have pos'd Adam to name' (*Satyre* iv, 20).

her country sister who is by far the more interesting. While the country maid remains a simple figure in more senses than one, the city nymph can be metamorphosed into different forms depending upon her specific environment: she may haunt the streets, the theatre, or a fashionable masquerade. As her roles overlap, her image becomes more complicated: 'drabs of quality' and 'nymphs of Drury-Lane' are sisters under the (painted) skin, and a writer may treat them with a deliberately histrionic touch, highlighting costume, façade, the sense of posturing unreality. Among seventeenth-century literary characters the whore figures as a symbol of disguised evil—'Her body is the tilted Lees of pleasure, dasht over with a little decking to hold colour'[6]—and the symbol survives into the eighteenth century. Certainly Defoe, who incidentally includes a form of prose character of the whore in *Roxana*,[7] gives her a less metaphoric, much more earthbound social context; nevertheless, she remains inevitably an object for fantasies, both male and female. In effect, Gay and Swift combine two forms of presentation: in their poetry, the nymph in the shape of the whore is not only a literal being, the professional who walks the London or Dublin streets; she is also a creature of the imagination, mocking reality by her travesty of beauty and desire. Like a society nymph, she dramatizes and disguises and indeed parodies nature. The literary parody expresses the living parody.

So far it appears that Gay and Swift are working within tradition when they pursue the nymph fiction, or, at least where pastoral is concerned, logically developing a tradition which permits its conventions to be adapted ironically while the essential moral value, 'what is true', remains intact. But they diverge from seventeenth-century lyric practice (whether pre-or post-Restoration) in one important respect. Although the satiric and pastoral conventions associated with art, nature, and the nymph may express attitudes to the female sex in general, it is true that in seventeenth-century lyrics the poet is more likely to identify the 'she' of his verses with a real or supposed mistress. Rochester flings the name 'whore' as a private gesture of abuse, a retaliation for an abortive love affair:

> Then if, to make your ruine more,
>   You'll peevishly be coy,
> Dye with the Scandal of a Whore,
>   And never know the Joy.
> (*Poems by John Wilmot, Earl of
> Rochester*, ed. V. de S. Pinto, 1964, p. 21)

This abusiveness is of a very different kind from Swift's descriptions of nymph prostitutes: it is emotionally complicated, because Rochester implies both degradation and lineaments of gratified desire in his choice of term, and because it requires at least an assumed involvement. As it happens, Defoe later draws the stanza's sting by making Moll Flanders paraphrase it to describe a literal social

---

[6]'A Whoore' (*The 'Conceited Newes' of Sir Thomas Overbury etc.*, ed. J. E. Savage, 1968, p. 112).
Cf. John Webster, *The White Devil*, III, ii, 78–101.
[7]*Roxana*, ed. Jane Jack, 1964, pp. 132–3.

predicament.[8] In any case, by the early eighteenth century the personal view-point which an imaginary relationship provides is less in evidence. The poets satirise the nymphs rather than sigh for them, although complimentary lyric still functions as social small coin. When Swift writes of his relationship to a real woman, he deliberately relegates the poetic mistress and muse to Grub Street, asserting that he and Stella belong to a different order of reality:

> Thou *Stella*, wert no longer young,
> When first for thee my Harp I strung:
> Without one Word of *Cupid's* Darts,
> Of killing Eyes, or bleeding Hearts.
> ('To Stella, Who Collected and
> Transcribed his Poems', 9–12)

Friendship and esteem take precedence of discredited romantic love. But we ought to avoid the trap of distinguishing too positively between the individual women of whom Swift and his friends write with personal feeling, and the nymphs who originate in social observation and literary convention. The poets themselves turn the distinction into a joke as well as a genuine compliment. Swift teases Stella on being unsuitable for nymphhood, and makes Venus petulantly remark of Vanessa

> 'She was at Lord knows what Expence,
> 'To form a Nymph of Wit and Sense.'
> ('Cadenus and Vanessa', 864–5)

Pope gallants it in his verse for Martha Blount without transforming her into a full-blown nymph like Belinda. For the nymph as true literary type comes into her own in poems where the poet is interested in the image or role, rather than in individuals or feelings. In other words, he gives art priority over nature: but it is his *own* art which concerns him most, and this immediately complicates the issue beyond the simple conflict of art and nature as a literary frame of reference. In fact, we return to the problematic truth-fiction-poetry triangle which is in a sense analogous to the nature-art-woman triangle.

One way of resolving the complication shifts responsibility for the fiction from the poet to the woman herself and possibly to society at large. In seventeenth-century Cavalier lyrics, a poet like Thomas Carew professes himself more than satisfied to be the creator of a woman's beauty, to make her desirable, after the manner of a court painter; after all, it gives him a bargaining position to be ironically exploited. The Restoration poets also regard themselves as 'Lords of Infamy and Praise', and, considering their flair for elegant vilification, probably in that order of priority. But as Gay and Swift move away from private pose to public satire, they become more preoccupied with confirming or destroying pre-existing images of the sex, whether created by literature, by social expectations, or by the woman concerned. This presupposes a moral distinction between the satirist's art and art

[8] *Moll Flanders* (first edition), ed. Bonamy Dobrée and Herbert Davis, 1961, pp. 74–5.

used irresponsibly. However, a more subtle literary approach, also open to them, is not to resolve the complication at all but to acknowledge the poet's ambiguous position and then play upon it. If it is easy to oversimplify the moral formula of art opposed to nature, the contrary idea that art enhances nature requires more expert handling, especially when both attitudes—appreciation and disapproval—exist simultaneously. For instance, in seventeenth-century poetry Marvell's teasing and beautiful pastorals have the exact quality of ironic consciousness required, and 'The Gallery' focuses this very problem, since both mistress and poet participate in the game between nature and art played out

> In all the Forms thou can'st invent
> Either to please me, or torment

to culminate in the final shepherdess image.[9] Congreve carries overt complicity (and social allusion) further in his opalescent lyric, 'A Hue and Cry after Fair Amoret':

> Fair *Amoret* is gone astray;
>   Pursue and seek her, ev'ry Lover;
> I'll tell the Signs by which you may
>   The wand'ring Shepherdess discover.
>
> Coquet and Coy at once her Air,
>   Both study'd, tho' both seem neglected;
> Careless she is with artful Care,
>   Affecting to seem unaffected.
>   (*Complete Works of William Congreve,*
>   ed. M. Summers, 1923, iv, 74)

Set this beside Herrick's earlier treatment of precisely the same motif, the pastoral search, where he uses the pastoral convention in its prelapsarian state, so to speak, and produces an effect of 'natural' spontaneous lyricism:

> Among the *Mirtles,* as I walkt,
> Love and my sighs thus intertalkt:
> Tell me, said I, in deep distresse,
> Where I may find my Shepardesse.
> Thou foole, said Love, know'st thou not this?
> In every thing that's sweet, she is.
> In yond' *Carnation* goe and seek,
> There thou shalt find her lip and cheek . . .
>   (*Poetical Works of Robert Herrick,*
>   ed. L. C. Martin, 1956, p. 106)

Herrick has the air of discovering beauty growing wild, which reminds us of a yet older song tradition. But for Congreve, the art revealed in the errant girl's behaviour is her own creation and as much an artistic illusion as a poem written

---

[9] *The Poems and Letters of Andrew Marvell*, ed. H. M. Margoliouth, 2nd edn. 1952, i, pp. 29–30. For a relevant discussion of this poem v. Winifred Nowottny, *The Language Poets Use*, 1962, pp. 94–6.

about it. The chief difference is that the one pleasure, the girl's coquetry, is precarious, the other, his poem, is permanent.

In the eighteenth century Pope develops this ambivalent nature/art theme far beyond the confines of the lyric: it is not however only the scale of *The Rape of the Lock* which accounts for increased complexity, but the awareness he displays in discriminating between different arts. Pope is investigating a world which has already evolved its own rival means of controlling or expressing nature through its etiquette, its social manoeuvres, even its *objets d'art*. Within this environment, the nymph also is an artist working in her own medium to transform nature. Consequently, the scenes concerned with Belinda's adornment have a certain moral and aesthetic elusiveness perfectly mediated through the fiction of the sylphs. When criticising *The Rape of the Lock*, John Dennis perceives art and nature to be important points of reference, and so delivers himself of a familiar little homily on gilding the lily. But his evidence from pastoral ironically betrays him into the very discrepancy he condemns in Pope:

> And our Ladies who spend so much Time at their Toilettes would do well to consider, that ... they who are most charm'd with their Persons, endeavour to retrieve their natural Beauty in Imagination at least, by divesting them of their borrow'd Ornaments, and cloathing them in the Simplicity of the rural Habit, when in their Sonnets they transform them to Shepherdesses.
>
> (*Critical Works of John Dennis,* ed. E. N. Hooker, 1943, ii, 334)

The fallacy contained in this argument is the age-old fallacy concerning what is 'natural': the critic fails to acknowledge that the poet's artifice embellishes nature as much as the lady's. When Pope uses pastoral convention to describe his heroine's beauty, he, and we, derive pleasure from art consciously heightening nature. Yet, as a whole, the poem's fiction insinuates a truth, as it progresses towards the final serious separation not just of art and nature but of art and art— one goes to dust, the other endures like a star.

When Gay makes use of the nymph fiction in his earlier poetry, he frames her in the conventional moral oppositions of town and country, art and nature. In *Rural Sports*, the fisherman's artificial fly images the society beauty throwing out her lures; both demonstrate art imitating nature for destructive purposes.[10] And, predictably, he pictures the country girl in terms of her opposite—

No Midnight Masquerade her Beauty wears
And Health, not Paint, the fading Bloom repairs.
(259–60)[11]

[10]*Rural Sports,* first version (1713), 135–8.

[11]Gay's alterations in his revised version (1720) do not substantially change his presentation in these particular instances, although he omits one couplet from the earlier description of the rural maid which is perhaps redundant through over-emphasizing the point:

Upon her Cheek a pure Vermilion glows,
And all her Beauty she to Nature owes.
(247–8)

All quotations from Gay's works are from *Poetical Works,* ed. G. C. Faber, 1926.

Such verse does not lack charm, but it is a charm tarnished with a breath of trite-ness. When Gay morally separates art and nature, he is often being sentimental: allowing the two ideas to coalesce gives him the chance of a much more fasci-nating and variable play of irony beneath the surface. Correspondingly, the roles of the nymph coalesce in his subtlest work. In *The Beggar's Opera* it is an open question (as for their male counterparts) whether fine ladies imitate whores, or whores fine ladies. By the time he writes *The Beggar's Opera* he has perfected his ability to have a literary convention both ways, so that reminiscences of the original, whether pastoral or heroic, both satirize and enhance his material. For instance, Macheath's sweet mocking song in praise of woman, 'If the heart of a man is deprest with cares', epitomises the bruised lyricism of many of these songs in their Newgate context: a few stage-moments later, the almost Eliza-bethan natural imagery 'Roses and lillies her cheeks disclose' gives place to Macheath's banter with the whores on the subject of 'the repairs of quality', cosmetic paint (*The Beggar's Opera*, II, iii and iv). Somewhere between the directness of *Rural Sports* and the indirectness of *The Beggar's Opera*, the description of the nymph-prostitute in *Trivia* appears to mark an intermediate stage in Gay's development of the fiction. On the one hand, with regard to its placing in the general scheme of the poem, Gay might have made more of possi-ble cross-references, as he does in *The Beggar's Opera* where fine filaments of style are constantly thrown out to connect different worlds, and different sets of social and artistic conventions. On the other hand, *within* the actual description of the nymph he captures a shuddering allurement as well as a moral judgment. He succeeds in suggesting the fantasy element surrounding such a figure: the whore's masquerade hints at a sinister imitation of the society masquerade, and also bears a kind of left-handed relation to the theatre. In addition to her line of patter, this nymph masks herself with what might almost be the remnants of stage costume, including, like Roxana, a Quaker guise:

> In riding-hood near tavern-doors she plies,
> Or muffled pinners hide her livid eyes.
> With empty bandbox she delights to range,
> And feigns a distant errand from the '*Change*;
> Nay, she will oft' the Quaker's hood prophane,
> And trudge demure the rounds of *Drury-Lane.*
> (iii, 275–80)

In every detail, highlighted like her hectic cheeks, Gay does not merely contrast art with nature but displays its active perversion. He pulls the entire fiction together through the corresponding town / country theme: corrupt town pastoral blights country pastoral in the person of the 'hapless swain' whom the 'fraudful nymph' entices and infects. It is vividly done; and yet, paradoxically, Gay is cre-ating a fantasy image at the same time as he ostensibly destroys it. There is some hiatus between moral intention and this vital travesty, which is less apparent in works where Gay pretends not to have a moral stance towards his fiction, or where his art can support a genuinely ambivalent attitude.

Such ambiguities are more available to him when he treats the subject of the society nymph and her masquerades, instead of the nymph-prostitute. Gay's shepherdesses inherit the mantle of Congreve's Amoret, in that they, too, consciously create an image to be admired: indeed the masquerade itself licences these disguises. The fine lady no longer depends on the poet to turn her into a nymph, but effects her own transformation with significant consequences:

> Last *Masquerade* was *Sylvia* nymphlike seen,
> Her hand a crook sustain'd, her dress was green;
> An am'rous shepherd led her through the croud,
> The nymph was innocent, the shepherd vow'd;
> But nymphs their innocence with shepherds trust;
> So both withdrew, as nymph and shepherd must.
> ('The Tea-Table', 21–6)

Gay duplicates this pastoral logic in another poem, the 'Epistle to Pulteney', in an exquisite mannered piece describing *la dolce vita*:

> When the sweet-breathing spring unfolds the buds,
> Love flys the dusty town for shady woods.
> Then *Totenham* fields with roving beauty swarm,
> And *Hampstead* Balls the city virgin warm;
> Then *Chelsea*'s meads o'erhear perfidious vows,
> And the prest grass defrauds the grazing cows.
> 'Tis here the same; but in a higher sphere,
> For ev'n Court Ladies sin in open air.
> What Cit with a gallant would trust his spouse
> Beneath the tempting shade of *Greenwich* boughs?
> What Peer of *France* would let his Dutchess rove,
> Where *Boulogne's* closest woods invite to love?
> But here no wife can blast her husband's fame,
> Cuckold is grown an honourable name.
> Stretch'd on the grass the shepherd sighs his pain,
> And on the grass what shepherd sighs in vain?
> (101–16)

In an emphatically moral reading, S. M. Armens defines this pastoral as a 'social perversion', equating the defrauded cows with the defrauded husbands (*John Gay, Social Critic*, 1954, pp. 172–3). But decadence of this kind is beautiful and amusing as well as morally deplorable, and Gay is caught up in his fiction for its own sake as he experiments here with literary convention. Certainly we are meant to see that this sexual behaviour could be more harshly termed prostitution and adultery, and this appears as 'truth' on one level. Yet the fiction allows for a more complex truth, because Gay persuades us, if only momentarily, that the springtime does indeed metamorphose courtiers into shepherds, that Arcadia does border on the environs of London. Instead of town and country as moral opposites, nature herself bewilderingly turns temptress. Gay so phrases the love invitation as to go beyond the simple nostalgic appeal of spring pastoral to a jaded city: in fact, he alludes to another form of pastoral, not the one which Armens claims is perverted. When Armens writes about 'the debasement of country love, simplicity, and innocence by . . . hypercivilized shepherdesses' he idealizes and limits the genre almost as much as the neoclassical theorists. Here (as elsewhere) Gay seems if anything closer to the Caroline tradition than to the neoclassical. He alludes ironically and specifically to the conventions of *libertin* pastoral, casting the passage into the mould of a Golden Age set-piece extolling free love, but giving it a post-Dryden satiric overtone by locating his Golden Age historically and geographically. Compared with the past, the present age is crass in its regulation of such affairs, and Gay mimics this lapse of taste in a couplet bridging Caroline irony and Augustan satire:

> But since at Court the rural taste is lost,
> What mighty summs have velvet couches cost!
> (131–2)

He makes an interesting parallel use of the Golden Age convention, demonstrating clearly the art/nature link, in his 'Prologue Design'd for the Pastoral Tragedy of *Dione*':

> There was a time (Oh were those days renew'd!)
> Ere tyrant laws had woman's will subdu'd;
> Then nature rul'd, and love, devoid of art,
> Spoke the consenting language of the heart.
> (1–4)

Again, morality is not the whole truth: he undercuts this opening sentiment, which could have affinities with Tasso or with Guarini,[12] by mischievously suggesting that he prefers 'tyrant laws' because they add spice to love affairs:

> I envy not, ye nymphs, your am'rous bowers:
> Such harmless swains!—I'm ev'n content with ours.
> But yet there's something in these sylvan scenes
> That tells our fancy what the lover means . . .
> (13–6)

Indeed there is, and it goes far towards explaining our response to the Pulteney passage. Even granting the evident irony, it is hard to accept the single-minded view of Gay as Augustan moralist. A further indication of the extent to which the almost Caroline quality of his verse modifies its Augustanism is the gap between Gay's pastoral irony and Swift's. The couplet

> Stretch'd on the grass the shepherd sighs his pain,
> And on the grass what shepherd sighs in vain?

---

[12]cf. Tasso's *Aminta* (1573), Guarini's *Il Pastor Fido* (1589), and the conflicting *libertin* and moral versions of the Golden Age convention in seventeenth-century English poetry (for instance, Carew and Randolph provide examples of the former, and the earlier poet, William Browne, of the latter).

compares with Swift's

> *Corinna*, Pride of *Drury-Lane*,
> For whom no Shepherd sighs in vain.
> ('A Beautiful Young Nymph
> Going to Bed', 1–2)

But where Gay conveys his innuendo with finesse, leaving the pastoral art intact, Swift lays bare his meaning in a manner which defiles pastoral convention itself by association.

When Swift demolishes art, he does not spare—indeed he singles out—the fictions of poetry. In his descriptions of nymph-prostitutes, he literally strips down the image and forces us to watch it fall apart. But nature can provide no moral alternative to art, since pastoral nature is tainted by literary illusion, and what is natural to human beings, mentally and physically, is yet more deeply corrupt. Starting from these premises, however, Swift can still develop the conjunction of art, nature, and the nymph in a number of poems in order to make statements about what is true and what is delusion. One especially interesting example occurs at the end of 'The Lady's Dressing Room', where the poet offers an apparent compromise solution to the problem of how Strephon should sort out the confusion of art and nature, appearance and reality, sharply impressed upon him by Celia's squalor:

> When *Celia* in her Glory shows,
> If *Strephon* would but stop his Nose;
> (Who now so impiously blasphemes
> Her Ointments, Daubs, and Paints and Creams,
> Her Washes, Slops, and every Clout,
> With which he makes so foul a Rout;)
> He soon would learn to think like me,
> And bless his ravisht Eyes to see
> Such Order from Confusion sprung,
> Such gaudy Tulips rais'd from Dung.
>
> (133–42)

The speaker implicitly condemns both Strephon's original illusion and his violent disillusion as ferments of a diseased imagination, but his own insinuating answer is no less ironic, and no more tenable. He invites Strephon to learn to think like him, yet at a price, for in order to do so Strephon cannot afford to admit reality through all his senses: he must look and stop his nose, smell no evil so to speak. In place of suppressed imagination, the speaker voices a disillusioned intelligence, prepared to accept Celia's image for the artefact it is. Without the irony, the argument that art produces order from confusion would be a perfectly respectable philosophical and poetic proposition. But Swift has forced 'Confusion' upon the reader too intimately and menacingly in the whole poem for 'Order' to be anything other than an abstract and highly satiric compensation (he does not create Celia's 'Glory' for us as Pope does

Belinda's: the difference in strategy corresponds to a different conception of the theme). His actual rejection of the nature/art compromise is confirmed by the final image 'Such gaudy Tulips rais'd from Dung' and its fascinating, if minor, literary history. Since the 1630s, when tulips were the rage of Europe, poets commonly associated references to these flowers with a certain type of beauty flaunting itself in the eye of the beholder. In the context of art and nature, the cultivation of tulips (especially the flamboyant streaked varieties) signifies a triumph of art. Consequently, an aura of moral ambivalence clings to the lyric image of the tulip (as to Perdita's gilly-flowers in *The Winter's Tale*, IV iii) ironically like a fragrance that the flower itself does not possess. James Shirley exiles both tulips and women from his melancholy lovelorn garden:

> Those Tulips that such wealth display,
> To court my eye, shall lose their name,
> Though now they listen, as if they
> Expected I should praise their flame.
> (*The Cavalier Poets,* ed. R. Skelton,
> 1970, p. 233)

Marvell represents nature corrupted by art (with a side-glance at female cosmetics) in his more celebrated tulip image from 'The Mower against Gardens':

> The Tulip, white, did for complexion seek;
> And learn'd to interline its cheek.
> (*Poems & Letters,* ed. Margoliouth, i, 40)

And Cowley provides a conclusive seventeenth-century example, highly detrimental to female beauty and tulips:

> *Beauty,* Thou *active, passive* Ill!
> Which *dy'st* thy self as fast as thou dost *kill!*
> Thou *Tulip,* who thy stock in paint dost waste,
> Neither for *Physick* good, nor *Smell,* nor *Tast.*
> (*Poems of Abraham Cowley,* ed. A. R. Waller,
> 1905, p, 116)

Nor are the nuances lost upon an eighteenth-century poet and garden enthusiast: Pope shows that the image survives transplantation to a different kind of poetry—[13]

> Ladies, like variegated Tulips, show,
> 'Tis to their Changes that their charms they owe;
> Their happy Spots the nice admirer take,
> Fine by defect, and delicately weak.
> (*Epistles to Several Persons,* ed. F. W. Bateson,
> 1961, p. 53)

---

[13]Claude Rawson draws attention to Pope and Swift's tulip images in 'Order and Cruelty: a Reading of Swift (with some comments on Pope and Johnson)', *Essays in Criticism,* Jan. 1970 (above, pp. 29ff.).

It is not necessary to suppose that Swift must have known and modelled his allusion on specific earlier examples; those quoted simply prove how strong the combined associations are, how easily poets might come to see the tulip as the harlot of the garden. The image of 'gaudy Tulips' to represent woman's art and beauty is unlikely to have been chosen at random.

Swift is perhaps most dazzlingly subversive in exploiting the pastoral fiction of the nymph when he writes 'The Progress of Beauty' and 'A Beautiful Young Nymph Going to Bed'. The descriptions spark and flare into their own wildfire poetic logic, again forming a dialectic of art and nature. In effect, the earlier poem 'The Progress of Beauty' has a regressive structure: the poet's art fails when simple rearrangement makes a mockery of all his metaphors; the nymph's cosmetic repairs prove futile against natural deficiency—

> But, Art no longer can prevayl
> When the Materialls all are gone—

art, the poor mortar of crumbling nature, has nothing left to hold together. Paradoxically, however, Swift's art does 'prevayl' because it has the makings of myth. The symbolic identification of whore and moon is more than a neat ironic antithesis of poetic praises addressed to the virgin goddess.[14] Perhaps unexpectedly, the image probes a nerve, touches upon much older and deeper human fantasies expressed in nature myth. The link between the moon and female sexuality is the dark reverse of the bright chastity image, a source of fear and possible repulsion. When Swift works out the parallel between a syphilitic moon, gradually eaten away night by night, and rotting Celia strolling the street, he follows his customary stylistic practice which compounds what is comic and what is intolerable. As in *A Modest Proposal,* he releases the imagination's own sources of power, but, for once, it is a power also generated in traditional poetry and myth. Through the chosen fiction, 'The Progress of Beauty' insinuates what is imaginatively as well as morally 'true' about its subject.

The later poem 'A Beautiful Young Nymph Going to Bed' also cuts deep, since it starts from a familiar erotic situation which is both literary topic and personal fantasy. Again, however, Swift goes beyond simple parody. Geoffrey Hill expresses a commonly felt uneasiness about this poem when he remarks that 'it may seem that the superior intelligence can assert itself only by extravagant gestures of revulsion' (*The World of Jonathan Swift,* p. 207). Surely, however, (as his own penetrating analysis of the final lines would bear out) the chief gesture made by the superior intelligence is precisely the art of the poem. Swift organizes it meticulously through a controlling metaphor made literal, one of his most impressive techniques. Just as he developed the whore-moon parallel in 'The Progress of Beauty', so here he develops a dominant image of physical dissolution on this side of the grave, the nightmare of a human creature falling apart into the components of a hideous art form:

[14]cf. Kathleen Williams's assessment of this poem (*Jonathan Swift and the Age of Compromise,* 1958, p. 149).

> Then, seated on a three-legg'd Chair,
> Takes off her artificial Hair:
> Now, picking out a Crystal Eye,
> She wipes it clean, and lays it by.
> Her Eye-Brows from a Mouse's Hyde,
> Stuck on with Art on either Side,
> Pulls off with Care, and first displays 'em,
> Then in a Play-Book smoothly lays 'em.
>   (9–16)

Nature takes her revenge on the nymph both in the physical ravages she suffers, and in the grotesque mauling of her property by the creatures. In the morning, Corinna must recreate her image—

> But how shall I describe her Arts
> To recollect the scatter'd Parts?
>   (67–8)

So the poet says, intimating that he and his 'bashful Muse' must withdraw; and by this point, the reader is only too ready to welcome the withdrawal as a heavily ironic concession to sensibility. But in fact, this attitude dovetails into the logic of the poem, and indeed of Swift's general treatment of art and the nymph. If the satiric poet's function is to strip the nymph-prostitute of the image which she creates for herself or which society and literature pervertedly apply to her, then the controlling metaphor in 'A Beautiful Young Nymph' exactly corresponds to this intention and theme. Swift ruthlessly takes apart Corinna's image in the going to bed sequence: he cannot participate as poet in the process of rebuilding this image. The poem as it stands is his creation set against hers; and for the poem—if not for its nymph heroine—the whole is more than the sum of the parts.

To return then to the initial question of how Gay and Swift differ in manipulating fiction and truth, and whether or not they are 'True Poets' according to Swift's definition: neither is as simple a case as the definition implies. For Gay, theatrical and pastoral illusions are—to adapt a phrase from Marianne Moore—like imaginary gardens inhabited by real toads. At his best, he solves the problem of truth and fiction, not by discrediting fiction but by exaggerating it to a point where we are forced to make comparisons with reality, as when he holds the deliberately framed fairytale ending of *The Beggar's Opera* against a known and real Tyburn. Swift, on the other hand, does not hesitate to debase fiction in the name of truth. Yet 'truth' in his poems is not therefore independent of fiction, a straight synonym for reality. If it were, we might argue, he would not be writing verse at all. However wary he may be of the power of poetry as an equivalent of private fantasy, reinforcing certain sexual images, for example, and repressing others, it is this same power that he harnesses as a destructive counter-force in his nymph poems. Where truth and nature *are* to be found, in the Stella poems, he uses fiction as a context, a test of their mutual integrity: the worth of human personality is weighed by plain statement, and truth shines the better in verse

which does not shine. And so in one of the birthday poems (1721) he tosses away
'Art or Time or Nature' as sops to the women who attempt to bribe this tyran-
nous triumvirate. For Stella such propitiation is needless, just as for her poet 'all
the Commonplaces / Worn out by Wits who rhyme on Faces' are eminently dispensable.

Both Gay and Swift make original poetry out of the nymph fiction because
they have the wit to see how, in conjunction with the concepts of art and nature,
this convention can relate to ultimately serious themes. But it must be said that
satire against the nymphs, like the antecedent pastoral convention, is all too easily trivialized by lesser talents. When this happens, the poets level meaningless
infamy with meaningless praise, and are lords no longer. Nevertheless the
theme, in one or other of its forms, continues to attract major artists. Yeats's version in *A Woman Young and Old*, which might stand as a splendid lyrical riposte
to Swift's satire, despite its totally different philosophical basis, further proves
the intellectual and imaginative vitality of the subject:

> If I make the lashes dark
> And the eyes more bright
> And the lips more scarlet,
> Or ask if all be right
> From mirror after mirror,
> No vanity's displayed:
> I'm looking for the face I had
> Before the world was made.

Swift as Lyricist:
The Poems to Stella and His Career
in Satire

Richard Feingold

No artist is more playful than Jonathan Swift, and no criticism more suited to his play than ours. He toys with and devastates meaning; we can at least understand the design of the assault. Our critical poise, moreover, is accompanied by a social one. Not like William Thackeray, fulminating in wonder at the human monstrosity of Swift, we can speak more easily of him even as we see as deeply into the horror managed by his play. As teachers, surely, more of us have encouraged our students to see the Swiftian worst than have advised them to spare themselves the experience.[1]

Certainly the Swiftian worst is a sublime cultural possession: Swift is a giant because he has defined a human possibility we might otherwise not have known. No other art springs so directly from the energies of hate as does his; no other art has, with hatred for its spring, revealed so much of reality. And no other artist has, with so small an estimate of the value of his enterprise and the worth of his audience, still urged himself toward the attention of the race. To accumulate these negative superlatives is to approach a judgment and a definition of Swift's achievement and of its anomalous character. Where could we find, until near our own time, a theory of art which could explain his imagination, which did not centrally affirm art as the work or the product of mankind's positive energies? And when was the pressure of this prejudice more heavily felt than by artists of Swift's own time, indeed, by Swift himself? The central judicial task of Swift's critics, therefore, will always be to explicate and insist upon the Swiftian worst even as they permit the pressure of positive ideas appropriate play in shaping their judgments. And the critical success we have been having with Swift is certainly explicable by the habitual poise we command as critics nowadays, poise

From Richard Feingold, *Moralized Song: The Character of Augustan Lyricism* (New Brunswick and London: Rutgers University Press, 1989), 52–93. Copyright © 1989 by Rutgers, The State University. Reprinted by permission of the author and the Rutgers University Press.

[1]Not so Thackeray to the audience for his lecture on Swift; to those in it fortunate enough not to have read the fourth voyage "I would recall the advice of the venerable Mr. Punch to persons about to marry, and say 'Don't.' " Excerpted in *Discussions of Jonathan Swift*, ed. J. L. Traugott (Boston: Heath, 1962), p. 19, from Thackeray's lecture in *The English Humorists of the Eighteenth Century*.

being essential to so delicate a management of worst and best as Swift demands. In our poise we can communicate at least *something* and come through such cognitive devastation as the digression on madness or the fourth voyage, not unscarred, but certainly not incapable of speech. We can follow the devastation of argument which *is* Swift's argument and acknowledge, for instance, the hatred of the poor issuing in the details of the Irish feast. Swift did not love those he labored for and to see his hatred still produce such strenuous moral exertion is indeed an experience we are enriched by, a human possibility we might not, by ourselves, have guessed at.

But poise may protect too well against the occasionally valuable benefits of misunderstanding. Johnson, for example, was plainly unsettled by Swift, and his discomfort led him to some illuminating misjudgments. Johnson's estimate of Swift's achievement was, of all things, that he mastered a style whose strength was the "safe and easy conveyance of meaning."[2] It is no wonder to us that Johnson, thinking that, would have to retreat in confused irritation from those features of Swift's work which are neither safe nor easy. Only in the last paragraph of criticism proper in his life of Swift does Johnson raise an issue he does not mean to pursue: "The greatest difficulty that occurs in analyzing his character, is to discover by what depravity of intellect he took delight in revolving ideas, from which almost every other mind shrinks with disgust . . . what has disease, deformity, and filth, upon which the thoughts can be allured to dwell?"[3] It is to Johnson's credit that even in his irritation he could recognize—the words "delight," "revolving," and "allured" prove it—the obsessiveness that springs forth in the characteristic Swiftian play. Sensing the obsessiveness and the allurement and the delight that Swift released and experienced, Johnson could not integrate such a perception into his judgment of Swift's achievement. The safe and easy conveyor of meaning becomes a mystery as a man, and Johnson speaks of Swift's character rather than his work when he confesses his bewilderment at the most characteristic feature of the work. So Johnson gives us a master of didactic style and a monstrosity of a man—one who took delight in what "almost every other mind shrinks [from] with disgust." Our criticism, on the other hand, more successfully brings together the two. To us, Swift is a safe and easy conveyor of meaning least of all—he is an anarchic, aggressive assaulter of it. And for us, the value of his art is precisely that, the release it provides through play of what we all shrink from with disgust and fear.[4]

[2]Samuel Johnson, "Swift," *Lives of the Poets*, ed. G. B. Hill, 3 vols. (Oxford: Clarendon, 1905), 3:52.
[3]Ibid., p. 62.
[4]A good example of our poise and its useful results is A. E. Dyson's excellent definition of the value to us of an art as playful and as subversive in its play as Swift's: "On a final balance, I fancy that we have to compromise: agreeing that *Gulliver* ends by destroying all its supposed positives, but deducing, from the exuberance of the style and the fact that it was written at all, that Swift did not really end in Gulliver's position . . . he always . . . enjoyed the technique of irony itself, both as an intellectual game, and as a guarantee of at least some civilized reality. Very often, even at the most intense moments, we may feel that pleasure in the intellectual destructiveness of the wit is of more importance to him than the moral purpose, or the misanthropy that is its supposed *raison d'être*. Irony, by its very nature, instructs by pleasing: and to ignore the pleasure, and its civilized implications, is inevitably to

And yet Swift would have valued Johnson's judicious approval could he have won it. Swift, for whom poise was always suspect, for whom poise and complacency were difficult to distinguish, would have honored the moral intelligence that could not stand gracefully before games as dangerous as he played. Poise before such games, such disfigurations of meaning, risks being no more than the bland sophistication Swift hated in the human race above all else. What is the target of his *Modest Proposal* if not poise—the social poise that can accept the sight of the poor and the literary poise that can discover the *Proposal's* joke. The two kinds can be the same, and John Traugott is right to say that the joke is on the reader who too quickly catches the joke of the *Proposal*—or who sees a joke in it at all.[5] If we consider that depopulation, either through celibacy, famine, or emigration, *has been* the historical politics of Irish poverty, we can sense the rightness of Traugott's judgment and the seriousness of Swift's proposal, his joke that is no joke at all. And if we consider that in writing down dreadful things there may be more strain than in doing them, we can recognize, beyond the positive intentions of the *Proposal,* the furious personal energy that seethed in ambiguous bondage to them. Swift must have hated the poor for the spectacle they presented; violent, filthy, promiscuous, abject—the poor of the *Proposal* are among his most horrific images of humanity, images that tell us how insulted he must have been by his daily sight of them, and may explain his detailed imagining of the uses to which their flesh could answer. In that imagination we should sense the desire. In this respect the *Proposal* is a great fiction as Plato understood fiction, the medium in which a mime becomes anything he wishes: thunder, wind, a wheel, a pulley, a dog, sheep, a cock, or, in this case, a murderer.[6]

Plato, who admired the safe and easy conveyance of meaning, despised the pantomimic gentleman. The trouble with him is that he does not speak in one voice—he has too much personality and not enough character for that; he needs

oversimplify, and falsify the total effect" ("Swift: The Metamorphosis of Irony," *Essays and Studies,* n. s. 11 [1958]: 67). The escape route here, of course, is quite properly Swift's artistry, and Dyson's judgment is in accord with Irvin Ehrenpreis's characterization of Robert C. Elliott's argument in *The Power of Satire* (Princeton: Princeton Univ. Press, 1960): "the element of satire which belongs to imaginative literature is the element that invites not action but contemplation" (*Swift: The Man, His Works and the Age,* 3 vols. [London: Methuen, 1962–1983], 2 [1967]: 295). John Traugott's studies of Swift have all emphasized the increment of consciousness which Swift's irony yields, but Traugott is especially alert to the danger of Swift's games. "Irony asks to be saved from itself by an arbitrarily imposed 'stop' . . . [but] the peculiar quality of Swift's irony is that he does not impose a stop." Instead he gives us laughter. "The terminal thing for Swift is a joke to remind us that though our case is hopeless we are alive. The jokes about Gulliver's stable-pleasures put to rout all philosophical instabilities that have to do with hatred of the Yahoo and love of the Houyhnhnm. It is a characteristic end-game, a trick, a feat of aesthetic legerdemain, not a faith. We need not forget to be" ("Gulliver in the Doll's House: *Gulliver's Travels* the Children's Classic," *Yearbook of English Studies,* 14 [1984]: 148).

[5]John Traugott, "Swift's Allegory: The Yahoo as Man of Mode," *Univ. of Toronto Quarterly*, 33 1 (Oct. 1963): 5.

[6]"For every Whig or Tory exterminator and every modest proposer that Swift invents and exposes, there is counterbalancing evidence of a primary Swiftian feeling which is unsettlingly similar, a Kurtz-like underside . . . wishing extermination, now of 'all the brutes,' now of selected types" (C. J. Rawson, "Nature's Dance of Death: Part I: Urbanity and Strain in Fielding, Swift and Pope," *ECS,* 3 [Spring 1970]: 317).

to be too many people. Art is his way of giving each part of him, whatever its value, its play. For Plato the process is destructive of meaning, whatever other worth it may have. And Swift's *Proposal* can stand as an example of this, for how can we speak of the meaning of that assault upon meaning: the joke that is no joke, the murderer's hatred disguising itself in the moralist's zeal, and the other way around. The *Proposal* is Swift's way of being several of the people he was, and Johnson's praise for his style—"that he always understands himself, and his reader always understands him"—seems especially wrong, though consistent with his other judgment about Swift's safe and easy conveyance of meaning.

But again, Swift would have wished to deserve this praise. For, whatever direction he finally takes, whatever energies he finally releases, whatever meanings he ultimately destroys, his art derives its peculiar character from what must have been his haunting wish that meaning—direct, pure, true—might still be known and communicated among human creatures.[7] Swift's way of imagining virtue was to imagine a time or place or condition that was safe and easy for the conveyance of meaning. It was his favorite fantasy and can be seen in the pattern of his production. The meaning he assaults in *A Modest Proposal*, he asserts in *The Drapier's Letters*; the church he takes down in *An Argument against Abolishing Christianity*, he justifies in *The Sentiments of a Church of England Man*. Each of the "satires" is a kind of companion piece to a "straight" piece, indistinguishable in its superficial stylistic character (so well described by Johnson) from the other. *The Drapier's Letters* presume a community that can be directly addressed: "Brethren, Friends, Countrymen and Fellow Subjects." "I will therefore first tell you the plain Story of the Fact." "But a Word to the Wise is Enough." "When once the Kingdom is reduced to such a Condition, I will tell you what must be the End." "Therefore my Friends, stand to it One and All, refuse this Filthy Trash."[8] Here there is no play, and perhaps, little opportunity for explication. This style of the Drapier is the style of the Dean, nor was there any desire for that identity to be a subject for playful speculation. Assertiveness is the style, didactic authority (not down-home plainness) the stance, just as in the sermons, in which we can hear the same ring: preaching on the Trinity, Swift says of his style and of his subject, "I hope to handle it in such a Manner, that the most ignorant among you may return Home better informed of your Duty in this great Point, than probably you are at present."[9]

---

[7]The dark side of this positive fantasy was, of course, clear to Swift; he reveals it in the questions he raises but does not bother to answer. Gulliver may be obtuse and evil when he attributes the giant king's horror at gunpowder to narrow principles and short views but, as Traugott asks, "Eschewing force, how did the King establish his rule of the Good, [and] maintain it? How is a lawyer to be kept to one interpretation of the law? Following Platonic utopias, the citizens presumably simply love the Good once they see it. But also following Platonic utopia, those who have not eyes to see are eliminated" as is demonstrated by the "chill and master-race eugenics of the Houyhnhnms or the genocide in store for the Yahoos" (pp. 147, 149).

[8]*The Drapier's Letters and Other Works*, ed. Herbert Davis, The Shakespeare-head edition of Swift's *Prose Works*, 14 vols. (Oxford: Blackwell, 1939–1968), 10: 3, 4, 5, 7, 11. Subsequent references to this volume and others in this edition are cited as *Prose Works*.

[9]*Prose Works*, 9:159.

This is language without play, the language of character—wise, authoritative, socially and intellectually stable—not the release of personality. It conveys meaning safely, easily, and confidently. "I will tell you" is the characteristic configuration. It is, as Plato would have approved, the language of the speaker's single self. More, the integrity of that self is a function of the presumed integrity and coherence of its audience.

"Brethren, Friends, Countrymen, and Fellow Subjects," this salutation to the readers of *The Drapier's Letters* defines an audience for the style Johnson said was Swift's special achievement, an audience to whom meaning could be safely and easily conveyed. It is also an audience before whom, as Plato preferred, a writer could speak in his own voice, be his sole self. Such an audience is open to didactic address because between it and the writer language is a common ground. A word to the wise is enough when words are not tricks, when the writer understands himself and is therefore understood by the reader. To take the didactic stance before such an audience is to join with them, to direct their attention to common beliefs, shared positives: to instruct is only to remind and almost to celebrate. In the program and pattern of Swift's writing he regularly takes the didactic stance, pursues a didactic intention, presuming to teach or remind, all on the assumption that between him and his reader meaning can be clear and easy.

If we ask, then, what distinguishes the great satires from the didactic and straight, purposeful pamphlets, one way to answer would be to say that the satires only imitate didactic manner, only pretend to speak to a good audience, only pretend to arise from the cognitively fruitful opportunity that such an audience provides. The great satires become in effect fictions whose central subject is the absence of the good audience, the consequent devastation of cognitive opportunity and the anarchy of language. A notorious sentence from *A Modest Proposal* can stand as an example: "But I am not in the least Pain upon that Matter; because it is very well known that [the poor, aged, diseased and maimed] are every Day *dying*, and *rotting*, by *Cold* and *Famine*, and *Filth*, and *Vermin*, as fast as can be reasonably expected."[10] This sentence is the speaker's answer to a request that he instruct the populace on the welfare of the aged and the sick, but its true subject is the revised meaning of the words "Pain" and "reasonably," or, more accurately, their meaninglessness. And the pamphlet as a whole is about the revised meaning, or the meaninglessness, of the Irish nation and community. In the vicinity of the butcher's stall, who is an Irishman? What is an Irishman? Is the question real, and with what resources of language can an answer now be even contemplated? The pamphlet becomes an imitation of a world and a state of mind whose linguistic experience is only prattle because its ostensible debates must be conducted with words that have no moral meaning— nation, Irishman, man, reason. If what distinguishes Swift's satiric art from his didactic polemic is irony, then his irony might be described as the inevitable

---

[10]*Prose Works*, 12:114.

result of meaning's decay. Irony is what we perceive as meaning when once the communal conditions for direct cognitive interchange have been lost.

What kind of meaning survives in Swift's irony, then? It is the kind of meaning art has.[11] Swift's irony is not the eloquent medium of his didactic purpose, although it arises in works whose strategy is to imitate the appearance of such purpose. It is instead the vehicle that transforms this ostensible end into the less immediately utilitarian processes of art. *A Modest Proposal* becomes, through its irony, not the agent of the author's reforming zeal, but rather the expression of his insight into the moral shapelessness of a world beyond reform. In this sense too the *Proposal* is less a satire (in Swift's own reformist's sense of satire) than a fiction, a self-enclosed poetic whole in which language is freed for play, the self-referential play possible where ordinary words are freed from the ordinary constraints and references by which they ordinarily take on meaning. Freed in this way, language may become as in poetry the vehicle of the most devastating inquiry into ordinary meaning. Whereas the initial utilitarian or reformist purposes of the *Proposal* may be, like those of *The Drapier's Letters,* based upon the values of community, patriotism, and reason, the artistic *effect* of the *Proposal* is to raise the most radical questions about those very positives. Are they real or illusory? Are they effective standards of conduct, rooted in experience, or are they instead the self-serving illusions by which human creatures indulge a pleasing complacency, sweetening their fantasies of what they are? The chill in the proposer's view of the aged and the maimed is generated by his play with the word "reasonable" in a way that excludes from it any overtone of "humane." The effect is double. It clarifies the richness of a lost usage by defining the values that healthy custom and healthy intellect have concentrated into the key words of a culture. "Reasonable" can be understood in its rich complexity as a lost concept, once encompassing "humane" in contrast to the proposer's implied simpler definition: "statistical." But at the same time, in its capacity as a fiction whose mimetic subject is a ruined culture, the *Proposal* tests that lost usage, toys with it, measures it against the facts of actual behavior, so that it becomes not so much the standard against which aberrant behavior is measured but rather the subject of a test for which aberrant behavior has become the measure. As a reformist's polemic, the *Proposal* vexes its readers by inviting them first to identify with the proposer, an irretrievable misstep, then to dissociate themselves from him; they may dissociate themselves from him by exclaiming "No, what you say is detestable, unreasonable, it is inhumane." But

---

[11]Edward Said argued that Swift's intentionally "literary" writing was less significant to him than the work he did in service to the Tory ministry. Said speaks of Swift's purely literary writing as "indicting itself in his mind for being an appendage to reality. . . . Correct writing for Swift did not merely conform to reality. . . . It was reality . . . an event necessitated by other events. . . . The Tory policy Swift supported and wrote about was policy in the world of actuality: the Whig opposition was projection, mere scribbling. . . . After 1714, Swift occupied no place except as outsider. . . . He had become the scribbler and projector he had once impersonated and attacked" ("Swift's Tory Anarchy," *ECS,* 3/1 (Fall 1969): 48, 54, 56–57). Following Said, it seems to me that Swift's overtly didactic writing, as in the sermons and *The Drapier's Letters*, would conform to his sense of what correct, ethical, and authentic expression could be.

this is to invoke precisely those concepts and that once rich usage which do not pass the test of actual behavior. The polemical purpose is superseded in this way as the *Proposal* proceeds to demonstrate the self-serving nature of our best words, the way they help us to dissociate ourselves from a project so exactly framed on our actual behavior. And in doing so it raises radical and subversive questions about the very positives we invoke when our actual behavior is challenged. Community, reason, humanity—they may survive Swift's scrutiny as speculative possibilities, but they do not survive intact as moral ideas that function feelingly in actual life. There they function as self-serving illusions of indistinct value, not guiding actual behavior but screening it. Because a satisfactory answer, based upon our actual behavior, to the question, "Why not eat the children?" is not possible for Swift's audience, the relevance to human life of man's moral ideas—his positives—is not clear. And A *Modest Proposal*, in so vexing its reader, ceases to function as a reformist document and becomes the fiction it is—the mimetic presentation of a world foundering without meaning, and of the quality of mind and feeling dominating such a world of cognitive disarray.

In *An Argument against Abolishing Christianity* the same dynamics are at work. This piece bears a relationship to *The Sentiments of a Church of England Man* similar to that between *A Modest Proposal* and *The Drapier's Letters*. The rational compromise supported in *Sentiments* becomes the nominal Christianity of *An Argument*, and once again "our actual behavior" becomes the subject of a fictional presentation, the actual behavior of a people subsisting upon the shards of indistinct custom and belief. But the edge of this piece is threateningly sharp. The nominal Christian or nominal Christianity is not so much the object of its polemical attack; instead, the phenomenon of "nominality" itself is the subject of its piercing inquiry. Issuing from Swift's involvement with the politics of the First Fruits and the Test Act, and probably initially intended to advance the same polemical ends as the later *Sentiments of a Church of England Man*, *An Argument* develops in oblique relation to the position of that moderate document. For, after all, despite the argumentative subtlety, despite the skill with which it preserves its appearance as a conciliatory document even as it acts to trap the dissenting party, *The Sentiments* advances a moderate's position, and demonstrates the polemical functioning of a moderate position against those who favor repeal. But in the *Argument* Swift seems to be examining the meaning and value of moderation itself, that is, the meaning and value of *any* religious settlement whose virtue is that it *can* stand as conformable with the needs of a political settlement. Moderation in *Sentiments* is "nominalism" in *An Argument*, and matters that are of casual concern in *The Sentiments* therefore become central in *An Argument*.[12] In *The Sentiments*, the writer can admit,

[12]Rawson comments that even the "Church of England man, an unusually sustained portrait of virtuous moderation . . . becomes at moments which are kindled by a real Swiftian intensity, a faintly unreal figure. And Swift's most powerfully realized moderates are not virtuous, but calm upholders of the world's wickedness, modestly proposing a nominal Christianity, or mass murder. Behind them stands a Swift whose more absolute moral denunciations . . . turn indistinct under strange pressures of self-implication and self-concealment" (p. 320).

as if to show his fairness, that "in the lists of the National Church," are many who by their behavior, writings, and conversation show that they need reminding that they "ought to believe a God and his Providence, together with revealed Religion and the Divinity of Christ."[13] But in *An Argument* this marginal belief of the Church-of-England man himself is the central source of the irony. In *The Sentiments* Swift notes that it "makes an odd sound" to advance the apparently minimal stipulation that the Anglican should be a believer, but in the *Argument* that odd sound and all its overtones ring through the piece. *An Argument* is no longer a defense of a reasonable religious and political compromise; it is rather about the spiritual meanness of such compromise and the meanness of institutions that make it possible. For the minimal demands of Occasional Conformity, understood as a virtue of the religious and political settlement praised in *The Sentiments,* are the very substance of the nominal Christianity that is the subject of *An Argument.* In this piece Swift has represented a situation that works: this is the speaker's central point, and Swift's goad. In this state of affairs the Sacramental Test and the practice of Occasional Conformity are identified with the Christian religion itself. In this politico-spiritual warp where Occasional Conformity sounds in our ears like casual Christianity, it becomes indeed conceivable that the Church can survive the abolition of its own proper foundation. That the abolition of Christianity only *may* put the Church in some danger is the possibility Swift sees into, a possibility that opens the subversive, generalized inquiry into the connection between spiritual ends and political means that the *Argument* in fact is. It is the very usefulness of a church, its undisturbing support of ordinary life, that enrages the writer we sense behind the speaker.

In this way *An Argument* probes the implications of "the settlement" celebrated in *The Sentiments,* probes them to raise questions not only about "the settlement," but about settlement in general. Swift does this simply by introducing into *An Argument* the notion of nominal Christianity, distinguishing the nominal from the primitive—that is, the true—version, and demonstrating the compatibility among the present settlement, current life, and nominal observance. The very Test Act that he labors for in his straight polemic he recognizes here as a support for a church whose connection with the Christian religion can be, for all essential purposes, accidental rather than necessary. He assures his readership that he is not

> so weak [as] to stand up in the Defence of *real* Christianity such as used in primitive Times . . . to have an influence upon Men's belief and Actions: to offer at the Restoring of that would indeed be a wild Project; it would be to dig up Foundations; to destroy at one Blow *all* the wit, and *half* the Learning of the Kingdom; to break the entire Frame and Constitution of Things; to ruin Trade, extinguish Arts and Sciences with the Professors of them; in short, to turn our Courts, Exchanges, and Shops into Deserts. . . . Therefore I think this Caution was in itself altogether unnecessary . . . since every candid Reader will easily understand my Discourse to be intended only in

[13]*Prose Works,* 2:4.

Defence of *nominal* Christianity; the other having been for some Time wholly laid aside by general Consent, as utterly inconsistent with our present schemes of Wealth and Power.[14]

As in *A Modest Proposal*, the joke here may well be on the reader who too quickly perceives this declaration as a joke. Actually, what has happened is that the attitude of "low-norm" satire (to use Northrop Frye's terms) in which Swift puts forth his defense of the settlement, has been simultaneously scrutinized from the perspective of high norms, of primitive, or real, Christianity.[15] From this perspective, such practices as occasional conformity and such acts as the Sacramental Test must themselves appear as shrewd compromises, wholly in accord with "our present schemes of wealth and power," which now emerge as the effective norms according to which a society judges and values its first things. This conclusion seems fairly to be drawn from the demonstration that the abolition of nominal Christianity only *may* put the Church in some danger. We can imagine Swift in writing *An Argument* warming toward that demonstration, seeing keenly and suddenly into the absolute incompatibility of true religion and any politics, and losing himself as a "low-norm" polemicist as he discovers himself as a high-norm satirist, a satirist who sees that the Church, its Test Act, and its dependence upon occasional conformity are all instruments of politics only, useful to civil society only insofar as they do not disturb its real business. In its furthest implications, *An Argument* is nothing less than a subversive inquiry into the general relations between spiritual and secular experience, advancing the most disturbing suggestions about people's efforts to seek institutional expression for their spiritual nature. The polemical Swift, to be sure, would define a healthy society as one that had met with some degree of honest success in discovering such a settlement. The satirical Swift sees in the effort only a prostitution—at best a compromise—of humanity's spiritual life, its first things. The mind that imagined nominal Christianity hated the Church, hated all churches, as mere instruments of nominality.[16]

[14]Ibid., pp. 27–28.

[15]Northrop Frye, *Anatomy of Criticism* (Princeton: Princeton Univ. Press, 1957), pp. 226, 234.

[16]Ehrenpreis's is the most comprehensive account we have of the *Argument*, discussing at length the difficult ironies of its endorsement of hypocrisy: "Swift cannot mean simply that it is absurd for men to keep the name when the thing it designates is gone; for in his scheme, nominal Christianity is parallel to the nominal communion demanded of officeholders by the Test Act; and we can be certain that the author wishes to defend the act. On the other hand, not only do we not like to suppose that he is counselling hypocrisy, but also we can hardly interpret the bitterly ironical style of the pseudo-defense, throughout the essay, as expressing anything but a ferocious derogation of *nominal* Christianity as contrasted with *real*." Ehrenpreis seeks to solve this dilemma by "looking into history," and recording that at the time of the writing of *An Argument against Abolishing Christianity* there were those "who felt indignant at the perversion of the sacrament" entailed in "occasional conformity," who "agitated for passage of the bill against occasional conformity," but who, "while they awaited this consummation, . . . felt no impulse to relax the law already in operation." In the terms of the *Argument* these were the "real Christians" to whom Swift appealed: they had no respect for nominal Christianity but they did not "see how its mere abolition 'unmitigated' by some form of coercive invigilation [could] do other than weaken the real institution" (2:282–284).

The special intensity of Swift's satiric art derives then from its unsettling movement toward possibilities whose radical and subversive character are out of kilter with the initially conservative pretensions of his didactic or polemical purpose. In this movement both Swift and his reader gain a kind of freedom, the freedom that distinguishes the poet from the rhetorician, the poet's reader from the rhetorician's audience. We move from a persuasive mode confident in its possession of utilitarian meaning to a mode that works to free meaning from any obligation to issue in action or decision. The only obligation of Swift's reader is to engage in the play against meaning now freed by his ironic art: we can surface from the *Proposal,* or the *Argument,* only as darkly delighted questioners, enjoying our freedom from certainty. Neither our assumptions about the humane and rational foundations of human community, nor an earlier audience's convictions about the Sacramental Test and the establishment that depends upon it, can have simply survived the play against meaning set loose in those pieces. This is the vexation Swift intends for the world, but in the freedom that accompanies it there is an increment of delight.

Swift's irony is both the agent and the effect of his shift from a didactic purpose to the satirical freedom that can trace down the fullest implications of such ideas as infanticide and nominal Christianity. But to take on the freedom of the ironic mode, though it yields its increment of delight, has costs of its own. One of these is the identity Swift loved to think of as his, the character of the Dean and patriot, the community leader, acknowledged as such and well beloved. "The Dean and his Merits we everyone know, / But this skip of a lawyer, where the De'il did he grow," he writes in an obscure broadside against a minor antagonist in some local affair.[17] But the broadside celebrates the pledge of some of his parishioners to protect him against his enemy, Sergeant-at-Law Richard Bettesworth, who had threatened to beat Swift for some lampoon the Dean had written against him. It is an obscure incident, played out in the dimness of Swift's last active years in Dublin, when his battles were mainly local, though consistent with those he had fought years earlier. But for all its obscurity, that Swift should occupy himself with a broadside celebrating a pledge of protection from a self-constituted neighborhood posse is noteworthy. "The Dean and his Merits we everyone know," he has them say of themselves. That is, he has them celebrate his own character, his well-established identity as Dean, with all its well-established merits. This portion of his

---

But it is not clear to me that this appeal to history for a solution to the "problem" of the *Argument* does anything but restate that problem. For there is no "solution" to be sought, no argument to be unraveled. In the satire Swift allows himself the freedom of his own deepest disdain for the institution he is committed to defending. The piece is remarkable because it can express also his contempt for (what he represents as) the debased and cowardly sophistication—the "radical chic"—of the Church's opponents. *An Argument against Abolishing Christianity* is, after all, not a problem to be solved. It is a great fiction about the shattering of a traditional culture, and its power is not in the convolutions of its argument in favor of hypocrisy, or even in the exuberance of its comic satire, but rather in its wide-ranging and freely distributed contempt for what is destroyed as well as for the destroyers.

[17]"The Yahoo's Overthrow" (1733–1734) in *The Poems of Jonathan Swift,* ed. Harold Williams, 2d ed., 3 vols. (Oxford: Clarendon, 1958), 3:814–817. Subsequent references to Swift's poems are to this edition and are cited by volume and page, where needed, and by line numbers.

identity, his public character, is sufficient authority for didactic and polemical address, even for furious invective. In *The Legion Club* for example—as furious an invective as any—Swift brings himself into the poem as a confidant of the keeper of the madhouse, Ireland's parliament, and as he releases a torrent of abuse, naming all his enemies, and directing the keeper to "Lash them daily, lash them duly"—he invokes, as the authority for his invective, his character as poet and patriotic philanthropist. The *Verses on the Death of Dr. Swift, D.S.P.D.* provides the best example of his cherishing that public character. To "One quite indiff'rent in the Cause" he assigns the job of summing it up; the details are familiar:

> "Fair liberty was all his Cry;
> For her he stood prepar'd to die;
> For her he boldly stood alone;
> For her he oft expos'd his Own.
> Two kingdoms, just as Factions led,
> Had set a price upon his Head;
> But, not a Traytor could be found
> To sell him for six hundred Pound."
>   [2:347–354]

But there are inaccuracies in this well-deserved panegyric. They have to do with his career in satire and are an index to his awareness that that career stood in uneasy relation to the character he wished to claim as his identity:

> Yet Malice never was his Aim;
> He lash'd the Vice, but spar'd the Name . . .
> His Satyr points at no Defect,
> But what all Mortals may correct . . .
>   [458–60, 463–464]

What, if not a universal malice, is the spur of Swift's most intriguing art? How many names did he spare, and which defects intrigued him more than those that were beyond correction—finally the smell and look of humanity itself?

In this very engagement with defects beyond correction Swift's cherished character fails him. Dealing with those matters upon which his thoughts were "allured to dwell," those matters "from which almost every other mind shrinks with disgust," was for him beyond the range of expression available to his public character. Invective, polemical rhetoric, didactic persuasion, the arts that assume a bond between audience and writer and are the expression of an integral and single self, knowing the strength of its own virtue, and reminding its audience of its own—these arts were insufficient to his allurement with ideas and feelings from which his did not, like "almost every other mind," shrink. His mind expanded into its greatest imaginative richness in its obsessive play beyond the frontiers of normal human concern.

Beyond those frontiers the force of character yields to the play of a personality whose stylistic agent is that vexatious irony we recognize as peculiarly Swift's and whose effect is the devastation, not, as in invective or persuasion, the assertion of utilitarian meaning. Everything that Swift so proudly claims in the signature, "D.S.P.D.," as in the verses on his own death and in his epitaph, becomes itself vulnerable to his personality's play. So *An Argument against Abolishing Christianity* releases those parts of his being which must have hated the church establishment he labored for in his public character—the establishment that depended upon occasional conformity and stood as the signature of political settlement. So *A Modest Proposal* releases as much hatred for the poor as labor for them—the brutalizers of their wives, the willing proprietors of butchers' stalls, which, we are reminded, "will not be wanting." All the interpretive difficulties these works create are a function of the play of personality against character, of passions released against meanings intended, of art's freedom against rhetoric's utility. Nor are these interpretive difficulties to be resolved: these works contain no "persona" whose consistent voice can be our key, only the constant play against one another of the author's character and his personalities, of that part of him that would speak in the single voice of virtue against those elements of his being all clamoring for recognition against it. For this reason the modest proposer can warn us against reminding him of virtuous alternatives: he knows them, for he is Swift, the statesman. But Swift the statesman is also the Swift who, in despair of virtuous statecraft, hated the race that proved itself incapable of it—the bestial poor and the unspeakable rich—and envisioned in that despair what every other mind shrinks from—the sight of human community in a butcher's stall, the sight that by itself denies the utilitarian meaning that alone can stand as an answer to the proposer's project. So it is that even the most furious of Swift's invective—which always issues from his character and assumes a bond with his audience—is not half so piercing as his irony, the agent and the sign of his break with all community and the release of all that was most peculiarly and most intensely his own.

The art that releases all that is most peculiarly and intensely Swift's own is tricky, playful, subtle. Its spring is in those elements of his being which played under the surface of his character and which his character would judge detestable. To the Dean and Drapier, this art of voices must have been as suspect as it was to Plato, who rejected the drama because its art speaks in a multiplicity of voices in which the playwright's own authentic and integral self is lost. Dr. Johnson's inability to integrate his sense of the most peculiar characteristic of Swift's mind—his obsession with disease, deformity, and filth—with his definition of the most distinctive quality of Swift's didactic style probably has a similar foundation. Johnson did not value art for its ability to offer surrogate experience for parts of our being we ordinarily deny; art's value, to him, was the help it could afford us in our efforts to recognize and energize our best self, the self of our moral consciousness. The Dean and Drapier sympathized with such attitudes. We can hear their ring throughout his work in a hatred of cleverness, subtlety, complication, and deviousness—in the admiration for the celebrative simplicity of the Houyhnhnms' poetry, in his approval of the minimal libraries of the giants, in his detestation of "the Free-Thinkers, the strong Reasoners, and Men of profound Learning." Much in Swift detests the playful intelligence that is a source of all irony and much art.

Our tendency today would be to attribute the virtue of authenticity to the art which releases the undersurface of Swift's consciousness; we can value his subtle play with his positives more readily than his assertion of them, play generally being more open to critical inquiry than assertion anyway. In the play of "Sweat, Dandriff, Powder, Lead and Hair" there may be more to consider than in the celebration of "Honor and Virtue, Sense and Wit" but it is still a real question why, and how, Swift ever managed to make this catalogue of the virtues resonate with the energies of his being in an art whose authenticity is as evident as the ironic brilliance of his subversive satire. This question seems to have intrigued Swift himself; he enjoyed toying with it, teasing with its implications. In the verses on his own death it leads him toward a not entirely accurate but still telling assertion of a positive literary identity, a celebrative assertion of a direct link between his public good works and his satiric manner. In the large body of poems he wrote to his intimates, he regularly raises the issue, apparently discovering in this kind of poem the opportunity to explore his literary identity, to explore it under conditions especially rich in opportunities for self-revelation.

The playfulness of his intimate poetry is obvious, but we should emphasize how regularly the character of that playfulness is determined by his aggressive insistence upon the mastery of his immediate audience. He creates this mastery by placing himself, as Dean, in a didactic situation, assuming his right to teach and his audience's interest in hearing him do so. In *An Epistle to a Lady, Who desir'd the Author to make Verses on Her, in the Heroick Stile,* Swift conceives of the poem as a response to Lady Acheson's request that he address her in a heroic style—that is, that his moral instruction ("You wou'd teach me to be wise; / Truth and Honour how to prize; . . . How to relish Notions high; / How to live, and how to die") be delivered with a dignity appropriate to its high positives, and a temperance in accord with some humane recognition of her virtues as well as of her faults ("'Tis but just, you shou'd produce, / With each Fault, each Fault's excuse: / Not to publish ev'ry Trifle, / And my few perfections stifle"). Swift succeeds in this peculiar poem in denying Lady Acheson's stylistic demand even as he acknowledges its aptness: "End, as it befits your Station; / Come to Use and Application" he has her say, linking her demand for stylistic and didactic dignity with his own sense that such dignity "befits" his station, that his character as Dean demands, or implies, a closer, more integral connection than he usually could manage between his high positives and his stylistic preferences. Those stylistic preferences are themselves a subject of the poem, and Swift uses the occasion to assert and demonstrate the didactic efficacy of his more violent manner even as he claims to be master of a gentler style. The poem's middle he gives over to a long invective digression against his political targets—a digression whose violence quite belies his assertion within the same poem that he "can easier scorn than hate" (2:634. 144):

Let me, tho' the Smell be Noisom,
Strip their Bums; let Caleb hoyse 'em;
Then, apply Alecto's Whip,
Till they wriggle, howl, and skip.
                        [177–180]

To this image of his aggressive satiric violence Swift imagines Lady Acheson to reply, "Deuce is in you, Mr. Dean; / What can all this passion mean?"—crediting the lady for recognizing in him an intemperance not in accord with the Dean's effort to see himself more mildly. The lady's perception of the inner violence that energizes Swift's satiric manner calls forth her demand that he reapply his attention to her, that he end as it befits his station: that is, in dignified address, with "use and application." The poem continues, but does not develop from this point. Having acknowledged, through the lady, that he perceives a disjunction among his station, his character, his high positives, and the manner he continually discovers as most congenial, Swift proceeds to ignore this issue. He concludes the poem by asserting once more his preference for a raillery that he has demonstrated to be far more brutal in practice than his own description of it—"I encounter vice with Mirth" (142)—can acknowledge.

Even here, in a poem written to and for a friend, we can discover a tonal range whose effect is to produce that play with his audience, that intimate approach toward it and then that tricky withdrawal, which characterizes Swift's special achievement in ironic art. We should note here his own concern about the decorum of his undertaking, his own sense that the positive didactic enterprise he defines as his is not easily served by or embodied in the manner that most naturally expresses the negative energies of his personality. In his play with Lady Acheson's request for dignified address, Swift becomes elusive to her, and he imagines her to search for him, a search necessarily unsuccessful as he lets loose his invective, disfiguring his composure, drawing from her the puzzled recognition of the devil in him and, seeing this, the impossible demand—"End as it befits your Station." The demand is impossible because the devil in him and the Dean could be reconciled only under the rare and special circumstances he elsewhere created, and which he could create only from his connection with another.

These are the circumstances, at once intimate and celebrative, of Swift's connection with Esther Johnson, his dearest friend and sometimes close companion. Esther Johnson was a young child in Sir William Temple's household when Swift, then Temple's secretary, first came to know her and briefly to tutor her. She is, of course, the Stella of his poems and letters and *Journal*. Perhaps Swift's renaming of Esther Johnson tells us also that Stella is Swift's literary creation, but if so, she is a creation unlike any of his others. She is fashioned out of all that we would call positive in his imagination, yet fashioned so that she serves also to test this idealism. Even a casual reading of his various writings to and about her will strike us for their concentration of panegyrical topics—her beauty, her wit, her honor, her piety. Those topics, in short, which for Swift were generally unendurable as the subjects of simply celebrative rhetoric, became, with Stella as the vehicle for his celebration of them, fully and positively available to him. We may, then, when we examine his poems to her, be too easily prone to think of Stella as a creation of dubious authenticity, an inevitable alternative to the horrific female creations we know so well from the "unprintable" poems. But to think so about this unusual segment of Swift's work would be a mistake. Stella is undoubtedly a literary creation, but as such she demands of us a critical tact that acknowledges her actual identity before her literary one. For striking us first about her appearance in Swift's work—whether in poems, letters, or journals—should be his insistence upon her biographical actuality, to which he almost *offhandedly* engrafted his idealism. For him Stella was a personal fact as well as a literary necessity, and it is just this that seems to have continuously awakened his wonder and determined the character he would give her as his literary subject. In even the most intense of his celebrations of her we can hear his insistence upon her plain actuality: "Never was any of her sex born with better gifts of the mind, or more improved them by reading and conversation. . . . She had a gracefulness somewhat more than human in every motion, word and action." This report, for all its idealizing superlatives, still has a decorum that allows for such tempering and actualizing detail as that Stella was "looked upon as one of the most beautiful, graceful, and agreeable young women in London, only a little too fat."[18] Swift's characteristic practice, both in this piece, written under great emotional pressure at her death, and in the poems celebrating their friendship, is to make Stella into an idea with enough flesh on it to bear the inspection of just such irony as proves, without undercutting, the virtues she is made to embody and which she helps him to experience and to explore.

In his poems to Stella Swift regularly invokes the facts of their initial relationship: in life he was, and in these poems he remains, her tutor. The poems he addressed to her have at their center a didactic situation; they are teaching occasions of lesser or greater intensity. At their most moving, their didactic force is both generalized and particularized, generalized so that the lesson amounts to a celebration of the delivered doctrine, particularized so that its application develops from the personal substance of Swift's and Stella's connection, the mutual honoring, which is the proof, and the poignant acerbities, which are the test, of the positives these poems celebrate. The special circumstances of Swift's and Stella's personal relationship—that it developed into intimacy from their initially and literally didactic connection as tutor and tutee—Swift seems to have seized upon as rich with opportunities of extraordinary importance to him. Her actuality, her closeness, her willingness to acknowledge the shaping force of his influence, all seem to have come together to make her, in his imagination, just such an idea as could endure the strain of his obsession with the disjunctive antagonism between high and low, the ideal and the actual—the obsession, in short,

[18]*Prose Works*, 5:227.

that energizes his most intriguing and devastating art. But in the didactic art of the Stella poems the strain does not break the positive effort, the peculiar energies of Swift's personality do not overwhelm the effort of his character—nor are they yet denied.

In Stella Swift discovered an audience that eluded even his penchant for elusive trickery, an audience immune to his intriguing and devastating irony. As the addressee of his poems, as the single being he knew who grew for a time under his tutelage and would acknowledge it, she was, in her actuality, his ideal audience. His characteristic and vexatious irony, that irony in which he withdraws from his positives and from his audience as he makes them his target, was not necessary to him in the special circumstances he enjoyed as Stella's tutor in life and in verse. In writing to and for her, Swift could assume and maintain that direct contact with a good audience which is the condition of didactic address and which makes the didactic occasion also a celebrative one. We can hear these two strains together in lines such as these:

> True Poets can depress and raise;
> Are Lords of Infamy and Praise:
> They are not scurrilous in Satire,
> Nor will in Panygyrick flatter.
> Unjustly poets we asperse;
> Truth shines the brighter, clad in Verse;
> And all the Fictions they pursue
> Do but insinuate what is true.
> [*To Stella, Who Collected and
> Transcribed His Poems,* 2:729. 53–60]

The assertive and declarative manner of these lines is obvious in the diction: True Poets, Lords, Truth, shines. The thematic concern has to do with satire and panegyric, and asserts, aria-like, Swift's sense that the two kinds are not necessarily distinct or mutually exclusive: satire without scurrility, panegyric without flattery, are possible, but possible only where poets are true and when their matter is truth. These lines, which seem to reflect self-consciously on Swift's career in literature, mark the turn in the poem to which they belong. In asserting the possibility of an expression whose confident union with truth creates a manner free of both scurrility and flattery, their celebrative manner contrasts sharply with the poem's preceding section—a characteristically Swiftian obliteration of idealizing poets, though somewhat tempered in its scurrility—and introduces the tonal dignity required in the section to follow—a realistic assessment of Stella's character in which Swift demonstrates quite literally what a panegyric without flattery can be. The preceding section is typical of what Swift will ordinarily do when his matter permits him to dwell upon the polarities of the ideal and the actual:

> A Poet, starving in a Garret,
> Conning old Topicks like a Parrot,
> Invokes his Mistress and his Muse,

And stays at home for want of Shoes:
Should but his Muse descending drop
A Slice of Bread, and Mutton-Chop,
Or kindly when his Credit's out,
Surprize him with a Pint of Stout,
Or patch his broken Stocking Soals,
Or send him in a Peck of Coals;
Exalted in his mighty Mind
He flies, and leaves the Stars behind,
Counts all his Labours amply paid,
Adores her for the timely Aid.
[25–38]

Swift develops his game by intensifying the negative opportunities obvious in the conception, so that the starving poet's inspiration, his tattered mistress, can be represented as "Bright *Phillis* mending ragged Smocks, / And Radiant *Iris* in the Pox" (46–47). The line of argument sustaining Swift's play is that he, as Stella's friend, is saved from the idealizing foolishness of a poet whose sustenance, as well as inspiration, is his mistress. "With Friendship and Esteem possesst, / I ne'er admitted Love a guest"—this describes the nature of his connection with Stella, and also its enabling opportunity, for

should my Praises owe their Truth
To Beauty, Dress, or Paint or Youth,
What Stoicks call *without our Power,*
They could not be insur'd an Hour . . .
[61–64]

What Swift does, then, is to attribute to the romantic coolness of his connection with Stella the opportunity for evading the (foolish) entrapment in the special dilemma his negative imagination revels in: the dilemma created in the antagonism of what was for him always a disjunct idealism and actuality.

But if Swift is honest enough to acknowledge that as Stella's friend he enjoys a freedom from one kind of poetic foolishness, he immediately complicates his task by assuming burdens the idealizing poet could never know: the burden of telling the whole truth about his subject:

Your Virtues safely I commend,
They on no Accidents depend:
Let Malice look with all her Eyes,
She dares not say the Poet lyes.

Stella, when you these Lines transcribe,
Lest you should take them for a Bribe,
Resolv'd to mortify your Pride,
I'll here expose your weaker Side.
[79–86]

What follows is a remarkable achievement: the tonal dignity that Swift introduced as he moved away from his rougher manner now sustains his anatomy of Stella's "weaker side." The result can probably be considered Swift's demonstration of the work of the "true poet," who, he had written, can both "depress and raise."

> Your Spirits kindle to a Flame,
> Mov'd with the lightest Touch of Blame,
> And when a Friend in Kindness tries
> To shew you where your Error lies,
> Conviction does but more incense;
> Perverseness is your whole Defence:
> Truth, Judgment, Wit, give Place to Spite,
> Regardless both of Wrong and Right.
> Your Virtues, all suspended, wait
> Till Time hath open'd Reason's Gate:
> And what is worse, your Passion bends
> Its Force against your nearest Friends;
> Which Manners, Decency, and Pride,
> Have taught you from the World to hide:
> In vain; for see, your Friend hath brought
> To publick Light your only Fau't;
> And yet a Fault we often find
> Mix'd in a noble generous Mind;
> And may compare to *Ætna's* Fire,
> Which, tho' with Trembling, all admire;
> The Heat that makes the Summit glow,
> Enriching all the Vales below.
> Those who in warmer Climes complain
> From *Phoebus* Rays they suffer Pain,
> Must own, that Pain is largely paid
> By gen'rous Wines beneath a Shade.
> Yet when I find your Passions rise,
> And Anger sparkling in your Eyes,
> I grieve those Spirits should be spent,
> For nobler Ends by Nature meant.
> One Passion, with a diff'rent Turn,
> Makes Wit inflame, or Anger burn;
> So the Sun's Heat, with different Powers,
> Ripens the Grape, the Liquor sours.
> Thus *Ajax*, when with Rage possesst
> By *Pallas* breath'd into his Breast,
> His Valour would no more employ;
> Which might alone have conquer'd *Troy*;
> But Blinded by Resentment, seeks
> For Vengeance on his Friends the *Greeks*.
>
> You think this Turbulence of Blood

From stagnating preserves the Flood;
Which thus fermenting, by Degrees
Exalts the Spirits, sinks the Lees.

   Stella, for once you reason wrong;
For should this Ferment last too long,
By time subsiding, you may find
Nothing but Acid left behind.
From Passion you may then be freed,
When Peevishness and Spleen succeed.
                                        [87–136]

In approaching this passage we should note that it answers to Swift's resolution
to "mortify" Stella's pride, and we should recall the imaginative resources he
could release elsewhere in the name of such a resolution: the Yahoos, the lady's
dressing room, the Struldbruggs. Recognizing this, I find that the unusual
achievement of these verses is their genuinely heroic manner, whose effect is to
heighten their didactic intent, to affirm the positives according to which Stella is
being scrutinized, and finally, to celebrate Stella in the very process of con-
fronting her with her "weaker Side." The heroic ring comes from the wholly serious use of mythological material (the references to Ajax, Pallas, and Troy) and
from the quality of the reference to Aetna's fire ("Which, tho' with Trembling,
all admire"). This kind of material Swift more usually uses to produce sophisticated comedy—the mythological material in *Cadenus and Vanessa* sustains that
poem's comedy through several hundred lines, for example. But here, though
comedy is present, it is impossible to feel it as the dominant mode. The reason is
that the mythological and heroic allusions are sustained by the didactic assertiveness of the passage, which is itself an effect of Swift's habit of cataloguing the
very virtues that are the subject of the poem's teaching intent: "a noble generous
Mind" is such an assertion, another is "Manners, Decency, and Pride," along
with "Truth, Judgment, Wit." These positives are compacted in lists so that they
literally occupy the space of the lines in which they appear, and accumulate
assertive force by the nature of their physical presence in those lines. At the
same time, these words are muted: either they occupy subordinate clauses, or
they do not fall into rhyming position. This explains, perhaps, why the heroic and
celebrative strain in the passage is felt as a coloring, not as a major mode. The
major mode, in fact, is hard to pin down, but I would call it a kind of social ease,
an offhandedness in keeping with the personal intimacy from which the passage
springs and which it so successfully communicates. Moreover, Swift's offhandedness in asserting his positives is entirely right in this poem, for he has maneu-
vered it toward celebrative assertion after an earlier movement that had lam-
pooned the easier celebrative manner of romantic idealizing. What he has aimed
for here, and reached, is expression true to his claim of freedom from that idealizing manner. It is a heightening of plain truth that simultaneously asserts the
reality of the virtues and the grandeur of the woman whose actual behavior is not
always adequate to them. In the simultaneous presence of the heroic coloring

and the social ease, Swift is able to contemplate the distinction between ideal and actual behavior without turning the one into proof against the other. This is a rare achievement for him and not something he has been remembered for.

Turning from its earlier manner which lampoons one form of celebration, the idealizing kind, the poem demonstrates the possibility of another celebrative style, one whose genuinely heroic coloring is still compatible with the realism Swift always insists upon. In his poem to Lady Acheson Swift had evaded her request to be instructed in a dignified and heroic strain and indeed, of that request, had made an occasion to let loose a torrent of invective abuse. We can attribute to Stella—to Swift's experience of her grandeur and of her actuality—his success in devising a style that meets Lady Acheson's unmet demand: "But, I beg, suspend a While, / That same paltry Burlesque stile: / Drop, for once, your constant Rule, / Turning all to Ridicule . . ." (49–53). For in this poem, *To Stella, Who Collected and Transcribed His Poems,* Swift can express a thoroughly positive experience of his own best beliefs. The sign of this experience is that union of didactic intent and heroic tone with which he liked to credit himself despite the regularity with which it eluded him. Indeed, in this poem we can feel the peculiar intensity that the best Augustan poetry regularly discovers in didactic address. This intensity develops, I think, from the association of didactic and celebrative purpose, as if the teaching occasion were a kind of ritual experience of society's best beliefs, a firm acknowledgment of shared identity in shared belief.

This association of didactic and celebrative purpose, moreover, may help to illuminate a peculiarity of the poem's beginning and ending. For Swift frames the poem by addressing Stella as the collector and transcriber of his verses and therefore imagines her experience of the poem itself as a test of the efficacy of his instruction. To put it another way, he imagines her as the poem's audience and *as such*, in a special way, as its *creator*:

> As when a lofty Pile is rais'd,
> We never hear the Workmen prais'd,
> Who bring the Lime, or place the Stones;
> But all admire *Inigo Jones*;
> So if this Pile of scatter'd Rhymes
> Should be approv'd in After-times,
> If it both pleases and endures,
> The Merit and the Praise are yours.
> [1–8]

This puzzling assertion characterizes the poet as the poem's mechanic, its editor and transcriber as its shaping genius, apparently reversing the relationship we know to be the true one. But the puzzle clarifies when we look at the concluding lines, in which Swift addresses Stella, assuming that, in her editing, she has experienced the lesson of the poem's body, the exposure, that is, of her weaker side, her passionate pride:

> Say, *Stella,* when you copy next,
> Will you keep strictly to the Text?

> Dare you let these Reproaches stand,
> And to your Failing set your Hand?
> Or if these Lines your Anger fire,
> Shall they in baser Flames expire?
> Whene'er they burn, if burn they must,
> They'll prove my Accusation just.
>   [137–144]

These lines in fact tell us that the poem's integrity and finally its survival depend upon its audience, the object of its didactic intent. And that, of course, is the point. The audience *is* the final maker of a didactic poem, the reason why it can rise to heroic and celebrative style. In responding positively to the doctrine, the audience acknowledges its possession of the doctrine, its understanding of manners, decency, pride, truth, judgment, wit. In the case of this poem, Swift has imagined Stella as just such an audience, like the audience he imagined for his didactic purpose in *The Drapier's Letters,* where his job was to remind his readership of what they already knew about virtuous community and patriotism. And, as in *The Drapier's Letters,* Swift in this poem can be arch, can be clever (as the "bite" in the last couplet demonstrates) without withdrawing from his audience and his positives in that characteristic irony of his, whose effect is to make his ideals dubious and his audience his victim, as in *An Argument* and *A Modest Proposal.* The opening and the end of this poem, along with the heroic and celebrative delivery of its doctrine in the middle, verify that bond that must exist between teacher and taught, poet and audience, if their best beliefs are to provide them the cognitive integrity that is the test and end of positive art. Swift's great negative art flourished in the absence of that cognitive integrity, which he could experience only rarely, and most intensely, as Stella's teacher and poet.

In Swift's writings for Stella readers have always felt a lyrical quality that is all the more moving for his general distrust of what he thought were the romantic sources of lyric expression. I want now to explore the nature and the sources of the special lyricism of these poems, a lyricism that I think is a function of their didactic movement. I call it a special lyricism because it arises from a didactic effort that we might more easily identify with Swift's public station rather than his private self. The achievement of these poems is to secure an integration of station and self that was difficult for Swift, whose satiric intensity elsewhere arises indeed in the very failure of that integration. In establishing Stella as the fit audience for the positive and celebrative assertion of his own best beliefs, Swift concentrates into one person the function and identity of the whole public audience whose goodness is the condition of the didactic address, the guarantor of its efficacy, the reason that the didactic occasion can be a celebrative one. But in these poems the lyric poignancy, which delicately evokes an unspoken intimacy, is surely a complex effect of Swift's awareness that his audience of one was a surrogate for that public community he knew did not exist. The intimacy we appreciate in these poems takes on much of its value for Swift precisely because he charges it with energies that could not find their proper public release—except in the satirical intensity not in keeping with his station. What he says to and for Stella communicates his poignant awareness that what he most owed her was the opportunity she provided him to stay in some kind of positive touch with the ideas he loved. The didactic movement of the best of these poems is, therefore, part of a larger mimetic intention—the representation, in the intimacy of two difficult people, of the reality, the value, the cost of virtue.

In *To Stella, Visiting Me in My Sickness,* what starts out as a discourse on honor becomes an imitation of gratitude, and in the movement from the one to the other the poem develops its lyric intensities. The discourse on honor begins aggressively:

> But (not in Wranglings to engage
> With such a stupid, vicious Age)
> If Honour I would here define,
> It answers Faith in Things divine.
> [2:723.7–10]

The discussion of honor is initiated in the first place as a compliment to Stella, but Swift's lesson, his effort to define and illustrate, proceeds independently of any reference to Stella for some thirty lines. They strike me as remarkable lines, characterized in part by an epigrammatic wit that registers the speaker's comfortable familiarity with a set of ideas he possesses not simply as ideas but as heritage:

> As nat'ral Life the Body warms,
> And, Scholars teach, the Soul informs;
> So Honour animates the Whole,
> And is the Spirit of the Soul.
>   Those num'rous Virtues which the Tribe
> Of tedious Moralists describe,
> And by such various Titles call,
> True Honour comprehends them all.
> Let Melancholy rule supreme,
> Choler preside, or Blood, or Phlegm,
> It makes no Diff'rence in the Case,
> Nor is Complexion Honour's Place.
>   [11–22]

"Scholars teach" and "the Tribe of tedious Moralists" and "Those num'rous Virtues" (the demonstrative adjective does it here) all contribute to create our sense that the lesson is a kind of recital. But as the recital continues, the wit sharpens. The lesson, for all its familiarity—perhaps because of its familiarity, because it is a social as well as moral possession—can be easily misused. The wit of the following passage arises directly from the fact that moral knowledge *is* a social possession, and, as such, can be mere ornamentation or worse:

> But, lest we should for Honour take
> The Drunken quarrels of a Rake,
> Or think it seated in a Scar,
> Or on a proud triumphal Car,
> Or, in the Payment of a Debt
> We lose with Sharpers at Piquet. . . .
>   [23–28]

These lines help explain the aggressiveness of the lesson's beginning; these are the social uses of moral knowledge, the same graceful or complacent corruptions of doctrine which create the cognitive anarchy of *A Modest Proposal* and of nominal Christianity, the "dullness" of a "stupid, vicious Age." (We can easily see in these verses the salon of the Goddess Dullness.) Swift delineates here precisely the socialized viciousness that, in its complacent appropriation of doctrine, displays man's unfitness for doctrine. It is just this socialized viciousness that elsewhere and most memorably drives Swift into the satiric irony within which he withdraws from doctrine and from his audience, and in the simple additive intensification of the examples he adduces (there are four more lines and in them two more examples of stupid viciousness) we can see the anger that elsewhere generates his irony and motivates his withdrawal. Once again we are at the point where the ideal and the actual can break apart.

Here they do not, however. As the anger intensifies and the examples multiply, the passage comes to a sudden stop: to all these social corruptions of moral knowledge, there is an answer:

> Let *Stella's* fair Example preach
> A Lesson she alone can teach.
>
>   In Points of Honour to be try'd,
> All Passions must be laid aside:
> Ask no Advice, but think alone,
> Suppose the Question not your own:
> How shall I act? is not the Case,
> But how would *Brutus* in my Place?
> In such a Cause would *Cato* bleed?
> And how would *Socrates* proceed?
>   Drive all Objections from your Mind,
> Else you relapse to Human Kind:
> Ambition, Avarice, and Lust,
> And factious Rage, and Breach of Trust,
> And Flatt'ry tipt with nauseous Fleer,
> And guilty Shame, and servile Fear,
> Envy, and Cruelty, and Pride,
> Will in your tainted Heart preside.
>   [33–50]

Swift speaks for Stella here, but her example preaches. He, as speaker, acts as the vehicle for *her* doctrine in a collaboration that is a kind of marriage of her virtue and his intensity. In this remarkable union much is accomplished. We should note first the appeal to Brutus, Cato, and Socrates, that is, to the sternest, purest, most strenuous creators and exemplars of the moral heritage that Swift had invoked in the earlier lines. The effect of invoking these names is to remind us of the initial pure vigor of doctrine prior to its codification as heritage. Swift had celebrated doctrine codified as heritage in the ease and familiarity of his recital in lines 11–22, but it was heritage corrupted into social complacency which he had attacked in the section immediately following. Bringing Stella into the poem at this point has the effect of revivifying doctrine; it points to a living exemplar, an actual being whose life stands as reminder and proof of the original force of what has been so viciously and gracefully corrupted.

But if Stella can serve in this capacity, Swift still interprets her meaning, and his presence in these lines is clear in their doctrinal and tonal intensity. The lesson, lived by Stella, spoken by Swift, taken from Cato, Brutus, Socrates, is now not a definition of honor but a prescription for honorable behavior. The prescription is designed above all to prevent that "relapse to Human kind" in which actual behavior vitiates doctrine, and it is realized in a renunciation of self— "Suppose the Question not your own"—a conversion of personality into character—"How shall I act? is not the Case, / But how would *Brutus* in my Place?" Stella thus enters the poem as an embodiment of the ideal, more precisely as one whose appropriation of the ideal does not strain against her experience of the actual. A sense of that strain, however, is not absent from these lines, the last six of which are an intense catalogue of the causes of that "relapse into Human kind" which Stella's example preaches against and Swift's words define. These six lines are at the edge of intense invective, a list of malicious passions which taken together shift the emotional emphasis of this moment in the poem from didactic celebration to satiric anger, precisely expressed in the force of the imputation, "your tainted Heart." Against the beauty of Stella's experience of the ideal, the verse expresses Swift's latent fury at the actual, and the poem at this point is emotionally uncertain, equally strong in its celebrative and invective energies.

This uncertainty does not, however, govern the poem's development toward its conclusion. Though we can recognize here the elements of an irreconcilable division similar to that in Gulliver's fourth voyage—irreconcilable because the alternative to virtuous conduct is a relapse into not evil only, but *Human Kind*— nevertheless Swift discovers a way out.

> Heroes and Heroins of old,
> By Honour only were enroll'd
> Among their Brethren of the Skies,
> To which (though late) shall *Stella* rise.
> Ten thousand Oaths upon Record,
> Are not so sacred as her Word:

> The World shall in its Atoms end,
> E'er *Stella* can deceive a Friend.
> By Honour seated in her Breast,
> She still determines what is best:
> What Indignation in her Mind
> Against Enslavers of Mankind!
> Base Kings and Ministers of State,
> Eternal Objects of her Hate.
>   [51–64]

Here the force of the invective anger that had been building is retained, but its purpose is transformed. Swift does not exacerbate the strain between the ideal and the actual, and he does not withdraw from his didactic and celebrative intention. Instead, he smartly reapplies his attention to Stella in lines whose heroic tonality is unmistakable. Explicitly identifying Stella with "Heroes and Heroins of old," Swift converts the angry energy of the preceding section into heroically colored celebration: we feel this in the powerfully assertive effect of the third, fourth, and fifth couplets, two of which are hyperbolic in their particulars ("Ten thousand Oaths . . . The World shall in its Atoms end") while the third generalizes its praise from these grand exaggerations, confident in Stella's determination of "what is best." In the two concluding couplets of this section the transformation of anger into celebration is complete. The first is an open, plain expression of wonder: "What Indignation in her Mind / Against Enslavers of Mankind!" This is the rhetoric of wonder, wonder as the transfiguration of anger. The directness of "Enslavers of Mankind" is as far from corrosive irony as one can come: the words confidently define and declaim against a known and understood evil. Here Swift's confidence in Stella's knowledge of and her indignation against a clearly perceived evil makes it possible for him to experience and express his wonder at her capacity for proper indignation. The final couplet rises to boldly particular denunciation of those enslavers of mankind as "Base Kings and Ministers of State," and to a hyperbolic description of Stella's moral energy, a capacity to keep before her the "Eternal Objects of her Hate." The assertive grandeur of this passage is possible because Swift can free himself of the burden of hatred; he can do this by *attributing to Stella* a capacity for righteous hatred. Because Stella is now responsible for righteous indignation, Swift is free to value in her an experience which, in himself, would be corrosive. Stella gives him, then, the opportunity to celebrate in another a moral energy that, in himself, will find expression only in irony or invective. That moral energy can find positive, heroic, celebrative expression as praise for Stella, and this expression truly fits Swift's station.

These strong lines, in their heroic rhetoric, express fully Swift's own direct and healthy experience of his own best beliefs. The lines join the didactic and the celebrative in a moving, because rare, moment for Swift. The lesson on honor has not intensified in irony or invective, but in assertion; the strain between the ideal and the actual has not overwhelmed the initial commitment to the ideal. Instead, that commitment has found a local habitation and a name. And because the Stella of these lines is an indignant, angry Stella, the man who celebrates her does not endanger his authenticity. His movement into heroic praise involves no softening of, no blinking at, an actuality that more usually draws from him a meaner language. Because of Stella an occasion for irony or meanness becomes for Swift an occasion for a grander manner.

The poem's movement through several ranges of feeling as it continually adjusts its tonal coloring is at once a rhetorical and a poetic achievement. The progress from anger to wonder may be seen as the rhetorically persuasive accompaniment of the poem's didactic effort. Swift explicitly says as much:

> Her Hearers are amaz'd from whence
> Proceeds that Fund of Wit and Sense;
> Which though her Modesty would shroud,
> Breaks like the Sun behind a Cloud,
> While Gracefulness its Art Conceals,
> And yet through ev'ry Motion steals.
> [79–84]

The focus here is on the general audience who benefit directly from Stella's example, experiencing the same wonder—"Her Hearers are amaz'd"—we have seen in Swift's response to her, as well as the direct knowledge of a series of implicated positives: wit, sense, modesty, grace. But at the same time, the emotive movement from anger to wonder directly expresses the progress of a curve of private feeling, the inner experience of the poem's maker. For the final movement of the verse is distinctly personal; it brings us for the first time to the situation from which the poem springs, announced in the title: *To Stella, Visiting Me in My Sickness.*

This is a complex conclusion to the poem, intimate in its account of Swift's behavior and Stella's nursing. Its effect is to isolate the two from the audience, "the world," which had been to this point of the poem the addressee of its didactic and celebrative rhetoric.

> How would Ingratitude delight?
> And, how would Censure glut her Spight?
> If I should *Stella's* Kindness hide
> In Silence, or forget with Pride.
> When on my sickly Couch I lay,
> Impatient both of Night and Day,
> Lamenting in unmanly Strains,
> Call'd ev'ry Pow'r to ease my Pains,
> Then *Stella* ran to my Relief
> With chearful Face, and inward Grief;
> And, though by Heaven's severe decree
> She suffers hourly more than me,
> No cruel Master could require
> From Slaves employ'd for daily Hire

What *Stella* by her Friendship warm'd,
With Vigour and Delight perform'd.
My sinking Spirits now supplies
With Cordials in her Hands, and Eyes.
Now, with a soft and silent Tread,
Unheard she moves about my Bed.
I see her taste each nauseous Draught,
And so obligingly am caught:
I bless the Hand from whence they came,
Nor dare distort my Face for shame.

                              [92–116]

This passage first is characteristically aggressive toward the larger audience outside the sickroom, seen as an armory of Censure, Ingratitude, Spite. But the aggression is absorbed by a more compelling feeling as Swift deftly gives the poem over entirely to Stella in a movement of praise which is at the same time a record of his gratitude toward her, and consequently a mimetic rendering finally of the full meaning of the poem's didactic subject—honor. This final movement completes that lesson in a mimesis of Stella's behavior to Swift, of Swift's full response to that moral beauty, and of his recognition of its costs.

The lyrical intensity of this movement is an obvious consequence of the abrupt introduction of intimate detail. But we must not miss how finely this detail has been fitted to Swift's didactic material. The intimacy of "Then *Stella* ran to my Relief / With chearful Face, and inward Grief" concretely illustrates the earlier instruction, "How shall I act? is not the Case, / But how would *Brutus* in my place?" transforming Stella from a pattern of stoic severity, with its subordination of personality to character, into an image of effective blessedness, fully revealing personality:

I see her taste each nauseous Draught,
And so obligingly am caught:
I bless the Hand from whence they came,
Nor dare distort my Face for shame.

There is affectionate joking in this picture—a Swift on his best behavior, heroically taking his medicine—but the joking also is made from the didactic situation. The image of childish bravery—"Nor dare distort my Face"—is just right: yet another effect of Stella's virtue, it contributes to the intimacies portrayed, and sets off the earlier, harsher reflection of self Swift alludes to in "no cruel Master could require." We are given a scene then, and the scene effectively lets us into the most private of details, the acerbities as well as delights of an often difficult, usually rewarding connection, the whole a mimetic rendering of honor in action, earning gratitude and a blessing, so that the didactic lesson, presented earlier in the most heroic of terms, can be felt now within the realistically diminished and very private sickroom.

By rendering this closing movement of the poem as a scene, Swift can make it fully responsive to the force of personal feeling. The didactic material—the lesson on honor—is assimilated to another purpose, the mimetic portrayal of the rewards of honor. These are simply the blessings Swift bestows, the signs of the gratitude honor earns. The personal, lyrical color now of the poem's mimesis of gratitude within the sickroom may be said to be the private, intimate transfiguration of the public experience of wonder the poem had earlier expressed at Stella's heroism. And as the poem narrows its focus onto the emotional communication between the two people, we can see the way in which the earlier portrayal of Stella as model yields to the celebration of Stella as person, the way, that is, Swift insists upon the real selfhood of the figure he had earlier pointed to as an example of stoic selflessness, one whose beliefs and behavior had been seen as proof against a "relapse to Human Kind." For the final didactic movement, coordinated now with the lyrical fullness of the poem's conclusion, is about the human costs of such virtue as Stella possesses:

> Best Pattern of true Friends, beware;
> You pay too dearly for your Care;
> If, while your Tenderness secures
> My Life, it must endanger yours.
> For such a Fool was never found,
> Who pull'd a Palace to the Ground,
> Only to have the Ruins made
> Materials for an House decay'd.
>   [117–124]

Here Swift speaks directly to Stella imagining her as the recipient rather than the teacher of the lesson; this had been her role throughout the poem as its pattern of honor. Indeed, Swift uses that word as he directly addresses her in his thoughts—"Best Pattern of true Friends, beware"—but he can so address her because the other term that he applies to her in this small, lyric homily, the affectionate term "Fool," declares his poignant awareness of her real selfhood, just as the entire passage declares his recognition of the cost to that self of its virtue: "You pay too dearly for your Care." In full coordination with the poem's didactic material, these last lines complete the curve of personal feeling from invective anger to wonder to elegiac celebration, making the lesson in honor, which had celebrated Stella as pattern, now into a source of lyrical awareness, yielding the recognition of Stella as person, vulnerable to her virtues. The vehicle of this last movement is an almost Aesopian parable, simple in its didactic character: "For such a Fool was never found, / Who pull'd a Palace to the Ground . . ." The didactic character of this Aesopian homily, however, is clearly subordinate to the deeply lyrical feeling that informs the passage: indeed, it helps to create that feeling, as if Swift were invoking the public manner of the homily the more fully to show to Stella how intensely private this emotional moment is. More, the moment is made to carry a charge of self-revelation, also through the homiletic image Swift applies to himself: "an House decay'd." The poem completes its emotive curve in this self-revelation with its elegiac tonalities, fully expressive of the human actuality of its pattern of virtue and of the intensities of two people, whose human experience of suffering and sacrifice becomes the poem's final subject, the vehicle for its fullest demonstration of the meaning of honor, its didactic subject. As pattern yields to person, honor is shown to be the costly virtue whose effects are finally known only in suffering and sacrifice.[19]

The finest, and the last, of Swift's celebrations of Stella marks the fullest integration he achieves of didactic and lyric expression. *Stella's Birthday, March 13, 1726/7* is a dramatic poem, entirely conceived as a mimesis of an inner action, and as such, dominated throughout by its charge of lyric feeling. To that feeling the didactic movement is grafted, quite unlike the previous poem which traces its emotive curve through several stages of public address toward a moment of private self-revelation. Now the private focus and intensity are immediately revealed in the opening lines, which set a scene toward which the previous poem had worked as its conclusion:

> This day, whate'er the Fates decree,
> Shall still be kept with Joy by me:
> This Day then, let us not be told,
> That you are sick, and I grown old
> Nor think on our approaching Ills,
> And talk of Spectacles and Pills;
> To morrow will be Time enough
> To hear such mortifying Stuff.
> [2:763.1–8]

We hardly need to point out how precisely and plainly the unadorned language defines the intimate privacy of this occasion and also its solemnity. Although Swift speaks of his intention to mark the occasion with joy, and despite the witty offhandedness of the detail, there is an almost ceremonial decorum to the moment. Stella's day is a day he "keeps," and in just a few lines he will show that "keeping" this day means, among other things, delivering some "serious Lines." Moreover, keeping this day with joy requires that he arrange its circumstances: for the proper observance of the occasion he will exclude all that "the Fates decree"; "let us not be told / That you are sick, and I grown old" is a poignant yet willful self-assertion, a necessary condition for the didactic meditation on virtue which is to compose the poem's body and be the celebrative commemoration of Stella's life. Yet if we look ahead to the poem's conclusion we can see that the poise of this first movement will give way to more complex and difficult feelings:

[19]John Irwin Fischer writes of Swift's account of Stella's care for him: "Pained by his pain she accepts her pain and turns it to good. . . . [In her ministering to Swift] she catches entire that 'True Honour' which comprehends all virtues and which, amidst man's allotted pain and frailties, both gives and receives blessings" (*On Swift's Poetry* [Gainesville: Univ. of Florida Press, 1978], pp. 143–44.) But Fischer dismisses the severe didacticism of the poem's first half as both "silly" and "unfortunate" (p. 142), missing, I think, its importance within the poem's dramatic and lyric *development* of its didactic material.

O then, whatever Heav'n intends,
Take Pity on your pitying Friends;
Nor let your Ills affect your Mind,
To fancy they can be unkind.
Me, surely me, you ought to spare,
Who gladly would your Suff'rings share;
Or give my Scrap of Life to you,
And think it far beneath your Due;
You, to whose Care so oft I owe,
That I'm alive to tell you so.
[79–88]

The plaintive urgency of these final lines, in language as unadorned as the poem's opening, clearly reveals the difficulty of maintaining the ceremonial poise of that opening. What had begun in poise ends in pleading. In the distinctly different tonal coloring of these framing sections of the poem we can sense the direction of the poem's movement, the inner emotional action it imitates.

The final lines, perhaps the most personal Swift ever wrote, are addressed to a difficult woman. Swift joins their personal urgency—"Me, surely me, you ought to spare"—to an elegiac acknowledgment of that woman's lifelong virtue—"You, to whose Care so oft I owe, / That I'm alive to tell you so." The plea of these lines is that Stella demonstrate, now when such a test is most difficult, that her life of virtue is not vitiated by the strain of her final crisis, that at this most difficult moment she sustain her moral biography so that its author may be vindicated. The personal urgency of the poem's conclusion expresses not only a poignant and realistic description of Stella's impatience now toward the beneficiary of her former selflessness, but also Swift's full awareness that the authenticity of his celebration of her, and of virtue, is at stake. This poem is as much a test of all he has written about Stella as it is of her, and it is no surprise that in its final lines it should record his sense that his moral and imaginative life is an adjunct of hers. Here he pleads for the value of his own life.

Of the results of that plea we can know nothing. The tact in this refusal to conclude and to assert is itself a moving acknowledgment of Stella's existential actuality, indeed of her physical being, now in its last painful illness. This final scene of Swift's final poem for Stella is brutally realistic in its presentation of a strained experience charged with retrospective significance, demanding of the sufferer that in her suffering she prove out the force of that virtue Swift had attributed to her throughout her life, the life that has provided the measure of the value of Swift's own. And yet, the poem is in no significant sense inconclusive. This intensely elegiacal final movement, for all of its contrast with the more poised and assertive opening, still develops naturally from the poem's body, that is, from those "serious Lines" that Swift delivers as his birthday gift, the sign of the joy with which he means to keep this day.

Those earlier lines are a didactic meditation on the efficacy of virtue, offered to Stella now as support for her effort to endure her present crisis, and their argument, simply, is that a life of virtue should "leave behind / Some lasting pleasure in the Mind, / Which by Remembrance will assuage, / Grief, Sickness, Poverty, and Age . . ." Swift announces this as a wisdom in keeping with his station: "From not the gravest of Divines / Accept for once some serious Lines?" (13–14). We should notice his invoking his station here as against Stella's more intimate knowledge of his personality, his identity as "not the gravest of Divines." The delivery of the doctrine that is to follow, then, is a special effort to realize for Stella the force of his character as against the more private energies of a personality that pulls against it. To be adequate to Stella now means to realize the identity he most fully experiences as her poet.

What then is the quality of the didactic movement that follows? Its substance, as I have said, is that virtue's force will sustain in the mind the moral identity now being assaulted by grief, sickness, poverty, old age.

> Were future Happiness and Pain,
> A mere Contrivance of the Brain,
> As Atheists argue, to entice,
> And fit their Proselytes for Vice;
> (The only Comfort they propose,
> To have Companions in their Woes.)
> Grant this the Case, yet sure 'tis hard,
> That Virtue, stil'd its own Reward,
> And by all Sages understood
> To be the chief of human Good,
> Should acting, die, nor leave behind
> Some lasting Pleasure in the Mind,
> Which by Remembrance will assuage,
> Grief, Sickness, Poverty, and Age;
> And strongly shoot a radiant Dart,
> To shine through Life's declining Part.
>   [19–34]

We must not miss here the blend of assertion and tentativeness, the organization of the lesson as a concession first to the other party, imagined here as "Atheists," and then as a response to them. But this response is muted in its strictly argumentative character. That is, it arises not from personal certainty but from personal need. Grant the atheists their rejection of future happiness and pain, "yet sure 'tis hard, / That Virtue, stil'd its own Reward . . . Should acting, die . . ." The word "stil'd" is peculiarly active here; it contributes to the passage's argumentative tentativeness, and seems a choice appropriate to the special impetus of the thought, the feeling that the other alternative—virtue as ineffective—were "hard" (not, we should note, "untrue").

Swift had earlier introduced these "serious Lines" as "A better and more pleasing Thought" (10). This better thought, however, he develops with a full sense of its willed character, its responsiveness to a compelling need, not its doctrinal certainty. It is an effect of that rational will that seeks to be adequate to the plain experience of such moral beauty as Stella's life has demonstrated. The didactic body of this poem, in fact, develops its "argument" in accord with this prompting of the rational will, and the lyric intensity toward which the poem builds is in great part created by our sense that the didactic argument is wholly shaped and tested by the private knowledge of Stella's worth that Swift brings to the occasion. His lesson, as lesson then, seeks to activate Stella's own moral being to fit itself to what Swift imagines, or hopes, are similar inner promptings. "Say, Stella, feel you no Content, / Reflecting on a Life well spent?" (35–36).

Organizing the poem's didactic matter in this way opens an opportunity for celebration, and the next movement is emphatically celebrative, a rehearsal of Stella's conduct (37–50). But this celebrative movement, after all, is introduced by the question just put to Stella, the answer to which we never do hear. It leads to the next step in the meditation, in which the personal urgency and lyric intensity become unmistakable:

> Must these like empty Shadows pass,
> Or Forms reflected from a Glass?
> Or mere Chimaera's in the Mind,
> That fly and leave no Marks behind?
> Does not the Body thrive and grow
> By Food of twenty Years ago?
> And, had it not been still supply'd
> It must a thousand Times have dy'd.
> Then, who with Reason can maintain,
> That no Effects of Food remain?
> And, is not Virtue in Mankind
> The Nutriment that feeds the Mind?
> Upheld by each good Action past,
> And still continued by the last:
> Then, who with Reason can pretend,
> That all Effects of Virtue end?
> [51–66]

I emphasize again the unadorned language in which this poem is delivered. In this passage the plainest homiletic similes are the vehicle of its didactic movement: shadows, forms reflected in a glass, the body and its food. These may be said to be the rhetorical adornment of the lesson. But the poetry here is to be found and felt in the form of the statements, all of which are presented as questions. Rhetorically an argument is presented and illustrated; poetically that argument is vindicated. For the poetic meaning of the passage is not that the argument is true; rather, it is that the rational will requires that the argument be made, and be insisted upon, even as its certainty is left in doubt, doubt acknowledged by the very questions in the form of which the argument is advanced. Poetically, however, the passage imitates the intensifying force of the speaker's need for this doctrine, and this we can feel only in the rhythms and repetitions of the questions within which it is shaped. The reader feels these insistent rhythms built into the progress from the "medial" summary ("Then, who with Reason can maintain . . .") toward the conclusion ("Then, who with Reason can pretend . . ."), the shift from "maintain" to "pretend" reflecting the intensification of Swift's inner commitment to a doctrine whose truth he feels as rational need, not rational certainty.

This delicate blend of assertion and skepticism, of belief and doubt, develops sufficient force to generate the assertiveness of the application as the poem returns its attention to the difficult woman whose pain and impatience are, as we have seen, its final subject. We hear this in the address of the next section—"Believe me, Stella"—and the next—"O then, whatever Heav'n intends." But by this time we have come to understand this assertiveness as an expression of need and love, of the fully charged rational will, which is all this poem will vindicate. Furthermore, we can recognize this strained style of assertion as entirely appropriate to the emotional character of the poem's conclusion, that is, its character as Swift's plea to Stella that she find her substantial identity and acknowledge his in his words to her, in his need for her. If we feel in this poem the lyric intensity I have claimed for it, we feel this intensity in the poem's joining of its didactic content to its personal urgency. These come together in a poetic mimesis of the inner movement of the rational will seeking to realize itself, in the most difficult of circumstances, with reference to its best beliefs. In representing fully both the forces against which that will must strive, and the resources it possesses, the poem provides Swift the opportunity for self-revelation that makes his embrace of his own positives always a lyric occasion.[20]

In Swift's poems for his friend we see the opportunities for self-discovery inherent in the didactic stance, the opportunities for introspection inherent in the fulfillment of a public charge. My line of argument has sought to account for the intensely moving success Swift achieves in this respect when we consider his poems to Stella against the achievements of his career in satire. In his satire the didactic stance is the platform for attack, the occasion for irony, for the feigned commitment to beliefs and to an audience from which he subsequently withdraws. He withdraws in these circumstances into the subversive experience of a personality whose energies cannot be contained by the commitment to culture presupposed in the purposes of a moralist. But in Swift's poems to Stella he succeeds in realizing those purposes, and in a manner fully responsive, though not vulnerable, to the impulses of his anarchic energy. The characteristic movement of these poems is from public toward intimate address, tracing a curve of feeling expressive of the moralist's inner experience as he strives to understand and to value his positive commitments. This curve of feeling creates the lyric charge of the poetry; it is the sign of the poetry's developing adequacy as a mimetic representation of the inner meaning of its initial didactic commitment. As the poetry

[20]Robert Uphaus has correctly pointed to this poem as an example of Swift's capacity for a "poetry of approval": Uphaus sees the poem as a "reaffirmation of the stability of friendship and proof of the invulnerable wholeness of a virtuous life" ("Swift's Poetry: The Making of Meaning," *ECS*, 5/4 (Summer 1972): 576–578.) I would not argue against this as a general judgment, but such terms as "proof" and "invulnerable" are not quite adequate to the strain with which Swift experiences and expresses his affirmations—his *need* for affirmation is more accurate—in this beautiful and trying poem.

intensifies, its readers, responsive to its emotive line, are no longer the object of its public address, but the overhearers of its inner music. We read a lyric poem.

We overhear the poignant melody that sustains and accompanies the speaker's commitment to his high station. In that poignancy we discover a language whose oblique dignity, whose truth to the love and to the strain Swift's best beliefs generated within him, still survive the anarchic energy he elsewhere directed against those beliefs. The oblique dignity of this language mirrors the manner in which the great Augustans experienced their best beliefs: with reverence and doubt. And this blend of reverence and doubt is the explanation for the inherent lyricism of their work, that tension of the personal against the public which so movingly expresses the strain they felt in maintaining their fidelity to what they loved best. When we speak, as we sometimes do, of the decline of lyric expression in Augustan art, we are missing its presence in works whose shape, though not nominally lyrical, is yet ultimately adequate to the impress of such personal pressure as writers could know in devoting their minds, hearts, and skills to the celebration and to the scrutiny of moral commitments they represented as essential to them even as they recognized their vulnerability and their cost. Dr. Johnson, the most responsible spokesman for Augustan culture, said it best in a prayer he composed near the end of his life: ". . . give me Grace always to remember that thy thoughts are not my thoughts, nor thy ways my ways. And while it shall please thee to continue me in this world where much is to be done and little is to be known, teach me by thy Holy Spirit to withdraw my Mind from unprofitable and dangerous enquiries, from difficulties vainly curious, and doubts impossible to be solved."[21] The Swift who wrote the poems to Stella merited, though he did not receive, the praise of the critic who could compose his own reverence and doubt into the poise of such a prayer.

[21]Samuel Johnson, *Diaries, Prayers, and Annals,* ed. E. L. McAdam, Jr., with Donald and Mary Hyde, in the Yale edition of *The Works of Samuel Johnson* (New Haven and London: Yale Univ. Press and Oxford Univ. Press, 1958), 1:383–384 (12 Aug. 1784).

Feminism and the Augustans:
Some Readings and Problems

Penelope Wilson

Early in 1715 Pope wrote, for decency's sake in the guise of their 'brother', to Martha and Theresa Blount, describing a visit with a doctor and a divine to inspect 'the most reigning Curiosity in the town', currently a hermaphrodite. The account is in Pope's rakish mode, a set-piece of the *risqué* rather than a personal reaction: the priest has to imitate the method of the Apostle Thomas, seeing and feeling, and the Doctor opines that 'upon the whole it was a woman; whatever might give a handle to think otherwise, was a trifle, nothing being more common than for a child to be mark'd with that thing which the mother long'd for'.[1] Since the letter was included in the 1735 editions of Pope's works, it was actually published in the same year as the *Epistle to a Lady*, the poem which ends with a tribute to the same Martha Blount as an androgynous ideal, a 'softer Man', a blend of elements picked from each sex. In the letter the 'brother' concludes—'As for this Party's temper of mind, it appears to be a most even disposition, partaking of the good qualities of both sexes . . . Of how obliging and complaisant a turn appears by this, that he tells the Ladies he has the Inclinations of a Gentleman, and that she tells the Gentleman she has the *Tendre* of a Lady'. We can hardly help noticing the natural slippage in this bawdily-tinged account from the best kind of fusion or tempering (like Martha Blount, 'Woman's at best a Contradiction still') to the nastiness of the Sporus portrait in the *Epistle to Dr Arbuthnot*, published one month earlier than *To a Lady*: 'His Wit all see-saw between *that* and *this*, / Now high, now low, now Master up, now Miss, / And he himself one vile Antithesis'. Thin partitions divide the good contradiction from the vile antithesis. The tribute to Martha Blount if set alongside that letter can be seen to hover on the borders of monstrosity: it is not only Calypso who is 'ne'er so sure our passion to create / As when she touch'd the brink of all we hate' (*To a Lady*, 51–2).

One of the earliest of the still relatively few pieces of feminist work on the

From *Critical Quarterly* 28 (1986), 80–92. Reprinted by permission of the author.

This essay is based on a paper given at the Humanities Research Centre in the Australian National University where the author held a Visiting Fellowship from April to July 1985.
[1] Pope, *Correspondence*, ed. George Sherburn (Oxford, 1956), I, 277–9. Quotations from Pope's poetry are from the one volume Twickenham edition of the *Poems*, ed. John Butt (London, 1963).

period bears the telling title 'The female monster in Augustan satire'.[2] If feminism has—until very recently—left Augustan satire alone, it is partly no doubt because it can expect few rewards from an area which offers more obvious scope for recrimination than for critical insight. To set alongside Pope's hermaphrodite, based this time on the 'curiosity' of the year 1708, there is the 'double mistress' episode of the *Memoirs of Martinus Scriblerus*, where the object of desire is literally monstrous, one of a pair of Siamese twins joined at the waist and with genitalia in common. The isolated figures of Vanessa and 'Stella' and Martha Blount, idealised largely by virtue of their transcendence of the differentially feminine, provide at best a frail counterweight to set against a well-documented gamut of misogyny which runs from attacks on particular women, and in particular on women writing, through satire on the *mores* and pastimes of the contemporary female world, to a representation of woman as species—whether as a physical being as in Swift's 'scatological' poems, or with the more ambivalent recoil of Pope's psychological characterisation in *To a Lady*—which is aptly enough summed up in that phrase, 'the brink of all we hate'.[3] Female sexuality is a focus for fear or derision, or both: Gulliver's climactic trauma in the land of the Houyhnhnms is after all the embrace of a young female Yahoo. Motherhood has no better a press. Breast-feeding in Brobdingnag provides Gulliver with one of the nastiest sights of his voyages, and in *The Dunciad*, where the 'Mother' is figured as a force of anti-creation, a black hole drawing everything back into her vortex, images of giving birth tend constantly towards transmogrification—as 'Sooterkin', for example (I.126), or embryo: 'How hints, like spawn, scarce quick in embryo lie, / How new-born nonsense first is taught to cry, / Maggots half-form'd in rhyme exactly meet, / And learn to crawl upon poetic feet' (I.59–62).

There is a striking, though not unpredictable, lack of awareness in most standard commentaries that there is an issue here at all. One doesn't have to be a very humourless feminist to identify the masculine clubbery which can see the 'broad humour and farcical action' of the Double Mistress episode in the Scriblerus *Memoirs* as a 'refreshing change', nor to query the latent sexism of several now classic readings of *The Rape of the Lock*—less overt, but perhaps no less objectionable than Dr Johnson's frank commendation of its moral as exposing 'the freaks, and humours, and spleen, and vanity of women, as they embroil families in discord, and fill houses with disquiet'. The notes to the Twickenham edition of *To a Lady* offer an unreconstructed litany of prejudice, randomly exemplified by the gloss on the line 'from loveless youth to unrespected age', where the parallel weighting given to two items of 'information' about the Duchess of Buckingham—that she obtained a separation from her first husband because of his brutality to her, and that 'in her old age she became one of the town's [i.e. Horace Walpole's?] jokes'—brings out all the potential insensitivity

[2]Susan Gubar, *Signs* 3 (1977), 380–94; see also comment by Ellen Pollak, and Gubar's reply, *ibid.*, 728–33.

[3]Recently adopted as the title of a study of the tradition of post-Restoration satire on women: see Felicity A. Nussbaum, *The Brink of All We Hate* (Lexington, 1984).

of Pope's zeugma. Pope *is* allowed to have been unfair, for 'political' reasons, to Queen Caroline ('the worst that can be said of such a sensible and tolerant woman is that she maintained an implacable hatred of her eldest son'): sexual politics, however, count for nothing. Because of its date, perhaps the most startling example of the general myopia comes from a work published as late as 1971 where we are told of Swift's *The Lady's Dressing Room* and other similar pieces that the scatological elements, the relentless recitations of the details of female grossness, 'dramatize the failure of people, *as represented by the young heroes, to reconcile the physical imperfections and animal nature of man with his decent and spiritual side*' (my italics).[4]

Clearly there is plenty of scope for a revisionary questioning of the ideological assumptions which tend to be brought into play as one reads these works: and teaching early eighteenth-century literature to today's undergraduates one is made perpetually aware of the dimensions of the challenge. But despite that real need to free readings from the pall of misogyny, there are acute problems for feminism in these uncongenial waters. The political importance of a more consciously resistant reading in this case seems to remain, disappointingly, out of all proportion to its usefulness as a critical tool. The potential creativity of entry into the text from the margins too easily loses itself either in a righteous cul-de-sac of recrimination or in a self-generating process of elaboration on the 'positions' of feminist theory. On the one hand there is a real danger of unproductive anachronism, the feminist reader of Augustan satire courting comparison with the hack author of Swift's *Tale of a Tub,* reading Homer, in current parlance, against the grain: 'What can be more defective and unsatisfactory than his long dissertation upon tea?' On the other hand, whereas in its own defence, to avert the charges, or more importantly the consciousness, of naivete or marginality to which it is so prone, feminism must meet academic criticism on its own terms, in doing so it can itself become at least stylistically complicit in forms of scholastic oppression to which it should be particularly sensitive. The justice of the cause, one wants to remind oneself, is not necessarily a measure of its availability for theoretical sophistication.

These problems—general problems, of course, for feminist criticism—are, I would argue, in a special way integral to this topic. Augustan satire is perhaps uniquely adept at constructing the terms of its own criticism and at pre-emptive disablement of the opposition. 'Augustanism', if more than a conventional denomination, is more usefully seen as a strategy, a range of rhetorics and tactics, than as a set of absolute beliefs. It is strongly anti-theoretical in stance. Like Barthes's 'mythology' representing History as Nature, it represents itself and its values as beyond the merely partisan, timeless rather than accidental, paradoxically 'universal' in that by these values most of the world will fall. Opposition is

[4]See *Memoirs of the Extraordinary Life, Works, and Discoveries of Martinus Scriblerus,* ed. C. Kerby-Miller (New Haven: Yale University Press, 1950), p. 294; Johnson, *Lives of the English Poets,* ed. G. Birkbeck Hill (Oxford, 1905), III, 234. Pope, *Epistles to Several Persons,* ed. F. W. Bateson (London: Methuen, 1951); Jae Num Lee, *Swift and Scatological Satire* (Albuquerque: University of New Mexico Press, 1971), pp. 82–3.

inevitably defined as partial. From the early *Essay on Criticism* to the final *Dunciad* the good critic is for Pope the one who looks to 'the whole' rather than to parts; and as the word 'Author' suggests in the following passage from *The Dunciad,* the bad critic connects closely with the scientific investigators approved by Dulness, who 'See Nature in some partial narrow shape, / And let the Author of the whole escape' (IV.455–6). Two tenets of characteristic circularity are hinted at here: that the proper concern of literature and criticism is with human nature in general rather than with the particular and the partisan, and that works are to be read not 'against the grain' but in the same spirit that the author writ. Feminism thus fits neatly if anachronistically into Pope's account of critical malpractice in the *Essay on Criticism.* It is particularly threatened by distinctions like those set up in the language of the following passages:

> Most Criticks, fond of some subservient Art,
> Still make the *Whole* depend upon a *Part,*
> They talk of *Principles,* but *Notions* prize,
> And All to one lov'd Folly sacrifice . . .
>
> Thus Criticks, of less *Judgment* than *Caprice,*
> *Curious,* not *knowing,* not *exact,* but *nice,*
> Form *short Ideas*; and offend in *Arts*
> (As most in *Manners*) by a *Love to Parts.*
> (263–6, 285–8)

In the face of such high-precision intimidation, there are few options but to hold out exactly for 'caprice' and 'curiosity' as, if not ends in themselves, at least the tools of exploration, necessary inroads into the apparent certainties embedded in 'judgement', 'knowing', and the confident representation of 'the whole'. One of the first premises of feminism is, of course, that the structures it has to confront are not those of a universal, all-embracing humanism, but are coloured by an unspoken androcentrism; that these part/whole statements can be, and need to be, turned on their heads, so that the shape of Pope's own construction of 'Nature' is recognised as 'partial' and 'narrow'. It is hardly accidental that Augustanism, coloured as it is by the ethos of a like-minded coterie, has remained something of a masculine preserve. The parallel drawn by Pope in the lines above between criticism and 'manners' is still a resonant one in academic circles, and highlights the fear endemic to women's studies of being *mal à propos,* of being ridiculous. humourless, or banal. In doing so it may help to focus our attention on the more particular problems of the voice of feminist resistance when confronted with the refractions and complexities of specific examples of Augustan wit.

In Pope's letter to the Blount sisters the hermaphroditic penis may be a 'trifle', but sexual difference is not: the joke places the phallus as the object of the woman's longing at the centre of sexual existence. The representation of sexual difference is at the heart of this topic, and on it must depend any further judgements about what seem to me the less interesting questions of whether or not the texts or their authors are sexist, misogynist, or partly or wholly 'recuperable'. In this essay I want to look at the question of sexual difference in two of the best-known of the Augustan poems on 'women', Swift's *The Lady's Dressing Room* and Pope's *To a Lady*, noting in passing that for these purposes there is an imbalance in the material available to us: there is, in this sense, no *Essay on Man*. It goes more or less without saying that here and elsewhere both Pope and Swift represent positions which are properly inimical to a modern feminist consciousness. Pope's poem calls constantly for such qualification: in its validation in advance in the first lines of a sexist discourse of dumb blondes and brunettes (' "Most Women have no Characters at all" . . . And best distinguished by black, brown, or fair'); in the relegation of women to a purely private, domestic realm; in the Miltonic sub-ordination effected through the image of the moon and its reflected light; in the collapsing of female obedience and desire—the one who 'by submitting sways'; in the notion of woman as charming in her weaknesses, 'fine by defect, and delicately weak', this last formulation being one directly challenged by Mary Wollstonecraft,[5] *The Lady's Dressing Room* is understandably regarded as one of the most notori-ous sites of anti-feminist animus, no less so for being, as Felicity Nussbaum and others have shown, in a long literary tradition of obscene and scatological satire against women.

Swift's dressing-room is a far cry from the narcissistic ritual presented to public view in *The Rape of the Lock* ('And now, unveil'd, the Toilet stands display'd'): instead we are drawn in to the stealthy inspection of the closed quarters of woman and maid which had been used since Lucretius, Juvenal, Ovid, as the paradoxical site of potential redemption for the love-pangs of the suffering suitor.[6] The accusatory *reportage* of Swift's dressing-room poem presents a room from which the lady herself has issued forth in the third line leaving the room 'void' for Strephon's inspection, 'void' only in a sense which one might most appropriately gloss as 'vacant', since in other respects it is all too full—of litter, debris, matter. In Pope's ceremonial set-piece the looking-glass is the site of beauty made manifest: here the absent image is transmogrified into the world of the magnifying glass and tweezers, of 'worms in the nose', bristles on the chin, ear-wax, snot, grease, sweat, the scrapings of teeth and gums. The catalogue of nouns, scarcely relieved by the sparse adjectival qualifiers of equal maculacy—'begumm'd, bematter'd, and beslim'd'—produces a verbal texture clogged like that of Celia's own combs, 'fill'd up with Dirt so closely fixt, / No Brush could force a way betwixt. / A Paste of Composition rare, / Sweat, Dandriff, Powder, Lead, and Hair'.

Strephon's investigations, and the narrator's rhetorical excitement—though not perhaps the reader's arc of revulsion—culminate with the discovery of the

[5] *The Rights of Woman*, ch. 4, 'Observations on the state of degradation to which woman is reduced by various causes' (London, 1970), p. 68.
[6] For a wide variety of commentaries, see the works listed in Pat Rogers's Penguin edition of *Swift's Complete Poems* (Harmondsworth, 1983), p. 827; and on the English 'dressing-room' tradition, see especially Harry M. Solomon, ' "Difficult beauty": Tom D'Urfey and the context of Swift's "The Lady's Dressing-room" ', *SEL* 19 (1979), 431–44. Quotations from Swift's poems are from the *Poetical Works*, ed. H. Davis (London, 1967).

commode and its contents. The trauma of his 'peeping' turns Strephon—now fittingly 'blind' to female charms—into an out-and-out misogynist:

> His foul Imagination links
> Each Dame he sees with all her Stinks . . .
> All Women his Description fits,
> And both Idea's jump like Wits:
> By vicious Fancy coupled fast,
> And still appearing in Contrast.

In the well-known coda, the narrator dissociates himself from the extremity of his hero's reaction: 'Should I the Queen of Love refuse / Because she rose from stinking Ooze?' If Strephon would but stop his nose—like Gulliver on his return from his final voyage?—

> He soon would learn to think like me,
> And bless his ravisht Eyes to see
> Such Order from Confusion sprung,
> Such gaudy Tulips rais'd from Dung.

Language and structure enable various utterly 'respectable' readings of the poem—Christian, proto-Freudian, straightforwardly didactic. The poem follows a characteristic Swiftian pattern: the hero, like Gulliver, is disillusioned in proportion as he had before been gulled into accepting a false and clichéd romantic construct. Indeed, since Strephon's case is presented to us not in his own voice but by a commenting narrator, the coda usefully makes explicit a way of diagnosing Gulliver's final hippophiliac disorder in terms of associative psychology—horses and rationality, man and bestiality bound into a dichotomy no less rigid for being inverted. As one considers that coda more closely, however, the apparent moderation of the narrator's pose is re-read as a hopeless and violent yoking together of its own constituent obsessions and refusals, compromised rather than a compromise, a symptom of that ambiguously 'ravisht' sight which constitutes a common ground between him and Strephon. The locus of insanity shifts backwards through the poem, with the narrator's attempts to impose a distancing literary order on Strephon's findings, and his perfunctory authorial gestures towards reticence or euphemism ('the Stockings, why should I expose . . .?', 'Why Strephon will you tell the rest?'), coming to seem an increasingly mad and irrelevant refrain to the catalogue of disgust: we could be again in the company of the hack of *A Tale of a Tub*. In the mythologising and metaphoric moves of the presentation of the excremental 'chest'—the comparison with Pandora's box, and the lingering mutton chops simile—the narrator quite overtakes the now 'cautious' Strephon in his unmediated involvement in the survey.

> But Strephon cautious never meant
> The Bottom of the Pan to grope,
> And fowl his Hands in Search of Hope . . .
>
> As Mutton Cutlets, Prime of Meat

So Things, which must not be exprest,
When plumpt into the reeking Chest;
Send up an excremental Smell
To taint the Parts from whence they Fell.[7]

All this undermining—of Strephon, of the narrator, and obliquely of the
reader who lends a complicit ear—may seem to deflect much of the attack from
'Celia' and her body on to the minds of men. A tactful, if incongruously bland,
reading is made available for the critical consensus in the way, directly analogous
with Swift's best-known prose writings, in which the poem both suggests and
explodes a schema of compromise. We are free to conclude that, like others in
the same *remedium amoris* mode—'A beautiful young nymph going to bed',
'Strephon and Chloe'—'woman' functions here simply as the clearest image of
the discrepancy between the human—and especially the literary—capacity for
idealisation and the gross materiality of things as they are. The poem is not
really, then, 'about' women: on the contrary, as we have seen, it is (although few
critics have felt entirely comfortable with it) about man's 'decent and spiritual
side'.

A feminist reading would want to resist the hermeneutic move to write out
the issue of gender from the poem. Granting that Swift's scatological satire is
not solely directed against women, it would not accept as merely accidental or
opportunist the association in this and in other poems of the feminine with dirt-
iness and decay. It is hardly a twentieth-century possibility that the poem
should be taken—as it largely was by contemporaries, with a brave literality—as
primarily practical in its aim, to reform women's boudoir habits. That even then
some sort of accommodation seemed necessary is suggested by the unlikely
shift of emphasis found in one of the earliest critiques of the poem; 'whenever
he offends against delicacy, he teaches it . . . And though it may reasonably be
supposed; that few English ladies have such a dressing-room as Celia's, yet
many may have given sufficient cause for reminding them, that very soon after
desire has been gratified, the utmost delicacy becomes necessary, to prevent
disgust'.[8]

It takes a rare reader to uncover here the lineaments of gratified desire; but
even without them, the operation of the poem is a complex one, at once moralis-
tic and cathartic. The generalising, homiletic impulse of a de-gendered reading
operates on a sophisticated level of interpretation, demanding to be decoded;
but the poem also enacts a much more primitive ritual of control of the unspeakable, cleansing through naming. Jean Hagstrum finds the author here less like a
wit or an outraged priest than 'a Freudian patient repeating compulsively the

---

[7]This is a rather different reading of what Herbert Davis sees as the bubbling up of Swift's 'irre-
pressible spirit of parody' throughout the poem: 'A modest defence of "The Lady's Dressing-Room" ',
in *Restoration and Eighteenth-Century Literature*, ed. C. Camden (Chicago, 1963), pp. 39–48.
The essay would serve as a good illustration of the 'sanitising' critical effect of devices like parody and
allusion.

[8]John Hawkesworth (1755): *Swift: The Critical Heritage*, ed. K. Williams (London, 1970), p. 154.

particulars that produced his trauma'.[9] The poem certainly has something pathological about it, a dimension which retrospectively, and sometimes anachronistically, taints even its more innocent locutions, as 'issues' and 'tissues' in lines 3 and 4. The purpose of this inventory, we are told in lines 9 and 10, is 'to make the Matter clear'; and in the context of this extravagant be-mattering (l.45) there seems a fleeting possibility that itemisation itself could somehow restore a kind of purity or transparence to the impurity of the congealed effluvia of the dressing-room debris.

In that context, and with sexual difference in mind, it is interesting to note the absence of disgust at any specifically feminine failures in hygiene; and one might compare a similar silence in *Strephon and Chloe,* where honeymoon disillusion is precipitated by the revelation of Chloe's bodily nature not through the menstrual anxiety which is the common currency of wedding-night jokes (hinted at no doubt in the narrator's use of the phrase 'no proper season') but through a unisex Swiftian variation: 'Carminative and diuretic / Will damp all passions sympathetic'. In anthropological terms matter issuing from the body is dangerous because of its marginal nature, and Mary Douglas suggests that the particular bodily margins to which the beliefs of each culture attribute power will depend on 'what situation the body is mirroring'.[10] What Celia represents in *The Lady's Dressing Room* is not the otherness of the menstrual body, with its attendant disgusts and fears: Swift's 'nymphs' do produce on their respective Strephons and Cassinuses effects nearly as dramatic as those feared by some cultures to result from contact with menstrual blood, but disillusion operates through a recognition of sameness, of shared excrementality, rather than through fear of otherness. The lines 'Should I the Queen of Love refuse / Because she rose from stinking Ooze?' very possibly contain an echo of some lines by Etherege where the reference is quite explicitly vaginal:[11] even allusion here seems to act rather as suppression, the insistence on the excremental nature of the 'smell' indicating the consistency of the urge to write sexuality out of the picture.

There is of course another side to Swift's views on women, even without an invocation of the *Journal to Stella*—the tough, unsentimental challenge of his arguments for female education, a concern introduced into the Utopian visions of Books I and IV of *Gulliver's Travels,* and expounded in his 'Letter to a very young lady on her marriage' without a vestige of the 'lullaby strains of condescending endearments' to which Mary Wollstonecraft was to take such strong exception in later male purveyors of 'advice' to young women. The 'Letter' is an important document in a version of feminism as integration, the whole direction of Swift's exhortations being that women should make themselves, and be allowed to make themselves, intellectually fit companions for men. Clearly of

[9]Jean Hagstrum, *Sex and Sensibility: Ideal and Erotic Love from Milton to Mozart* (Chicago and London, 1980), p. 148.

[10]Mary Douglas, *Purity and Danger: an Analysis of Concepts of Pollution and Taboo* (London: Routledge and Kegan Paul, 1966), p. 121: cf. also p. 147. See in general Janice Delaney, Mary Jane Lupton, and Emily Toth, *The Curse: a Cultural History of Menstruation* (New York, 1976).

[11]*Poems*, ed. James Thorpe (Princeton, 1963), p. 38.

limited acceptability from the viewpoint of modern feminism, the letter is uncompromisingly hostile to the forms of female bonding ('A Knot of Ladies got together by themselves, is a very School of Impertinence and Detraction'); like some of the poems (e.g. 'The furniture of a woman's mind'), its most positive tribute to women is anger at what Swift sees as the almost universal misdirection of their energies. The fact that Swift has found a place in studies both of misogyny and of feminism in the eighteenth century is only apparently a paradox, as is perhaps most economically illustrated by one characteristically unconvivial statement from that letter, a statement to which I should like to give emphasis as a focal point for this paper: *'there is no Quality whereby Women endeavour to distinguish themselves from Men, for which they are not just so much the worse.'*[12]

The androgynous emphasis of Swift's construction of the acceptable woman is clear in several works addressed to his female friends—the poems to Stella, or *Cadenus and Vanessa.* His commitment is to the need for women to overcome sexual distinctions, and however enlightened a position that may be in educational terms, in physical terms the rejection—or the suppression—of femininity must be an irredeemably misogynist position. Turning from Swift to Pope we move, despite all their similarities (and it is interesting to note the incidence of Swiftian touches in *To a Lady*), into a very different mode. The difference is usefully signalled by a revealing variation of emphasis in Johnson's strikingly parallel formulation of the mechanism of disgust in Swift and in Pope. On Swift, he finds that 'the greatest difficulty that occurs, in analysing his character, is to discover by what depravity of intellect he took delight in revolving ideas, from which almost every other mind shrinks in disgust'. With Pope there is a new sense of the reader's complicity in the process of 'revolving': 'we feel all the appetite of curiosity for that from which we have a thousand times turned fastidiously away'. As a comment on *The Rape of the Lock* this is itself something of a *faux pas*, but it will serve to point to the intrusion of a new concept, essentially that of 'charm'. In Pope's words, ' 'Tis to their Changes that their charms we owe': the concept is now bereft of its magic and its danger, denoting an ambiguous fascination with the potentially evil or disruptive disabled of its power, a weakened and more manageable version of the passion created on the brink of hatred.

It has been suggested that the peculiarly bald negativity of Swift's views on women may be accounted for as a failure to accept, or more positively a dissociation from, the essentially middle-class sexual ideology which was crystallising during his lifetime, a myth of feminine idleness and domestication which would offer a new register to which Pope—twenty years Swift's junior—was to find no difficulty in acceding.[13] At any rate, if in Swift the otherness of women, and of a woman's world, is something to be as far as possible eliminated, Pope in the

---

[12]*Prose Works*, ed. Herbert Davis, IX (Oxford, 1948), pp. 83–94.

[13]See Ellen Pollak in *Signs* 3 (1978), 728–32. One might compare the myth written out by Addison in the story of the sexually segregated commonwealths in *The Spectator*, nos. 433–4.

Epistle to a Lady is from the outset accepting and building on an acceptance of 'contra-distinction' between the sexes and their worlds. The addressee, the listener, is a woman who transcends femininity not by quelling 'the feminine' in herself, the difference of her sex, but rather by an apotheosis of it—'Woman's at best a Contradiction still'.

Martha Blount's androgyny bears a closer relation to the angels than to the hermaphrodite, her desire not so much ambiguous as collapsed into submission. Female sexuality is a strongly negative presence in the poem, a recurrent synecdochic representation of selfishness, social disruption, or a disturbing power of detachment which begins to call into question the simplification of woman's sexuality as unbridled lust—as with Chloe who, 'while her Lover pants upon her breast, / Can mark the figures on an Indian chest' (167–8). Nevertheless, sexual difference is overtly presented by Pope as a matter of degree rather than of absolute distinctions. Woman is 'a softer Man'; women are more inconsistent within themselves than men but more uniform in general character. It is notable, however, that the subject of 'women' induces a significant qualitative modification to Pope's psychological schema of the Ruling Passion, the providential *laissez-faire* expounded in the *Essay on Man* and the *Epistle to Cobham* which ensures with an easy optimism that 'the two extremes of a vice serve like two opposite biasses to keep up the balance of things', that 'one man's weakness grows the strength of all'. The difference with women is not just one of degree:

> In Men, we various Ruling Passions find,
> In Women, two almost divide the kind;
> Those, only fix'd, they first or last obey,
> The Love of Pleasure, and the Love of Sway . . .
>
> Men, some to Bus'ness, some to Pleasure take;
> But ev'ry Woman is at heart a Rake:
> Men, some to Quiet, some to public Strife;
> But ev'ry Lady would be Queen for life.

The uncertainty signalled by that slippage from a divided kind to blanket inclusiveness lies near the surface here, but can be seen more subtly to inform the whole poem. The 'ruling passions' in women are no longer self-cancelling in the larger scheme of things, but dialectically interactive in one individual: 'They seek the second not to lose the first'. The collapsing of those separate and divergent principles into this more challenging pleasure/power dialectic carries with it, as numerous readers have recognised, a new charge of poetic engagement. The struggle to characterise 'woman' seems to take Pope to a new level of general truth. It would be hard to argue that the portraits of some of these 'difficult women' do not in some way dramatise the poet's own awareness of a divided consciousness—that of Atossa, for example, her life, like that of a wit in Pope's 1717 preface to his own poems, 'a warfare upon earth', her schizophrenia surely the nightmare of the satirist ('Shines, in exposing Knaves and painting Fools, / Yet is, whate'er she hates and ridicules'), or even of the chameleon poet ('Scarce once herself, by turns all Womankind'). As in the curiously masculine orientation of the line, 'But ev'ry Woman is at heart a *Rake*' we can here observe another version of androgyny, one which involves the poet in much the same way as the female impersonation of the early epistles, the translation of Ovid's 'Sapho to Phaon' as well as the better-known *Eloisa to Abelard.*

Ellen Pollak, in an exposition of what she sees as 'the conventional ideological imperatives regarding gender' inscribed by *To a Lady,* rightly points out that the ambiguities and complexities of a well-wrought poem do not in themselves guarantee its ideological innocence; and she goes on to argue, more problematically, that the illusion of complexity generated by Pope's paradoxes is actually a sophisticated rhetorical strategy for obscuring an ideological simplicity.[14] One is reminded of Dr Johnson's report that Pope 'hardly drank tea without a stratagem'; and if *To a Lady* is in general more resistant than Pollak allows to the dropping down of an ideological barrier against the play of meaning, it is at any rate possible to identify in its central device of address to a friend just such a muddying of the waters. Pope's satire on women takes the form of a tribute to one woman, and for many readers the tribute so radically qualifies the satire as to free the poem from any taint of misogyny.[15] The use of the exemplary woman can, obviously, however, be an anti-feminist device in itself. The technique is a commonplace of rhetorical strategy—used in an anti-feminist context as early as Simonides, who sets nine types of women reincarnated from nasty animals against the one useful type derived from the bee.[16]

In *To a Lady* the woman could be said to be constituted from the outset in the role of traitor to her sex, and her mostly silent participation in the quizzing of the figures in the portrait gallery raises a more general question about the nature of this kind of collusive adversarial relationship. The power play in wit of this sort very obviously depends on the existence, or the construction, of a suitable third party to receive and validate it. The representation of sexual difference here is not simply a product of an ideology, or of individual or communal neurosis, but is substantially informed by the interplay of poet and listener in the satiric game. We can take this further: it may be that one of the most suggestive models for feminist criticism in relation to Augustan literature is that of the triangulating technique of the 'tendentious' joke.[17] In *The Lady's Dressing Room* we have at one level what is perhaps the classic structure of the anti-feminist joke, the aggression of the male narrator directed past the woman (and at least overtly past Strephon as well) to a third person, the colluding listener, inevitably

---

[14]Ellen Pollak, 'Pope and sexual difference: woman as part and counterpart in the "Epistle to a Lady"', *SEL* 24 (1984), 461–81. See now the same writer's *The Poetics of Sexual Myth: Gender and Ideology in the verse of Swift and Pope* (Chicago and London, 1985), which appeared while this essay was in the press.

[15]See, e.g., Howard Weinbrot, *Alexander Pope and the Traditions of Formal Verse Satire* (Princeton, 1982), pp. 189–98.

[16]Paraphrased by Addison in *Spectator* 209: ed. D. F. Bond (Oxford, 1965), II, 320.

[17]See Freud, *Jokes and Their Relation to the Unconscious* (translation by James Strachey published in Pelican Freud Library, 1976), esp. pp. 140ff. on jokes about women.

inscribed as male. In Pope's *Epistle* (and in the letter describing the visit to the hermaphrodite) the fact of address to a woman interferes with that triangulation, apparently defusing its hostility, as the brother–sister fiction of the letter 'apparently' renders its very bawdiness innocent. In each case a social interplay is set up in which the voice of feminist resistance can hardly seem other than unmannerly, shrill, or gauche.

The first recorded voice of feminist resistance to *The Lady's Dressing Room* is that of Lady Mary Wortley Montagu, refreshingly untroubled by any such qualms in her own octosyllabic Augustan wit, diagnosing the poem as simple revenge for sexual misadventure in a critical approximation to the knee in the groin:

> Perhaps you have no better Luck in
> The Knack of Rhyming than of —[18]

Laetitia Pilkington, whose mother deserves a place in the Critical Heritage as having simply thrown up her dinner on reading *The Lady's Dressing Room,* has an anecdote which may serve as one last example of the repertory of techniques brought by Augustan satire to the anti-feminist animus of its wit. Interesting partly for the way in which Swift, as so often, executes a move which leaves Pope's stratagems looking transparent, it also captures the voicelessness to which one may be reduced by such 'civility', and perhaps in capturing it enacts its own more indirect revenge. She is relating 'a compliment of [Swift's] to some ladies, who supped with him, of whom [she] had the honour to be one': 'The Dean was giving us an account of some woman, who, he told us, was the nastiest, filthiest, most stinking old B—ch that ever was yet seen, except the Company, Ladies! except the Company! for that you know is but civil. We all bowed: could we do less?'[19]

[18]See Robert Halsband, ' "The Lady's Dressing-Room" explicated by a contemporary', *The Augustan Milieu,* ed. H. K. Miller, E. Rothstein, and G.S. Rousseau (Oxford, 1970), pp. 225–31.
[19]*Memoirs* (Dublin, 1748) II, 144–5.

Part 5
POLITICS

Swift's Politics:
A Preface to Gulliver's Travels

Ian Higgins

the modern Question is only, Whether he be a *Whig* or a *Tory*

—*The Sentiments of a Church-of-England Man*
(1708; published 1711)

But, I confess, that after I had been a little too copious in talking of my own beloved Country; of our Trade, and Wars by Sea and Land, of our Schisms in Religion, and Parties in the State; the Prejudices of his Education prevailed so far, that he could not forbear taking me up in his right Hand, and stroaking me gently with the other; after an hearty Fit of laughing, asked me whether I were a *Whig* or a *Tory*.

—*Gulliver's Travels*, II, iii (1726)

If possible, to learn his Story,
And whether he were *Whig* or *Tory*? . . .
In State-Opinions *a-la Mode*,
He hated *Wh—n* like a Toad;
Had giv'n the *Faction* many a Wound,
And Libell'd all the *Junta* round

—*Part of the Seventh Epistle of the First
Book of Horace Imitated* (1713)

Swift's politics is a large, complex and controversial subject upon which there is a considerable corpus of commentary. This paper is an attempt to consider briefly some of the contested issues in interpretation of Swift's political writing and to examine aspects of the politics of *Gulliver's Travels*, a general satire which had topical polemical resonance at the time of its publication.[1]

From *Monash Swift Papers*, 1 (1988), ed. Clive T. Probyn and Bryan Colebourne, 41–65. Reprinted by permission of the author.

[1]Swift intended *Gulliver's Travels* as a polemical act against the Whig government and a satire on contemporary European civilization and the vices and follies of humanity: see *The Correspondence of Jonathan Swift*, edited by Harold Williams, 5 vols (Oxford, 1963–65), III, 102, 138, 226; hereafter cited as *Correspondence*. For an illustration of how Swift's satire has particular political and 'universal' meaning, see the discussion of the satire on the Emperor of Lilliput's 'Mercy' by R.F. Kennedy, 'Swift and Suetonius', *Notes and Queries*, n.s., 16 (1969), 340–41. On the contemporary reception and significance of *Gulliver* as an Opposition work, see Bertrand A. Goldgar, *Walpole and the Wits: The Relation of*

As Swift described in his violent sermon 'On Brotherly Love', 'Party' division profoundly pervaded his society.[2] There is at least nominal inconsistency in Swift's own party political attachment. After writing Odes to both King William III and the deprived Archbishop of Canterbury, William Sancroft, in the early 1690s, Swift's first political tract *A Discourse of the Contests and Dissentions Between the Nobles and the Commons in Athens and Rome, With the Consequences they had upon both those States* (1701) was published for a specific Court Whig political cause, although Swift's Tory answerers were able to demonstrate unwhiggish tenets in the work.[3] *A Tale of a Tub* (1704) is dedicated to the Junto Whig Lord Somers, although hostile contemporaries remarked that the ironic 'Bookseller's Dedication' to Somers was disrespectful.[4] The Dedication remained in the fifth edition of 1710. Swift's opposition to Whig ecclesiastical policy is well-documented and well-known and in 1710 for principled and personal reasons Swift began to write for what he later described as 'the immortal Tory Ministry'[5] of the last four years of Queen Anne's reign.

Swift's own statements about his political principles and party allegiance in this Age of Party might seem to illustrate a Swiftian 'Thought': 'How inconsistent is Man with himself!'[6] Regularly charged in the Whig press after 1710 with venal political apostasy, and clearly sensitive to charges that he had deserted the Whigs for the Tories in 1710, Swift frequently claimed personal political consis-

---

Politics to Literature, 1722–1742 (Lincoln, Nebraska, 1976), esp. pp. 30, 49–63 and J.A. Downie, 'Walpole, "the Poet's Foe," ' in *Britain in the Age of Walpole*, edited by Jeremy Black (London, 1984), pp. 171–88. However, on the tenuousness of the consistent political allegories and much of the particular and personal allusion commonly alleged in criticism of the book, see Phillip Harth, 'The Problem of Political Allegory in *Gulliver's Travels'*, *MP*, 73 (1976), S40–S47; J.A. Downie, 'Political Characterization in *Gulliver's Travels'*, *YES*, 7 (1977), 108–20; Ragnhild Hatton, *George I: Elector and King* (London, 1978), p. 259; F.P. Lock, *The Politics of 'Gulliver's Travels'* (Oxford, 1980), esp. pp. 89–112.

[2]*The Prose Writings of Jonathan Swift*, edited by Herbert Davis and others, 16 vols (Oxford, 1939–74), IX, 176–77; hereafter cited as *PW*.

[3]See the excerpts from *The Source of Our Present Fears Discover'd* and from Charles Leslie, *The New Association. Part II* and 'Supplement' reprinted as appendices in *A Discourse of the Contests and Dissentions Between the Nobles and the Commons in Athens and Rome, With the Consequences they had upon both those States. By Jonathan Swift*, edited by Frank H. Ellis (Oxford, 1967), pp. 228–51. Leslie, who assumed the work was by the eminent Whig polemicist Bishop Gilbert Burnet, triumphed at one point: 'Ah! *Doctor, Doctor*, Was this *Always* your *Doctrine*? Are you come to see it at last? And yet never *Mend*!' (p. 247). See the extended study of the pamphlet in F.P. Lock, *Swift's Tory Politics* (London, 1983), pp. 146–61, esp. pp. 160–61.

[4]See the extracts from William King's *Remarks* and William Wotton's *Observations on A Tale of a Tub* reprinted in *Jonathan Swift. A Tale of a Tub and Other Works*, edited by Angus Ross and David Woolley (Oxford, 1986), pp. 182–91 (pp. 183, 190).

[5]*PW*. V, 265.

[6]*PW*. IV, 245. Swift also wrote: 'IF a Man would register all his Opinions upon Love, Politicks, Religion, Learning, and the like; beginning from his Youth, and so go on to old Age: What a Bundle of Inconsistencies and Contradictions would appear at last?' (*PW*. I, 244). Patrick Reilly remarks in his study of Swift that 'Swift is consistent only in his inconsistency, partisanly utilising or discarding any argument to secure his overall aim'. That no single formula accommodates all the contradictions and inconsistencies in Swift's writing 'for his judgements were provisional and piecemeal', see Reilly's *Jonathan Swift: the brave desponder* (Manchester, 1982), pp. 28, 120.

tency.[7] Sometimes he averred that there was no real difference between the essential principles of Whig and Tory and that he was moderate and bipartisan. In a letter to the Earl of Peterborough in 1711, for instance, Swift wrote:

> This dispute [about the principle of passive obedience] would soon be ended, if the dunces who write on each side, would plainly tell us what the object of this passive obedience is in our country. For, I dare swear, nine in ten of the Whigs will allow it to be the legislature, and as many of the Tories deny it to the Prince alone: And I hardly ever saw a Whig and a Tory together, whom I could not immediately reconcile on that article, when I made them explain themselves.[8]

It was only circumstantial and personal reasons, Swift claimed in *The Sentiments of a Church-of-England Man* (published in 1711), that had associated him with one party more than another:

> I converse in full Freedom with many considerable Men of both Parties; and if not in equal Number, it is purely accidental and personal, as happening to be near the Court, and to have made Acquaintance there, more under one Ministry than another.[9]

In his *Memoirs, Relating to that Change which happened in the Queen's Ministry in the Year 1710* (written in 1714 although not printed until 1765) Swift states that in 1702 'I first began to trouble myself with the difference between the principles of Whig and Tory'. The formulation of his position is careful:

> I talked often upon this subject with Lord Sommers; told him, that, having been long conversant with the Greek and Roman authors, and therefore a lover of liberty, I found myself much inclined to be what they called a Whig in politics; and that, besides, I thought it impossible, upon any other principle, to defend or submit to the Revolution: But, as to religion, I confessed myself to be an High-churchman, and that I did not conceive how any one, who wore the habit of a clergyman, could be otherwise.

Despite the strong inclination he expressed to Somers to be a Whig in politics, and thus to make his adherence to the Revolution settlement unquestionable, the High Churchman attempts to vindicate himself in the *Memoirs* from the charge that he 'was a favourer of the low-party'.[10] In 1716 it is the High Church Tory Bishop of Rochester, Francis Atterbury, to whom Swift looks to preserve

---

[7]Frank H. Ellis, ('"A Quill worn to the Pith in the Service of the State": Swift's *Examiner*' in *Proceedings of The First Münster Symposium on Jonathan Swift*, edited by Hermann J. Real and Heinz J. Vienken (München, 1985), pp. 73–82; hereafter cited as *Proceedings*), comments: 'Although *The Examiner* attacks some Whigs whom Swift defended in *A Discourse of the Contests and Dissentions* (1701) and many Whig practices of 1690–1710, it attacks only one Whig principle'. With the exception of an apparent alteration in his attitude on the issue of an Occasional Conformity bill 'Swift did not "change any Principles relating to Government, either in Church or State", when he undertook *The Examiner*' (p. 74n).

[8]*Correspondence*, I, 212. See also: *PW*. II, 13–14; VIII, 71–72; *Swift vs Mainwaring. 'The Examiner' and 'The Medley'*, edited by Frank H. Ellis (Oxford, 1985), pp. 34–37 (*Examiner*, 16 November 1710); pp. 313–14 (*Examiner* 22 March 1711); pp. 450–58 (*Examiner*, 31 May 1711).

[9]*PW*. II, 2.

[10]*PW*. VIII, 120, 122.

the nation from slavery.[11] Swift seeks to assure Atterbury in 1717 of his fidelity to 'my party'.[12] Swift had of course credit and acquaintance with a remarkable number of prominent Jacobite Tories.[13] Yet in his post-1710 correspondence he professed to have always been a member of the Whig party in politics.[14] The inquest into his party political identity imagined in *The Life and Genuine Character of Doctor Swift* is in disagreement about him:

> He was an *honest man* I'll swear:
> Why Sir, I differ from you there,
> For, I have heard another Story,
> He was a most *confounded Tory!*[15]

The exegesis of Swift's political principles and party political allegiance is a matter of continuing disagreement in modern Swift studies. Essentially there are three basic and contradictory accounts of Swift's politics. One position is that Swift is a post-Revolution Tory who was temporarily allied by circumstance to the Whigs. The case for Swift as a Tory in politics and ecclesiology has been advanced principally and recently in the work of F.P. Lock.[16] A second position in Swift studies tends to see Swift as a paradoxical, idiosyncratic political figure whose political attitudes include elements from Tory and Whig extremes of contemporary political argument; that there are conservative Tory and reactionary and radical Whig and libertarian strands in his political ideology. This

---

[11]*Correspondence*, II, 198–99.

[12]*Correspondence*, II, 278–80.

[13]See for instance the list of persons in Swift's letter to Mrs. Barber of 23 February 1731, *Correspondence*, III, 439–40.

[14]For descriptions of himself as a Whig, see *Correspondence*, I, 359 (27 May 1713, to Richard Steele); II, 236 (22 December 1716, to Archbishop King); III, 484 (27 July 1731, to the Countess of Suffolk); IV, 100 (8 January 1733, to Lady Elizabeth Germain); IV, 230 (23 March 1734, to Francis Grant).

[15]*The Poems of Jonathan Swift*, edited by Harold Williams, second edition, 3 vols (Oxford, 1958), II, 547; hereafter cited as *Poems*.

[16]F.P. Lock, *Swift's Tory Politics* (London, 1983) and 'Swift and English Politics, 1701–14', in *The Character of Swift's Satire. A Revised Focus*, edited by Claude Rawson (Newark, Delaware, London and Toronto, 1983) pp. 127–50. Harold Williams remarked: 'Swift, by upbringing and association, regarded himself as a Whig, and continued in that belief after it had ceased to be true in fact and meaning. By 1710 his ecclesiastical and political views had nothing in common with Whig doctrine' (*PW*, XV, xxi). On Swift's High Church and Tory politics, see among others: Robert W. Babcock, 'Swift's Conversion To The Tory Party', *University of Michigan Publications in Language and Literature (Essays and Studies in English and Comparative Literature)*, 8 (1932), 133–49; J.R. Moore, 'Was Jonathan Swift a Moderate?', *South Atlantic Quarterly*, 53 (1954), 260–67; David P. French, 'Swift, the Non-Jurors, and Jacobitism', *MLN*, 72 (1957), 258–64; R.M. Adams, 'The Mood of the Church and *A Tale of a Tub*', in *England in the Restoration and Early Eighteenth Century: Essays on Culture and Society*, edited by H.T. Swedenberg, Jr. (Berkeley, Los Angeles, London, 1972), pp. 71–99 and see his 'In Search of Baron Somers', in *Culture and Politics from Puritanism to the Enlightenment*, edited by Perez Zagorin (Berkeley, Los Angeles, London, 1980), pp. 165–202; Richard I. Cook, *Jonathan Swift as a Tory Pamphleteer* (Seattle, 1967), esp. pp. ix–xxxiv; Isaac Kramnick *Bolingbroke and His Circle: The Politics of Nostalgia in the Age of Walpole* (Cambridge, Mass., 1968), esp. pp. 205–17) describes a bias 'traditional and Tory, idealizing an aristocratic and gentry society' shared by Swift. For Swift as a Tory reactionary see Perry Anderson, *Arguments Within English Marxism* (London , 1980), pp. 83–99, esp. pp. 94–97 which contests the reading by E.P. Thompson (see for example *Whigs and Hunters: The Origins of the Black Act* (London, 1975), esp. p. 293) of Swift as a Tory radical.

second position argues that it is probably a futile exercise to try to site Swift in the terrain of post-Revolution party politics or that both 'Whig' and 'Tory' descriptions of Swift are appropriate.[17] A third view is that Swift is essentially a Whig in state politics and remained so despite his 'conversion' to the predominantly Tory administration of 1710–14. This view, which can be found stated or expounded in the work of many distinguished Swiftians, would appear to be the present scholarly orthodoxy although the critical shorthand 'Tory satirists' applied to Swift and the Scriblerian circle still has currency.[18] The Whig case for Swift squares with a literal reading of Swift's repeated profession that he was 'a Whig in politics' although a 'High-churchman' in religion; that he was 'of the old Whig principles, without the modern articles and refinements'.[19] Swift's hostility to 'modern whiggery' and particularly to the Walpolean regime is not

[17]See the acute readings in Daniel Eilon, 'Did Swift Write *A Discourse on Hereditary Right*', *MP*, 82 (1985), 374–92; 'Private Spirit: A Moral and Political Theme in Swift's Prose' (unpublished Ph.D. dissertation, University of Cambridge, 1986); David Nokes, 'The Radical Conservatism of Swift's Irish Pamphlets', *BJECS*, 7 (1984), 169–76 and his *Jonathan Swift, A Hypocrite Reversed, A Critical Biography* (Oxford, 1985). The phrase 'Tory-anarchist' has long had currency in studies of Swift. But see especially Carole Fabricant, *Swift's Landscape* (Baltimore and London, 1982), p. 37.

[18]For some modern studies that, despite other differences, identify Swift's fundamental Whig politics: Arthur E. Case, *Four Essays on Gulliver's Travels* (Princeton, 1945; rpt. Gloucester, Mass., 1958), pp. 107–09; J.C. Beckett, 'Swift as an Ecclesiastical Statesman', in *Essays in British and Irish History in Honour of James Eadie Todd*, edited by H.A. Cronne, T.W. Moody and D.B. Quinn (London, 1949), rpt. in *Fair Liberty Was All His Cry: A Tercentenary Tribute to Jonathan Swift 1667–1745*, edited by A. Norman Jeffares (London, 1967), pp. 146–65 (pp. 150, 152, 159); Kathleen Williams, *Jonathan Swift and the Age of Compromise* (Lawrence, Kansas, 1958), pp. 100–03; James A. Preu, *The Dean and the Anarchist* (Tallahassee, 1959), esp. pp. 33, 99–102; Bertrand A. Goldgar, *The Curse of Party: Swift's Relations with Addison and Steele* (Lincoln, Nebraska, 1961), pp. 63–67, 83, 169; Basil Hall, ' "An Inverted Hypocrite": Swift the Churchman', in *The World of Jonathan Swift: Essays for the Tercentenary*, edited by Brian Vickers (Oxford, 1968), pp. 38–68 (p. 60); W.A. Speck, 'From Principles to Practice: Swift and Party Politics', in *The World of Jonathan Swift*, pp. 69–86 (pp. 80–81) and 'The Examiner Examined: Swift's Tory Pamphleteering', in *Focus: Swift*, edited by C.J. Rawson (London, 1971), pp. 138–154 (p. 138); Donald Greene, 'Swift: Some Caveats', in *Studies in the Eighteenth Century II: Papers presented at the Second David Nichol Smith Memorial Seminar 1970*, edited by R.F. Brissenden (Canberra, 1973), pp. 341–58 (pp. 341–47); Lee Horsley, 'Vox Populi in the Political Literature of 1710', *HLQ*, 38 (1974–75), 335–53 (p. 353). Like W.A. Speck, J.A. Downie (*Robert Harley and the Press: Propaganda and Public Opinion in the Age of Swift and Defoe* (Cambridge, 1979), pp. 127–29, and *Jonathan Swift: Political Writer* (London, 1984), esp. pp. 259–60), presents the argument that Swift straddled the contemporary party division between Whig and Tory. His anachronistic political ideology was Old Whig or Country. Irvin Ehrenpreis (*Swift: The Man, His Works, and the Age*, 3 vols (London, 1962–83)), sees Swift as an 'Old Whig' in politics but Tory with regard to the Church. J.G.A. Pocock ('*The Machiavellian Moment* Revisited: A Study in History and Ideology', *Journal of Modern History*, 53 (1981), 49–72 (p. 63)), remarks 'the presence in opposition of Tories of the style of Swift, Bolingbroke, and Pope, whose ideology differed surprisingly little from that of the Old Whigs'. The relation of Swift's political theory to Lockean radical whiggism is traced in: Irvin Ehrenpreis, 'Swift on Liberty', *JHI*, 13 (1952), 131–46 and his *Swift*, II, 127; III, 142, 255–58, 273, 286–88; Louis A. Landa in *PW*, IX, 123; Myrddin Jones, 'Further Thoughts on Religion: Swift's Relationship to Filmer and Locke', *RES*, 9 (1958), 284–86; Ricardo Quintana, *Two Augustans: John Locke, Jonathan Swift* (Madison, 1978), pp. 71–82. Liberal and republican politics have of course been derived from Swift's writings: for examples see Caroline Robbins, *The Eighteenth-Century Commonwealthman* (Cambridge, Mass., 1961), p. 153. Swift's political ideology has been related to the classical republican, neo-Harringtonian traditions described in the scholarship of Z.S. Fink, Caroline Robbins, J.G.A. Pocock and others; see generally F.P. Lock, *The Politics of 'Gulliver's Travels'*, ch. 2, 'The Lessons of History', pp. 33–65.

[19]*PW*. VIII, 120; *Correspondence*, IV, 100.

contested but it is argued that his opposition to the modern Whig party leadership reflects his fundamental Whig principles rather than disaffected Tory politics. A forceful expression of the case for Swift as a true Whig opposed to Tory ideology and Hanoverian Court Whiggism is found in a recent essay by J.A. Downie. He sees a continuity in Swift's political discourse from his first prose work of 1701 defending Whig lords through to his alliance with the Whig Archbishop King in Ireland during the affair of Wood's halfpence, *The Drapier's Letters* and *Gulliver's Travels.* J.A. Downie concludes that in *Gulliver's Travels* Swift

> refers to the way in which old Whig ideals have been allowed to become corrupted since the Revolution by men like Walpole. Swift, in Gulliver's conversations with the King of Brobdingnag (and elsewhere), compares Modern Whig government with Old Whig political ideology . . . In this, his greatest statement on politics, Swift, through implication, outlines his ideal political system. And this turns out to be not Tory in inspiration, but Whig.[20]

We are all familiar with the problems involved in negotiating Swift's radically ironic style and disorientating rhetorical strategies. But it is, I think, a measure of the complex nature of the issues involved in historical criticism of Swift's politics and the effect on Swift criticism of current historiographical controversy about the nature of party politics and ideology after the Revolution, and especially in the early Hanoverian period, that two authoritative scholars working on Swift's politics who appear to share a Hirschian critical methodology, who rehearse much the same evidence in their historical criticism of Swift's texts, and who are in agreement about the 'Country' critique informing Swift's political satire in *Gulliver's Travels,* should have arrived at such spectacularly opposed verdicts on Swift's politics. For F.P. Lock, Swift is a natural Tory. For J.A. Downie, Swift is an unreconstructed Revolution Whig.[21]

The problem for historical criticism of Swift's political language is to register the full complexity of contemporary political argument and ideology within which Swift's political formulations at various times are to be situated and the meanings determined. For instance, it seems too undisturbed a reading now to state that 'Pope and Swift are still occasionally accused of Jacobitism, despite the

---

[20]J.A. Downie, 'Swift's Politics', in *Proceedings*, pp. 47–58 (p. 58).

[21]For reviews (from different perspectives) of the historiographical debate about Tory politics and about whether the primary dichotomy in post-1714 politics is Court-Country or Whig-Tory (with party political identity continuing beneath the bipartisan 'Country' attitudes of opposition Whigs and Tories on specific issues), see the following: Linda Colley and Mark Goldie, 'The Principles and Practice of Eighteenth-Century Party', *The Historical Journal*, 22 (1979), 239–46; J.C.D. Clark, 'The Politics of the Excluded: Tories, Jacobites and Whig Patriots 1715–1760', *Parliamentary History*, 2 (1983), 209–22; Nicholas Rogers, 'Party Politics during the Whig Ascendancy', *Canadian Journal of History*, 18 (1983), 253–60; Linda Colley, 'The Politics of Eighteenth-Century British History', *Journal of British Studies*, 25 (1986), 359–79; Eveline Cruickshanks, 'Right and Might', *Journal of British Studies*, 25 (1986), 500–04; John A. Phillips, 'Peers and Parliamentarians versus Jacobites and Jacobins: Eighteenth-Century Stability?', *Journal of British Studies*, 25 (1986), 504–14. J.A. Downie directs Swiftians to the scholarship on neo-Harringtonian, classical republican, 'Country' and radical Whig political languages and argues that the context in which Swift's politics is to be understood is that of an independent Old Whig tradition and Swift is located in a political world characterized by Court–Country rather than a Whig–Tory division after 1714.

fact that, in reality, they are predominately influenced by "Country" or "Old Whig" principles, though one was a Roman Catholic and the other vehemently High Church'.[22] 'Country' principles are a significant strand in Jacobite ideology and polemical argument.[23] It has been argued that Swift is 'uncompromisingly Whig' in politics because he 'believed in the Whig principles current at the time of the Revolution', opposed 'Corruption' and 'the threat posed by an encroaching executive', insisted on the separation of the executive and the legislature, agreed with the Declaration of Rights of 1689, opposed Septennial bills, approved annual parliaments and detested standing armies.[24] But historical criticism of Swift also needs to note contemporary Tory polemical languages. A few examples must suffice. The Tory M.P. Archibald Hutcheson, for instance, in his speech against the Septennial Bill in 1716 approves annual parliaments (confirmed in the ancient constitution) and the Triennial Act, sees the liberties of a people threatened by the executive and 'corruption', detests Henry VIII's tyrannical invasion of 'the liberties of his people' and traces the encroachments of the crown's prerogative to his reign. Hutcheson also argues that the Act of Habeas Corpus is 'essential to the being of a free people', reminds the parliament 'of the prerogatives claimed and exercised by king James the 2d, to dispense with the laws . . . recited by the Claim of Rights' from which the Revolution rescued the nation, reflects on 'how wanting we were to ourselves upon that turn, in not retrieving and securing for ever, by the Claim of Rights, our ancient constitution of frequent new parliaments', and so on.[25] The Jacobite Tory, William Shippen, in the same debate said:

> I think you ought not to repeal the Triennial Act, except in the last extremity, and in the most imminent danger of the State. This law was one of the fruits of the Revolution: This law restored the freedom and frequency of parliaments, so far as was consistent with the circumstances of that reign, which was involved in a war, and had occasion for constant and heavy taxes.[26]

[22]T.N. Corns, W.A. Speck and J.A. Downie, 'Archetypal Mystification: Polemic and Reality in English Political Literature, 1640–1750', *Eighteenth Century Life*, 7 (1982), 1–27 (p. 24).

[23]See especially: Howard Erskine-Hill, 'Literature and the Jacobite Cause: was there a Rhetoric of Jacobitism?', in *Ideology and Conspiracy: Aspects of Jacobitism, 1689–1759*, edited by Eveline Cruickshanks (Edinburgh, 1982), pp. 49–69; Paul Chapman, 'Jacobite Political Argument in England 1714–1766' (unpublished Ph.D. thesis, University of Cambridge, 1983); J.G.A. Pocock, 'Radical Criticisms of the Whig Order in the Age between Revolutions', in *The Origins of Anglo-American Radicalism*, edited by Margaret Jacob and James Jacob (London, 1984), pp. 33–57 (esp. pp. 36–37); F.J. McLynn, 'The Ideology of Jacobitism on the Eve of the Rising of 1745—Part I', *History of European Ideas*, 6, no. 1 (1985), 1–18 (p. 1) and 'The Ideology of Jacobitism—Part II', *History of European Ideas*, 6, no. 2 (1985), 173–88; Paul Monod, 'Jacobitism and Country Principles in the Reign of William III', *The Historical Journal*, 30 (1987), 289–310. For recent scholarship on Jacobitism after 1714, see J.C.D. Clark, *Revolution and Rebellion: State and society in England in the seventeenth and eighteenth centuries* (Cambridge, 1986), Appendix B, pp. 174–77.

[24]J.A. Downie, 'Swift's Politics', *passim*.

[25]*Cobbett's Parliamentary History of England*, Vol. VII (London, 1811), cols. 339–67. On Hutcheson, see the entry by Eveline Cruickshanks in *The House of Commons 1715–54*, edited by Romney Sedgwick, 2 vols (London, 1970), II, 163–64; Linda Colley, *In Defiance of Oligarchy: The Tory Party 1714–60* (Cambridge, 1982), see pp. 28–29, 98–99; Jeremy Black, 'Archibald Hutcheson as Author', *Notes and Queries*, n.s., 32 (1985), 207–08.

[26]*Cobbett's Parliamentary History*, VIII, cols. 317–18.

Bolingbroke's *Craftsman* extols '*that Act,* which is call'd the *Declaration of Rights*; by which, we hope, an End is put to the dangerous Claims and Practices of some *former Reigns*; such as That of a Power in the Crown to *dispense with the Execution of the Laws*; as also That of keeping up a *standing Army in Time of Peace, without Consent of Parliament*; and some other Particulars, which are contained in *that Act.*'[27] The Jacobite *Fog's Weekly Journal* supports annual parliaments, the separation of the legislative and executive parts of the government, and contractual resistance, for example.[28] And Robert Walpole stated:

> No man of common prudence will profess himself openly a jacobite . . . Your right Jacobite, Sir, disguises his true sentiments; he roars out for revolution principles; he pretends to be a great friend to liberty, and a great admirer of our antient constitution; and under this pretence there are numbers who every day endeavour to sow discontents among the people, by persuading them that the constitution is in danger, and that they are unnecessarily loaded with many and heavy taxes.[29]

The Country opposition and the 'Country' political critique of excessive power in the executive, corruption, placemen and pensioners, high taxation and standing armies became increasingly Tory after the early 1690s.[30] Despite the Whig associations and influences of his early political career and intellectual inheritance, Swift may be recognized as a 'naturalized' Tory of the Queen Anne and Hanoverian period. The consonance of Swift's political and ecclesiastical attitudes with identifiable Tory party political positions can be noted in his attack on dissent and occasional conformity in *A Tale of a Tub* (1704); in his hostility to the Union with Scotland expressed, for example, in his 'Verses Said To Be Written on the Union' (1707); in his support for the Lower House of Convocation; in his commitment to an exclusive Anglican monopoly of public office and resistance to any extension of religious toleration; in his hostility to Protestant immigration and the Naturalization Act; in his support for a noninterventionist foreign policy;[31] and revealingly, in his animus against the Dutch.

Attention to the possible polemical provenance and resonance of some of Swift's political statements allows us to understand how a contemporary might have construed aspects of Swift's political discourse as Tory and disaffected speech acts. It is a hermeneutic injunction, but both the conceptual meaning of words on the page *and* their functional meaning in a polemical moment need to be recognized in interpretation of Swift's political texts. Certainly this was a reading procedure of politically literate contemporaries. Daniel Defoe, for example, in his *Review* in 1705 considered the 'Reception to my Exhortation to

[27]*Lord Bolingbroke. Contributions to The 'Craftsman'*, edited by Simon Varey (Oxford, 1982), p. 153 (no. 375, 8 September 1733).

[28]*Select Letters taken from Fog's Weekly Journal*, 2 vols. (London, 1732), II, 26, 158–59, 172–73.

[29]*Cobbett's Parliamentary History of England*, Vol. X (London, 1812), cols. 400–01. See Eveline Cruickshanks, *Political Untouchables: The Tories and the '45* (London, 1979), pp. 14–16.

[30]See David Hayton, 'The "Country" interest and the party system, 1689–c.1720', in *Party and Management in Parliament, 1660–1784*, edited by Clyve Jones (Leicester, 1984), pp. 37–85.

[31]Hayton notes that it is Swift's attitude to foreign policy which renders him 'Tory as much as Country'; see 'The "Country" interest and the party system', p. 64.

Peace' in one of his previous papers and found that 'it seem'd absolutely necessary for me to Enquire, What is meant by *this Peace*? And not only what Peace it
self means, but what every particular sort of People *mean by it*, and why they all
pretend to it, and yet so few pursue it'.[32]

In 'A Letter from Dr Swift to Mr Pope', written in the election year of 1722,[33]
Swift declared:

> I ever abominated that scheme of politicks, (now about thirty years old) of setting up a
> monied Interest in opposition to the landed. For, I conceived, there could not be a truer
> maxim in our government than this, That the possessors of the soil are the best judges of
> what is for the advantage of the kingdom: If others had thought the same way, Funds of
> Credit and South-sea Projects would neither have been felt nor heard of.[34]

The 'neo-Harringtonian', 'Country' opposition to the City 'monied Interest'
expressed here also had party political significance as Swift was well aware. In a
private letter to the Tory leader Bolingbroke in September 1714 Swift had written:

> if I see the old Whig-measures taken in the next elections, and that the court, the bank,
> East-India, and South-sea, act strenuously, and procure a majority, I shall lie down and
> beg of Jupiter to heave the cart out of the dirt.[35]

The Tory political character of Swift's support for a 'Country' measure such as a
Triennial bill is revealed in the following comment on William III's veto of the
Triennial bill in 1693 in his autobiographical fragment: 'The Consequence of
this wrong Step in His Majesty was very unhappy; For it put that Prince under a
necessity of introducing those People called Whigs into power and Employments, in order to pacify them.'[36] Swift wrote to Lady Elizabeth Germain in
1733: 'I know you have been always a zealous Whig, and so am I to this day . . .
I am of the old Whig principles, without the modern articles and refinements'
and he drew Francis Grant's attention in the election year of 1734 to 'Standing
armies in times of peace; projects of excise, and bribing elections . . . not forget-
ting septennial Parliaments, directly against the old Whig principles, which
always have been mine'.[37] But in October 1733 the *Craftsman* noted: 'the *Body*
of the *present Tories* have adopted the Spirit of the *old Whigs*'.[38] Swift knew well
enough that to advance 'certain old whiggish principles' was to pass 'for a disaffected person.'[39]

Swift's description of himself as a 'Whig' in politics but a 'High Churchman' in
religion is obviously problematic at a time when ecclesiastical and political issues,
and Tory and clerical causes are interconnected. Work on the Tory party, partic-

---

[32]*Review*, 28 April 1705.
[33]The letter is dated 1722 in Irvin Ehrenpreis, *Swift*, III, 136.
[34]*PW*. IX, 32.
[35]*Correspondence*, II, 129.
[36]*PW*. V, 194.
[37]*Correspondence*, IV, 100, 230.
[38]Cited in Paul Langford, *The Excise Crisis: Society and Politics in the Age of Walpole* (Oxford,
1975), p. 13.
[39]*PW*. IX, 33.

ularly by Mark Goldie, has shown that the Tory party was (as Swift termed it) a 'Church-party' and then a Court or monarchy party. A long clericalist tradition of the Church's corporate rights and independence informed the transition of Toryism from Court to anti-executive stances and the High Church response to James II and to the Courts of William III, Anne, and the Hanoverians.[40] It is arguable, for instance, whether Swift's opposition to James II really derives from a basic Whig ideology as is often supposed in Swift studies. Swift viewed events leading to the Revolution in religious terms. He saw a design by Peter and Jack to dispossess Martin. He repeatedly argued that it was the Church of England clergy who principally opposed James II's use of the dispensing power and 'Invasions of our Rights' before the Revolution, whereas the dissenters revealed themselves to be in collusion with Roman Catholics basely complying with James II's policy of prerogative toleration.[41] Swift did his best in print to subsume the Revolution in traditional, conservative Anglican political theory. The nation supposed the throne was vacant; it was a case of necessity *in extremis* which however left the Church-of-England Man's principle of non-resistance to the supreme magistrate intact. 'As to the Abdication of King *James* . . . I think a Man may observe every Article of the *English* Church, without being in much Pain about it'.[42] Jack was now at large and tolerated, however. The 'old Republican Spirit, which the Revolution had restored, began to teach other Lessons: That, since we had accepted a new King from a Calvinistical Commonwealth, we must likewise admitt new Maxims in Religion and Government'.[43] Those who 'were only able to give Reputation and Success to the Revolution, were not only laid aside, as dangerous and useless; but loaden with the Scandal of *Jacobites,* Men of *Arbitrary Principles,* and *Pensioners* to *France*'.[44] It was for Swift 'the Constancy and Sufferings of the Bishops and Clergy; or of the Head and Fellows of *Magdalen* College; that furnished the Prince of *Orange*'s Declaration with such powerful Arguments, to justify and promote the Revolution'.[45]

It is also perhaps suggestive of the interconnection of religion and politics that Swift instinctively compares Ireland's slavery under the English parliament with the erastian bondage of Anglican Convocations.[46] And that one of his most dramatically libertarian declarations—'I have lived, and by the grace of God will die, an enemy to servitude and slavery of all kinds'—was actually occasioned by a matter of clerical privileges (Swift is responding to Archbishop King's provocative demand that the Dean of St. Patrick's supply a proxy for the Archbishop's visitation).[47]

---

[40]Mark Goldie, 'The Nonjurors, Episcopacy, and the Origins of the Convocation Controversy', in *Ideology and Conspiracy: Aspects of Jacobitism, 1689–1757,* edited by Eveline Cruickshanks (Edinburgh, 1982), pp. 15–35.
[41]For examples see, *PW.* I, 131; II, 9; III, 46–47; V, 285, 286, 318.
[42]*PW.* II, 20.
[43]*PW.* VII, 5.
[44]*PW.* III, 12.
[45]*PW.* II, 9.
[46]*Correspondence,* II, 342 (4 April 1720; Swift to Charles Ford).
[47]*Correspondence,* III, 210.

Swift never seems to have called himself a Tory. But then Swift seemed unwilling to admit that Jacobites and Tories existed at all in Ireland. An attack on occasional conformity in A *Letter From a Member of the House of Commons in Ireland To a Member of the House of Commons in England, Concerning the Sacramental Test* is put this way:

> the Parties among us are made up, on one side, of *moderate Whigs*, and, on the other, of *Presbyterians* and their *Abettors*; by which last I mean, such who can equally go to a *Church*, or a *Conventicle*; or such who are indifferent to all Religion in general; or, lastly, such who affect to bear a personal Rancor towards the Clergy.[48]

In 1725 he wrote to Sheridan (who had preached a sermon on the anniversary of the accession of the House of Hanover from the text 'Sufficient unto the day is the evil thereof') that:

> It is safer for a Man's Interest to blaspheme God, than to be of a Party out of Power, or even to be thought so . . . I tell you there is hardly a Whig in *Ireland* who would allow a Potato and Butter-milk to a reputed Tory.[49]

Swift stated publicly in 1735 that he professed to be of the Whig party in politics.[50] But to Lord Bathurst in 1737 Swift remains 'a disaffected person, such y" will be reputed as long as y" live, after y' death perhaps y" may stand Rectus in Curia.'[51] A significant and much discussed annotation Swift made in later life in the margin of a copy of Gilbert Burnet's *History of His Own Time* on the arguments propounded in 1688–89 takes us to the heart of the difficulties in understanding his politics. Swift appears to confess himself both a contractarian Whig and an ultra-Tory loyalist. Against Burnet's account of a 'party . . . made up of those who thought that there was an original contract between the kings and the people of England,' Swift wrote: 'I am of this party, and yet I would have been for a regency'.[52] At the constitutional Convention called by William of Orange which assembled in January 1689 the proposal for a regency in King James II's name was advanced by High Anglican Tories. The regency proposal if implemented would have preserved James II's legal authority and the Anglican political doctrine of passive obedience. A regency would have prevented a transfer of the crown or alteration of the hereditary succession. In Burnet's words the proposers of the regency thought,

> their expedient would take in the greatest, as well as the best, part of the Nation: Whereas all other expedients gratified a Republican party, composed of the Dissenters, and of men of no religion, who hoped now to see the Church ruined, and the government set upon such a bottom, as that we should have only a titular King; who, as he had his power from the people, so should be accountable to them for the exercise of it, and

[48]*PW.* II, 118. See also *PW.* X, 132–33.
[49]*Correspondence*, III, 93–94.
[50]'Swift's Advertisement to *Poems*, 1735', in *Swift: Poetical Works*, edited by Herbert Davis (London, 1967), pp. xxix–xxx (p. xxix); Downie, 'Swift's Politics', p. 48.
[51]*Correspondence*, V, 79 (6 December 1737, Lord Bathurst to Swift).
[52]*PW.* V, 291.

should forfeit it at their pleasure. The much greater part of the House of Lords was for this, and stuck long to it: And so was about a third part of the House of Commons. The greatest part of the Clergy declared themselves for it.

Swift commented: 'And it was certainly much the best expedient'.[53] Considering the views of 'those who were for continuing the government, and only for changing the persons', Swift approves not the radical Whig assertions described by Burnet, but the *in extremis* argument put by those who 'avoided going into new speculations, or schemes of government'.[54] He also appears to be sympathetic to the Tories in the debate on the word 'abdicated' and the vacancy of the throne.[55]

Despite Swift's support for a regency and aspersion on William in the marginalia,[56] Swift's statement of identification with the party that thought there was an original contract between the kings and people of England is quoted in Swift studies as an important instance of Swift identifying with contractarian Whig principles at the Revolution. But it might also be worth observing that in a letter to Thomas Swift of 1692 Swift writes that he used 'to converse about 2 or 3 years ago' with the nonjuring Bishop of Ely, Francis Turner.[57] Turner, a Jacobite Tory, was a leading advocate of the regency scheme (for him it was an expedient until James II could be restored). In the constitutional debate at the Convention, Turner accepted that there was an original contract between kings and people, he argued that the law settling the hereditary succession was part of the original contract, and that laws can only be altered by the legislative power of King, Lords and Commons in parliament.[58] For Swift to accept a contract theory and support a regency is not contradicting the publicly-professed views of the Jacobite Bishop of Ely. It is arguable too whether Swift's identification with the party at the Revolution, which thought that there was an original contract (as described by Burnet), means that he was endorsing extreme Whig versions of contract theory.[59]

[53]Gilbert Burnet, *Bishop Burnet's History of His Own Time*, 2 vols. (London, 1724, 1734), I, 811; *PW*. V, 291. See also: *PW*. III, 163; IX, 229–30.
[54]Burnet, *History of His Own Time*, I, 814; *PW*. V, 291.
[55]*PW*. V, 291.
[56]*PW*. V, 270, 275, 277, 285, 288, 290, 292.
[57]*Correspondence*, I, 9.
[58]See *The Debate at Large, Between The House of Lords and House of Commons, at the Free Conference, Held in the Painted Chamber, in the Session of the Convention, Anno 1688. Relating to the Word, Abdicated, and the Vacancy of the Throne, in the Common's Vote* (London, 1695; rpt. Shannon, 1972), pp. 49, 51–60. Swift owned this book: see Hermann J. Real and Heinz J. Vienken, 'A Catalogue of an Exhibition of Imprints from Swift's Library', in *Proceedings*, p. 363. On Turner at the Convention, see George L. Cherry, 'The Legal and Philosophical Position of the Jacobites, 1688–1689', *The Journal of Modern History*, 22 (1950), 309–21; Robert Beddard, 'The Loyalist Opposition in the Interregnum: a Letter of Dr. Francis Turner, Bishop of Ely, on the Revolution of 1688', *Bulletin of the Institute of Historical Research*, 40 (1967), 101–09, and his 'The Guildhall Declaration of 11 December 1688 and the Counter-Revolution of the Loyalists', *The Historical Journal*, 11 (1968), 403–20; Lois G. Schwoerer, *The Declaration of Rights, 1689* (Baltimore and London, 1981), esp. pp. 216–19. For a summary of our fragmentary knowledge of Swift's acquaintance with Turner, see Edward W. Rosenheim, Jr., 'Swift's *Ode to Sancroft*: Another Look', *MP*, 73 (1976), S24–S39 (S30–S32).
[59]See Burnet, *History of His Own Time*, I, 811–13; J.R. Western, *Monarchy and Revolution* (London, 1972), p. 310; J.P. Kenyon, 'The Revolution of 1688: Resistance and Contract', in *Historical*

The presence of anti-executive and classical republican elements in Swift's writing—the language of Old Whig radicalism—is usually regarded as key evidence for a 'Whig' rather than 'Tory' Swift. So to take an extreme example, manifestations of the tyrannicide Marcus Brutus in Swift's texts are of particular interest to students of Swift's politics. In the *Examiner* of 15 March 1711 Swift tries to find an historical parallel to illustrate for the *Examiner's* readers the horror of an assassination attempt on Robert Harley: '*Caesar's* Murder being performed in the Senate, comes nearest to the Case; but that was an Affair concerted by great Numbers of the chief Senators, who were likewise the Actors in it, and not the Work of a vile, single Ruffian'.[60] Marcus Brutus, though a principled Senatorial assassin, is here beyond the pale for a ministerial, Tory propagandist. However, the appearance of Marcus Brutus along with Cato in *Some Reasons to Prove, That no Person is obliged by his Principles, as a Whig, to Oppose Her Majesty or Her Present Ministry. In a Letter to a Whig-Lord* (1712) represents an audacious appropriation of Brutus for the Tory party against that modern Caesar the Duke of Marlborough. Those icons of Roman virtue, Cato and Brutus, the Whig Lord learns, 'joined heartily on that side which undertook to preserve the Laws and Constitution, against the Usurpations of a victorious General, whose Ambition was bent to overthrow them'.[61]

But the most famous of Swift's references to Brutus occurs in Part III of *Gulliver's Travels* when Gulliver is in Glubbdubdrib, the island of sorcerers or magicians. When antiquity is summoned into Gulliver's presence by the island's governor there is this remarkable celebration of the uncorrupted Senate of Rome, Brutus and tyrannicide:

> I desired that the Senate of *Rome* might appear before me in one large Chamber, and a modern Representative, in Counterview, in another. The first seemed to be an Assembly of Heroes and Demy-Gods; the other a Knot of Pedlars, Pick-pockets, Highwaymen and Bullies.
>
> The Governor at my Request gave the Sign for *Caesar* and *Brutus* to advance towards us. I was struck with a profound Veneration at the Sight of *Brutus*; and could easily discover the most consummate Virtue, the greatest Intrepidity, and Firmness of Mind, the truest Love of his Country, and general Benevolence for Mankind in every Lineament of his Countenance. I observed with much Pleasure, that these two Persons were in good Intelligence with each other; and *Caesar* freely confessed to me, that the greatest Actions of his own Life were not equal by many Degrees to the Glory of taking it away.

Gulliver candidly tells us:

> I chiefly fed mine Eyes with beholding the Destroyers of Tyrants and Usurpers, and the Restorers of Liberty to oppressed and injured Nations.[62]

Perspectives, edited by Neil McKendrick (London, 1974), pp. 43–69 and his *Revolution Principles* (Cambridge, 1977), p. 2; Erskine-Hill, 'Literature and the Jacobite Cause: was there a Rhetoric of Jacobitism?', esp. p. 50.

[60]*PW*. III, 106.
[61]*PW*. VI, 134. Brutus is a Swiftian hero, as *PW*. I, 222; *Poems*, II, 724.
[62]*PW*. XI, 195–96.

Swift's vicarious entertainment of tyrannicide in this passage and in his account of the Lindalinian rebellion against the court of Laputa (not in any edition of *Gulliver's Travels* in Swift's lifetime), but whose final sentence reads: 'I was assured by a great Minister, that if the Island had descended so near the Town, as not to be able to raise it self, the Citizens were determined to fix it for ever, to kill the King and all his Servants, and entirely change the Government'[63], have startling analogues in seditious 'Old Whig' and 'Tory' Jacobite writing especially of the 1720s. For example, in defending the Bishop of Rochester (convicted of Jacobite conspiracy) *The True Briton* found this analogue for Atterbury's public spirit in this time of Whig tyranny:

> The Great *Brutus* who stabb'd *Caesar,* is a Noble Mark of Publick Spirit. *Caesar* was his Friend, and had served him in many Instances; yet, when he trampled on the Laws, the general Good was preferr'd to his private Inclinations; and when he imbrued his Hands in his Blood, it was the *Tyrant,* not the *Friend,* he struck.[64]

The following passages are quoted from a Jacobite Tory work of 1722, George Granville, Baron Lansdowne's *A Letter from a Noble-Man Abroad, to His Friend in England.* The parallels between the political expression in this work and that in *Gulliver's Travels* are readily apparent:

> At this critical Conjuncture when the Rumour of a new Parliament sounds like the last Trumpet, to awaken the Genius of Old *England,* and raise departed Liberty to Life, it would be a Crime to be silent . . .
>
> In those Times of Distraction, so like our own, when the Will of a Triumvirate, supported by a Majority of bribed Senators, and an Army at Command was the sole Law; when *Cato* and *Cicero* were in Danger of being torn to Pieces in the Street; when to be honest was to be prescribed [sic; 'proscribed']; what Course could good Men take overpower'd by Numbers, and dispairing of the Commonwealth, but to retire to Athens, or some remote Corner to lament in Silence, and to seek for Comfort in the Study of Philosophy . . .
>
> We have lived to see our antient Constitution in a manner dissolved, and the most important Articles of our new Contract, upon settling the Protestant Succession, evaded, suspended, or set aside; the Wealth and Strength of the Kingdom exhausted in Foreign Quarrels, and for Foreign Acquisitions; the very Nation it self sold to make Purchases abroad, and to enrich Strangers.
>
> We have lived to see the first Honours of Peerage bestowed to dignifie Prostitution, the Freedom of the People, the most inestimable Article of their Freedom, the Freedom of Elections, betrayed by their own Representatives, so that the most precious Part of our Liberty may be justly said to have been stabbed by its own Guard . . .
>
> We have lived, and yet we live to be trampled upon, by the vilest, the most ignominious of all Tyranny, the Tyranny of Ministers, the Tyranny of Fellow Subjects, raised from the Dirt of Faction, supported by Senates, chosen and directed by Corruption . . .

---

[63]*PW.* XI, 310. Compare *Poems,* II, 550 (*The Life and Genuine Character of Dean Swift,* lines 190–92); *PW.* VIII, 218; IX, 31.

[64]*The True Briton,* 9 August 1723. The Old Whig, regicidal element in Jacobite political argument has been described by Paul Chapman (see note 23 above).

By the Artifice of cunning and designing Men we have been too long kept divided in Parties . . .

Let then no other Denomination be heard among us, no other Distinction but that of good *English-men*; let all who would merit that Name unite, embrace, and take a *Roman* Resolution to save their Country, or perish with it.

Brutus was a sworn Enemy to *Pompey*, the Murderer of his Father; but when it happened that *Rome* must perish, or *Pompey* be supported, *Brutus* became *Pompey's* Friend.

Brutus took an Oath to *Caesar*, but *Brutus* never swore to be an Enemy to his Country.

Brutus owed much to *Caesar*, but *Brutus* thought private Benefits as well as private Injuries were to be sacrificed to the Publick Safety. And *Brutus* was an honourable Man.

The militant cry is: 'stand for Liberty and Old *England*.'[65] In Glubbdubdrib Gulliver has raised to Life before him 'some *English* Yeomen of the old Stamp . . . once so famous for the Simplicity of their Manners, Dyet and Dress; for Justice in their Dealings; for their true Spirit of Liberty; for their Valour and Love of their Country'. Such 'pure native Virtues were prostituted for a Piece of Money by their Grand-children; who in selling their Votes, and managing at Elections have acquired every Vice and Corruption that can possibly be learned in a Court'.[66] It is interesting that in the 'Advertisement To The Reader' of the *Memoirs of Captain John Creichton* (1731) which Swift prepared for the press, the Stuart loyalist Captain Creichton is described as '*a very honest and worthy Man; but of the old Stamp: And it is probable, that some of his Principles will not relish very well, in the present Disposition of the World. His* Memoirs *are therefore to be received like a Posthumous Work*'. The old soldier's Memoirs are offered '*in their native Simplicity*' and the man himself is distinguished by his '*personal Courage and Conduct*'.[67]

Swift's satire in *Gulliver's Travels* on such topics as the 'clemency' of despots, George I's regular journeys to Hanover, the degenerate hereditary nobility, the corrupt management of the treasury, foreign military intervention, mercenary standing armies, corrupt elections, informers, faction and corruption, have analogues in Tory Jacobite pamphleteering of the 1720s. The satire on Walpole's decypherers and the Whig government prosecution of Atterbury distinguishes *Gulliver's Travels* as a 'Tory' satire. In May 1715 John Barber had written to Swift: 'We have 20 frightfull Accounts of your being sent for up, and your papers

[65][George Granville, Baron Lansdowne], *A Letter from a Noble-Man Abroad, to His Friend in England* (London, 1722), *passim*. This work is reprinted in full in Howard Erskine-Hill, 'Alexander Pope: The Political Poet in His Time', *ECS*, 15 (1981–82), 123–48 (pp. 143–46). On Lansdowne, see Elizabeth Handasyde, *Granville the Polite* (Oxford, 1933). On the *Letter*, see Erskine-Hill, 'Literature and the Jacobite Cause: was there a Rhetoric of Jacobitism?', 55–56 and Eveline Cruickshanks and Howard Erskine-Hill, 'The Waltham Black Act and Jacobitism', *Journal of British Studies*, 24 (1985), 358–65 (p. 360 n). Also compare William Shippen, *Faction Display'd* (1704), lines 486–87: 'Where is the Noble *Roman* Spirit fled, / Which once inspir'd thy antient Patriots dead?' (in *Poems on Affairs of State. Augustan Satirical Verse, 1660–1714*, Vol. 6: 1697–1704, edited by Frank H. Ellis (New Haven and London, 1970), p. 671.
[66]*PW*. XI, 201–02.
[67]*PW*. V, 121–22.

seized, for you are the reputed Author of every good thing that comes out on our side'.[68] The political critique in works of Tory or Jacobite provenance such as Francis Atterbury's *English Advice to the Freeholders of England* (dated 1714; published 1715 and to which Barber in his letter to Swift probably refers); and *The Second and Last English Advice, To the Freeholders of Englan[d]* (1722) can be readily identified in *Gulliver's Travels*.

M.B. (perhaps Marcus Brutus) Drapier knew very well that Old Whig language was perceived as a discourse of disaffection. In a letter to Charles Ford of 15 April 1721, in which Swift says he is at work on the *Travels*, he refers to 'The letter of Brutus to Cicero', one of the classic Old Whig *Cato's Letters* (1 April 1721) which Swift feels 'should have been better translated'. He then remarks that the English 'Ministry seems to me to want Credit in suffering so many Libells published against them; and here there is a worse Matter; for many of the violent Whigs profess themselves perfect Jacobites, and plead for it the Miseryes and Contempt they suffer by the Treatment of England'.[69] Swift forged political links with radical Whigs in the 1720s as did Tory M.P.s such as Archibald Hutcheson and Sir Thomas Hanmer.[70] He said of his fellow nationalist Lord Molesworth in 1723, 'excepting in what relates to the Church, there are few Persons with whose Opinions I am better pleased to agree', though Swift is antagonized by the Old Whig's political attack on clerical '*Liberty and Property*'.[71] The Drapier dedicated a Letter to Molesworth and voiced traditionally Whig radical doctrine found in the writings of Molesworth and others in attacking the Whig English government.

Is the author of *Gulliver's Travels* still best understood as an Old or Real Whig even though Old Whig principles and rhetoric were by 1726 appropriated by Jacobites and Tories? Despite the contingency and nominalism of political argument in contemporary pamphlet and periodical literature some real differences between 'Old Whig' and 'Tory' political positions can be registered. Considering some of the differences, it is evident that Swift's politics are 'Tory'.

An essential element of Old Whig or Country Whig ideology is its religious heterodoxy and anticlericalism—its opposition to 'priestcraft'.[72] True Old Whigs such as the third Earl of Shaftesbury, Robert Molesworth, John Trenchard, Thomas Gordon, John Toland, Matthew Tindal and others were never really able to identify with a party hostile to religious dissent and toleration even though the Tories became the party synonymous with Country political ideology. Swift, however, a High Church Anglican in religion, had no trouble identifying with the modern 'Church party'. Conformity to the established religion is a positive in *Gulliver's Travels*.[73] Robert Molesworth complained in his *Principles*

---

[68]*Correspondence*, II, 168.
[69]*Correspondence*, II, 380.
[70]See Colley, *In Defiance of Oligarchy*, pp. 98–99.
[71]*PW*. IX, 58–60.
[72]See Mark Goldie, 'The Roots of True Whiggism 1688–94', *History of Political Thought*, i (1980), 195–236.
[73]*PW*. XI, 50, 60, 131.

of a Real Whig that 'there has been such chopping and changing both of Names and Principles, that we scarce know who is who'. But his ideal is a cosmopolitan, tolerant polity and he notes that a 'Genuine *Whig* is for promoting a *general Naturalization*'.[74] Swift was not a genuine Whig.[75] Also, Swift's complete and unqualified opposition to mercenary standing armies in times of peace and war is more 'Tory' than 'Old Whig'.[76] Molesworth wrote:

> A *Whig* is against the raising or keeping up a Standing *Army* in Time of Peace; but with this Distinction, that if at any time an *Army* (though even in Time of Peace) should be necessary to the Support of this very Maxim, a *Whig* is not for being too hasty to destroy That, which is to be the Defender of his Liberty.[77]

Molesworth of course became a placeman after the accession of George I and supported a standing army.[78] Opposition Whigs (and Walpole when in opposition) tended to argue for only a reduction in the size of the standing army.[79] Walpole was in Swift's mind when an acute Gulliver reports that one of the 'Methods by which a Man may rise to be Chief Minister' is 'by a *furious Zeal* in publick Assemblies against the Corruptions of the Court. But a wise Prince would rather chuse to employ those who practise' this method 'because such Zealots prove always the most obsequious and subservient to the Will and Passions of their Master'.[80] It was Jacobites and Tories who consistently denounced and voted against standing armies.and septennial parliaments. The canonical Old Whig publication Trenchard and Gordon's *Cato's Letters* in the issue of 20 April 1723 reflected on '*The spirit of the conspirators, accomplices with Dr.* Atterbury': 'They exclaim against armies and taxes, and are the cause of both, and rail at grievances of their own creating. Who make armies necessary, but they . . .'.[81]

Swift in 1714 had hoped that the new Hanoverian monarch would be forced to rule with the Church party. What he witnessed, however, was the proscription of the Tories. On 6 October 1714 Swift wrote to his acquaintance Knightley Chetwode:

> I am as much disquieted at the turn of public affairs as you or any men can be. It concerns us spiritual men in a tender temporal point. Everything is as bad as possible; and I think if the Pretender ever comes over, the present men in power have traced him the way.[82]

[74]See the 'Sentiments of the late Lord *Molesworth*' in *The Memoirs of John Ker, of Kersland in North Britain Esq*, 3 pts. (London, 1726), III, 191–221 (pp. 191, 207).

[75]*PW*. VII, 94–95.

[76]*PW*. V, 80; IX, 31–32; XI, 131. For the eclectic sources behind Swift's invective on standing armies, see Heinz J. Vienken and Hermann J. Real, ' "Ex Libris" J.S.: Annotating Swift', in *Proceedings*, pp. 305–19 (pp. 314–15).

[77]*Memoirs of John Ker*, III, 210–11.

[78]*Cobbett's Parliamentary History*, VII, 536–37; see Hayton, 'The "Country" interest and the party system', p. 51.

[79]Observed in Eveline Cruickshanks, 'The Political Management of Sir Robert Walpole, 1720–42', in *Britain in the Age of Walpole*, edited by Jeremy Black, pp. 23–43 (p. 33).

[80]*PW*. XI, 255.

[81]*Cato's Letters: Or, Essays on Liberty, Civil and Religious, And Other important Subjects*, 4 vols. (n.p., 1754), IV, 146 (no. 125, 20 April 1723).

[82]*Correspondence*, II, 135–36.

The 'temporal point' is the Anglican doctrine of passive obedience and non-resistance, and the oath of allegiance taken to the King in possession. There appears to be no clear evidence extant of Jacobite commitment or activism on Swift's part. Rather, he expounded to the Jacobite Chetwode the doctrine of allegiance to any prince in possession according to present law in force.[83] Swift seems not to have hazarded all 'on Revolution principles' like his 'brother Orrery.'[84] There are political dramatic ironies in Swift's remark to Bishop Atterbury in a letter of 18 April 1716:

> I congratulate with England for joining with us here in the fellowship of slavery. It is not so terrible a thing as you imagine; we have long lived under it, and whenever you are disposed to know how you ought to behave yourself in your new condition, you need go no farther than me for a director.[85]

Despite the violence of Swift's satire on Hanoverian Court Whiggism and vicarious entertainment of revolt, it is the Tory doctrine of non-resistance and passive obedience that is exemplified and endorsed in *Gulliver's Travels* in the passive conduct of the oppressed Lord Munodi—whose patience under extreme provocation is intended to be poignant and admirable.[86] High Church Tory ideologists of absolute non-resistance represented submission, prayer, appeals and petitions, or leaving the country as the subject's options when lawful governors acted tyrannically.[87] Gulliver in his Travels goes through these routines of a loyal subject. In the third voyage Swift has Gulliver act out the principle of passive obedience in a 'text-book' exigency—when his religion and the law of the State conflict. Gulliver is expected by the Emperor of Japan to perform the ceremony 'of *trampling upon the Crucifix*'. Gulliver petitions to be excused from active obedience to this law of Japan to which Dutchmen (one of whom he pretends to be) are subject.[88] A despairing Gulliver in the fourth voyage is obedient to the (literally inhuman) rational rigour of a Houyhnhnm Assembly '*Exhortation*'.[89] Swift generally represents Gulliver as an abject and servile figure before authority. But Swift professed himself to be a slave in Hanoverian Ireland. Gulliver feeds his eyes on 'the Destroyers of Tyrants and Usurpers' but as a subject in Lilliput he seems to know the duty of a Church-of-England Man:

> Once I was strongly bent upon Resistance: For while I had Liberty, the whole Strength of that Empire could hardly subdue me, and I might easily with Stones pelt the

---

[83]*Correspondence*, II, 384 (29 April 1721). See also II, 213 (30 August 1716; Swift to Alexander Pope).

[84]See Swift's letter to Robert Cope, *Correspondence*, II, 435 (9 October 1722).

[85]*Correspondence*, II, 198.

[86]*PW*. XI, 176.

[87]See for instance Luke Milbourne, *The Measures of Resistance To The Higher Powers, So far as becomes a Christian: In a Sermon Preach'd on January the 30th 17 $\frac{09}{10}$* (London, 1710), pp. 27–29.

[88]*PW*. XI, 216.

[89]*PW*. XI, 280.

[90]*PW*. XI, 73.

Metropolis to Pieces: But I soon rejected that Project with Horror, by remembering the Oath I had made to the Emperor.[90]

This is Swift's authentic High Church Tory voice:

no true Member of the Church of England, can easily be shaken in his Principles of Loyalty, or forget the Obligation of an Oath by any Provocation.[91]

As Swift wrote to Archbishop King in 1727:

My Lord, I have lived, and by the grace of God will die, an enemy to servitude and slavery of all kinds: And I believe, at the same time, that persons of such a disposition will be the most ready to pay obedience wherever it is due.[92]

---

[91]*PW*. VIII, 95. Swift however was in sympathy with those disaffected from the Hanoverian government, see *PW*. V, 252: 'Suppose a King grows a Beast, or a Tyrant, after I have taken an Oath: a 'prentice takes an Oath; but if his Master useth him barbarously, the lad may be excused if he wishes for a Better'.

[92]*Correspondence*, III, 210.

Parables of the Younger Son: Swift and the Containment of Desire

Michael McKeon

1

For a brief time fellow servants of the Tory ministry, Defoe and Swift were never on close, or even cordial, terms. The cultural gulf between the two men, evident enough in their educational and religious differences, can be felt most palpably as a matter of social status. Swift's utter disdain—in 1706 he disingenuously referred to Defoe as "the fellow that was *pilloryed*, I have forgot his name"— elicited an exasperated defensiveness that supports the contention that Defoe "lashed out at Swift less as an individual than as the representative of a social class which treated him and his dearest social aspirations with contempt." Yet Swift hardly saw himself as patrician. To Bolingbroke he said that "my Birth although from a Family not undistinguished in its time is many degrees inferior to Yours . . . I a Younger Son of younger Sons, You born to a great Fortune." Swift had no brothers; the stance of the younger son served as a delicate rebuke of the nobleman for assuming that their material hardships were remotely comparable.[1]

In his panegyric to Sir William Temple many years earlier, Swift had adopted this same stance, complaining that nature unjustly denied to the indifferent poet what she lavished on his esteemed patron:

Shall I believe a Spirit so divine
   Was cast in the same Mold with mine?
Why then does Nature so unjustly share
Among her Elder Sons the whole Estate?
   And all her Jewels and her Plate,
Poor we *Cadets* of Heav'n, not worth her Care,
Take up at best with Lumber and the Leavings of a Fate . . .

Here the conceit is that Swift by nature is without deserts and yet deserves more than he gets. The posture of the younger son defined for him a condition of

From Michael McKeon, *The Origins of the English Novel* (Baltimore: Johns Hopkins University Press, 1987), 338–56. Reprinted by permission of the author and the Johns Hopkins University Press.

[1]Michael Shinagel, *Defoe and Middle-Class Gentility* (Cambridge: Harvard University Press, 1968), 81, 86; Jonathan Swift to Viscount Bolingbroke, Oct. 31, 1729, in *The Correspondence of Jonathan Swift*, ed. Harold Williams (Oxford: Clarendon Press, 1963), III, 354.

extraordinary instability. Swift believed that the delusions of freethinking were most likely to thrive "amongst the worst Part of the Soldiery, made up of Pages, younger Brothers of obscure Families, and others of desperate Fortunes." But he also wistfully imagined that the *"New-men"* whom the crown was periodically obliged to raise to the pinnacles of state service were "sometimes younger Brothers." It is the distressing spectacle of unrecognized merit that most feeds the conservative psychology of the deprived younger son, and Swift was often inclined to see his own career as a series of missed opportunities for advancement—missed not for a lack of talents in the aspirant but for a lack of gratitude and justice in his masters. Inadequately rewarded for his services to the great, Swift learned a cynicism toward them and their favorites that was consonant with his broader reading of recent English history. On occasion he represented this experience of political and social deprivation in terms of aimless mobility and exile. In the ode to Temple he is "to the Muse's Gallies ty'd," perpetually and vainly struggling to reach shore. To his friends he later described himself, torn between countries and employments, as "a vexed unsettled Vagabond." "I may call my self a stranger in a strange land."[2]

The life of Swift's greatest character shares some of these general features. Lemuel Gulliver begins his travel narrative with the following words:

> My Father had a small Estate in *Nottinghamshire*; I was the Third of five Sons. He sent me to *Emanuel-College* in *Cambridge,* at Fourteen Years old, where I resided three Years, and applied my self close to my Studies: But the Charge of maintaining me (although I had a very scanty Allowance) being too great for a narrow Fortune; I was bound Apprentice to *Mr. James Bates* an eminent Surgeon in *London,* with whom I continued four Years.[3]

Gulliver is one of those younger sons whose "fortunes and employments," in the words of William Sprigge, "are not correspondent to the grandure of their birth and education."[4] Having the foresight to acquire skills "useful in long Voyages," which "I always believed it would be some time or other my Fortune to do," Gulliver studies navigation and physic, and he does make several voyages before resolving "to settle in *London,* to which Mr. *Bates,* my Master, encouraged me" (I,

---

[2]Jonathan Swift: "Ode to the Honble Sir William Temple" (1962), ll. 178–84, in *The Poems of Jonathan Swift,* ed. Harold Williams, 2nd ed. (Oxford: Clarendon Press, 1958), I, 32: (Irish) *Intelligencer,* no. 9 (1728), in *The Prose Works of Jonathan Swift,* vol. 12: *Irish Tracts, 1728–1733,* ed. Herbert Davis (Oxford: Blackwell, 1964), 47; *A Letter to a Young Gentleman, Lately enter'd into Holy Orders . . .* (1721), in *Prose Works,* vol. 9: *Irish Tracts, 1720–1723 and Sermons,* ed. Louis Landa (Oxford: Blackwell, 1948), 78; "Ode to Temple," l. 191, in *Poems,* I, 32; Swift to John Arbuthnot, July 3, 1714, and Swift to Alexander Pope, Aug. 11, 1729, in *Correspondence,* II, 46, and III, 341. On Swift's sense of physical alienation, and on his profound attachment to Ireland, see Carole Fabricant, *Swift's Landscape* (Baltimore: Johns Hopkins University Press, 1983), chap. 6. On the conservative reading of recent English history and the psychology of the younger son, see above, chap. 6, sec. 3.

[3]Jonathan Swift, *Travels into several Remote Nations of the World. In Four Parts. By Lemuel Gulliver . . .* (1726), vol. 11 of *Prose Works,* ed. Herbert Davis (Oxford: Basil Blackwell, 1941), I, i, 3 (hereafter cited as *Travels*); all parenthetical citations in the text are to this edition, and consist of part, chapter, and page number.

[4]See McKeon, *Origins of the English Novel,* chap. 4, n. 62.

i, 3). So he marries and sets up in practice; but his master soon dies and his business begins to fail. Gulliver goes to sea again, grows "weary" of it, resumes his practice unsuccessfully, and "after three Years Expectation that things would mend," enters employment on the ship that will take him to Lilliput (I, i, 4).

Thus Gulliver's first travels are undertaken in default of a more settled and upward mobility at home. After the voyage to Lilliput, however, the idea of physical travel takes on more of the financial and moral ambiguity it has in other narratives I have discussed, and the change in tone is effected by familiar narrative strategies. The second voyage begins with "my insatiable Desire of seeing foreign Countries," but also "in Hopes to improve my Fortunes." This expectation is not unreasonable, for Gulliver has already "made a considerable Profit by shewing my Cattle to many Persons of Quality" (I, viii, 63–64). But events soon conspire to cast ethical doubts on such "improvements." The tables are turned in Brobdingnag, when the avaricious farmer, "finding how profitable I was like to be, resolved to carry me to the most considerable Cities of the Kingdom" and "to shew me in all the Towns by the Way . . . to any Village or Person of Quality's House where he might expect Custom" (II, ii, 83). The echo is unmistakable: "The more my Master got by me, the more unsatiable he grew" (II, iii, 85). It is no doubt this dangerous connection between physical mobility and the indulgence of unlimited appetite that evokes, as in *Robinson Crusoe,* the retrospective voice of the repentant Narrator. Cornered in the Brobdingnagian cornfield and waiting for the enormous reapers to descend upon him, Gulliver, "wholly overcome by Grief and Despair," "bemoaned my desolate Widow, and Fatherless Children: I lamented my own Folly and Wilfulness in attempting a second Voyage against the Advice of all my Friends and Relations" (II, i, 70). But like Robinson, Gulliver is also able to disown responsibility and to project his desire for a fortune onto Fortune. Part II begins with his "having been condemned by Nature and Fortune to an active and restless Life," and it ends as his "Wife protested I should never go to Sea any more; although my evil Destiny so ordered, that she had not Power to hinder me; as the Reader may know hereafter" (II, i, 67, 133).

The success of the younger son in Defoe's narrative depends on his ability to internalize providence and to naturalize his appetites; less sympathetically, we might say that he learns how to project his desire and then to forget that he has done it. Gulliver never attains that comfort. He undertakes his third voyage because he receives an advantageous proposal, "the Thirst I had of seeing the World, notwithstanding my past Misfortunes, continuing as violent as ever" (III, i, 137–38). His decision to make the fourth interrupts a brief period at home "in a very happy Condition, if I could have learned the Lesson of knowing when I was well" (IV, i, 205). Like Robinson, Gulliver undergoes a decisive island conversion. Inseparable from his conversion experience, however, is the necessity of remaining in the physical presence of the godlike Houyhnhnms and in exile from human society. "But it was decreed by Fortune, my perpetual Enemy, that so great a Felicity should not fall to my Share" (IV, vii, 242). In fact it is a decree of the Grand Council of the Houyhnhnms, "from whence I date all the succeeding

Misfortunes of my Life" (IV, ix, 257). Character and Narrator merge at the end, but it is scarcely an act of reconciliation or "atonement." For Gulliver ends radically at odds with himself, violently repudiating his own human nature yet spurned by that other nature with which he has learned to identify so closely. The expectations of the younger son so absolutely and permanently exceed all possibility of reward that status inconsistency becomes a biological condition of existence.

I will return to the land of the Houyhnhnms. For the moment it is enough to see that Swift's narrative both imitates the general movement of the spiritual autobiography and subverts it, by giving us a protagonist whose conviction of depravity issues not in repentance and faith but in the paradoxically prideful mortifications of misanthropy. By the same token, Gulliver's career (and those of several surrogates) both recapitulates that of the progressive, upwardly mobile younger son and parodically negates it in two distinct, and characteristically conservative, trajectories: that of industrious virtue insufficiently rewarded, and that of upstart ambition rewarded beyond all deserts. F. P. Lock is right to compare *Gulliver's Travels* not only to More's *Utopia* but also to Machiavelli's *The Prince*, for Swift's plot is profoundly concerned with questions of state service, and throughout his travels Gulliver repeatedly assumes the role of the "new man," symbolically and unequivocally sundered from any past "inheritance" by his status as a wandering alien who wades ashore willing and eager to serve the reigning prince and receive his due recompense.[5]

The notoriously discontinuous quality of Gulliver's character throughout much of his travels has frequently been cited to confirm the status of *Gulliver's Travels* as a "satire" rather than a "novel." But the retrospective standards by which we judge what is "novelistic" are of problematic relevance to the generically uncertain narratives that are native to the period of the novel's gradual stabilization. It may therefore be more instructive to see the discontinuity of Gulliver's character as a strategy that permits him to reflect satirically upon the serviceable hero of progressive ideology in two very different ways. On the one hand, he is the obsequious sycophant who seems always in the act of "prostrating" himself "at his Majesty's Feet," devoting his "Life to her Majesty's Service," embracing the role of "useful Servant," "most humble Creature and Vassal," and "Favourite," and humbly forbearing to rehearse for us just how honorably he has been treated (I, iii, 28; II, iii, 85–86, 90, iv, 97, viii, 123). Of course, his pride ensures that we will know this very well; a case in point is his vain and insistent allusion to his robe nobility after being honored with the Lilliputian title *Nardac*—"the highest Title of Honour among them"—in reward for the theft of the Blefuscudian fleet (I, v, 37, 39, vi, 49–50). Gulliver's rivalries for court precedence with the Lilliputian High Treasurer and the Brobdingnagian dwarf are equally demeaning, and like the theft of the fleet, his "signal Service" to the enormous king (blandly advising absolute despotism)

[5]F. P. Lock, *The Politics of Gulliver's Travels* (Oxford: Clarendon Press, 1980), 22. Machiavelli was of fundamental importance to both progressive and conservative ideology; for a discussion primarily of the former influence, see above, chap. 5, nn. 16–18.

and to the tiny queen (urinating on her palace) do not speak highly of his virtue and merit (II, iii, 91–92; I, v, 39–40; II, vi, 111, vii, 118). And as we watch Gulliver behaving like a reprehensible upstart, we also hear how this particular career pattern of status inconsistency has come to dominate the modern world. In Lilliput, the "Skills" that earn court preferment are those of the "Rope-Dancer," and honorific "Girdles" are awarded on the basis of *"leaping* and *creeping"* (I, iii, 22–23). To the Brobdingnag king it is evident that despite Gulliver's assurances, it is the great exception "that Men are ennobled on Account of their Virtue" in England (II, vi, 116). Later Gulliver is able to confirm that in modern Europe the most scandalous vices are likely to win "high Titles of Honour, and prodigious Estates," and he goes so far as to admit that even in England, our ancestors' "pure native Virtues [are] prostituted for a Piece of Money by their Grand-children" in pursuit of political interest (III, viii, 184, 185–86). Once in Houyhnhnmland, Gulliver has become quite trenchant on the "three Methods" by which an Englishman "may rise to be Chief Minister," and "Scoundrels [are] raised from the Dust upon the Merit of their Vices" (IV, vi, 239, x, 261).

But Gulliver's example also teaches the equally conservative lesson of, not "vice rewarded" but "merit punished." While his industrious virtue often looks more like obsequious ambition, we also find throughout Part I the thread of a sober and dignified complaint at the "immeasurable . . . Ambition" and "Passions" of princes and their ingratitude to those who serve them well (I, v, 37, 38, vii, 57, viii, 61). Fully "conscious of [his] own Merits and Innocence," Gulliver learns that his enemies at court have secretly obtained his impeachment for treason, and that he has been sentenced to blinding and to starvation by slow degrees. The punishment is deemed lenient; and after all, "it would be sufficient for you to see by the Eyes of the Ministers, since the greatest Princes do no more." "Yet, as to myself," Gulliver reflects, "I must confess, having never been designed for a Courtier, either by my Birth or Education, I was so ill a Judge of Things, that I could not discover the *Lenity* and Favour of this Sentence" (I, vii, 52, 54, 56).

The episode enacts Castiglione's dilemma of the omnicompetent courtier, still nominally in service yet in fact far greater (in this case physically so) than the prince he serves. A rather different deficiency in the established system of state service is reflected in Gulliver's voyage to Laputa and Balnibarbi, for there the ideals of civic humanism have been quite superseded by those of the new philosophy and its modernized conception of reform.[6] By that conception, both the "great Lord at Court" and his retired friend Lord Munodi, although they "had performed many eminent Services for the Crown," are judged men of little utility or understanding. This disregard for affairs of state, however, does not preclude in the king of Laputa a modicum of ambition for absolute power (III, iv, 157, 159, iii, 155). The trip to Luggnagg returns Gulliver to a more traditional political landscape— that of an arbitrary despot and his murderous court—and although he is made some "very honourable Offers" of favor, he prudently avoids entering into service

---

[6] See McKeon, *Origins*, chap. 5, n. 22. On Castiglione see above, chap. 5, n. 14.

(III, ix, 188–90). Responding, at the end of the narrative, to the suggestion that it was his duty in the several lands he discovered to have taken "Possession in my Sovereign's Name," Gulliver admits to "a few Scruples with relation to the distributive Justice of Princes upon those Occasions," and in the following account of the rapacious founding of "a *modern Colony*," we may recognize writ large the familiar principles of princely ambition (IV, xii, 278–79). But Gulliver's career is not our only source on the failure of princes to reward merit justly. In Glubbdubdrib, the survey of dead kings yields the consensus that preferment is never made for "Virtue" or "Merit," and when Gulliver summons up those responsible for truly "Great Services done to Princes and States," he is confronted by people he has never heard of, most of whom "died in Poverty and Disgrace, and the rest on a Scaffold or a Gibbet" (III, viii, 183–84).

2

So the conservative disclosure of status inconsistency is made from two distinct but complementary directions in *Gulliver's Travels*. And because this two-pronged attack on the injustice of the modern, progressive system incorporates the progressive critique of tradition, Swift is characteristically ambivalent with respect to aristocratic ideology. His scorn for the fiction of noble birth is as strong here as anywhere. Thus, Gulliver gives the Brobdingnag king a ludicrously earnest account of the English peers of the realm, "worthy Followers of their most renowned Ancestors, whose Honour had been the Reward of their Virtue; from which their Posterity were never once known to degenerate." And when he calls up the ancestral lineages of royalty and nobility in Glubbdubdrib, Gulliver is surprised to find not just that the descendants have decayed from their ancestors, but that the originating ancestors of aristocratic lines are themselves of uncertain status. Everywhere he finds, like Defoe in *The True-Born Englishman*, "an Interruption of Lineages by Pages, Lacqueys, Valets, Coachmen, Gamesters, Fidlers, Players, Captains, and Pick-pockets." Later his Houyhnhnm Master, assuming the ideal standard of consistency that obtains in his own country, remarks that Gulliver "must have been born of some Noble Family, because I far exceeded in Shape, Colour, and Cleanliness, all the *Yahoos* of his Nation." And the disillusioned Gulliver ruefully assures him "that, *Nobility* among us was altogether a different Thing from the Idea he had of it . . . That a weak diseased Body, a meager Countenance, and sallow Complexion, are the true Marks of *noble Blood*" (II, vi, 112; III, viii, 182–83; IV, vi, 240–41).

But in the conservative mentality, the absence of noble blood tends also to persist as a conventional sign, never too closely examined, of the absence of merit. Thus when Gulliver reflects that in Houyhnhnmland, unlike England, "no Scoundrels [are] raised from the Dust upon the Merit of their Vices," he adds: "or Nobility thrown into it on account of their Virtues" (IV, x, 261). We have two instances (albeit less drastic) of such a decline in Lord Munodi and his friend, both of whom are manifestly meritorious, have done great service to the Laputan monarch, and are held in utter contempt for their incapacity for abstraction—and whose virtues, we sense, are due at least in part to their ancient and eminent nobility (III, iv, 157, 159). And when Gulliver depicts the type of upstart found in his native England—"where a little contemptible Varlet, without the least Title to Birth, Person, Wit, or common Sense, shall presume to look with Importance, and put himself upon a Foot with the greatest Persons of the Kingdom"—his list of what is lacking here characteristically gives at least a symbolizing precedence to lineage (II, v, 108). This ghostly insinuation of belief in the justice of a traditional, aristocratic stratification is entirely consistent, I have argued, with conservative ideology. It is a socially useful fiction, a cautiously instrumental faith that germinates in the soil left by the flowers of progressive belief once the conservative critique has, to its own satisfaction, quite deracinated them. This fiction is inseparable from the utopian element in conservative ideology. In *Gulliver's Travels* we fleetingly sense its presence in the "*English* Yeomen of the old Stamp" summoned up at Glubbdubdrib (III, viii, 185). We hear it articulated more fully in the account of the militia of Brobdingnag, "which is made up of Tradesmen in the several Cities, and Farmers in the Country, whose Commanders are only the Nobility and Gentry, without Pay or Reward . . . Every Farmer is under the Command of his own Landlord, and every Citizen under that of the principal Men in his own City" (II, vii, 122).[7] In Lord Munodi we see an aristocratic landowner, joined by "some few other Persons of Quality and Gentry," who "was content to go on in the old Forms; to live in the Houses his Ancestors had built, and act as they did in every Part of Life without Innovation" (III, iv, 161). Munodi's estate combines, more certainly than those other instances, the conservative utopian elements of a status consistency somehow underwritten by tradition and the stable reality of landed property. But the crucial utopian enclave in *Gulliver's Travels* is, of course, Houyhnhnmland.

On first encountering the oddly equable horses, our serviceable hero naturally expects that it is he, the human, who will be "served" by them (IV, i, 211, ii, 213). He is soon disabused of this error, not by any conventional signs of dominion, as in his earlier voyages, but through the gradual and insensible growth of a natural deference toward the Houyhnhnms. He observes first that the household he is engaged with distinguishes itself into "Master" and "Servants," and after speaking to us for a while of "the Master Horse," he offhandedly refers to "my Master (for so I shall henceforth call him)" (IV, ii, 213, iii, 216, 218). Soon it seems natural to call "my Master" "his Honour," and Gulliver sits in long dialogue with his master about the state of European affairs, much as he had once done with the King of Brobdingnag (IV, v, 229). But although he does indeed come to see himself as in "Service" to his master, the nature of the relationship is very different from those he has experienced in the past: "I did not feel the Treachery or Inconstancy of a

---

[7]Swift's immediate model here is less the old Cavalier army (see above, chap. 5, n. 19), than the Machiavellian republican tradition.

Friend, nor the Injuries of a secret or open Enemy. I had no Occasion of bribing, flattering or pimping, to procure the Favour of any great Man, or of his Minion" (IV, x, 264, 265, 260).

This negative model of service is still available in Houyhnhnmland, among the Yahoos, for "in most Herds there was a Sort of ruling *Yahoo*" whose fawning and servile "*Favourite* is hated by the whole Herd" and befouled by it when he comes to be replaced in the affections of the ruler (IV, vii, 246–47). But when Gulliver receives favor now, it is "the Favour of being admitted to several *Houyhnhnms*, who came to visit or dine with my Master," and he is happiest in "the Station of an humble Auditor in such Conversations" (IV, x, 261). If we hear an echo of the old obsequiousness in such statements, we must keep in mind (as Gulliver himself knows) that nothing is to be gained by such arts of the courtier. In Houyhnhnm-land, service and its rewards appear indistinguishable; they are something like a religious discipline, the contemplation of virtue. Before his banishment Gulliver had resolved "to pass the rest of my Life among these admirable *Houyhnhnms* in the Contemplation and Practice of every Virtue" (IV, vii, 242). And after it his only ambition is "to discover some small Island uninhabited," where he might "reflect with Delight on the Virtues of those inimitable *Houyhnhnms*," "which I would have thought a greater Happiness than to be first Minister in the politest Court of *Europe*; so horrible was the Idea I conceived of returning to live in the Society and under the Government of *Yahoos*" (IV, xi, 267).

The very terms of the old dynamic of service and reward are altered by the utopian nature of Houyhnhnm culture because the enabling premise of that dynamic, status inconsistency, has vanished. It is not only their morality that is pervaded, in the apt words of C. J. Rawson, by "an absolute standard of congruity or *fittingness*," but also their very existence as natural and social beings. When Gulliver assures the Brobdingnag king of the purity of noble lineages in England, he is acting in bad faith. When the Houyhnhnm master assumes Gulliver's nobility, he is simply and truthfully speaking from his own experience, for "among the *Houyhnhnms*, the *White*, the *Sorrel*, and the *Iron-grey*, were not so exactly shaped as the *Bay*, the *Dapple-grey*, and the *Black*; nor born with equal Talents of Mind, or a Capacity to improve them; and therefore continued always in the Condition of Servants, without ever aspiring to match out of their own Race, which in that Country would be reckoned monstrous and unnatural" (IV, vi, 240). The appetite for upward mobility—through state service, intermarriage, or whatever means—never arises here, because the very conditions of status inconsistency by which it is generated, the very possibility of expectations that are "relative" to anything but one's own race, are absent. We are reminded of the aristocratic ideal—enforced by the futile stratagem of sumptuary legislation—of a correspondence between internals and externals so absolute that even mind and body are in complete accord. But here the romance convention whereby the noble are instantly recognizable through the purity of their complexions or the fineness of their hair has become a social reality.[8]

---

[8]C. J. Rawson, *Gulliver and the Gentle Reader: Studies in Swift and Our Time* (London: Routledge and Kegan Paul, 1973), 19. On sumptuary legislation see above, chap. 4, nn. 2, 29.

True, the smooth running of the social order requires more than the unrationalized operation of a purely natural "instinct." But the Houyhnhnms' recourse to "culture" is a good deal more candidly naturalized to the social order than a stealthy, "convenient fiction" like Socrates' myth of autochthonous origins, for it takes the form of a system of eugenics, which is rationally pursued in order "to preserve the Race from degenerating." It is to this end, and neither for love nor for the consolidation of the estate, that marriages are made, and the young couple is pleased to participate in the system because "it is what they see done every Day; and they look upon it as one of the necessary Actions in a reasonable Being" (IV, viii, 252–53). In such policies we see how socially useful conventions are subtly incorporated within Houyhnhnm social practice and obtain the tacit authority of behavior that is at once socialized and natural. The Houyhnhnm institution of marriage is based neither on the progressive fiction of the freedom of choice of the individual, nor on the aristocratic fiction of sacrifice to the greater end of familial lineage, but on their dialectical mediation.[9]

The Houyhnhnm economy is similarly suffused with a principle of congruity or consistency. In the insatiable avarice of the Brobdingnag farmer, we have already seen an ironic reflection of Gulliver's own insatiable desire for profit and mobility after Lilliput. The rest of the narrative does much to argue that these appetites, and the economic base that permits their unlimited growth, are endemic to English culture. The status inconsistency that nourishes the endless round of service and reward is itself fueled, as the Brobdingnag king discerns, by monetary corruption (II, vi, 113–16; III, viii, 185–86). And in Houyhnhnmland, Gulliver describes to his master how the English economy, unlimited by any principle of necessity or subsistence, thrives on the satisfaction of luxurious appetites, all the while creating fanciful new desires that will in turn need slaking. The key to this, Gulliver explains, is the exchange value of money, with which a European Yahoo "was able to purchase whatever he had a mind to . . . Therefore since *Money* alone, was able to perform all these Feats, our *Yahoos* thought, they could never have enough of it to spend or save," and the result is both conspicuous consumption and avaricious accumulation (IV, vi, 235–37). The only example of this sort of behavior in Houyhnhnmland is found, not surprisingly, among the Yahoos. Although Gulliver's master had long known of their fondness for a certain kind of shining stone, "he could never discover the Reason of this unnatural Appetite, or how these *Stones* could be of any Use to a *Yahoo*; but now he believed it might proceed from the same Principle of *Avarice*, which I had ascribed to Mankind." The same could be said of the principle of luxury and uncontrolled consumption, for there is nothing more odious about the Yahoos "than their undistinguishing Appetite to devour every thing that [comes] in their Way" (IV, vii, 244–45).

Among the Houyhnhnms things are, needless to say, very different. Like the Brobdingnag people, they are committed in general to a limiting principle of util-

[9]But while status distinctions are thereby reinforced, like many utopian communities, the Houyhnhnms (and the Lilliputians) are opposed to the extreme socialization of sex difference; see *Travels,* I, vi, 46; IV, viii, 253. For other utopian practices in this regard, see McKeon, *Origins,* chap. 6, n. 38. On Socrates see chap. 4, nn. 8–9.

ity (II, vii, 120; IV, iv, 226, viii, 252). Just as the Houyhnhnm master could not see the use of the Yahoos' stones, so "I was at much Pains to describe to him the Use of *Money*" (IV, vi, 235). For the use of money lies paradoxically in its alienation, in its exchange, and the Houyhnhnms have no use for exchange, because they have no desire for products that are obtainable only through the circulation of commodities (or indeed for the process of circulation itself, the taste for which is one of the most highly developed in capitalist culture). Theirs is not a "free" but a planned economy, whose principle of privileged communism Swift nicely articulates as the "Supposition that all Animals had a Title to their Share in the Productions of the Earth; and especially those who presided over the rest" (IV, vi, 235). In Houyhnhnmland, the manifest reality of social inequality is seen as quite consistent with economic egalitarianism. The closest the Houyhnhnms come to a system of exchange is a mechanism for the redistribution of goods: every four years, "whereever there is any Want (which is but seldom) it is immediately supplied by unanimous Consent and Contribution" (IV, viii, 254). And despite his deficient preparation for it, Gulliver learns to practice here his "little Oeconomy"—the account both invites and resists comparison with Robinson Crusoe's ostentatiously noncapitalist improvements—so that the very simple wants of his life are fully satisfied by an equally simple productive regimen (IV, x, 260).

3

Thus the conservative utopia of Houyhnhnmland so successfully dispels the imaginary values and unnatural wants of contemporary English civilization that it seems, finally, to establish a "consistency" between nature and culture. And if this is the achievement of Swift's utopia, the analogy of nature and culture, of biological and social existence, is also, of course, the method by which he has entangled his protagonist in adventure all along. In accord with the tradition of the imaginary voyage, Gulliver's travels are an experience of both sociopolitical and physical transformation, and it is clear that Swift would have us understand and ponder the analogical nature of this relationship. When Gulliver recalls the English variety of the "little contemptible Varlet," for example, it is as "the Moral of my own Behaviour" in Brobdingnag, when he acts the diminutive mock-hero in bombastic defense of his honor against his mortal enemy, the palace monkey (II, v, 107–8). And when he tells us soon after that "I was the Favourite of a great King and Queen, and the Delight of the whole Court; but it was upon such a Foot as ill became the Dignity of human Kind," we are obliged to see that he is describing not just the unique status of a pygmy among giants but the typical indignity of a court favorite (II, viii, 123). As we first know him Gulliver is, of course, much more physically than socially conscious. Like Robinson Crusoe, he is a practical man: a student of "Physick," a pragmatic "Projector," and a "Mechanical Genius," "curious enough to dissect" a Brobdingnag louse, "so curious [as] to weigh and measure" a Brobdingnag hailstone, inclined to wander from his shipmates in order "to entertain [his] Curiosity" (I, i, 3, v, 35; II, i, 69, iv, 97, v, 100, vi, 110; III, iv, 162). Entirely devoted to the evidence of the senses, Gulliver is one of those "plain, diligent, and laborious observers" celebrated by Thomas Sprat, who bring their "eyes uncorrupted" to their work, and he is quite preoccupied with an assortment of instruments—spectacles, pocket perspective, pocket compass—with which he hopes artificially to improve upon "the Weakness of [his] Eyes" (I, ii, 21).[10]

In Gulliver we are confronted with the man of science, a naive empiricist whose modernized version of the old sin of *libido sciendi* consists in the reduction of knowledge to sense impressions. In the problems that plague him in Parts I and II, we first encounter the theme that comes to the center of Swift's narrative in Part III, the critique of scientific empiricism as "the new romance." Already in Brobdingnag we learn that the category of the *"Lusus Naturae"* of "the Modern philosophy of *Europe"* is, whatever Gulliver believes, no better than "the old Evasion of *occult Causes,* whereby the Followers of *Aristotle* endeavour in vain to disguise their Ignorance" (II, iii, 88). By the time he meets Munodi, Gulliver is content to characterize a projector in terms not of vigorous skepticism but of "much Curiosity and easy Belief," and the Academy of Projectors in Lagado in a monument to the ironic reversal by which the objectivity of scientific projects for reforming the world is shown to entail a stealthy projection of subjective fancy upon it (III, iv, 162; cf. III, v–vi).[11]

But the demystification of objectivity is first enacted in the collisions between Gulliver's quantifying method and the respective standards of Lilliput and Brobdingnag. At the beginning of Part I, Gulliver's careful spatial estimates in leagues, degrees, inches, feet, and miles are soon confounded by phenomena that seem to defy an absolute and unitary measure ("The great Gate . . . about four Foot high"; leg chains "almost as large" as "those that hang to a Lady's Watch in *Europe"*; a prince big enough—"taller by almost the Breadth of my Nail, than any of his Court"—"to strike an Awe into the Beholders") (I, i, 4–5, 11–12, ii, 14). At the outset in Part II, we pass quickly from an account of the ship's movement "by my Computation" to an account of "Trees so lofty that I could make no Computation of their Altitude" (II, i, 68, 69). And now the fact of relativity, the reduction of objective quantification to a completely subjective perception, is impressed upon the bewildered Gulliver with all the force of an ontological theory of relative expectations: "Undoubtedly Philosophers are in the Right when they

[10]See also *Travels,* I, vi, 35–36, viii, 62, and, for the utility of the magnifying glass and the looking glass in Brobdingnag, II, i, 76, iii, 88, 91, viii, 131. For Sprat see above, chap. 3, n. 31. Gulliver likes to keep his instruments of sight in his most private and secret pockets, and he tells us of his gratitude when the pirates of Part III and the mutineers of Part IV refrain from a pocket search: *Travels,* III, i, 139; IV, i, 206. Given this empiricist investment in his eyesight, it is particularly disturbing that the punishment with which Gulliver is threatened in Lilliput is blinding: ibid., I, vii, 54, 56. On the potential "corruptions" of the telescope see the comments of Swift's skeptical predecessors in the critique of the new philosophy, Henry Stubbe and Samuel Butler, above, chap. 2, nn. 14–15.

[11]David Renaker has argued that only the science of Lagado represents Newtonianism and the experimental method of the Royal Society, and that the abstracted speculators of Laputa represent Cartesian rationalism: "Swift's Laputians as a Caricature of the Cartesians," *PMLA,* 94, no. 5 (Oct., 1979), 936–44.

tell us, that nothing is great or little otherwise than by Comparison: It might have pleased Fortune to let the *Lilliputians* find some Nation, where the People were as diminutive with respect to them, as they were to me. And who knows but that even this prodigious Race of Mortals might be equally overmatched in some distant Part of the World, whereof we have yet no Discovery?" (II, i, 71). But even under these extreme conditions of ontological vertigo, Swift is careful to ensure that physical relativity continues to operate as an analogy for social relativity. Thus Gulliver, although disgusted by the smell of the Brobdingnag "Maids of Honour," through an effort of will concedes that they may be "no more disagreeable to their Lovers . . . than People of the same Quality are with us in *England*" (II, v, 102). But the appalling sight of a nurse's "monstrous Breast, which I cannot tell what to compare with," makes him "reflect upon the fair Skins of our *English* Ladies," and he himself is flatteringly perceived by the Brobdingnags as having "a Complexion fairer than a Nobleman's Daughter of Three Years old" (II, i, 75–76, ii, 80).

The relativizing of physical standards of objectivity is an undeniable accomplishment of the first three voyages, but if we take this to be irreversibly damaging to the equilibrium of the modern empiricist-traveler, we do him an injustice. In fact, Gulliver's fundamental appetite of curiosity—the "insatiable Desire of seeing foreign Countries," that "insatiable Desire I had to see the World in every period of Antiquity"—is only whetted by the experience of indefinite relativity, for this is after all precisely what he is seeking: the experience of difference. And like all good travelers, he is well equipped for the experience. Despite his disclaimers, he is very adept at comparison, which permits him, at any single moment, to equilibrate difference, and the result is that he is extraordinarily adaptive to change. If "going native" is a cross-cultural version of social assimilation,[12] Gulliver's assimilative powers are so strong that even Brobdingnag is as much an experience of upward as of downward mobility for him. True, when the English ship comes upon his traveling box in the open sea, he imagines it will be an easy matter for one of the crew to slip his finger through its ring and lift it on board (II, viii, 127). But early on, Gulliver also learns to internalize the standards of what he sees around him and to recall with contempt the affectations of *"English* Lords and Ladies": "My Ideas were wholly taken up with what I saw on every Side of me; and I winked at my own Littleness, as People do at their own Faults" (II, iii, 91, viii, 132; cf. iv, 98, viii, 131, 133).

Gulliver's facility for assimilative comparison depends upon his ability to abstract himself from the fact of difference onto a plane of similarity, to manipulate a kind of epistemological exchange value that accommodates qualitatively dissimilar objects to a more general and equalizing standard. For this reason it is not surprising that like the mobile and serviceable seaman Edward Coxere, Gulliver is a master of languages (like language, "money is," in the words of Anthony Ascham, "an invention onely for the more expedite permutation of things"). Gulliver's facility with languages is so great, and his vanity as translator, purveyor of specialized

---

[12]See McKeon, *Origins*, chap. 6, n. 37.

terminologies, and amateur linguist is so well developed, that he appears to aspire in his own being to fulfill the utopian fantasy of seventeenth-century language projectors, the dream of a universal language. And in the Academy of Projectors at Lagado he is greatly taken with the several schemes by which language would be mechanized, materialized, or allegorized by method so as to render it a universal and transparent medium of exchange (III, v, 166–70, vi, 174–76).[13]

But in Houyhnhnmland this complacent dream is shattered. Here Gulliver is put "to the Pains of many Circumlocutions to give my Master a right Idea of what I spoke" (IV, iv, 226). At first it appears that this is the result of the primitive state of the Houyhnhnms' understanding, reflected in their regrettable paucity of words and expressions. But it soon becomes clear that what they lack is rather the superfluity of vicious desires that make language obscure and complicated and that are symbolized in the confusion of the Tower of Babel (IV, iii, 219, iv, 228). Ironically it is Houyhnhnm speech that approximates most closely, in *Gulliver's Travels*, a universal language. It is employed simply "to make us understand one another, and to receive Information of Facts." The Houyhnhnms have no "Occasion to talk of *Lying*, and *false Representation*," not only because their wills are not infected, but because in their speech there is a perfect correspondence and consistency of word and thing (IV, iv, 224). In Houyhnhnmland, the absence of a highly elaborated language is directly analogous to the absence of a highly elaborated economy. And Gulliver, frustrated in his attempts to translate between English and Houyhnhnm speech—to equalize them on the linguistic market of exchange—humbly acknowledges, with John Bunyan, the persistence and intractability of the old problem of mediation, and strives "to express [him] self by Similitudes" (IV, iv, 227).[14]

4

As in *Robinson Crusoe*, questions of virtue in *Gulliver's Travels* are never widely separated from questions of truth, and at times Swift is willing to juxtapose them quite directly. When the King of Brobdingnag concludes his attack on the inconsistency of status and virtue in England, for example, Gulliver, despite his "extreme Love of Truth," freely admits to having given the king a more favorable account of the matter "than the strictness of Truth would allow"

---

[13]Gulliver's facility with languages and translation: *Travels*, I, i, 4, ii, 15, 18–20; II, i, 73; IV, ii, 216. Nautical terminology: ibid., p. xxxv, II, i, 68. Gulliver as a linguist: ibid., II, ii, 79; III, ii, 145–46. On the concern of imaginary voyages with the universal language see McKeon, *Origins*, chap. 6, n. 38. For Ascham see chap. 5, n. 50. For Coxere see chap. 6, nn. 41–42.

[14]Compare Hosea 12:10: "I have used . . . similitudes," which provides the epigraph for *The Pilgrim's Progress*. In his account of the Brazilian Indians, Michel de Montaigne similarly associates economic with linguistic simplicity: "It is a Nation wherein there is no manner of Traffick . . . no use of Service, Riches or Poverty, no Contracts, no Successions, no Dividents . . . no Agriculture, no Mettal, no use of Corn or Wine, and where so much as the very words that signifie, Lying, Treachery, Dissimulation, Avarice, Envy, Detraction and Pardon, were never heard of" (*Essays of Michael seigneur de Montaigne* . . . , trans. Charles Cotton [1685], "Of Cannibals," I, 368–69).

(II, vi–vii, 116–17). And in Glubbdubdrib, immediately after telling us of the remarkable "Interruption of Lineages" among royalty and nobility, he narrates how "disgusted" he was "with modern History" and with "how the World had been misled by prostitute Writers" (III, viii, 183). *Gulliver's Travels* is adorned with all the claims to historicity and all the authenticating devices of "modern History" in general, and of travel narrative in particular. The claim itself is made early, late, and with considerable insistence (pp. xxxv–viii; II, i, 78; IV, xii, 275–76). The narrative is interspersed with documents—letters, maps—that attest to its own documentary objecthood (pp. xxxiii–viii, 2, 66, 136, 204), and it makes reference several times to the "Journal Book" on which, in accordance with the Royal Society's instructions, its own historicity is based (I, ii, 21; IV, iii, 218, xii, 276). The prefatory letter added in 1735 alludes to the spurious continuations and keys that have been published since the first printing, thereby buttressing its founding authenticity, but at the same time it complains of some spelling and other errors in that printing, the most serious of which are editorial deletions and insertions that raise the dilemma of quantitative completeness (pp. xxxiii–xxxvi). We encounter familiar hints that the narrative seems strange and therefore true; that "there is an Air of Truth apparent through the whole"; and that the author has chosen "to relate plain matter of Fact in the simplest Manner and Style" (II, iv, 98–99; p. xxxvii; IV, xii, 275). Finally, we are reminded throughout that what we are reading is indeed a book of travels and may be judged accordingly.[15]

The results of such a judgment are not entirely straightforward. *Gulliver's Travels* is, of course, a satire of the travel narrative, and of the naive empiricism with which it is so closely associated. But just as Swift's critique of progressive ideology shares with that ideology a contempt for the fictions of aristocratic honor, so the subversion of the claim to historicity proceeds from a common, if more relentlessly indulged, skeptical impulse. The conventions of imaginary and "real" voyages were the same, and Swift's wide reading in the form bespeaks (as is so characteristic of his interests) an equivocal fascination composed of attraction as well is repulsion.[16] When Gulliver couples his claim to historicity with the aim of moral "Reformation," he is echoing, to be sure, the sort of state-

[15]See *Travels,* II, i, 78, iv, 98–99, viii, 131; III, xi, 198; IV, ii, 216–17, viii, 251, x, 266, xii, 275–77. Documentation: Part I also contains Gulliver's "Word for Word" translations of several official Lilliputian documents; ibid., I, ii, 18–20, iii, 27–28, vii, 52–53. Gulliver makes clear his intellectual affiliation with the Royal Society by telling us that he has donated several Brobdingnag wasp stings to that institution; ibid., II, iii, 94. Printing errors: The printer has erroneously transformed "Brobdingrag" into "Brobdingnag"; compare Edward Cooke, *A Voyage to the South Sea, and Round the World . . .* (1712), II, vi, where "Selkirk" is corrected to "Selcrag." On quantitative completeness see also *Travels,* II, i, 78, vii, 117.

[16]Many narrators of travels, both real and imaginary, made the plausible argument that our doubts concerning the existence of things—lands, peoples, extraordinary animals—we do not know may reflect only our skepticism, not their unreality; e.g., see above, chap. 3, nn. 48–50. John Arbuthnot told Swift of readers who behaved as though *Gulliver's Travels* was authentic; see Arbuthnot to Swift, Nov. 5, 1726, in *Correspondence,* III, 180. On the complexity of Swift's attitude toward travel narratives see also Percy G. Adams, *Travel Literature and the Evolution of the Novel* (Lexington: University Press of Kentucky, 1983), 142–44.

ment that preceded not only some of Defoe's works but numerous exercises in quasi-spiritual autobiography and travel as well (p. xxxv). But the coexistence of that aim with his disgusted repudiation of "so absurd a Project as that of reforming the *Yahoo* Race in this Kingdom" is entirely typical also of Swift's own lifelong ambivalence about the utility of satiric schemes of reformation (p. xxxvi). By the same token, the Swiftian attack upon the incredibility of "true history" would not be as profound as it is if Swift were not deeply committed to some species of historical truth.[17]

What are the implications of Swift's epistemological double reversal for how he would tell the truth in narrative? Obviously he does not underwrite Gulliver's claim to have related "plain matter of Fact." The Houyhnhnms can use language to convey and "receive Information of Facts," but that is because they are Houyhnhnms. Gulliver's commitment to the factual veracity of his factually vulnerable narrative is thus one clear sign of his error. But he is also committed, however fallibly, to the wisdom of the Houyhnhnms, and in his transmission of their wisdom to us he practices another sort of truth-telling in narrative, which he articulates when he says that "a Traveller's chief Aim should be to make Men wiser and better, and to improve their Minds by the bad, as well as good Example of what they deliver concerning foreign Places" (IV, xii, 275). This formulation of how history teaches truth and virtue by example is in fact rather more traditional than Gulliver's—and Swift's—actual practice would warrant, for the texture of circumstantial and authenticating detail is too dense to be dissolved by our somewhat anxious insistence that it is "all ironic."[18]

The epistemology of *Gulliver's Travels* can be usefully compared with that of the most acute and self-conscious of the spiritual travelers at the end of the previous century, whose plain style and historicity were instruments by which to arrive

---

[17]Lock has made an important objection to the common and uncritical assumption that much of the political allegory that has been attributed to *Gulliver's Travels* was intended by Swift. But he is wrong to suggest that reference to particular historical cases was foreign to Swift's aim in that work, and to maintain that "to bury the meanings so deeply that the allegory could neither be recognized nor certainly interpreted if discovered was self-defeating" (*Politics of Gulliver's Travels*, 106). I have earlier argued that the uncertainty of allegorical interpretation provides Swift and his contemporaries with a crucial focus for investigating the problem of mediation, especially as that problem was trivialized and aggravated (for people like Swift) by naive empiricist or enthusiastic beliefs in the possibility of an immediate access to truth. This is nowhere more clear than in *A Tale of a Tub* (1704), where Swift attacks simultaneously the opposed but complementary errors of deep and superficial reading. In the episode of the political allegorizers in *Gulliver's Travels* (III, vi, 175), Swift creates a similar sort of double-bind for his readers by calling them "the Natives called *Langden*" "in the Kingdom of *Tribnia*." Lock thinks these are "crudely intrusive anagrams that make the satire . . . needlessly specific." (*Politics of Gulliver's Travels*, 82). But the effect of the names is to implicate us inextricably in the problem of interpretation, for by automatically deciphering them as "England" and "Britain," we replicate the behavior of the projectors whom Swift obliges us to scorn. (Another way of saying this is to suggest that Swift here employs a second-order satire whose principal target is not really "the English" at all, but overly elaborate interpretation—like that required to read the currently popular secret histories and *romans à clef* [see McKeon, *Origins*, chap. 1, nn. 99–100].) Here Swift has a little joke at our expense. But the critical problem of interpretive indeterminacy, although it may feel self-defeating, is a serious one that ramifies into many areas of his thought.

[18]See the intelligent discussion of how we are to take Gulliver's claim to historicity in Rawson, *Gulliver and the Gentle Reader*, 9–10.

at a truth that lay through, but not in, the factual.[19] But Swift's parable is noticeably non-Christian, and since we are not asked to acknowledge the Author who lurks behind the author, we are not overly occupied with attributing to an ultimately higher source Swift's creation of the artifice Gulliver has disavowed. As a result, by subverting empirical epistemology, Swift contributes, as fully as Defoe does by sponsoring it, to the growth of modern ideas of realism and the internalized spirituality of the aesthetic. Swift's parabolic pedagogy can tacitly justify its return to an anachronistic attitude toward how to tell the truth in narrative in part because it has, as it were, earned the right to it through a self-conscious evisceration of the more modern alternative, and in part because that modern alternative is learning how to reconcile itself to notions of aesthetic universality through the resuscitation of Aristotelian doctrine. In this respect, as well as in its inevitable dedication to the weapon of perceptual subjectivity, which it employs to attack empirical notions of objectivity, Swift's narrative method is at the forefront of the "modern alternative." The attack would be ineffective if it were based only on the old unsearchability of the divine spirit and its intentions. Yet in substituting for the traditional a modernized critique of materialist sufficiency, Swift participates, as surely as Defoe, in the modern replacement of Spirit by Mind.[20]

But there are also other ways of understanding why *Gulliver's Travels* is non-Christian. In *Robinson Crusoe* Defoe is willing, quasi-metaphorically, to speak of Robinson's "original sin" because in the optimistic spirit of progressive ideology he is willing to conceive that status inconsistency, for which original sin stands as its most irrevocable instance, can be indemnified and overcome. Swift does not speak of original sin because his social vision is too thoroughly infiltrated by a conviction of it, and in the Houyhnhnms he wants to posit a race of mortals—humanoid but necessarily nonhuman—that has no experience of status inconsistency. In Brobdingnag, Gulliver has already shown remarkable powers of resistance to negative socialization. Bestialized at every turn—compared to a weasel, a toad, a spider, a splacknuck, a canary, a frog, a puppy, a diminutive insect, a little odious vermin—it is testimony to his resilience that he is yet able to identify as fully as he does with his enormous human hosts. In Houyhnhnmland the Yahoos confront Gulliver with the similar challenge of an effective theriomorphy, and for a while he fends it off.

When he first encounters the Yahoos they are "Beast[s]," "ugly Monster[s]," deformed "Animals" who bear no relation to the "many Tracks of human Feet" he has earlier observed, a "cursed Brood" that presumably served "the Inhabitants" as "Cattle" (IV, i, 207–8). As the alarming resemblance becomes harder to avoid, he tries to conceal "the Secret of [his] Dress, in order to distinguish [himself] as much as possible" (IV, iii, 220). But at length Gulliver is obliged to acknowledge "that entire Congruity betwixt [himself] and their *Yahoos*," and when a young female, observing him bathe, becomes "inflamed by Desire . . . [he] could no longer deny,

---

[19]E.g., cf. William Okeley, McKeon, *Origins*, chap. 3, n. 56.
[20]On these matters see McKeon, *Origins*, chap. 3, sec. 6.

that [he] was a real *Yahoo*" (IV, vii, 242, viii, 250–51). Still he entertains some hope that the Houyhnhnms "would condescend to distinguish [him] from the rest of [his] Species," but he is overcome with despair when the General Council exhorts his master "either to employ [him] like the rest of [his] Species, or command [him] to swim back to the Place from whence [he] came" (IV, x, 262, 263).

So Gulliver is obliged against his will to "go native." What is the precise meaning of this assimilation? It is of course in the interest of Gulliver's self-esteem for him to understand himself as the pure form of the species, from whom the "corrupted" Yahoos have "degenerated" (IV, iii, 222, viii, 249). This view receives some support from his master's interpretation of the traditional story of the origins of the Yahoos, "whereof," Gulliver significantly adds, "he had indeed borrowed the Hint from me" (IV, ix, 256).[21] But Gulliver's account of European culture, the impartial observation of the Yahoos, and the wisdom of the Houyhnhnms all point toward the contrary conclusion: that the tincture of reason possessed by the Europeans has aggravated, corrupted, improved, and multiplied the vices and wants that they naturally share with the Yahoos, and made them unquestionably the degenerate and bestial form of the species (IV, v, 232, vii, 243–48, x, 262, xii, 280). The "corruptions" of money, it would appear—its ability to create new and unheard-of desires and vanities—are a subcategory of the "corruptions" of reason. Both are peculiar to that segment of the human race whose vicious appetites have become so unlimited by the constraints of nature and custom as to demand the final and appalling sanction of being, themselves, the standard of what is natural.[22]

One basic argument of the "soft school of interpretation" concerning Part IV of *Gulliver's Travels* is that Swift tacitly and tellingly discredits the Houyhnhnms by making them passionless and cold—an argument which ignores how consistently the containment of the passions operates in Swift's writings as a positive norm. In fact Swift tells us that the language of the Houyhnhnms is well suited to the expression of the passions (IV, i, 210). True, their passions and wants are fewer than ours; but among the appetites they lack is "the Desire of Power and Riches," whereas the detestable type of the first minister of state in England—possessed of rather fewer passions, apparently, than even the Houyhnhnms—"makes use of no other Passions but a violent Desire of Wealth, Power, and Titles" (IV, iv, 226, 228, vi, 239; see also IV, vi, 236, viii, 253, for passions the Houyhnhnms do not know). It is precisely because the passions of the Houyhnhnms are few, and because they place natural and discretionary limits on them—planned marriages, the practice of abstinence, the selective censorship

---

[21] In the first edition, Gulliver elaborates this interpretation to suggest that the Yahoos are the "very much defaced" descendants of specifically English people; see *Travels*, "Textual Notes," 306.

[22] See McKeon, *Origins*, chap. 5, sec. 4. The idea that human reason works to corrupt rather than to enhance human nature was a familiar one in political and utopian literature; e.g., in [Gabriel de Foigny], *A New Discovery of Terra Incognita Australis* ... (1693), 75–76, the wise old man tells Sadeur that his countrymen "have some *Sparks of Reason*, but they are so weak, that instead of enlightning them, they only serve to conduct 'em more surely in their Error."

and eventual banishment of Gulliver—that they have avoided the degenerations and corruptions of the human race (IV, v, 231–32, viii, 252–53, x, 263).[23]

For the wisdom of the Houyhnhnms entails not an invulnerability to corruption but the foresight and will to prevent it. And their wisdom in banishing Gulliver is evident in the fact that his assimilationist vanity is in no way limited by his acceptance of his status as a Yahoo, which instead only whets his appetite to become a Houyhnhnm. In what is surely an extreme case of upwardly mobile ambition, Gulliver aspires to the status of a higher species. And when we call up the image of him trotting and whinnying like a Houyhnhnm, we are struck by the justice with which the materialist sufficiency of this man of science is now expressed in the hopelessly physical mode through which he would imitate moral excellence (IV, x, 262–63).[24] Gulliver's impersonation of a horse is his equivalent of Robinson's figures of absolute dominion and divine providence. Both men are engaged in postconversion projects of "improvement"; but whereas Robinson is permitted by his author to project English society upon his island with impunity and to introject a divinity that sanctions his desires, Gulliver's ethnocentric attempts to find an ideal England abroad are consistently frustrated, and the Houyhnhnms absolutely resist introjection.

Although we might be tempted to draw the easy lesson that only this particular conversion has failed, Swift is really reflecting on all suspect conversions that consist in the psychological process of introjection, conversions that succeed if their subjects are complacent enough to be certain that they have. And so he gives us a protagonist whose utopia cannot be internalized, who cannot "make" himself, whose social mobility manifestly cannot signify spiritual achievement, because try as he might, he cannot become what he is not—a truth that is demonstrated most of all in his very willingness to try. Robinson Crusoe's honest old Portuguese captain serves to reflect back to him his heightened spiritual status, to provide the external accreditation of the community. Gulliver's honest Portuguese captain, Don Pedro de Mendez, exists to provide this same assurance, and the fact that Gulliver barely tolerates him bespeaks a fine doubleness. For it supports both a painful truth—even the best of men are only human (and Gulliver has renounced easy confirmations)—and a painful delusion—Gulliver's distaste for Don Pedro is inseparable from his continuing conviction of his own differentness.

[23]Like other conservative writers, Swift thus implicitly mocks the progressive claim that the indulgence of the avaricious passions may help countervail more destructive ones; see McKeon, *Origins*, chap. 6, nn. 25, 53. On the soft and hard schools of interpretation see James L. Clifford, "Gulliver's Fourth Voyage: Hard and Soft Schools of Interpretation," in *Quick Springs of Sense: Studies in the Eighteenth Century*, ed. Larry S. Champion (Athens: University of Georgia Press, 1974), 33–49.

[24]The amusing silliness of a Houyhnhnm threading a needle, on the other hand, is Swift's mild self-mockery of the inadequacy of his own efforts (a very minor version of his hero's failings) to mediate Houyhnhnm to human nature by way of physical resemblance. But note that even here it is Gulliver who creates the incongruity by lending the mare a needle: *Travels*, IV, ix, 258. With Gulliver's vain ambition compare the desperate and self-censored aspiration of Mary Carleton to be a different sex (McKeon, *Origins*, chap. 6, nn. 32–34). It is easy to sympathize with her ambition, as it is not in the case of Gulliver's, because hers amounts to a just desire to obtain the power she merits rather than a vain emulation of a status that is beyond her internal capacities.

So the inwardly divided Gulliver returns to England, makes a "small Purchase of Land," and retires to cultivate "my little Garden." And by that movement he completes, in the double trajectory with which he began, a characteristically circular conservative plot pattern: the embittered return of the disdained country gentleman to his landed enclave (and the type embraces also the retirement of Munodi and Swift himself); and the comic rustication of the unsuccessful younger son, bloated with pride and incomprehendingly indignant at his failure to make it in town or at court (pp. xxxiv, xxxvi; IV, xii, 279). The power of *Gulliver's Travels* as a narrative explanation of status inconsistency cannot be detached from the force of its will to explain, parabolically, our more general condition of mutability and discord. The ironic theme of historical degeneration and cyclical decay is everywhere: in the testimony of Aristotle at Glubbdubdrib when he enunciates the conservative maxim "that new Systems of Nature [are] but new Fashions," and new truths only recapitulate the errors of those they replace; in the case of the Struldbruggs, who seem to Gulliver to promise an "antient Virtue" that may "prevent that continual Degeneracy of human Nature," but who in fact are a terrible emblem of physical and mental decay (III, viii, 182, x, 192, 194).[25]

But the generality of the problems Swift investigates in *Gulliver's Travels* can be overstated. At crucial moments in the critique of ambitious courtiers and ungrateful princes, we are told that our concern is with the modern period and the modern world. The familiar-sounding crises that we hear of in Lilliputian politics began with the present emperor's great-grandfather and continue to very recent times (I, iv, 32–34, vi, 44). The present era of Brobdingnag stability dates from the reign of this king's grandfather, who ended a civil war (II, vii, 122). The virtues of the old English yeomen have been prostituted by their corrupted grandchildren, who are even now at large (III, viii, 185–86). The volatile period to which Swift alludes most insistently, in other words, is the previous century. In the last analysis it seems important to recognize that *Gulliver's Travels* intertwines the microplot of Lemuel Gulliver with these allusive invocations of the macroplot of seventeenth-century English history in order to specify, and explain, a species of error and corruption that, to a very important degree, Swift saw as a modern phenomenon.

---

[25]On the circular patterns of conservative plots see McKeon, *Origins*, chap. 6, nn. 21–22.

Swift's Satire on "Science" and the Structure of *Gulliver's Travels*

Douglas Lane Patey

When the philosophers of the last age were first congregated into the Royal Society, great expectations were raised of the sudden progress of useful arts; the time was supposed to be near when engines should turn by a perpetual motion, and health be secured by the universal medicine; when learning would be facilitated by a real character, and commerce extended by ships which could reach their ports in defiance of the tempest.

But improvement is naturally slow. The society met and parted without any visible diminution of the miseries of life. The gout and stone were still painful, the ground that was not plowed brought no harvest, and neither oranges nor grapes would grow upon the hawthorne. At last, those who were disappointed began to be angry; those likewise who hated innovation were glad to gain an opportunity of ridiculing men who had depreciated, perhaps with too much arrogance, the knowledge of antiquity. And it appears from some of their earliest apologies, that the philosophers felt with great sensibility the unwelcome importunities of these who were daily asking, "What have ye done?"

—Samuel Johnson, *Idler* 88 (1759)

Long before Marjorie Nicolson and Nora Mohler demonstrated the topical referentiality of Swift's satire in book 3 of *Gulliver*, readers understood that among its targets is what we have come to call the "new science" of the Royal Society.[1] When writing *Idler* 88 in 1759 (a year when both science and travel writing occupied much of his attention), Johnson had *Gulliver* clearly in mind. Here are Swift's targets, from efforts at perpetual motion to Bishop Wilkins's "real character"; here (in Johnson's characteristically gentler manner) is Swift's satire on the "philosophers'" failure to achieve their much-advertised practical results ("utility"). What especially links *Idler* 88 and *Gulliver* is Johnson's characterization of these "philosophers" as *Moderns*—proponents of "progress" who arrogantly depreciate "the knowledge of antiquity." But from Johnson's time to ours, there has been little agreement about the precise substance of Swift's sup-

From *ELH* 58 (1991) 809–39 © 1991 by The Johns Hopkins University Press. Reprinted by permission of the author and Johns Hopkins University Press.

I would like to thank Professor Paul Pickrel for his thoughtful comments on the argument of this essay.

[1]Marjorie Nicolson and Nora Mohler, "The Scientific Background of Swift's *Voyage to Laputa*," *Annals of Science* 2 (1937): 299–334.

posed objections to science or the function of those objections in the *Travels* as a whole. Has Johnson, like many critics since, read too literally Munodi's deliberately overstated remark that "as for himself, being not of an enterprizing Spirit, he was content to go on in the old Forms; to live in the Houses his Ancestors had built, and act as they did in every Part of Life without Innovation"?[2]

Debate over the range of Swift's satire in book 3 in fact began among *Gulliver's* first readers: to the Earl of Orrery's claim that book 3 was "in general written against chymists, mathematicians, mechanics, and projectors of all kinds," Deane Swift replied: "Certainly DR. SWIFT has laughed egregiously in the voyage to *Laputa*, and exerted a vein of humour, not against the whole tribe of chymists, projectors, and mathematicians in general; but against those, and those only, who despise the useful branches of science, and waste their lives in the pursuit of aerial vanities and extravagances."[3] The debate between Orrery and Deane Swift persists, with the difference that among Orrery's twentieth-century descendants Swift has become the enemy of "science" *tout court*. Thus, for instance, despite the warnings of many modern Deane Swifts, R. G. Olson argues in a new essay on "Tory-High Church Opposition to Science" that "what began for Arbuthnot as one scientist's concern for the unintended errors and excesses of his colleagues, in the hands of Jonathan Swift turned into a full-blown antagonism to the scientific enterprise," with the result that "A *Tale of a Tub* and *Gulliver* . . . contain classic statements of conservative antiscientific sentiment."[4] Predictably, such extreme argument generates equally implausible

[2]*The Prose Works of Jonathan Swift*, ed. Herbert Davis, 16 vols. (Oxford: Basil Blackwell, 1959), vol. 11, *Gulliver's Travels*, 177. All subsequent references are to this edition and are cited parenthetically in the text.

[3]John Boyle, Earl of Orrery, *Remarks on the Life and Writings of Dr. Jonathan Swift* (London, 1752), 147; Deane Swift, *Essay on the Life, Writings and Character, of Dr. Jonathan Swift* (London, 1755), 214.

[4]Richard G. Olson, "Tory-High Church Opposition to Science and Scientism in the Eighteenth Century: The Works of John Arbuthnot, Jonathan Swift, and Samuel Johnson," in John G, Burke, ed., *The Uses of Science in the Age of Newton* (Berkeley: Univ. of California Press, 1983), 182, 185; Olson even repeats the canard about Swift's poor performance in "science" courses in college (184). See also John Sutherland: "Swift does more than attack the excesses of would-be scientists: he attacks science itself . . . he recognized that man's analytic use of his intellect in an attempt to examine and manipulate the natural world as one of the best possible examples of the sin of pride in action" ("A Reconsideration of Gulliver's Third Voyage," *Studies in Philology* 54 [1957]: 46). More recent treatments of book 3 in this vein include: John Hill, "Corpuscular Fundament: Swift and the Mechanical Philosophy," *Enlightenment Essays* 6 (1975): 37–49; Dennis Todd, "Laputa, the Whore of Babylon, and the Idols of Science," *Studies in Philology* 75 (1978): 93-120; and Eric Rothstein, "*Gulliver* III: or the Progress of Clio," *Proceedings of the First Münster Symposium on Jonathan Swift*, ed. Hermann Real and Heinz J. Vienken (München: Wilhelm Fink, 1985), 216-31.

The scholar probably most influential in keeping Orrery's view alive among literary critics in our century has been Richard Foster Jones, whose view of Swift follows from his larger theory of the antiscientific stance of the Ancients in the quarrel between Ancients and Moderns (see for instance "The Background of the Attack on Science," in *Pope and his Contemporaries*, ed. James L. Clifford and Louis Landa [London: Oxford Univ. Press, 1949], 96–113). Jones's influence among critics persists despite widespread dissatisfaction among historians of science themselves with that theory (see especially Peter Mathias Rattansi's review of Jones's *Ancients and Moderns*, *British Journal for the Philosophy of Science* 18 [1967]: 250-55).

defenses of Swift's "scientific" sympathies and attainments—indeed, of his proficiency even in technical mathematics and physics.[5]

What is needed to resolve this controversy, especially in its modern form, is not so much a more careful reading of the *Travels* as its fuller contextualization. We must place Swift's satire more securely within the conceptual terrain of the early eighteenth century, attending to the ways the disciplines of knowledge were divided in Swift's time, and to Swift's particular concern, as an Ancient, over certain nascent shifts in those divisions. For it is only in the eighteenth century, in the context of the quarrel between Ancients and Moderns, that our notions of "science"—of the "sciences" as distinct from and opposed to the "arts" and "humanities," and of "science" as distinctively progressive—begin to emerge.[6] Like his fellow Ancient Pope, Swift is aware of this shift and satirizes the new division of knowledge from the point of view of an older one.

We may note that neither Orrery nor Deane Swift (nor for that matter Johnson or Swift himself) speaks of "science" in its modern sense; for them, the term still means, first of all, knowledge in general. Neither has a word with which to separate out "the whole tribe of chymists, projectors, and mathematicians in general"; Johnson has only "philosopher." In book 3 Swift uses "science" only in its widest sense, speaking for instance of "an Analogy between the two Sciences" of mathematics and politics (164); his experimenters are not "scientists" but "artists." Nor does Swift possess what was only emerging in this time, a distinct concept of what were coming to be understood as "fine" arts. It has been most tempting to read a modern distinction (and opposition) between science and art (or the sciences and the humanities) into Gulliver's famous summary of Laputan deficiencies:

> Imagination, Fancy, and Invention, they are wholly Strangers to, nor have any Words in their Language by which those Ideas can be expressed; the whole Compass of their Thoughts and Mind, being shut up within the two forementioned Sciences ["Mathematicks and Musick"]. (163–64)

But Gulliver does not adduce this lack of imagination in the context of poetry or painting, the arts of beauty or the realm of taste; he is speaking much more generally, and in fact dwells here on Laputan unimaginativeness specifically in politics ("They are very bad Reasoners, and vehemently given to Opposition . . . passionately disputing every Inch of a Party Opinion"). The Grand Academy of

---

[5]Such implausible defenses include S. H. Gould, "Gulliver and the Moons of Mars," *Journal of the History of Ideas* 6 (1945): 91–101, which would make Swift a careful student of both Kepler's *System of the World* and Newton's *Principia*, and Colin Kiernan, "Swift and Science," *The Historical Journal* 14 (1971): 709–22, which tends to construe Swift's satire as a straightforward scientific treatise. A much more trustworthy survey of Swift's lifelong interest in the sciences is George Reuben Potter, "Swift and 'Natural Science,' " *Philological Quarterly* 20 (1941): 97–118.

[6]The roots of the new division of knowledge have been traced by Paul O. Kristeller, "The Modern System of the Arts," *Journal of the History of Ideas* 12 (1951): 496–527; 13 (1952): 17–46; Ronald S. Crane, "The Idea of the Humanities," in *The Idea of the Humanities and Other Critical Essays*, 2 vols. (Chicago: Univ. of Chicago Press, 1967), 1:3–170; and Douglas Lane Patey, "The Eighteenth Century Invents the Canon," *Modern Language Studies* 18 (1988): 17–37.

Lagado, finally—to some extent like the early Royal Society—freely mixes "scientific" with political and even what we would call artistic concerns, just as the projector whose machine combines words at random predicts that his device will be equally fruitful in the production of "Books in Philosophy, Poetry, Politicks, Law, Mathematicks and Theology"; the Academy distributes its buildings not between schools of science (or even "natural philosophy") and politics, but between practical and "speculative Learning" (182–84).

I do not mean to argue that *Gulliver* contains no satire on science because (modern) "science" did not yet exist—though in important ways this is true (the "natural philosophy" of Swift's time differs from modern science both extensionally and intensionally, in both range and meaning). Swift indeed means, as many readers have noted, to protest the illegitimate importation of "scientific" methods into "arts" where they do not belong; but he does not mean by these terms what we do. He does not, that is, use these terms as they were redefined by the Moderns; rather, he uses them to mark a division of knowledge familiar since Aristotle (a figure the *Travels* more than once defends). Swift's science is still what centuries of thinkers would have recognized as the realm of certainty, whose instrument is logical demonstration; his arts are not the fine arts or humanities, but the older arts of prudence—those fields in which, because of the limitations of the human mind, demonstrative certainty is not to be had. The arts of prudence comprise not science but opinion; they can aspire only to probability. Here, traditionary authority must largely supplant logical proof; the instrument of such arts is therefore not demonstration but *imitation*. Swift's vision of the proper conduct of natural philosophy thus emerges from and supports his belief in the limitedness of human capacity (of human nature)—limitedness that makes the method of imitation not merely an "aesthetic" choice but an epistemic necessity: imitation is the necessary means of cultural transmission under conditions of uncertainty. His account of science is thus not far distant from the theory of proper criticism propounded by Pope in the *Essay on Criticism*, which argues that since demonstrative knowledge of critical "rules" is impossible, both critic and poet must proceed by merely probable methods, in particular by imitation.[7]

Once we recover the division of knowledge Swift takes as normative, we will not only be able to make better sense than heretofore of the faults of the Laputans; we will find that Swift's comments on science, in book 3 and elsewhere, are more various and acute, and more fully integrated into the fabric of the *Travels* as a whole, than has commonly been realized. Of course, most statements about the *Travels* "as a whole" are eventually exploded. Readers by now generally agree not to identify Swift's book as a "novel," and so do not look to it for the kinds of consistency and progressive development of character and nar-

---

[7]For readings of Pope's *Essay* along these lines, see David B. Morris, "Civilized Reading: The Act of Judgment in *An Essay on Criticism*," in *The Art of Alexander Pope*, ed. Howard Erskine-Hill and Anne Smith (London: Vision Press, 1979), 15–39, and Douglas Lane Patey, *Probability and Literary Form: Philosophic Theory and Literary Practice in the Augustan Age* (Cambridge: Cambridge Univ. Press, 1984), 126–33.

rative that we expect in longer works by Fielding, Richardson, and even Defoe. Instead, the *Travels* are satire, more specifically satire in the form of (fictional, even mock) travel literature.[8] These identifications lead us to look elsewhere for the work's unity, to Swift's themes and more particularly to the rhetorical procedures he uses in elaborating them. But, I will argue, the travel genre itself embodies for Swift as for other Augustans a certain view of experience and knowledge, a view we might call probabilism. When seen in this larger context, Swift's comments on science not only provide additional ordnance in his attack on human pride; they outline a satiric alternative to the epistemological and moral commitments implied by the travel form itself.

Gulliver Against the Dogmatists

> That heavy Bodies descend by *gravity,* is no better an account than we might expect from a *Rustick*: and again; that Gravity is a *quality* whereby an heavy body descends, is an impertinent *Circle,* and teacheth nothing.
>
> —Joseph Glanvill, *The Vanity of Dogmatizing* (1661)[9]

One of the most familiar banners of the "new science" and the Royal Society was their rejection of what Hobbes called "insignificant speech," including especially such scholastic terminology as "occult quality," "substantial form," and "intelligible species."[10] These terms became objectionable particularly when used (as they were designed to be) in explanations, as in the example made famous by Molière: Why does opium produce sleep? because of its dormitive power (*vis dormitiva*). To the new scientists, such explanations and terms were the relics of an earlier kind of science, a demonstrative *scientia* which supposed it possible to know the "real qualities" of things (such as their "powers")—to know them either directly or by a mysterious kind of "scientific induction" (different from the problematic induction of later science)—and so to invoke them as explanations for particular effects (*qualitas* in its scholastic sense meaning a *cause* of the attributes of bodies). But with the seventeenth-century revival of a distinction between primary and secondary qualities, we are cut off from direct knowledge of such real qualities and can only conjecture them from their effects; such knowledge of causes is not demonstrative, but only hypothetical

---

[8]See most recently J. Paul Hunter, *"Gulliver's Travels* and the Novel," in *The Genres of Gulliver's Travels,* ed. Frederik N. Smith (Newark: Univ. of Delaware Press, 1990), 56–74, and on the generic construction of book 3 in particular, Jenny Mezciems, "The Unity of Swift's 'Voyage to Laputa': Structure as Meaning in Utopian Fiction," *Modern Language Review* 72 (1977): 1–21.

[9]Joseph Glanvill, *The Vanity of Dogmatizing* (London, 1661), 171. Glanvill adds: "The accounts that this [Aristotelian] *Philosophy* gives by other *Qualities,* are of the same *Gender* with these: So that to say that the *Loadstone* draws *Iron* by *magnetick attraction* . . . were as satisfying as these *Hypotheses,* and the solution were as pertinent" (171–72).

[10]See for instance Thomas Hobbes, *Leviathan,* chaps. 4-5; John Locke, *Essay,* ed. Peter H. Nidditch (Oxford: Clarendon Press, 1975), 3.10 ("Of the Abuse of Words"); Glanvill (note 9), chap. 16; and Gulliver himself of the Brobdingnagians: "As to Ideas, Entities, Abstractions and Transcendentals, I could never drive the least Conception into their Heads" (136).

(probable). (We might select as a historical turning point in this development Descartes's *Optics* of 1637, which argues in chapter 5 that our ideas are only nonresembling *signs* of their objects.) From such new theories of epistemology and perception emerges, for instance, Locke's doctrine of the unknowability of "real essences"; natural science itself changes from demonstrative *scientia* (wherein underlying natures can be *known*) to the probabilistic study outlined by Gassendi, Mersenne, and Locke with which we are familiar today. In this new context, the old explanations through qualities appear circular and *ad hoc,* the objectionable terms tautologous restatements of the effect. As Newton put it, "To tell us that every Species of Things is endow'd with an occult specifick Quality by which it acts and produces manifest Effects, is to tell us nothing"; and Glanvill devotes an entire chapter of *The Vanity of Dogmatizing* to the circularity of "Peripatetick Explanations."[11]

I do not mean to attribute all this philosophy to Swift, to turn him into a Locke or a Glanvill; but neither is he simply the Luddite antagonist of science some have imagined. Swift read widely and enjoyed lifetime friendships with many natural philosophers; and more important, the conceptual shift outlined above was intelligible to any attentive observer of seventeenth-century thought, such as the author of *Gulliver* demonstrably was. It is in fact in his treatment of contemporary canons of scientific explanation that Swift's satire on science is most knowing and sly. Swift shares with Molière the new scientists' complaint against the old, but turns it against them by suggesting that, with their own new entities and forces, the new scientists are as guilty as the old of using insignificant speech to frame explanations that do not explain. Swift chooses his examples for making this point carefully, from among the most celebrated subjects of inquiry by the new science: gravity, magnetism, and the new emphasis on the world's government by a few simple, regular "laws of nature."

In Brobdingnag "three great Scholars" seek to provide some account of Gulliver; with that pride everywhere visible in the *Travels* which seeks always to take the measure of others' coats by the height, depth, and breadth of one's own, they find that Gulliver "could not be produced according to the regular Laws of Nature." He must then be (in the technical sense) a monster, though he appears neither "an Embrio, or abortive Birth" nor a dwarf.[12] Instead:

> After much Debate, they concluded unanimously that I was only *Remplum Scalcath,* which is interpreted literally *Lusus Naturae,* a Determination exactly agreeable to the Modern Philosophy [i.e., the new science] of *Europe:* whose Professors, disdaining the old Evasion of *occult Causes,* whereby the Followers of *Aristotle* endeavour in vain to disguise their Ignorance; have invented this wonderful Solution to all Difficulties, to the unspeakable Advancement of human Knowledge. (104)

[11]Isaac Newton, Cambridge Univ. MS, quoted in Richard S. Westfall, *Force in Newton's Physics* (London: Macdonald, 1971), 386; Glanvill, chap. 18.

[12]Monsters, understood as nature's teleological failures (beings that mix forms or incompletely realize a single form), were the subject of the science of teratology; see for instance Ambroise Paré's treatise of 1573, *On Monsters and Marvels,* trans. Janis L. Pallister (Chicago: Univ. of Chicago Press, 1982).

Swift's point here is first that, consigned as we are to reason by analogy, which is limited (we can and do reason but from what we know), claims to the discovery of nature's laws must be uncertain and often premature; and second, that explanations drawn from such "laws" are in these circumstances no better than the old references to occult causes. (We should note, too, that Gulliver shields Aristotle from censure, criticizing only his scholastic "Followers.")

Swift parodies the same kind of non-explanation again in book 3, when Gulliver blandly reports the Laputans' theories why their island cannot "rise above the Height of four Miles" or "move beyond the Extent of the Dominion below":

> For which the Astronomers (who have written large Systems concerning the Stone) assign the following Reason: That the Magnetick Virtue does not extend beyond the distance of four Miles, and that the Mineral which acts upon the Stone . . . is not diffused through the whole Globe, but terminated with the Limits of the King's Dominion. (170)

These explanations are no better than references to a "dormitive power" not merely because they rely on terms (such as "Magnetick Virtue") of which, as the new philosophers would say, their users have "no clear idea"; they are *ad hoc* in presuming more knowledge of nature—a more certain knowledge of its "regular laws"—than the explainers can justly lay claim to. Since these examples come (by way of parody) not from the old but the "new" science, Swift means them as instances of modern dogmatizing.[13]

Swift makes the point most comprehensively in the famous scene in Glubbdubdrib wherein Gulliver calls up the spirits of scientists both ancient and modern:

> I then desired the Governor to call up *Descartes* and *Gassendi,* with whom I prevailed to explain their systems to *Aristotle.* This great Philosopher freely acknowledged his Mistakes in Natural Philosophy, because he proceeded in many things upon Conjecture, as all Men must do; and he found, that *Gassendi,* who had made the Doctrine of *Epicurus* as palatable as he could, and the *Vortices* of Descartes, were equally exploded.

[13]Swift could easily have learned such arguments by attending to the conduct of internecine debate among the new scientists themselves. Leibniz had notoriously accused Newton of reintroducing occult qualities into philosophy (see Nicholas Jolley, *Leibniz and Locke* [Oxford: Clarendon Press, 1988], 56), and accusations like the following, made in 1709 by the Cartesian mathematician Antoine Parent, become typical:

> [Newton] aime bien considérer la pesanteur comme une qualité inhérente dans les corps, et ramener les idées tant décriées de qualité occulte et d'attraction. Il ne faut pas nous flatter que dans nos recherches de physique nous puissons jamais nous mettre au-dessus de toutes les difficultés; mais ne laissons pas de philosopher toujours sur des principes clairs de méchanique; si nous les abandonnons, toute la lumière que nous pouvons avoir est éteinte, et nous voilà replongés de nouveau dans les anciennes ténèbres du péripatétisme, dont le ciel nous veuille préserver. (*Mémoires de l'Académie royale des Sciences* [Paris, 1709], 149)
>
> Newton likes to consider gravity as a quality inherent in matter, and so to revive the much-decried notions of occult qualities and of attraction. We should not deceive ourselves that in our physical researches we can ever overcome all difficulties; but let us always philosophize upon clear mechanical principles; if we abandon these, all the light that we might achieve is extinguished, and we are thereupon plunged once again into the ancient peripatetic shadows, from which heaven preserve us. (translation mine)

He predicted the same Fate to *Attraction,* whereof the present Learned are such zeal-ous Asserters. He said, that new Systems of Nature were but new Fashions, which would vary in every Age; and even those who pretend to demonstrate them from Mathematical Principles, would flourish but a short Period of Time, and be out of Vogue when that was determined. (197–98)

The passage reveals the responses of an acute mind to contemporary science and the polemics surrounding it. Swift does more here than predict that Newton's gravity will go the way of Gassendi's Epicurean atomism and Descartes's circu-lar motion in a plenum: he suggests *why* this will be so. Each is a "system," a loaded term by which Swift implies a fanciful body of explanations that goes beyond what is given in experience; as such, each account of causes can be only "conjectural" (probable). And again shielding Aristotle from Modern abuse, Swift in a surprising reversal identifies Aristotle as the proponent of probabilis-tic science (one who knows it must "proceed upon Conjecture"), the Moderns as claimants to certainty (for instance, in his echo of the title of Newton's *Philosophiae naturalis principia mathematica*), which purports to "demonstrate" "from Mathematical principles." The new scientists are unmasked as old-fash-ioned scholastic Aristotelians, while Aristotle himself appears the cautious empiricist, a kind of forerunner of the author of *Conjectures and Refutations,* Sir Karl Popper.[14]

To understand the passage, we need to keep in mind the excited claims of the new scientists to have broken with the past and so provided a new beginning for knowledge, a great instauration. Through its new methods, polemicists from Bacon and Hartlib onward claimed, science was finally to achieve a secure foun-dation. (This is the spirit of renewal we hear, for instance, in Dryden's epistle to Dr. Charleton.) It was in fact on the basis of appeal to such methods that Modern polemicists grounded their new distinction between the (cumulatively progressive) "sciences" and the (merely traditionary) "arts." And what of the new methods themselves? Descartes had claimed to prove his most fundamental physical principles, including the doctrine of the plenum, with certainty, through an *a priori* physics. Newton himself, despite his different metaphysical commitments, had still his supposedly "crucial" (demonstrative) experiments and his famous claim not to feign mere hypotheses. Even Bacon had argued that his new method of induction would eventually yield certain knowledge of the "simple natures" of things (in effect, their real essences).[15] All this while criticiz-ing the "dogmatism" of their benighted forebears. New scientists in fact criti-cized old precisely for failing to move beyond the evidence of their senses. Thus for instance in his *Experimental Philosophy* (1664), Henry Power castigates the

---

[14]Such treatment of Aristotle can be traced to the beginnings of humanism, which already with Vives distinguishes the revered ancient writer from the accretions of his scholastic commentators. See Elaine Limbrick's remarks in her introduction to Francisco Sanches, *That Nothing Is Known* (*Quod Nihil Scitur*) (Cambridge: Cambridge Univ. Press, 1988), 28–29.

[15]On Bacon's method of certainty in discovering "simple natures," see Mary Hesse, "Francis Bacon's Philosophy of Science," in *Essential Articles for the Study of Francis Bacon,* ed. Brian Vickers (Hamden: Archon Books, 1968), 114–39.

Aristotelians as "Sons of Sense" while himself recommending inquiry into a more "hidden" level of reality; as Glanvill writes, "While we know but [nature's] more sensible ways of working, we are but vulgar *Philosophers,* and not likely to help the *World* to any considerable *Theories*"; "For by [the peripatetic] way of disquisition there can be no more truly comprehended, than what's known by every common Ignorant."[16]

Twentieth-century students too seldom realize that the familiar posture of the new scientists in rejecting previous authorities was less often an attempt to clear away past errors in order to make room for a new probabilistic experimental science than to clear away the probabilism of Renaissance humanists in order to make room for a new philosophic and scientific certainty. Little wonder then that some old-fashioned Aristotelians such as Thomas White should join the new scientists in arguing their master to have been in fact more an empiricist than those who sought to dethrone him—or that Swift, always skeptical of high claims, should identify a contradiction in those being made for the "new" science.[17] In its largest sense, then, Swift's satire on contemporary canons of explanation is grounded in a suspicion that Modern method is not really so new after all, and hence that Modern divisions between science and art—between the realms of progress and tradition—are finally ill-grounded.

Science and the Arts of Prudence in Laputa

> Practical experience in life, gained through the examples of our ancestors, together with the knowledge of present-day affairs makes a man, as the Greeks name him, a *Polyhistor* as much as to say multiscius (a many-sided man). Such a man, however, we, following a better nomenclature, term a man of practical wisdom (*prudens*) and his province we call practical wisdom (*prudentia*).
>
> —Juan Luis Vives, *De tradendis disciplinis* (1530)[18]

We all know what Swift finds wrong with the natural philosophers of Lagado. Gulliver witnesses experiments that serve no practical human use, or that would do harm by inverting the uses of nature (breeding sheep without wool); in seeking to reverse the order of nature (extracting sunshine from cucumbers, returning excrement to its original food), Lagadan projects are utopian—the external equivalent, we might say, of the failure to know one's self. And if throughout the

---

[16]Henry Power, *Experimental Philosophy* (London, 1664), preface; Glanvill (note 9), 170, 172.

[17]See Thomas White, *An Exclusion of Scepticks From all Title to Dispute: Being an Answer to the Vanity of Dogmatizing* (London, 1665), 55–56.

[18]Foster Watson, *Of Education: A Translation of the "De Tradendis Disciplinis" of Juan Luis Vives* (1913; reprint, Totowa: Rowman & Littlefield, 1971), 42–43. The term "prudence" enters Western discussion especially with Cicero, who used *prudentia* (which he defines as "knowledge of what should be done and what avoided") to translate Aristotle's *phronesis*, a practical wisdom of which we read in the *Rhetoric*: "The young may be experts in geometry, mathematics, and other similar branches of knowledge, but *phronesis* requires a knowledge of particular cases, which comes from experience, which a young man does not possess, since experience is the fruit of years" (Cicero, *De Officiis* 1.43; Aristotle, *Rhetoric* 1.1.1355b15; translation mine).

Travels the customs of nations seem to follow *ad exemplum regis,* the prince who misguides this nation flies overhead in an island disconnected both literally and metaphorically from the earth below; Swift was fond of the maxim first used of Thales, that the philosopher who fixes his eyes always on the heavens may find his lower parts seduced into a ditch.[19]

More generally, Swift organizes his portrayal of the Laputans around a distinction crucial to intellectual debate in his time, especially to the theories of mind and education that by the end of the seventeenth century divided the Ancients from the Moderns. The Laputans "were indeed excellent in two Sciences," mathematics and music—with the exception of that friend of Munodi, out of favor at court, whose tutors could not "without extreme Difficulty teach him to demonstrate the most easy Proposition" (173); they fail miserably at the practical, applied, and "mechanic." The Laputans—like all Moderns, Swift argues—have forgotten the ancient distinction between the sciences of demonstration and the arts of prudence. I do not mean simply to point to their misguided worry over such distant and unlikely eventualities as the collision of comets with the earth or what nineteenth-century scientists such as Lord Kelvin would call "heat death" (the extinction of the sun), contingencies the Laputans could in any case do nothing about—though such worries are symptoms of their failure of prudence. In a larger way, Swift suggests, they have mistaken the nature and limits of human knowledge.

In Aristotle's famous maxim, we should expect no more certainty in any field than its subject matter permits:

> The same exactitude is not to be looked for in all fields of knowledge, any more than in all kinds of crafts. It is the mark of an educated mind to accept just that exactitude in any subject that the nature of the matter permits. For it is unreasonable to accept merely probable arguments from a mathematician, or to demand formal demonstrations from an orator.[20]

As Swift learned at university, only some subjects are capable of yielding to human minds *scientia* in its truest sense (demonstrative knowledge of causes, or at least knowledge reducible to axiomatic form); in others we must rest content with probability. From Aristotle's time until the seventeenth century, mathematics—in particular geometry—was the paradigm of demonstrative science. Other subjects (called by historians "high" sciences) might be assimilated to the methods of geometry, most notably theology, some parts of physics, and music (the theoretical part of music, in effect the arithmetic of ratios, as distinct from *musica practica*). When Swift pairs music with mathematics in Laputa, then, he is not merely recalling (as many readers have noted) the mystical musicology of earlier thinkers such as Kepler (the last great scientist to believe in that literal

---

[19]Jonathan Swift, "A Discourse concerning the Mechanical Operation of the Spirit," in *Prose Works* (note 2) 1:190; Cf. Gulliver on the higher class of Laputan: "He is always so wrapped up in Cogitation, that he is in manifest Danger of falling down every Precipice, and bouncing his Head against every Post" (159–160).

[20]Aristotle, *Nicomachean Ethics*, 1.3.1–4, 1094b (translation mine).

music of the spheres the Laputans claim to hear). He would have learned at Trinity that if study of integers belongs to arithmetic, fractions are the domain of music; even Moderns such as William Wotton—who unlike Swift does subscribe to the new division of arts and sciences, though without yet possessing adequate terms for it—continue to think of music as a special branch of mathematics. Wotton writes of what he calls the "Physical Sciences" in his *Reflections upon Ancient and Modern Learning* (1694):

> These are Things which have no Dependence upon the Opinions of Men for their Truth; they will admit of fixed and undisputed *Mediums* of Comparison and Judgment: So that, though it may be always debated, who have been the best Orators, or who the best Poets; yet it cannot always be a Matter of Controversie, who have been the greatest *Geometers, Arithmeticians, Astronomers, Musicians, Chymists, Botanists,* or the like.[21]

From all these fields were distinguished the "low" (or "empirical") sciences—medicine, mineralogy, etc.—not *scientiae* in the truest sense. Further down the epistemic scale come the various "arts" (as that term had been understood since Aristotle), the arts of making by rule-governed imitation of nature, from horsemanship, tailoring, cookery, and conversation to poetry, architecture, military strategy, and statesmanship. In all these fields where true science is impossible, knowledge must proceed from "opinion" (probability). And in the formulation of two millennia of textbooks, "That Axiome is probable which seems so to all, to many, or them that are wise"; the probable includes especially the "common sense" of mankind, traditionally approved examples (models for imitation, from which rules may be educed), and other forms of traditionary authority.[22] As Vico was to put it, in the probable arts of living we depend on "common sense supported by erudition."[23] We must proceed, that is, as Pope advises the poet and critic in *An Essay on Criticism*: by conjecture. Because we cannot reason in these fields *a priori*, we must infer probabilistically from successful examples to the general "rules" they embody: "Just *Precepts* thus from great *Examples* giv'n"; "Thence form your Judgment, thence your Maxims bring."[24]

John Locke thus takes a revisionary stance when he argues in the *Essay concerning Human Understanding* that while "natural Philosophy" (physics, chemistry, etc.) "is not capable of being made a science," *ethics* can be known

---

[21]William Wotton, *Reflections upon Ancient and Modern Learning* (London, 1694), 78.

[22]Thomas Spencer, *The Art of Logick* (London, 1628), 288; and more generally Patey, *Probability* (note 7), chap. 1.

[23]Quoted in Yvon Belaval, "Vico and Anti-Cartesianism," in *Giambattista Vico: An International Symposium*, ed. Giorgio Tagliacozzo (Baltimore: Johns Hopkins Univ. Press, 1969), 82.

[24]Alexander Pope, *An Essay on Criticism*, lines 98, 126. The term "maxim" (probably a shortening of *maxima sententia*, a proverb or formulation of "common sense" possessing authoritative weight) had of course a long history in ethics, rhetoric, and all the "low" sciences (such as medicine) wherein general rules of universal application cannot be had, nor can rules be demonstrated; "maxims" thus possess only what St. Thomas called a "probable certitude." See Albert R. Jonsen and Stephen Toulmin, *The Abuse of Casuistry: A History of Moral Reasoning* (Berkeley: Univ. of California Press, 1988), 252–53 and passim.

demonstratively.[25] Locke here recalls the more startling claim his fellow Modern Hobbes had made earlier in the century, that whereas the world had before known only one science—geometry—he would be the first to give it a second: politics. Swift has the author of *Leviathan* (among others) in mind when Gulliver offers the king of Brobdingnag that standard item in the trinity of Modern inventions, gunpowder; when the king refuses this means of becoming "absolute Master of the Lives, the Liberties, and the Fortunes of his People," Gulliver reflects: "I take this Defect among them to have risen from their Ignorance; by not having hitherto reduced *Politicks* into a *Science,* as the more acute Wits of Europe have done" (135).[26]

Thus in chapter 2 of book 3, having established that the Laputans make the demonstrative sciences of mathematics and music the measures of all things, Swift proceeds to survey their failures and ignorance, producing what any humanist reader would recognize as a catalogue of the arts of prudence. The Laputans fail not only in what we would call fine arts, but also in "practical Geometry"—tailoring and building, "which they despise as vulgar and mechanick"; they fail in all the arts which should guide "the Common Actions and Behavior of Life" (including those arts so dear to Swift, conversation and cookery). Most of all, as we have seen, they fail in politics:

> But what I chiefly admired, and thought altogether unaccountable, was the strong Disposition I observed in them towards News and Politicks; perpetually enquiring into publick Affairs, giving their Judgments in Matters of State; and passionately disputing every Inch of a Party Opinion. (164)

It is in this context that Gulliver diagnoses the Laputans' failure of "Imagination, Fancy, and Invention"; lacking these, the Laputans lack the faculties that in Renaissance divisions of knowledge guide all the arts of prudence, including especially the chief of such arts, politics. Thus George Puttenham writes in *The Arte of English Poesie*:

> Of this sorte of phantasie are all good Poets, notable Captaines stratagematique, all cunning artificers and enginers, all Legislators Polititiens and Counsellours of estate, in whose exercise the inuentiue part is most employed and is to the sound and true Judgment of man most needful.[27]

[25]Locke (note 10), 4.12.10. This claim for ethics is of course a direct challenge to Aristotle (for example, *Eth. Nic.*, 6.5.1–4, 1140a–b; 7.7, 1141b; 12.1–6, 1144b).

[26]Jeffrey Bergner presents a fine account of Hobbes's claims in *The Origins of Formalism in the Social Sciences* (Chicago: Univ. of Chicago Press, 1981), chap. 1. At about the same time as Hobbes, both Pufendorf and Pascal argue that ethics can be known demonstratively (can be a science): Pufendorf even writes his early *Elementorum jurisprudentiae universales* (1658) in the manner of Spinoza and later Newton, *more geometrico*; and under the influence of Descartes, Pascal writes of ethics in his fifth *Provinciale* (1656): "I am not satisfied with probability. I want certainty" (*The Provincial Letters*, trans. A. J. Krailsheimer [Baltimore: Johns Hopkins Univ. Press, 1967], 81). On gunpowder in the trinity of modern inventions (including also printing and the compass), see Roy S. Wolper, "The Rhetoric of Gunpowder and the Idea of Progress," *Journal of the History of Ideas* 31 (1970): 589–98.

[27]George Puttenham, *The Arte of English Poesie* (London, 1589), 35; see also Juan Huarte, *The Examination of Mens Wits* (London, 1594): "From a good imagination spring all the Arts and Sciences,

Hence the significance, too, of those particular areas of knowledge about which the Laputan king "discovered not the least Curiosity"—"the Laws, Government, History, Religion, or Manners of the Countries where [Gulliver] had been"—instead confining "his Questions to the State of Mathematics" (166). The list was a familiar one: it is a syllabus of the topics of the humanist theory of travel as education and of the prudential arts educational travel was to foster.[28] What Swift has in fact done in Laputa is to recreate a special skirmish in the quarrel between Ancients and Moderns, as that quarrel entered the educational philosophy of his time. In the second half of the seventeenth century a number of educators sympathetic to the new science, such as Arnauld, Nicole, and Bernard Lamy, following the Cartesian rejection of rhetoric and probability in favor of demonstrative methods, created a self-consciously Modern educational program. The chief pedagogic texts of the movement include the Port Royal *Logic* and *Grammar* and especially Lamy's *Entretiens sur les sciences* (1683), which argues in its central chapter (titled "Idée de la logique") that logic must replace rhetoric, mathematics replace history, and demonstrative methods replace topical in the education of the young. (Lamy even laments youthful enthusiasm for books of travel.) Elements of this program underpin Locke's defense of a "single method" of knowledge in later works such as his *Conduct of the Understanding.*[29] The program was thus a rejection of humanist educational theories in place since the time of Vives and Valla; it had already been opposed by such Ancients as Obadiah Walker in his immensely popular *Of Education* (1683) and most powerfully by Vico, who argued in his inaugural dissertation *On the Study Methods of our Time* (1709) that the Modern educational program (which he calls "criticism") destroys "imagination," "invention," and "prudence" in its pupils, and hence also those fields in which the ancient world excelled, the probable arts. Which are we to choose, Vico asks bluntly, Arnauld or Cicero? Laputans choose the former, Vico and Swift the latter.[30] The debate was to continue throughout the century, especially in France, where the

---

which consist in figure, correspondence, harmonie, and proportion; such are Poetrie, Eloquence" but also "the governing of a Commonwealth" and "the art of Warfare" (103).

[28]See George B. Parks, "Travel as Education," in *The Seventeenth Century*, ed. Richard Foster Jones et al., (Stanford: Stanford Univ. Press, 1951), 264–90.

[29]Bernard Lamy, *Entretiens sur les sciences, dans lesquels on apprend comment l'on doit étudier les sciences, & s'en servir pour se faire l'esprit juste et le coeur droit* (edited with an introduction which discusses the educational context by François Girbal and Pierre Clair [Paris: Presses Universitaires de France, 1966]); John Locke, *Of the Conduct of the Understanding*, ed. Francis William Garforth (New York: Columbia Univ. Teachers College Press, 1966), 69, 123. See also in general Howard Clive Barnard, *The French Tradition in Education: Ramus to Mme Necker de Saussure* (Cambridge: Cambridge Univ. Press, 1922), chap. 5, and Geoffrey H. Bantock, *Studies in the History of Educational Theory, I: Artifice and Nature* (London: Allen & Unwin, 1980), 215–27.

[30]See Ernesto Grassi, "Topical Philosophy or Critical Philosophy? Meditations on the *De nostri temporis studiorum ratione*," in *Giambattista Vico* (note 23), 39–50, and more generally Joseph Levine, "Giambattista Vico and the Quarrel between the Ancients and the Moderns," *Journal of the History of Ideas* 52 (1991): 55–79. Obadiah Walker's *Of Education, Especially of Young Gentlemen* (Oxford, 1683) was the most popular treatise on the subject to appear in England until Locke's *Thoughts on Education;* it reached six editions before 1700 and was the model for the *Tristrapædia* in *Tristram Shandy.*

Modern program remains most clearly identified with Cartesianism's *esprit de géométrie*; thus in 1741 the Abbé Du Resnel argues in a discourse presented in the Académie des Inscriptions et Belles-Lettres, "the Disadvantages Caused by the Exclusive Taste Which Seems to be Established in Favor of Mathematics and Physics":

> We must be careful not to confuse the philosophical mind with the calculating mind. . . . We will not hide the fact that our century is beginning to lose sight of this distinction; that in taking pride in geometry—or rather, in its desire to reduce everything to calculation, to apply that method everywhere, or to erect it as a universal instrument—our century has practically ceased to be philosophical.

Du Resnel's solution is a balancing of "geometry" with "erudition," gained especially through study of Ancient "letters": "By maintaining the taste for truth which the Ancients gave us, letters . . . will teach us to contain [the calculating mind] within its limits."[31]

The debate on education brings into high relief those elements of the quarrel between Ancients and Moderns that most concern Swift in *Gulliver's Travels*. Replacing imitation with logic, Moderns and Laputans would extend demonstrative methods through all education and knowledge, thereby ruining prudence and its arts, whereas for the Ancients, because there can in these arts be no "high priori Road," we must rely on probability in the form of traditionary authority. Such authority does not preclude progress: Prudence in the familiar artistic iconography looks ahead as well as forward and behind; the discipline of imitation meant to the Augustans both preserving a tradition and correcting it from within. In the arts of living as of writing, "good imitation is continual invention"; one should always seek, as the king of Brobdingnag puts it, to make two blades of grass grow where only one grew before (135).[32] But because traditional authority usually takes the form of approved examples, models that each generation must laboriously imitate, educing relevant precepts (maxims) from examples in order to guide its own practice, there is always the danger, to which Swift is sensitive throughout the *Travels*, of degeneration. A society may decay by failing to be guided by or live up to its examples (as Gulliver finds both of Lilliput and of Europe's nobility), or it may go mad by rejecting them altogether (like the Laputans). Once again the *Essay on Criticism* provides an instructive parallel. Pope explains how criticism has become corrupted through improper imitation and improper models; he provides a list of models and instruction in their imitation so that criticism may regain the usefulness it had when it functioned according to its proper nature (in accord with limited human nature).

---

[31]Quoted in Jean Starobinski, "From the Decline of Erudition to the Decline of Nations: Gibbon's Response to French Thought," in *Edward Gibbon and the Decline and Fall of the Roman Empire*, ed. Glenn Warren Bowerstock et al. (Cambridge: Harvard Univ. Press, 1977), 146. See also on the continuing French debate Jean Seznec, "Le Singe antiquaire," in *Essais sur Diderot et l'antiquité* (Oxford: Clarendon Press, 1957), 76–96.

[32]The equation of imitation with invention is the Chevalier de Jaucourt's, from his entry "Imitation" in the *Encyclopédie* (1765, 8:568).

For Swift as for Pope, then, progress is possible, but not in the Modern way: human capacity being limited, progress comes not of rejecting but of embracing (imitating) inherited forms. Thus in book 3 Swift concentrates his opposition to the Laputans in the approved example of Munodi, a gifted conversationalist and preserver from decay whom Gulliver celebrates specifically for his "Prudence." And it is Munodi who, explaining how his allegiance to traditionary authority has resulted in his low esteem at court, explicitly connects the concerns of book 3 with the conflict of Ancient and Modern, begun "about forty years ago" (175, 176). A master of the arts of living, Munodi imitates proper models and so is a proper model for imitation himself. It is through such imitation, Swift believes, that we realize ourselves—our proper dignity—and so by rejecting Munodi and the arts of prudence, the Laputans have in effect defeated themselves, resigned their proper humanity: their science is indeed the external equivalent of a failure to know one's self. That certainty which humans can only sometimes reach through demonstration is possible in all things only for God, or (as Swift sometimes portrays them) for God-like Houyhnhnms; Modern Laputans in effect proudly claim for themselves the powers of unfallen, angelic reason. Theirs is a version of the vice Walker Percy calls "angelism," a pride near allied to the madness that overtakes Gulliver at the end of book 4.[33]

---

[33]Walker Percy, *Love Among the Ruins; the Adventures of a Bad Catholic at a Time near the End of the World* (New York: Farrar, Straus & Giroux, 1971). On the consistency of Swift's portrayal of the Houyhnhnms, see Irvin Ehrenpreis, "Swiftian Dilemmas," in *Satire in the 18th Century,* ed. John Dudley Browning (New York: Garland, 1983), 214–31.

Swift goes to some trouble in characterizing Houyhnhnm intellect. Theirs is not so much the immediate intuition of angels as the perfection of human discursive reason, that is, a perfectly orderly psyche in which all faculties remain within proper bounds: "Neither is *Reason* with them a point problematical as with us, where Men can argue with Plausibility on both Sides of a Question; but strikes you with immediate Conviction; as it must needs do where it is not mingled, obscured, or discoloured by Passion and Interest" (267). All thought for them thus possesses the certainty of demonstration; they cannot "understand the Meaning of the Word *Opinion*" (opinion of course being the status of merely probable knowledge). Theirs is thus the condition of intellect generations of thinkers had attributed to Adam before the Fall: prelapsarian man had no "opinions." (As Cowley wrote in 1656 of "The Tree of Knowledge," its "Apples were demonstrative"; but eating them gave us not "Science" but only "Opinions," "Probabilities," "Rhetoric," and "Fallacies." On the tradition of differences between man's prelapsarian and fallen intellect, see Patey (note 7), 12–13). For fallen man, as Gulliver's Houyhnhnm master points out, *"Natural Philosophy"* can be only a "Knowledge of other Peoples Conjectures"—of probabilities (267–68).

What to do with the Yahoos is for the Houyhnhnms a matter of debate, "indeed, the only Debate that ever happened in their Country" (271), again because of the analogy Swift has set up between Houyhnhnm and unfallen man. Like unfallen man the Houyhnhnms possess "no Conceptions or Ideas of what is evil in a rational Creature" (267): Having no knowledge of evil (knowledge in this case requiring acquisition of the quality, a kind of learning by doing), they can neither explain nor understand it. We might say, taking into account what Swift tells us of their religious views, that the Houyhnhnms possess (as all men may) natural theology, but that since they have not fallen (and so have no need of regeneration), they can neither understand nor explain the problem of evil. "Nature and Reason" may be "sufficient guides for a reasonable Animal," but not for one in whom that faculty is "corrupted" (248). (We can draw a useful analogy here between Swift and Defoe: Robinson Crusoe finds natural theology sufficient to instruct Friday only until Friday raises the problem of evil, asking "Why God no kill the Devil?" Natural theology [reason] alone cannot help Crusoe with this question; he must turn to revelation.)

The Epistemology of Travel

By the way it will not be amiss to take notice, that as there is no *new thing* under the Sun, *so neither any new action*; but the same are represented over again under varying circumstances; so that he, who intends to be a wise man, must endeavour to distinguish the Action (as Physicians do in judging diseases) from the circumstances; that he may be able to give a good judgment and prognostick; and afterwards to frame a *generall rule*, which may stand him in stead at other times and occasions.

—Obadiah Walker, *Of Education* (1683)[34]

I have argued that Swift's references to science in *Gulliver's Travels* comprise an attack not on the new science itself but on strident claims for its method and on the new division of knowledge the Moderns were erecting on those claims. Swift's notions of science turn out to be not so different from those of Locke, who argued that natural philosophy "is not capable of being made a Science." Nowhere in fact is Swift more a Lockean than in his choice of the travel genre itself. We have long recognized among the Augustans a renewal of the ancient connection between travel (and travel writing) and education, and between both and empirical philosophy. At bottom, what held all these concerns together, giving Augustan travels their characteristic rhetorical procedures and shape, were the new accounts of perception developed in the seventeenth century, most notably Locke's "way of ideas."[35] Both the extraordinary vitality of Augustan travel writing and the assimilation of travel procedures into literary forms from lyric to novel—from prospect poetry to the educational journeys of Fielding and Smollett—reveal alike the way in this period, in the context of new theories of mental functioning, travel can serve as metaphor for fundamental principles of how the mind operates and how education proceeds. The literary form of travel writing thus implies fundamental epistemic commitments, including especially a kind of probabilism; Swift makes his commitment to this view clearest in his remarks on science, but in fact it underpins the structural procedures of *Gulliver* as a whole.

Let us first review the epistemic commitments the travel form embodies. The Lockean mind gathers its "ideas" in "sensation" and proceeds to inspect and compare them in the act of "reflection" (Locke identifies the comparison of ideas as "judgment"). From the first conception ultimately stems the perceptual basis of so much Augustan writing and its reliance on procedures of spatial extent; converted into narrative, survey or prospect become travel (movement through a natural or human landscape), wherein we encounter varied ideas for comparison (on which to exercise judgment).[36] Comparison implies grounds of

---

[34]Walker (note 30), 175.

[35]See Ray William Frantz, *The English Traveler and the Movement of Ideas, 1600–1732* (1934; reprint, Lincoln: Univ. of Nebraska Press, 1967), chaps. 1–2, and Charles L. Batten, *Pleasurable Instruction: Form and Convention in Eighteenth-Century Travel Literature* (Berkeley: Univ. of California Press, 1978).

[36]The pioneer work on Augustan procedures of spatial extent is Ralph Cohen's "The Augustan Mode in English Poetry," *Eighteenth-Century Studies* 1 (1967): 3–32.

similarity in the objects compared, and so travel writing tends toward repetition, repetition of the same sorts of actions or events in differing guises: in Walker's words, "The same are represented over again under varying circumstances." Thus the travel form becomes useful especially for enacting the procedure of "abstraction," of canvassing varied particulars in order to abstract from them what is essential to the type. This is how Locke himself makes use of the evidence of travelers in the *Essay concerning Human Understanding*. In book 1, addressing the question whether the idea of deity is culturally constructed or innate, Locke turns not merely to *a priori* reasoning but to the accounts of voyagers who have seen humanity differently diversified by varying cultures. Some travelers report societies innocent of any conception of deity, so the idea cannot be innate; it is not essential to human nature, but only accidental. Locke's procedure here reminds us of the probabilistic basis of the investigation, and by extension of the travel form itself: we cannot reason to essential human nature *a priori* but must descend to things, conjecturing from the signs observable in varied instances, because the "real essences" of things are beyond the limits of our knowledge.[37]

By positioning their readers as surrogate travelers, Augustan authors dramatize this view of mind and so create works structured so that the very activity of reading them enacts a process of education (a process which is often also their explicit subject). Thus in *Roderick Random*—organized, as John Barrell has argued, as a prospect or "georgic of society"—Smollett uses the travel form to present a repetitive sequence of situations, partly the same, partly different, whereby readers can sort out accidentals and so infer the essential nature of the "gentleman" and his role in society; in *Joseph Andrews*, Fielding uses the same procedure to enact (and so teach) the process by which we assemble complex concepts such as the nature of charity.[38]

Gulliver's Travels too uses this form to provide varied contexts for discrimination and inference, comparisons that have in fact formed the basis of nearly all interpretations of Swift's book. Books 1 and 2 (which are richest in references to optical instruments) present what might be considered a series of controlled laboratory experiments based on comparisons of size: differences in size permit parallel situations, both within and between books, through which we are led to compare (most memorably) man's physical body with his pretensions (to beauty, power, wisdom, etc.).[39] In book 4 the lines of comparison run not Lilliputian-Gulliver-Brobdingnagian, but Yahoo-Gulliver-Houyhnhnm. We compare condi-

---

[37]On the idea of deity, see Locke, *Essay* (note 10), 1.4.8–17; on real *vs.* nominal essences, 3.3.15–20.

[38]John Barrell, *English Literature in History 1730–1780: An Equal, Wide Survey* (New York: St. Martin's, 1983), chap. 3; on *Joseph Andrews*, see *Probability and Literary Form*, chap. 7.

[39]In book 2, where because of his (relatively) small size, Gulliver acts as a kind of human microscope, examining natural details (especially of the human body) too small for the unaided eye normally to see, Swift is of course capitalizing on the unsettling discoveries made with the first microscopes only a few decades earlier, but we too often forget the reasons why natural philosophers found these discoveries so unsettling. That previously unknown creatures might be discovered seemed to conflict with Genesis 2:19–20, where Adam is said to have named all the creatures (though this could be

tions in Houyhnhnmland with those in Brobdingnag, Lilliputians with Lagadans. And travel itself becomes a ground of comparison: the kings of Lilliput and Laputa are not concerned to ask Gulliver about his voyages, whereas their ministers do so; Munodi asks "to be informed of the Affairs of *Europe,* the Laws and Customs, the Manners and Learning of the several Countries where [Gulliver] had travelled," demonstrating a proper understanding of the uses and practice of travel which he shares with the King of Brobdingnag and Gulliver's Houyhnhnm master.[40]

In its largest purposes *Gulliver* uses the epistemic procedures of the travel form to explore human nature itself, to abstract away accidentals until we have a view of the essential. Because in Swift's Christian view we are moral creatures, defined by what it is our task to become (that best self we must realize), a better name for what Swift seeks to isolate is that used by writers from Pico della Mirandola to Alexander Pope: the "proper dignity" of man. And because like his predecessors Swift understands improper pride as at root a failure of self-knowledge, the question as to what is essential human nature becomes equivalent to the question: of what can human beings properly be proud? Under what aspects can we examine ourselves without (to use one of Gulliver's favorite words) *mortification?* Through Swift's play with perspective (relative size and its implications) in books 1 and 2, this search is enacted as the question: what is there in us that survives comparison—what that cannot be rendered ludicrous, shameful, or disgusting when magnified to Brobdingnagian proportions or shrunk to Lilliputian?

Books 1 and 2 establish, along with much else, that physical beauty ("pride of the body," as churchmen put it) does not survive comparison, nor do those dreams of human power and importance which appear so foolish when embodied in a Lilliputian; our proper dignity must reside elsewhere. Where that is comes clearest in a striking passage in book 2, chapter 6, at the moment when the king of Brobdingnag begins to take Gulliver seriously as a fellow being, and so as a potential source of wisdom (as a traveler who may provide useful comparative contexts on which the king may exercise his judgment, perhaps even suggesting models for imitation):

> I one day took the Freedom to tell his Majesty, that the Contempt he discovered towards *Europe,* and the rest of the World, did not seem answerable to those excellent Qualities of Mind, that he was Master of. That, Reason did not extend itself with the

---

handled by attributing special acuity to Adam's prelapsarian senses). Much more disturbing, it had been a central tenet of scholastic philosophy that no animal or other matter can exist below the threshold of our senses: as Aquinas wrote, "It is not possible that there should be certain parts of flesh and bone which are non-sensible because of smallness" (*Commentary on Aristotle's Physics,* trans. Richard J. Blackwell [London: Routledge & Kegan Paul, 1963], 340). To believe otherwise was to challenge the cardinal doctrine, rooted in both philosophy and theology, of the completeness of our senses. The new science, with its invisible material mechanisms, had of course to challenge this doctrine, prompting comments such as Montaigne's: "I make a question whether man be provided of all naturall senses, or not." (*Essayes,* trans. John Florio [London, 1886], 302). For Swift (as for Pope in *An Essay on Man*), we might say, the senses are mercifully incomplete.

[40] GT, 127, 166, 173–74, 243. Fielding similarly makes differing views of travel a context for discrimination in *Joseph Andrews.*

Bulk of the Body: On the contrary, we observed in our Country, that the tallest Persons were usually least provided with it. That among other Animals, Bees and Ants had the Reputation of more Industry, Art, and Sagacity than many of the larger Kinds. And that, as inconsiderable as he took me to be, I hoped I might live to do his Majesty some signal Service. The King heard me with Attention; and began to conceive a much better Opinion of me than he had ever before. He desired I would give him as exact an Account of the Government of *England* as I possibly could; because as fond as Princes commonly are of their own Customs (for so he conjectured of other Monarchs by my former Discourses) he should be glad to hear of any thing that might deserve Imitation. (127)

Comparison proves that reason, unlike beauty or strength, does not "extend itself with the bulk of the body"; here, at the conclusion of Swift's laboratory experiments based on differences of size, we find it is reason that survives comparison, and so is essential to human nature, not accidental. Our proper dignity, that which would survive comparison even if instanced in men the size of insects, is predictably our moral intellect (for Swift's "reason" is of course not merely the calculating faculty defined by Hobbes or Hume, but *ratio recta,* an orderly psyche embodying knowledge of ends as well as means). Books 3 and 4 proceed much more explicitly than 1 and 2 to investigate this faculty, especially its limitations and weaknesses—first of all in its application to the sciences. Book 3 examines the misuses of human reason (how, as the name *Laputa* suggests, it can be prostituted), book 4 its imperfections (since unlike Houyhnhnms, we are fallen human creatures).

Swiftian Physico-theology: The Necessity of Art

As in the figure, so in the Stature and Size of Man's Body, we have another manifest Indication of excellent Design. Not too Pygmean, nor too Gigantick; either of which Sizes would, in some Particular or other, have been incommodious to himself, or to his Business, or to the rest of his Fellow-Creatures. Too Pygmean would have rendered him unfit to manage the inferior Creatures; would have exposed him to the Assaults of the Weakest Animals, to the ravening Appetites of voracious Birds, and to have put him in the Way, and endangered his being trodden into the Dirt by the larger Animals.

—William Derham, *Physico-Theology: or a Demonstration of the Being and Attributes of God from his Works of Creation* (1712)[41]

"Physico-theology" is of course the term William Derham coined for that most Augustan form of natural theology (of the argument from design), which looks through nature up to nature's God by examining in scientific detail how

---

[41]William Derham, *Physico-Theology: or, a Demonstration of the Being and Attributes of God from his Works of Creation* (London, 1732), 288, quoted in Eric Rothstein, "In Brobdingnag: Captain Gulliver, Dr. Derham, and Master Tom Thumb," *Etudes anglaises* 37 (1984): 131–32. Rothstein points out the popularity of such argument: *Physico-Theology* was in its sixth edition in 1726, John Ray's *Wisdom of God Manifested in the Works of the Creation* (1691) in its eighth.

throughout the natural world means conduce to ends, parts to a harmonious whole, revealing (to paraphrase the title of John Ray's great botanical text) the wisdom of God manifested in the works of creation. Physico-theology was central to Augustan thinking about the relation of God to nature, providing scientific insight into the role of Providence in human affairs. In Augustan literature physico-theological argument found a natural home in prospect and survey poems, and in their parent genre, the georgic—a genre devoted to celebrating such harmonious wholeness and to recreating it through poetic form. This georgic impetus contributed, for example, to a century of imitations of that most famous rhetorical representation of such unity, the Thames couplets from Denham's *Coopers Hill*; the same passage, suitably deformed, could serve equally well in satire, the Augustan obverse of georgic, the genre devoted to treatment of fragmentation and disunity. But Swift rarely produces either straightforward physico-theology or straightforward georgic. As is well known, he found echoes of Denham tiresome, and he delights, as in his mock-georgic "Description of a City Shower," in transforming the familiar georgic *topos* of unity in variety into what Ralph Cohen has called "a harmony of garbage":

> Here various Kinds by various Fortunes led,
> Commence Acquaintance underneath a Shed. . . .
>
> Sweepings from Butchers Stalls, Dung, Guts, and Blood,
> Drown'd Puppies, stinking Sprats, all drenched in Mud,
> Dead Cats and Turnip-Tops come tumbling down the Flood.[42]

Such passages resemble the zany lists Swift is so fond of, lists generally used to survey (and convey) wild disorder. Swift's practice of turning the georgic procedure of *e pluribus unum* on its head is rooted in his suspicion of harmonies too easily asserted—of order simply found, unearned, in a fallen world rather than achieved through hard moral work—which manifests itself equally in *Gulliver's* satire on science used in the service of religion.

---

[42]Cohen (note 36), 7; *The Poems of Jonathan Swift*, ed. Harold Williams, 2nd ed. (Oxford: Clarendon Press, 1958), 137, 139; see also the conclusion of Swift's "grand Survey" in "The Lady's Dressing Room": "Such Order from Confusion sprung, / Such gaudy Tulips rais'd from Dung" (530) and the echo of Denham (identified by Swift in a note) in "Strephon and Chloe": "Her Hands the softest ever felt, / Tho' cold would burn, tho' dry would melt" (585). Swift condemns over-frequent use of Denham's formulation in "Apollo's Edict": "For know I cannot bear to hear, / The Mimickry of *deep yet clear*" (271). Swift expresses this view specifically of poems celebrating political harmony, for example that of "ANNA'S happy Reign"—poems such as Pope's *Windsor-Forest*, a georgic containing satiric passages built around straightforward and deformed versions of the rhetoric of unity in variety. Pope echoes Denham most audibly in this poem in lines 225–26. Throughout his poetry, though, when he wishes to express a conception of harmony or unity, Pope habitually turns to the techniques of georgic, and especially to prospect poetry; see for instance the many inset passages of prospect poetry used to explain the nature of literary unity in the *Essay on Criticism*, a poem which argues that proper reading is itself a kind of physico-theology, of tracing "the Muses upward to their Spring" (extended examples of such "prospects" occur at lines 158–60, 171–75, and most famously in the simile of the Alps, 220–32). Among his frequent uses of Denham's lines in a satiric context, see especially the famous echo at *Dunciad* (1729) 3.163–66.

Swift carries out this part of his satire on science by subjecting Gulliver himself to physico-theological scrutiny, especially in books 2 and 4, in nations whose inhabitants are generally wiser than he. In both cases, the familiar argument (in the title of Galen's famous treatise) *de usu partium corporis humani* reveals not harmony but deficiency, means that by themselves do *not* conduce to ends. Thus the Brobdingnagian scholars

> agreed that I could not be produced according to the regular Laws of Nature; because I was not framed with a Capacity of preserving my Life, either by Swiftness, or climbing of Trees, or digging Holes in the Earth. They observed by my Teeth, which they viewed with great Exactness, that I was a carnivorous Animal; yet most Quadrupeds being an Overmatch for me; and Field-Mice, with some others, too nimble, they could not imagine how I should be able to support myself. (103–4)

Gulliver's Houyhnhnm master assembles an even longer catalog of malfunctions and malformations, comparing human skin, nails, hands, feet, face, nose, eyes, and joints with those of other animals (especially himself) to show that "considering the Frame of our Bodies, and especially of mine, he thought no Creature of equal Bulk was so ill-contrived, for employing that Reason in the common Offices of Life" (242). This is physico-theology in reverse, a prospect not of benevolent design but painful limitations. All these physico-theologians reveal their own limitations (their limited point of view) through the way they judge others' coats only by their own, but we cannot doubt that Swift's irony here cuts two ways—that he intends as well to ridicule the easy self-celebration of such writers as Derham, Dr. Bentley, and the other Boyle lecturers.

At the root of Swift's objections to physico-theology, then, is his suspicion that its harmonies are too easy; they are found rather than made. Bentleys and Derhams fail properly to emphasize that other element of georgic, crucial to the form since Virgil: *culture*—georgic striving, which produces order in recalcitrant fallen nature through human labor, human art. Swift's inversion of natural theology can best be compared with Voltaire's in a work that has strong affinities to *Gulliver: Candide*. That work converts the argument from design into an argument from disaster to show the hollowness of metaphysical optimism. But Voltaire no more than Swift doubts the role of Providence in human affairs. Rather, Voltaire means to short-circuit those misuses of the design argument which feed human pride (we might think here of Jack's personal and *ad hoc* appeals to Providence at the end of *A Tale of a Tub*), and especially those misuses of it that discourage human striving. Voltaire understands with special acuity the usefulness of arguments from providential design in defenses of the existing social order and of political quietism. But more generally, *Candide* is a defense of the georgic values of human industry, art, and labor, in the form of a journey through a series of symbolic gardens to the final garden that Candide and his friends agree to cultivate.[43]

---

[43]See William F. Bottiglia, "Voltaire's *Candide*: Analysis of a Classic," *Studies on Voltaire and the Eighteenth Century* 7 (1959): 88–113.

Swift makes clear the connection between his larger satire on science (including physico-theology) and his belief in the necessity of art in a complex passage that occurs toward the end of book 2. In chapter 7—at the center of the *Travels*, just before he leaves Brobdingnag and before Swift turns his attention from pygmies and giants to the different procedures of books 3 and 4—Gulliver spends a long paragraph describing a small book. The passage has received little attention, perhaps because it is so much in keeping with all that surrounds it, and because Gulliver himself dismisses the "little old Treatise" as cliché:

> I have perused many [Brobdingnagian] Books, especially those in History and Morality. Among the latter was I much diverted with a little old Treatise, which always lay in *Glumdalclitch's* Bedchamber, and belonged to her Governess, a grave elderly Gentlewoman, who dealt in Writings of Morality and Devotion. The Book treats of the Weakness of Human Kind; and is in little esteem except among Women and the Vulgar. This Writer went though all the usual Topicks of *European* Moralists . . . [and] drew several moral Applications useful in the Conduct of Life, but needless here to repeat. (137)

Gulliver's dismissive tone is a warning: Swift delights in sweeping aside as trivial and hackneyed those truths which in reality he believes most deeply. And if the book is "in little Esteem except among Women and the Vulgar," these are often in Swift's satire wiser than the learned (in Laputa it is the "Wives and Daughters" who "lament their Confinement on this Island," while Gulliver foolishly thinks it "the most delicious spot of Ground in the World" [165]). Might we even speculate that Swift, the friend and educator of young women, the writer who enjoys impersonating common folk (especially women), is in some part of his mind casting himself as Glumdalclitch's "Governess, a grave elderly Gentlewoman, who dealt in Writings of Morality and Devotion"?

So many parallels connect this little book with the larger one which surrounds it that the treatise appears to be a microcosm of the *Travels* as a whole. Both illustrate

> how diminutive, contemptible, and helpless was Man in his own Nature; how unable to defend himself from the Inclemencies of the Air, or the Fury of wild Beasts: How much he was excelled by one Creature in Strength, by another in Speed, by a third in Foresight, by a fourth in Industry. (137)

Like *Gulliver* itself, this is a book whose lessons have been gathered through comparison. But ironically, its lessons soon go wrong, and begin to sound no wiser than those of the Brobdingnagian scholars:

> He added, that Nature was degenerated in these declining Ages of the World, and could now produce only small abortive Births in Comparison of those in ancient Times. He said, it was very reasonable to think, not only that the Species of Men were originally much larger, but also that there must have been Giants in former Ages; which, as it is asserted by History and Tradition, so it hath been confirmed by huge Bones and Sculls casually dug up in several Parts of the Kingdom, far exceeding the common dwindled Race of Man in our Days. He argued, that the very Laws of Nature absolutely required that we should have been made in the Beginning, of a Size more large and robust, not so

liable to Destruction from every little Accident of a Tile falling from an House, or a Stone cast from the Hand of a Boy, or of being drowned in a little Brook.

Swift completes our sense of the passage as a representation in little of the *Travels* as a whole by adding another, final ironic turn in the form of Gulliver's response to what he has read:

> From this Way of Reasoning the Author drew several moral Applications useful in the Conduct of Life, but needless here to repeat. For my own Part, I could not avoid reflecting how universally this Talent was spread of drawing Lectures in Morality, or indeed rather Matter of Discontent and repining, from the Quarrels we raise with Nature. And, I believe upon a strict Enquiry, those Quarrels might be shewn as ill-grounded among us, as they are among that People. (137–38)

In one way Gulliver is right; quarrels with nature, "Discontent and repining" at the state in which God has placed us, are ill-grounded expressions of pride. But again Swift's irony cuts two ways. To the extent that the treatise's "moral Applications" really are "useful in the Conduct of Life," Gulliver's flip rejection of them constitutes a misunderstanding of his own nature, and so another form of pride. The conclusion of this passage thus parallels that of book 4, another "Lecture in Morality," at whose end we find Gulliver proudly quarreling with his own human nature.

When the little treatise (like *Gulliver* itself) speaks of "how diminutive, contemptible, and helpless was Man in his own Nature," the operative phrase is "in his own Nature." This is the nature man was born with—nature unassisted by grace, unaugmented by art (for Swift as for Pope, the two are related). In Swift's inverted physico-theology, all the limitations cited in humankind—in "Man in his own Nature"—instance weaknesses that must be overcome by human labor, human art. To defend himself from the "Inclemencies of the Air" he must invent shelter; against the beasts he needs weapons; to acquire the "Strength" and "Speed" of other creatures he needs tools: everywhere he must exert (in the sense outlined above) "Imagination, Fancy, and Invention." Just as the "Bees and Ants" (whose "Industry, Art, and Sagacity" Gulliver recalls to the king of Brobdingnag) are models of such qualities in Virgil's *Georgics*, the model that Swift presents in book 3 of humanity best pursuing its purposes—best realizing its proper nature—is the agricultural cultivator Munodi, a kind of georgic hero.[44] Swift inverts physico-theology because, like Voltaire, he sees in the misusers of such argument (as in the scientists of Laputa) the enemies of georgic striving, which is itself, as Virgil had argued, the parent of the prudential arts. And finally, because it is our task in realizing our proper nature to strive to cultivate these arts, the human deficiencies pointed up by inverse physico-theology can themselves become grounds in an argument for providential design. The argument was first made by Virgil himself in the so-called "Jupiter theodicy" in book I of

[44] See Margaret Doody's splendid essay on Swift's use of Virgil, "Insects, Vermin, and Horses: *Gulliver's Travels* and Virgil's *Georgics*," in *Augustan Studies: Essays in Honor of Irvin Ehrenpreis*, ed. Douglas Lane Patey and Timothy Keegan (Newark: Univ. of Delaware Press, 1985), 145–74.

the *Georgics*. That Swift could share Virgil's view is made clear by an entry in his *Thoughts on Various Subjects*, a paraphrase of the Jupiter theodicy ending in a quotation from it:

> One Argument used to the Disadvantage of Providence, I take to be a very strong one in its Defense. It is objected, that Storms and Tempests, unfruitful Seasons, Serpents, Spiders, Flies, and the like Kind, discover an Imperfection in Nature; because human Life would be much easier without them: But the Design of Providence may clearly be perceived in this Proceeding. The Motions of the Sun and Moon; in short, the whole System of the Universe, as far as Philosophers have been able to discover and Observe, are in the utmost Degree of Regularity and Perfection: But wherever God hath left to Man the power of interposing a Remedy by Thought or Labour, there he hath placed Things in a State of Imperfection, on purpose to stir up human Industry; without which Life would stagnate, or indeed rather could not subsist at all: *Curis acuens mortalia corda.*[45]

The Brobdingnagian author thus goes wrong in arguing—like the most extreme proponents of the Ancients—that "the Species of Men were originally much larger," that "there must have been Giants in former Ages." Not only does his "little" book (huge to Gulliver) raise the ludicrous possibility of a kind of infinite titanic regress, it fails to recognize the relation between human limitation and the arts: need spurs progress (just as at a later stage of development luxury may still it). In rejecting the Brobdingnagian's argument, Swift makes clear his own stance in the debate on decay that had occupied Ancients and Moderns in the late seventeenth-century phase of their Quarrel and which so often surfaces in *Gulliver's Travels.* The Moderns had then defended the possibility of cumulative progress by rebutting the Ancient view, found in polemics such as Godfrey Goodman's *Fall of Man* (1619), that the whole earth, including the human frame, had been degenerating since ancient times; some extreme Moderns, such as Thomas Burnet in his *Telluris theoria sacra* (1681), even argued that the physical world itself continually improves.[46] On this issue Glumdalclitch's book sides with the most extreme Ancient proponents of decay. But we should no more identify its views here with Swift's than we should identify Swift with the Brobdingnagian scholars whom the passage echoes. Swift characteristically enjoys taking even his own views to extremes, meeting the enemy, as it were, on his own foolish terms; and as we have seen, Swift no more than Pope is the enemy of "progress" properly understood—as must of course be true of authors so much given to advancing their own suggestions for social improvement.

Swift's own views would appear to be those of Gulliver in Glubbdubdrib, where he observes "how much the Race of human Kind was degenerate among

[45]Swift, *Prose Works* (note 2), 4:245. The Jupiter theodicy, through which Virgil explains the origin of human arts, occurs in *Georgic* 1, lines 121–46. Swift's quotation comes from line 123, and is translated by Dryden: "And [God] whetted Humane Industry by Care." For further connections between the passage and *Gulliver's Travels,* see Doody (note 44).

[46]See Ernest Tuveson, "Swift and the World-Makers," *Journal of the History of Ideas* 11 (1950): 54–74.

us, within these Hundred Years past," such that even our bodies have "short-ened" (201). Such decay, Gulliver finds, has resulted not from any global natural processes but from simple human "Vice" (in this passage, from that vice so many of Swift's so-called "dirty" poems preach against: fornication, resulting in "the Pox"). Characteristically, Swift analyzes the old debate on progress down to the level of individual moral choice—the same individual moral choice Swift appeals to in kings, ministers, or gentlefolk when he himself turns serious projector in such works as *A Project for the Advancement of Religion and the Reformation of Manners* (1709), *A Proposal for Correcting the English Tongue* (1712), or *A Proposal for the Universal Use of Irish Manufacture* (1720), all of which begin with diagnoses of recent ills and go on to suggest prudent techniques (arts) by which decay may probably be reversed. If Swift's approach as projector changes during his career, it is in the same direction that both his politics and his views of science change: just as the Examiner focuses most on problems of corruption (failure to live up to valued established institutions), the Drapier on the more general problem of tyranny, earlier proposals begin with reviews of particular corruptions, later ones with larger ills; so too *Gulliver* generalizes the concern of *A Tale of a Tub* with particular "corruptions in religion and learning" to a more philosophically searching exploration of the limitations of the human mind, limitations that create for us at once the division between the realms of prudence and certainty, and the necessity of artful imitation in the transmission and progress of culture.

The Unity of Swift's "Voyage to Laputa": Structure as Meaning in Utopian Fiction

Jenny Mezciems

Method is good in all things. Order governs the world. The Devil is the author of confusion.[1]

Swift's own views on the importance of order are expressed in intimate confidences as well as in public pronouncements and do not, on the surface, suggest any inconsistency of belief to account for a gap between preaching and practice. Thus, though he wrote some exceedingly untidy works, the purpose of these was to mock practices and attitudes which he abhorred. The reader of *A Tale of a Tub*, for instance, becomes quickly aware of the criteria by which he is to judge what is before him. This is less true in the case of *Gulliver's Travels*, and particularly the *Voyage to Laputa* over which there still hangs the critical imputation that Swift's ordering energies were flagging, in matters of structural coherence and of style as related to overall theme. This paper aims to show that, on the contrary, the *Voyage to Laputa* is as carefully structured as any other Voyage, that its placing is part of a pattern essential to the whole work, and that particular effects are achieved by particular methods which can be recognized if we examine the procedures of certain literary genres and especially the genre of utopian fiction.

I. *Structures and Genres*

Some of the difficulties encountered by readers of *Gulliver's Travels* are not peculiar to Swift. The works of Rabelais, notorious for their looseness of form and apparent structural incoherence, are recognized as a source for some of Swift's material.[2] But it is perhaps more interesting that Rabelais, like Swift, provokes in the reader such a strong need, not only to discover order but for this

From *Modern Language Review*, 72 (1977), 1–21. Reprinted by permission of the author, the editors and the Modern Humanities Research Association.

[1]Swift to Stella, 19 October 1710. *Jonathan Swift: Journal to Stella*, edited by Harold Williams, 2 vols (Oxford, 1948), I, 72. For some cautionary comments on the varying degrees of seriousness among Swift's formulations of his views, see C. J. Rawson, 'Order and Misrule: Eighteenth-Century Literature in the 1970s', *ELH*, 42 (1975), 471–505 (p. 482).

[2]See, in particular, W. A. Eddy, *Gulliver's Travels: A Critical Study* (Princeton, New Jersey, 1923).

order to contribute to the meaning of the work before him. An editor of Rabelais describes the situation thus:

> Parmi les droits que l'œuvre littéraire donne au lecteur dès qu'elle se présente à lui comme telle, figure comme l'un des plus graves celui d'en organiser les parties, d'en apercevoir la forme particulière de cohérence . . . de la cohérence, il est (Dieu merci) d'autres formes que celle d'un exposé didactique ou d'une démonstration de géométrie.[3]

'La forme particulière de cohérence' is perhaps even more of a puzzle to Swift's reader than to the reader of Rabelais, since in Swift's fiction both didactic and geometric elements are insistently and equally to the fore. The relationship between meaning and form in *Gulliver's Travels* is almost too immediately evident, and still the search for unity and coherence continues as though there were never to be any certainty of arrival (*Dieu merci*). It is all the fault of Books I and II, which provide gratuitously a pattern so satisfyingly neat and complete as to engender in the reader certain expectations with regard to Books III and IV. These expectations are, of course, frustrated: the reader feels cheated of his 'right' to 'organize the parts', and from his disappointment or indignation springs a whole deluge of critical interpretation. Book IV has been most frequently the focus of attention but there the problem of what we are meant to make of Swift's Houyhnhnms has not depended particularly on structural considerations or on relationships between the last Voyage and others. In fact the most formally coherent 'structures' arising from discussion of Houyhnhnmland are probably the ranked forces of pro-Houyhnhnm and anti-Houyhnhnm judgements on Swift himself.[4] The part is examined by many critics not so much as though it were a key to the whole but as though it might replace the whole: if you can once get the Houyhnhnms right the rest will not really matter any more. Defeated in the attempt to form any consistent relationship with Gulliver we give up and look instead for Swift. This makes us rather like Laputans: 'one of their Eyes turned inward, and the other directly up to the Zenith'.[5] Too often the one thing we avoid looking at is the fiction, as a fiction, as a whole, with its meaning in its wholeness.

If Book IV, however, has borne the brunt of critical attention, and has been distorted sometimes in consequence, Book III has been much less fairly treated, regarded often as a fascinating irrelevance to the rest of *Gulliver's Travels* or, worse, as a flaw, a disappointment, an anticlimax. The opposing viewpoints reflect the degree to which readers are prepared to take the part on its own or, on the other hand, feel let down by an apparent failure of meaning to allow itself to be conveyed through structure. Few modern readers would be as dismissive as Coleridge ('Laputa I would expunge altogether. It is a wretched abortion, the product of spleen and ignorance and self-conceit').[6] Some modern

---

[3]V. L. Saulnier, *Le Dessein de Rabelais* (Paris, 1957), p. 11.

[4]See W. E. Yeomans, 'The Houyhnhnms as Menippean Horses', *College English*, 27 (1966), 449–54.

[5]*Gulliver's Travels*, p. 159. Quotations are from *The Prose Works of Jonathan Swift*, edited by Herbert Davis, 14 vols (Oxford, 1939–55), Volume XI (revised edition, 1959).

[6]*Coleridge's Miscellaneous Criticism*, edited by Thomas M. Raysor (Cambridge, Massachusetts, 1936), p. 130. In fact, I have found that students in 1976 can be almost as dismissive, finding Book III 'boring and irrelevant' on a first reading.

work on the third Voyage has been successful and engaging but has had the effect, while reasserting its value, of furthering the alienation of that Voyage from the rest, making it comprehensible in terms of the real world of Swift rather than the fictional world of Gulliver.[7] Even those who claim to be particularly interested in unity or coherence tend to propose schemes whereby the *Voyage to Laputa* can be related better to the outside world than to the fiction, so that it is still cut off from narratives on either side of it. Thus A. E. Case prevented us from shrugging off the whole episode as a mere hotchpotch of miscellaneous satire by saying that 'the third voyage is much more unified in purpose than has commonly been supposed'[8] and proceeded to show that that unification was all a matter of contemporary politics, important to Swift but having little connexion with Gulliver or his narrative. Gulliver is really the crux of the unification problem. It may well be that in Book III he 'in effect, vanishes', as Kathleen Williams says,[9] but we are not therefore at liberty to forget him or to disregard him as a central structure linking the four Voyages together. I call Gulliver a structure rather than a character: it is essential to this discussion to see him as such, and fortunately the days are over when problems of misreading arose chiefly from mistaken assumptions that *Gulliver's Travels* was a novel and Gulliver a novel-character.[10]

One of the dangers, however, of discovering that *Gulliver's Travels* is not a novel has been that of reducing it to a too simple allegorical relationship with fact. Direct equations may indeed be made between the particularities of real life and those in the fiction, but fiction can no more be confined to the concept of allegory than to the terms of the novel: it has traditional uses and forms older and wider than either of these, and to understand how Swift makes fiction serve his satirical purposes we have to turn from the local to the general, from the contemporary to the universal, remembering that Swift was an Augustan and on the side of the ancients. This obliges us to think in the conceptual terms of themes and genres and to take up suggestions made, but not exhaustively explored, by Northrop Frye and Martin Price and Robert C. Elliot[11] in order to restore the

---

[7]See Marjorie Nicolson and Nora M. Mohler, 'The Scientific Background of Swift's *Voyage to Laputa*' and 'Swift's "Flying Island" in the *Voyage to Laputa*', *Annals of Science*, 2 (1937), 299–334 and 405–30; Pat Rogers, 'Gulliver and the Engineers,' *MLR*, 70 (1975), 260–70. There have been a number of defenders, in recent years, of Book III as a unit necessary to the structure of *Gulliver's Travels* as a whole. Among those closest in approach to this article are John H. Sutherland, 'A Reconsideration of Gulliver's Third Voyage', *SP*, 54 (1957), 45–52; Clarence Tracy, 'The Unity of *Gulliver's Travels*', *Queen's Quarterly*, 68 (1961–2), 597–609; John H. Munro, 'Book III of *Gulliver's Travels* Once More', *English Studies*, 49 (1968), 429–36; I. D. Traldi, 'Gulliver the Educated Fool: Unity in the *Voyage to Laputa*', *Papers on Language and Literature*, 4 (1968), 35–50; Roberta S. Borkat, 'Pride, Progress, and Swift's Struldbruggs', *Durham University Journal* (June 1976), 126–34.

[8]*Four Essays on Gulliver's Travels* (Princeton, 1945), p. 80.

[9]*Jonathan Swift and the Age of Compromise* (Lawrence, 1958), p. 175.

[10]See Robert C. Elliott's useful discussion of genre features in *The Powers of Satire: Magic, Ritual, Art* (Princeton, 1960), pp. 184 ff. However, Gulliver as a novel-character lives on to some extent in Sutherland's article, cited above.

[11]*Anatomy of Criticism* (Princeton, 1957), pp. 305 ff.; *To the Palace of Wisdom: Studies in Order and Energy from Dryden to Blake* (Carbondale, 1970), pp. 197 ff.; Elliott, *Power of Satire*.

Voyage to Laputa to a position in which it can be seen as a contributing part, instead of an aberrant one, of *Gulliver's Travels* as a whole. The consideration of large, perhaps even vague, generalities need not lead to oversimplification: what is needed is some frame within which consistencies and apparent inconsistencies may be reconciled, whereby concrete narrative details may be linked to abstract concepts which will contain them and which will themselves stand up to close examination, so that structure and meaning may be properly united. Thematically, *Gulliver's Travels* is an attack on human pride, a satire on civilized society, an exposé of the truth about human nature as Swift saw it, and an analysis of the quality of human reason. Thematically the four Voyages are perfectly consistent: there is no individual Voyage from which any of these themes is absent, nor is the treatment of them noticeably uneven in emphasis. The themes are constant and the variations do not stray from the expression of a consistent meaning through narrative detail. In this respect the *Voyage to Laputa* has no less a part to play in the whole than any other Voyage.

The problems of coherence and unity are thus quickly identified as matters not of theme but of structure. For structure we need genre definitions, frames of reference within which to consider vital relationships between themes and forms, subjects and their appropriate modes of expression: in the reading and the criticism of all literature it is surely an agreed assumption that structure does contribute to meaning. (A comment by Quintana provides a good example of the way in which *Gulliver's Travels* can have its structure misread, and an even better one of the fact that it is in a structural sense that critics fail to justify Book III by means of its placing. For Quintana this Voyage stands as an anticlimax with the function of strengthening the climax of Book IV.[12] This suggests criteria of a kind more appropriate to a work for the theatre and is just as misleading as the old tendency to read the work as a novel.) Perhaps the structure of *Gulliver's Travels* is hard to understand just *because* it has features of a generic kind which nevertheless do not allow us to fix it firmly within any single genre. It may also be that the attempt to define any genre in terms of its structural features is itself a search after an ideal which been pursued vainly from Aristotle onwards. Seeming structural imperfections in *Gulliver's Travels* might then illustrate, as other features do, Swift's views on such a pursuit. Unity and coherence may seem to be lacking because we fail to understand how central a part of Swift's theme the concern with structure is, and the nature of that concern.

There is certainly a relationship between structure and genre, and two genres make legitimate claims on *Gulliver's Travels*. The first is the fantastic voyage. *Gulliver's Travels* contains four of these, and they provide a patterned framework of travel away from home and back again. The repetition strengthens the pattern and there is no suggestion of divergence or flaw. The fantastic voyage has to have a traveller and/or narrator, who need not be a 'character' but who is

---

[12]*Swift: An Introduction* (London, 1962), Oxford Paperback edition, p. 161. Quintana goes right outside literature, in fact, describing this Voyage as 'like the scherzo in a traditional four-movement symphony'.

an essential structural link and to whom the framing narrative belongs. Whatever happens to Gulliver in Book III the frame pattern of setting out and returning is not broken, and the disappearance mentioned by Kathleen Williams is virtual and temporary, not actual or permanent. The second genre is utopian fiction. This, too, has structure in the shape of an alien society, contained within boundaries, self-sufficient, and not susceptible to change. (It may, like Plato's Republic, be *threatened* by change or, like Lilliput, show signs of corruption from its original institution.) In *Gulliver's Travels* the essence of such a structure is provided four times over, as in the case of the fantastic voyage. The multiplicity of societies in Book III brings variety internally but no inconsistency in the relationship between that Book and others. The narrator figure, himself a structure, is common to both genres, may in either case be a traveller, and forms a link between the two genres. Thus the genres may be distinguished apart though often they overlap.

The fantastic voyage is thus a genre with a definable structure. So is utopian fiction. But in addition to the figure of the narrator, linking the two genres, we should consider one other form, that of language as a structure of expression which will vary with the requirements of each of these genres. The language of the fantastic voyage will be such as to persuade us of the veracity of things beyond experience or common sense, using much concrete detail of description and measurement, exact exaggeration of numbers, and so on. The language of utopian fiction will also be a structure based on the rhetoric of persuasion, a manoeuvring of comparisons between the ideal unknown and the real-and-known. If we then consider these four types of structure (voyage, utopia, narrator, and language) and the two genres (utopian fiction and fantastic voyage) it becomes evident that the features sought as aids to definition and distinction tend to overlap considerably, causing confusion and a temptation to avoid the structural issue altogether by taking refuge under the umbrella of a genre less demanding in formal terms. I refer to Menippean satire, which is a kind of 'mélange adultère de tout' but has the advantage of allowing a mixture of forms, modes, and structures whole or broken and varying in their degrees of compatibility, to come together in some sort of harmony of intent.[13] In this genre, though it may sound paradoxical, meaning and structure are as interdependent as in any other, for only through formlessness can certain preoccupations with form be expressed with any real force. In *Gulliver's Travels* I believe it is Swift's purpose to clarify and purify certain concepts, and that he achieves this in Book IV by means of techniques of purgation and polarization. In Book IV he presents a utopia (whether his own or Gulliver's I shall discuss in my conclusion) but the context from which the utopia emerges must be provided in Book III, where the setting is necessarily one of mixture, multiplicity, and muddle, conveyed through every available structure; those of language, of the figure of Gulliver, and of the encounter with alien societies, leaving only the essential voyage framework of the fiction intact (though even that is used for a particular kind of comment, as I shall show).

[13]See Elliott, pp. 186–7.

One more genre must be mentioned, because it has a bearing on the complex relationships between the other genres I have mentioned, and above all on the question of language. This is the travel book, which has an obvious connexion with the fantastic voyage and with utopian fiction. The travel book itself is based on real experience, the fictional variants on make-believe experience. The fictions are often used for satirical purposes, to criticize real life through direct comparison with an imaginary alternative, *or* to criticize a world of illusion created by a lying narrator and sold to an equally guilty, because gullible, reading public. The satirist's work must depend for its success not only on the forms used but on the study, critical understanding, imitation, and parody of the rhetoric of persuasion. The language he uses will be not only a means of expression but a part of his theme, whether he is concerned with folly or vice, credulity or prevarication, or the interdependence between all of these. Just as utopian fiction, the fiction of ideals, can criticize both the real world and the world of illusion, so the language of such fiction can criticize both the language of factual truth and the language of illusion: between truth and deception lies metaphor. Utopian fiction is itself metaphor. It has to present the ideal in terms of fiction, to protect it from reality, and to enable it to transcend illusion. The utopian writer's concern with language, from Plato to George Orwell, from the unexpectedly poetic Myth of Er to the Appendix on Newspeak, is too evident and too important to be given adequate treatment here. But if it is possible to justify the *Voyage to Laputa* by reference to traditional literary genres, then it is also important to remember that Swift's allusions, imitations, and parodies will have as much to do with language as with any other elements of theme and structure.

Whether *Gulliver's Travels* is utopian fiction or merely Menippean satire it clearly belongs to a canon which includes Plato's *Republic*, Lucian's *True History*, More's *Utopia*, the works of Rabelais, and Bacon's *New Atlantis*, and is commonly discussed in connexion with these works.[14] All are constructed around the concept of an ideal world, a utopia, and all were familiar reading to Swift. The first two Books of *Gulliver's Travels* are rooted in the real world, in spite of the fantasy. The device of the telescope, on which the fantasy depends, is a real and physical aid to vision, and Swift's inversions and distortions are equally real and physical. Books III and IV are rooted in the ideal and the vision is abstract and spiritual, as are the distortions. Swift's ideal is in literature and the ancient world, and it is through these literary spectacles that he looks at present reality. He uses the conceptual terms of utopian fiction not only for the utopia of Book IV but for the dystopia of Book III, and as with Books I and II the technique by which the pair are related is that of inversion. The Houyhnhnm utopia is an indirect imitation of Plato: the Laputan dystopia is an indirect parody of Bacon. The third Voyage is the most local, contemporary, personal, and 'original' (in a sense

---

[14]The most valuable single essay on *Gulliver's Travels* as a utopian fiction, and one to which my own debt is too extensive for me to be able to recognize its limits, is John Traugott's 'A Voyage to Nowhere with Thomas More and Jonathan Swift: *Utopia* and *The Voyage to the Houyhnhnms*', *Sewanee Review*, 69 (1961), 534–65.

which Swift would recognize and use as a term of condemnation), and at the same time the most imitative, the most conventional, and the most dependent of all on the authority of tradition. For all its apparent fragmentation there is one special kind of coherence in this Voyage, in that it is built on the ironic paradox that if the moderns are guilty of fragmenting the world the joke is on them because the ancients did it better. It is, in a sense, another and more sophisticated *Battle of the Books*.

II. *Imitations and Parodies*

Book III does not have to present us with a utopia in order to make its comments on utopianism. Plato, Lucian, Rabelais, More, and Bacon are all present, directly or indirectly as seems appropriate. More and Rabelais are not ancients, but they are on the right side, against contemporary vulgarities and firmly in the imitative tradition. Plato and Lucian represent utopian concepts from the ancient world, one describing the ideal, the other mocking the illusion. Bacon is there for an obvious reason: *New Atlantis* is the arrogant dream of a modern disguising himself as an ancient. Lastly, an episode (the whole Voyage) which is clearly fragmented can perhaps only be recognized as such by reference to concepts of unity and wholeness which are not merely utopian but more generally both Platonic and Christian. The name *Laputa* itself may suggest a dystopia or, rather, a perversion of utopia. Speculation on the process by which Swift invented names is perhaps a dubious enterprise but, since he enjoyed puns, anagrams, and near-anagrams, his reader is entitled to consider those he finds, if not to look for them. *Laputa* is a near-anagram of *utopia*. *Utopia* means *nowhere*. *Nowhere* contains an anagram of *whore*. *Laputa* means *whore*. The association of words and concepts is not so loose as to be untenable if my interpretation of Swift's use of Bacon's fantasy is accurate.

It is perhaps not necessary here to detail every specific borrowing or parody. In the case of Rabelais this work has been done by Huntington Brown,[15] and W. A. Eddy traces links with various sources. Many details in Laputa come directly from Rabelais, for instance some of the projects in the Academy at Lagado and the carving of food into geometrical shapes; the idea of the loadstone may owe something to Rabelais's use of a similar device in his account of the military power of Messere Gaster, though I have not seen this anywhere suggested.[16] Although the projects of the Academy make fun of contemporary scientific experiments, and borrow from contemporary records, Swift's attack takes its force from the fact that he can intersperse examples from reality with examples from fiction, as though defying us to recognize the difference, and the tone and

[15]*Rabelais in English Literature* (Cambridge, Massachusetts, 1933; London, 1967).
[16]*Le Quart Livre*, Chapter 62. Messere Gaster was a great inventor, particularly, and most ominously, of military devices. Later, and more probable, sources for Swift's loadstone are interestingly discussed by Paul J. Korshin, 'The Intellectual Context of Swift's Flying Island', *PQ*, 50 (1971), 630–46 (pp. 637–42).

intention are those of Rabelais, mocking the same tendency to abstraction in his own day by reference, in his turn, to older sources; the point being for both Swift and Rabelais that the moderns are not even modern. ('Moderns' may seem an inappropriate term to use when speaking of Rabelais's enemies except that they, like those Swift attacked, were mostly devotees of systems of abstract reasoning who thought they could afford to forget their origins.[17]) Gulliver's encounters with the spirits of the dead, apart from Faustian echoes (his dream of power in immortality amongst the Struldbruggs smacks of the same kind of unnaturalness and autonomous modernity), are borrowed from Lucian, and again it is a matter of tone as well as of detail, since both authors are using the traditional literary visit to the underworld for particular satiric ends. Knowing the pattern in Lucian's *True History,* the reader is better able to appreciate Swift's adaptation. For instance, where Lucian is concerned to reveal the illusory glow which history throws over all reputations indiscriminately, Swift wishes to use history in proof of a theory of degeneration. Lucian's traveller makes contact with Homer, and hears news of Plato living alone in obedience to his own laws: no revered figure is immune from ridicule. But Gulliver distinguishes between Aristotle and his commentators, and finds Thomas More among that 'Sextumvirate to which all the Ages of the World cannot add a Seventh' (p. 196). His nostalgia for '*English* Yeomen of the old Stamp' leads to a comment on the way in which their 'pure native Virtues were prostituted for a Piece of Money by their Grand-children' (pp. 201–2).

For reference to Plato in the *Voyage to Laputa* Swift uses something less direct than simple imitation or parody, and I shall discuss the use of certain imagery, as well as elements in the figure of Gulliver himself, when considering the contribution of the framework of Book III to the whole, in terms of unity and coherence. With regard to Bacon, and to More also, there are features which properly belong to an examination of the structure of language and its contribution to the meaning of the Voyage, and cannot be fully discussed here. But immediately and directly, of course, the Academy of Lagado cannot express Swift's views on the ambitions of the Royal Society without paying tribute to Bacon's advance dream of that institution: that it should, in a sense, have been founded on a fiction suits Swift's purposes very well.[18] One point is worth noting here about the relationship between fact and fantasy in the utopian fictions mentioned so far. There is a common pattern of structure whereby a formal description of the real world leads into a formal fiction of an ideal world. Plato's *Republic* finally transcends the dialogue form with the Myth of Er. More's *Utopia* begins with dialogue description of conditions in Europe before Hythlodaye is allowed to launch into his uninterrupted monologue on Utopia. Even Rabelais's untidy fiction spends three Books on the state of the real world, to the point at the beginning of Book IV where the company, led by Pantagruel,

[17]Compare C. J. Rawson, *Gulliver and the Gentle Reader* (London and Boston, 1973), p. 109.

[18]See J. B. Bury, *The Idea of Progress: An Inquiry into its Origin and Growth* (London, 1920), pp. 92 and 96.

voyage off into a much stranger unknown. And if we seek a logical pairing of Swift's third and forth Voyages, in the irresistible desire to make them as balanced as Books I and II, we can do so in terms of the pattern of utopian fiction by saying that the fragmentation of Book III is indeed Swift's portrayal of actuality in all its craziness, necessarily preceding and providing the occasion for the utopian idealism of Houyhnhnmland.

In the same way Bacon's *New Atlantis* can be seen as a fantasy rendering of the theme he pursues in the *Advancement of Learning*. That earnest recommendation to his prince, of an undertaking which will bring honour to him and the nation, is spiced with an appeal to the popular imagination in the form of a glorious, if uncompleted, fiction. To Swift there might well seem to be something disingenuous about Bacon's use of the power of fiction to persuade, especially when a comparison with More's *Utopia* is taken into account. More plays with this power, shows us his own vulnerability to it, and teaches us how to resist it or keep it in its place. Bacon, in his turn, has plenty to say about the easy domination of reason by imagination in the *Advancement of Learning* and Swift chose to parody Bacon's argument in *A Tale of a Tub*.[19] But Bacon, having warned us of a weakness, proceeds to exploit this weakness: there is no irony in either the *Advancement of Learning* or *New Atlantis*. In *Gulliver's Travels,* therefore, it is as though Swift is making Gulliver suffer the consequences of becoming Bacon's victim. More, like Plato himself, uses fantasy to show the otherness of the ideal; to show that it is defined by its difference from actuality. But Bacon (in what I believe to be Swift's view) dishonestly tries to fuse the two in an attempt to make the old seem compatible with the new and the advanced and progressive compatible with the traditional. Thus, though he shows through the society of Bensalem that there may be certain fallings-off in the European practice of the Christian way of life, his qualification for entry is a mere matter of improvement on what we already are and requires no basic change in human nature of the type that would be needed for More to travel with Hythlodaye or make Gulliver acceptable to the Houyhnhnms.

Swift uses features from Bacon's fiction and reverses their effect in the *Voyage to Laputa*. In both cases a central and mysterious institution provides scientific knowledge which brings political power. With Bacon the effects spread out beneficially into society without disturbing its traditional structure. In Swift's Laputa, however, knowledge without understanding spills over in the form of rumour and speculation, resulting in all kinds of nervous compulsions towards self-destruction. As, in Bacon, we see the effects before the cause, the social harmony explored before the traveller is initiated into the secrets of the College, so, in Swift, we learn of the disordered life of Laputa before we hear of the astronomer's cave and the loadstone.[20] The influence of this centre of control

---

[19]See Brian Vickers's discussion in *The World of Jonathan Swift: Essays for the Tercentenary,* edited by Brian Vickers (Oxford, 1968), pp. 87–128 (p. 97).

[20]For reference to Baconian uses of the idea of truth hid in a mine, see Vickers, p. 93, and compare Erasmus, 'Sileni Alcibiadis': 'At semen, in quo vis est omnium, quam est res minutula, quam abdita, quam non lenocinans adspectui, quam non ostentatrix sui? Aurum et gemmas in altissimas terrae latebras abdidit natura.'

is everywhere felt in the neglect of practical concerns while the population broods over 'Apprehensions' which 'arise from several Changes they dread in the Celestial Bodies' (p. 164). Effect and cause work together to set society on a disaster course. In Bensalem the College and the society surrounding it are, instead, mutually supportive: harmony depends on singleness of purpose and balance of function. Swift, characteristically, makes disharmony come about through multiplication and division. The Academy at Lagado is set up *in imitation* of Laputan manners and, worse, is apparently only one among a proliferation of such imitative institutions, for 'there is not a Town of any Consequence in the Kingdom without such an Academy'. The Academy itself 'is not an entire single Building, but a Continuation of several Houses' and 'every Room hath in it one or more Projectors; and I believe I could not be in fewer than five Hundred Rooms' (p. 179). Bad enough if a Royal Society imitates Bensalem's College: worse if every ambitious aspirant believes he need recognize no limit or control over his search for knowledge ('I had myself been a Sort of Projector in my younger Days' is Gulliver's modest claim (p. 178)).

The Academy at Lagado has the same kind of unquestioned authority as the College in Bensalem. Lord Munodi hardly dares speak aloud of his doubts about the wisdom of the prevailing rules for living. Projectors in both societies have about them the aura of a priesthood or of a closed but powerful monastic order. Swift's projectors, once inside the Academy, do not seem ever to emerge. They are discovered to be ugly, dirty and smelly, and totally uninterested in each other or in the world outside, and yet their activities are the pride of their society. When, however, one of the Fathers of Salomon's House appears in public the visit is a state occasion, full of confirmatory ceremony, the streets lined by a silently reverent populace for the procession of a splendidly dressed figure, with 'an aspect as if he pitied men', who 'held up his bare hand as he went, as blessing the people' (p. 237) in a papal gesture which justifies his existence and indicates exactly the relationship between the College and society.[21] (The effect is undermined for a reader who remembers a similar street procession in *Utopia*, where the populace is far from silent and is able to make its own judgement upon any emperor's new clothes. But Bacon knows, quite as well as More does, which things need to be made religiously impressive and which things are to invite rational assessment.) Bacon carries the air of religious mystery into the College itself, with an effect in his lists of projects and achievements which suggests vague and limitless benefits. He carefully avoids any too specific application of the knowledge acquired, and thus suggests infinite potential. It is this feature which Swift picks up and uses to negative ends, for as each separate Laputan project is described in isolation and carried through to its end it becomes self-enclosed, useless, impossible, or destructive.

Bacon's favourite word is 'divers' and his favourite proof of the superiority of knowledge in the College is that it consists of things 'yet unknown to you'. Thus:

---

[21]The text cited throughout is *'The Advancement of Learning' and 'New Atlantis'*, edited by Arthur Johnston (Oxford, 1974).

'We have also divers mechanical arts, which you have not; and stuffs made by them; as papers, linen, silks, tissues . . . excellent dyes, and many others'; 'We find also divers means, yet unknown to you, of producing light originally from divers bodies'; 'We have also furnaces of great diversities, and that keep great diversity of heats . , . these divers heats we use, as the nature of the operation which we intend requireth' (p. 243). Bacon in fact lists a wealth of available materials and processes for which the application is left open: the effect is heightened by his frequent use of such phrases as 'and the like', 'and many others', 'and divers other things' as a conclusion. This is a technique which Swift uses with different effect in other places,[22] but in Laputa his list of projects is always of particular natural materials turned into something else for a specific purpose but without success. Sunbeams may one day be extracted from Laputan cucumbers,[23] but Bacon's list of heat sources suggests great reserves of power far beyond immediate needs. Both authors depend for effect on large discrepancies between needs and resources, but in opposite proportions. Thus the opening irony of Chapter 6 in the *Voyage to Laputa*, on political projectors, fits Swift's satirical scheme perfectly, and is not merely an example of Gulliver's inconsistency of outlook. Properly read, the passage suggests that it is the puny capacities of those who misuse their natural resources which makes success unlikely even where the results might chance to be good. The satire is on this, and on the lack of distinction which the Laputans would make between good ends and bad: they simply do not relate beginnings to ends.

Bacon's fiction is utopian and Swift, using it here as a model to be inverted, is making his own comment on a particular kind of utopianism. In the *Voyage to Laputa* he plays on the differences between More and Bacon to show Bacon cheating on the whole utopian concept by bringing the ideal and the actual too close together, and the general pattern of events in the *Voyage to Laputa* is one whereby the same process is taken to the point of logical absurdity. All this is part of the thematic attack on pride. For Swift's purposes in the third Voyage he draws on the several models I have mentioned, but chiefly uses Bacon, as the modern betraying tradition, which is why the specific borrowings from Rabelais and the references to More and Plato are necessary as support. The utopist pride of Laputa, or of Bacon, is one in which life is treated as though it were a fiction, human nature glossed over by the powers of rhetoric and idea. In Houyhnhnmland the tables are then turned. Ideal and actual are pushed as far apart as they were formerly brought together. Human nature uncomfortably returns and the self-conscious Gulliver is unable to live in a purified fable which provides no middle ground for living because it is too formal, with the stark formality of this particular kind of fiction.[24] The punishment for being convinced by

---

[22]Discussed in *Gulliver and the Gentle Reader*, pp. 92 and 99.

[23]See Bonamy Dobrée, 'Swift and Science and the Placing of Book III', in *English Literature in the Early Eighteenth Century* (Oxford, 1959), pp. 454–7.

[24]'A marvelous or fantastic fable', as R. S. Crane suggests in his essay 'The Rationale of the Fourth Voyage', in *Gulliver's Travels: An Annotated Text with Critical Essays*, edited by R. A. Greenberg (New York, 1961), pp. 300–7 (p. 302).

your own utopian dream is to find that it will not accommodate you. It is the use of utopian concepts which makes the later pair of Voyages as neatly complementary as the earlier ones, as soon as we see how they illustrate the relationships between form in fiction and form in life. Book III is fragmented and messy because life becomes so as a result of the pride which enthuses with false idealism about form and control and ignores the difference between life and fiction. (Swift might well have seen the rise of the novel, as a major literary form in the modern world, as fulfilment of his fears.) Plato was suitably wary of fiction and of the dangers of that state of illusion which occupies the lowest of his four levels of apprehension: he uses myth with rigorous control. More's *Utopia* is also a controlled exercise in the use of fiction, and he, like Erasmus, admired Lucian as well as Plato because their concern was with the fight against illusion in art and superstition in faith.[25]

Swift of course recognizes and plays with the temptation to put life right by means of a fiction, but the severity with which Gulliver is made the victim of Swift's own self-indulgence shows particularly when the character emerges from the inner fiction and makes himself ludicrous in his speeches, his expectations of Yahoos, and his spleen at their failure. Swift also plays with similar temptations in the reader, those 'droits d'en organiser les parties' defended by Saulnier. It is only the expectation of perfect order which makes the reader uneasy about the structural qualities of the third Voyage, and his expectations in this instance are not so different from those of Gulliver. Book III shows that if fiction can escape our ordering compulsion we would be arrogant indeed to expect life to be more biddable. If the temptation to order were not real there would be nothing to be gained by Swift in using it.[26] In the end the only way we have of separating ourselves from Gulliver and restoring everything to its rightful place and function is by recognizing the degree to which *Gulliver's Travels* is a literary exercise to be judged by literary criteria. We can then indulge our passion for order without doing any harm and without accepting Bacon's invitation to assume control of the natural universe, including our own nature.[27]

III.   *Departures and Returns*

Thus it is important that the 'exposé didactique' should be in the form of a 'démonstration de géométrie'. The framework of the purely fictional fantastic voyage need have no quarrel with reality, because it can contain the tension

---

[25]See, for instance, Erasmus, *On Copia of Words and Ideas*, translated by Donald B. King and H. David Rix (Milwaukee, 1963), pp. 86–7. For Erasmus on Lucian, see *Collected Letters of Erasmus*, Volume II, *Letters 142–297 (1501–1514)*, translated by R. A. B. Mynors and D. F. S. Thomson (Toronto, 1975), Letter 193, to Christopher Urswick, 1506, and Letter 199, to René d'Illiers, 1506; pp. 116 and 122.

[26]See Price, p. 188, on Swift and irresponsible systems of order.

[27]But see Charles Peake, 'The Coherence of *Gulliver's Travels*', in *Focus: Swift*, edited by C. J. Rawson (London, 1971), pp. 171–95 (p. 195), on some of the traps awaiting those who try to 'order' *Gulliver's Travels*.

which Swift explores. The tension is that between, on the one hand, the obvious perfection and balance in the numbers two and four, opening up possibilities and returning to a state of self-enclosure, and, on the other, an intractability in the quality of narrative material which eludes the control of form. Such tension has both moral and aesthetic significances, and is caused by contrary impulses in the fiction which echo those in life: one towards circularity, completeness, stasis; the other towards movement, growth, infinite progression (or regression), and resistance to form.[28] It is this interest in tension rather than in form for its own sake which makes the work dynamic. Symmetry is a lure and a trap. I believe Swift means us to see this and to find ourselves caught between two illusions so that we may recognize and distinguish them. One illusion is that of the shape taken by each of the four Voyages, repeating and reinforcing a complete and perfect pattern, so that the possible pairings (Books I and II, III and IV or I and III, II and IV) create something like a formal dance, with a thematic curtsey and change of partner at measured intervals. The other illusion is that contained in the figure of Gulliver, who promenades through the four Voyages intent on his own linear progress onward, outward, and presumably upward. Swift's fiction illustrates an Augustan preoccupation with ideals which conflict and have yet to be made compatible in a resolution of stasis with progress, and this is why the concepts of utopian fiction, moved by identical impulses, are particularly useful. Plato's Republic, if it ever came into being, would begin at once to degenerate, he tells us. The myth which ensures its continuance (III.414–15) stays firmly within the fiction: the book of the *Republic* is itself a myth of the possibility of achievement. As for any lack of neatness about Swift's *Voyage to Laputa,* the apparent threat to unity may turn out to be the most important factor of all. In his essay, 'La Dissymétrie', Roger Caillois shows how a live organism must have a growth point, an unevenness, a flaw breaking its own protective symmetry, if it is to survive.[29] In Swift's fiction this growth point is Book III; his concern is for the survival, by distinction between them, of the separate forms of life and literature, even if his method reveals the unfortunate superiority of fiction to fact.

The conflicting patterns and impulses are clear in the framework structure of the four Voyages and in the relationship between this framework and the figure of Gulliver. For although the same frame is used four times, Gulliver himself imposes on it certain changes merely as a result of his belief that he is progressing (for instance the variations in the pattern of arrival home and setting out again).[30] Paradoxically it is also Gulliver's belief in progress which causes the repetition in cycles, as we shall see most particularly in the opening of Book III. Gulliver has a well developed sense of purpose and direction, his general aim in

[28]See Emrys Jones, 'Pope and Dulness', *Proceedings of the British Academy,* 54 (1968), 231–63, an essay with an enormous grasp of ideas to do with this kind of tension, and which incidentally makes relevant links between Lucian, More, Erasmus, and Swift in terms of utopian fiction.

[29]*La Dissymétrie* (Paris, 1973).

[30]See Joseph Horrell, 'What Gulliver knew', *Sewanee Review,* 51 (1943), 476–504. The pattern I have followed for the framework and its changing features comes mainly from this essay, and particularly Horrell's point about the cowardice of Gulliver's companions in Book II.

life being to improve his fortune. There is a strange confusion in the use of the word *fortune*. On the one hand it is something Gulliver seeks: he participates actively in a game of chance.[31] On the other hand it is a force in whose hands he is passive and which may be for or against him. A further confusion arises because Gulliver distinguishes throughout between his fortune and his nature. Yet finally they seem to prove one and the same thing. His nature is responsible for actions and choices in which he blames fortune; and where he thought he could take a hand in controlling his fortune he cannot eventually control his nature (which is what his fortune actually consists of). Gulliver is brought home in spite of himself: his movement forward has been as much an illusion as his idea of the extent to which he has been in control.

At the opening of Book I we hear of Gulliver's preparations for life: 'my Father now and then sending me small Sums of Money, I laid them out in learning Navigation, and other Parts of the Mathematicks, useful to those who intend to travel, as I always believed it would be some time or other my Fortune to do' (p. 19). A willed participation in the adventure of life, the knowing allowances made for the balance between what one can control and what must be left to chance, are passed over comfortably by the reader who so far shares Gulliver's illusions, one presumes. And fortune does play its part: Gulliver travels, gaining 'some Addition to my Fortune' (p. 20: here the dual use of the word, and some of the implications, become evident). But fortune is also fickle: one of the voyages 'not proving very fortunate' he tries staying at home, which does not mend matters. Fortune is already a part of the nature of other people, a finding which should teach Gulliver enough about himself to obviate any necessity to travel, away from crooked businessmen. The voyage which is to take him to Lilliput has the traditional device of the disorientating storm, to separate Gulliver from his companions. Though all trusted themselves 'to the Mercy of the Waves' it is Gulliver who 'swam as Fortune directed' him and came safe to land (p. 21). The illusion of some generally beneficial conspiracy between Gulliver and fortune continues to the end of this Voyage.

Gulliver arrives home with some material gains and is thus encouraged to travel again 'in Hopes to improve my Fortunes' (p. 80). Book II, however, opens on a new and threatening note: 'Having been condemned by Nature and Fortune to an active and restless Life; in two Months after my Return I again left my native Country' (p. 83). The innate internal factor is acknowledged, though the reader may pass over it and have no sense that the mention of 'Nature' and 'my native Country' has any significance beyond that of conventional rhetoric. On this occasion human nature in fact adds its contribution to that of the unsympathetic elements in deciding Gulliver's fate. There is no viciousness but there is a natural *cowardice* in his companions which causes Gulliver to be left alone on an alien shore. And at the end of the Voyage there

---

[31]See Price, pp. 183–4: 'Swift is always prepared to represent vice as choice', and John F. Reichert, 'Plato, Swift, and the Houyhnhnms', *PQ*, 47 (1968), 179–92: 'Capable of reason, and therefore of happiness, we choose to be irrational and unhappy. It is this in us which Swift refuses to endure' (pp. 191–2). Gulliver's emphases on the part played by fortune are a denial of responsibility.

have been more losses than gains, though we may not immediately recognize them: 'my Wife protested I should never go to Sea any more; although my evil Destiny so ordered, that she had not Power to hinder me' (p. 149). This is fortune being blamed where the fault is with nature. It is, of course, not only natural for Gulliver to travel, but *perversely* natural, since it is also natural for his wife to try to dissuade him (the criterion by which one decides that Mrs Gulliver is *not* perverse might comfortably suggest that harmony between nature and reason in the reader which is supposed to be peculiar to Houyhnhnms). Natural reason is surely on the side of Gulliver's wife: there is really no more for Gulliver to learn by travelling.[32] But his nature begins to show that it includes a large element of false reasoning which is to alienate him from natural sympathies. The first two Voyages should by rights have been enough, paired opposites in so many ways that suggest completion. Gulliver is now motivated, however, by pride of the kind which resists education, a passion supported by false rationalization, a refusal to recognize that he is what he is and that home is where he belongs.

The perversity is obvious in Gulliver's reasoning: 'the Thirst I had of seeing the World, notwithstanding my past Misfortunes' is a lame excuse supported by lamer, perhaps even vicious, reasons disguising secondary passions. Gulliver is persuaded (though his wife's persuasions failed) by a captain who 'had always treated me more like a Brother than an inferior Officer'; who 'made me a Visit, as I apprehended only out of Friendship' and 'plainly invited me, although with some Apologies . . . that I should have another Surgeon under me, besides our two Mates; that my Sallary should be double to the usual Pay; and that having experienced my Knowledge of Sea-affairs to be at least equal to his, he would enter into any Engagement to follow my Advice, as much as if I had Share in the Command' (p. 153). There is nothing in any of this which is defensible by reason: the very proliferation of excuses shows us how Gulliver's pride makes him susceptible to flattery, and at the same time sets the pattern for the other proliferating weaknesses of Book III. What occurs is an internal betrayal of nature by nature: Gulliver begins to stray outside his terms of reference. Events follow in the usual orderly way a pattern set by the framework introduction. Nature turns viciously against itself when an assumption of authority is not backed up by the necessary qualifications (this is even clearer in Book IV, as I shall show). Gulliver's improved status and pay do not make him able to alleviate or prevent the sickness of his sailors. The pirates who board the ship show the 'natural' viciousness of man to man, and the Dutchman who should be both a political and a religious ally (as though civilized ethics might correct the perversities of

---

[32]It is interesting to compare the relationship between Gulliver and his wife in this episode with that between Thomas More and Dame Alice, in the reference made by Cresacre More (*The Life of Sir Thomas More*, edited by Joseph Hunter (London, 1828), pp. 107–8) to Dame Alice as perhaps portrayed by More (in 'his book of Comfort in Tribulation'): 'one, who would rate her husband because he had no mind to set himself forward in the world, saying unto him: "Tillie vallie, tillie vallie: will you sit and make goslings in the ashes; my mother hath often said unto me, it is better to rule than to be ruled." "Now in truth," answered Sir Thomas, "that is truly said, good wife; for I never found you yet willing to be ruled" '.

nature) proves a traitor.[33] Gulliver betrays himself first, through lack of self recognition: this failure brings a dangerous vulnerability towards recognition by others, so that betrayal from outside follows inevitably. The return home completes Gulliver's 'disappearance': he no longer dares to 'be' what he thinks he is, that is, a Christian Englishman, and is obliged to disguise himself as a heathen and a Dutchman.

It is essential to Swift's purpose that life at home goes on normally and unchanged. Mrs. Gulliver and family, at the end of the third Voyage, are found simply 'in good Health,' and the understatement is part of that sustaining thread of common positive values that Swift weaves into the texture of the whole book (and particularly in framework narrative), not to be ignored except by Gulliver, and reminding us of the difference between Gulliver as the utopist and Swift as the critic of utopianism. Swift writes while Gulliver travels and his armoury, unlike Gulliver's, includes imagination and the ability to use fantasy as a way back into the real world. The irony of Gulliver's situation is underlined at the beginning of Book IV: 'I continued at home with my Wife and Children about five Months in a very happy Condition, if I could have learned the Lesson of knowing when I was well. I left my poor Wife big with Child, and accepted an advantageous Offer made to me to be Captain of the *Adventure*' (p. 221).[34] Among the advantages is that of extra money (improved fortune), though it is an advantage which Gulliver himself seems to discount, on looking back. But he is now to be captain, a post for which he is qualified not by training but by his own estimation of what he has learned by experience. Ironically (though not with irony) he makes a passing reference to the good and honest sailor whose fate was the result of his being 'a little too positive in his own opinions, which was the Cause of his Destruction' (p. 221). Gulliver's assumption of authority over himself and others results in mutiny, betrayal of a different kind from that in Book III. Here it is active revolt, not only in the framework events but in Gulliver himself amongst the Houyhnhnms, where he revolts against being human. As in Book III the revolt is from within. Again the outward voyage has its pattern echoed in the voyage home, and as Gulliver is imprisoned by his own rebellious crew, so he is chained in his cabin by Don Pedro's command, to prevent his doing himself some mischief.

Such parallels and pointers need to be pursued only so far as will show that Gulliver's illusion of progress (which may be seen as regression) is superimposed on the circular voyage structure; that the structure of the Voyages and the structure of Gulliver himself are consistently ordered and coherent in accordance with Swift's treatment of his theme and the terms in which he uses the fictional form; and that there is nothing irrelevant or different about the third Voyage. With regard to the structure of Gulliver there are two aspects to be considered.

---

[33]Gulliver's comment, on being 'sorry to find more Mercy in a Heathen, than in a Brother Christian' (p. 155), is a reminder, perhaps, of the main irony in More's *Utopia*, intensified in Swift's rational and benevolent horses.

[34]Kathleen M. Swaim, *A Reading of 'Gulliver's Travels'* (The Hague, 1972), manages to find significance in the names of Gulliver's successive ships, and her discussion of framework details is interesting, if somewhat strained in support of her thesis.

The Gulliver who narrates his story, who returns unhappily to the world of men, and who seems too shifting and inconsistent to be regarded as a character is an apparently ill-constructed artefact to whom I intend, nevertheless, to give the last word. At this point I want to return to the question of Swift's use of Plato in Book III, and to the figure of Gulliver as traveller in a utopian fiction which owes so much both to Plato and to Thomas More.

I refer primarily to Gulliver's status in the last two Voyages as, first, adviser to the ship's captain, and then captain himself. One of the rare but memorable metaphors in the *Republic* is that where Plato uses the image of the ship of state, describing the qualifications needed by the captain and his relationship with his crew (VI. 487–9). The subject, as in an important passage in Book I of More's *Utopia,* is that of the role of the philosopher and his usefulness to the king or, as expert on government, to his society. The practicability of the utopian dream, when the fiction is presented straightforwardly, depends on the acceptability of the dreamer as a rational political philosopher whose authority is recognized. Plato admits that such a situation is almost impossible. More argues, in the 'Dialogue of Counsel', for a pragmatic instead of an abstract philosophy which might bring hope of success. Bacon's optimism, in *New Atlantis,* seems to carry no reservations, which is why he becomes such a target for Swift's attack on pride. Swift may be asking us to follow Plato's injunction and to 'observe those who imitate [the philosophic] nature and usurp its pursuits and see what types of souls they are that thus [enter] upon a way of life which is too high for them and exceeds their powers' (VI. 491).[35] Gulliver does in a sense pretend to be a philosopher: he is regularly in a position to advise rulers, and the kind of advice he gives is based on his experience of England, as Hythlodaye's advice in *Utopia* is based on his experience of that land. Gulliver is the type of modern man that has replaced the philosopher, but not in the way that More intended Hythlodaye to be replaced. Swift's ideal of the modern man might presumably be More, whose commitments at home made him humble and pragmatic in action but firm in principle, a man aware of double standards, replacing one idealism with 'another philosophy, more practical for statesmen, which knows its stage, adapts itself to the play in hand, and performs its role neatly and appropriately'.[36]

Gulliver, as early as the end of the first Voyage, shows signs of being the same kind of irresponsible idealist as Hythlodaye, who has to be clearly distinguished from More.[37] Hythlodaye is free to travel because he has shared out his property among his relatives and feels he owes them, and society at large, no more. Similarly Gulliver travels with an easy mind, having fixed his wife in a good

---

[35]*The Republic,* translated by Paul Shorey, 2 vols, Loeb Classical Library (London, 1956), II, 31. On Gulliver as philosopher and ship's captain, see Reichert, p. 190.

[36]*The Complete Works of St. Thomas More,* Volume IV, *Utopia,* edited by Edward Surtz, S. J., and J. H. Hexter (New Haven and London, 1965), p. 99.

[37]See W. B. Stanford, *The Ulysses Theme: A Study in the Adaptability of a Traditional Hero* (second edition, Oxford, 1963) for a study which makes possible some interesting links between the figures of philosopher, traveller, and leader.

house at Redriff and being in no danger of leaving his family upon the Parish. But Gulliver's rise in status aboard ship fits Plato's image exactly, particularly at the opening to Book IV where Gulliver has been promoted to captain. Gulliver suffers the mutiny of sailors who bind him hand and foot, just as the sailors bind their captain in Plato's illustration. In Plato's image the perversity is in the sailors, who do not accept the authority of the captain, but in Gulliver's case the assumption of authority is as perverse as the mutiny. In Plato, More, and Swift alike the crucial question is that of who is fitted to lead whom. More, in the passage quoted above, himself uses the image of the ship, this time to argue that its captain should not abandon it in a storm because the winds will not obey him. More's captain has other things than his own advantage to consider.

That it should be a metaphor which links Plato so specifically with *Gulliver's Travels* (more generally of course he supplies the origin of the Houyhnhnm ideal) is apt. Plato does not often use metaphors, but when he does so it is in order to bridge a difficult middle ground between real-life experience and abstract philosophical argument. And the *Voyage to Laputa* is itself a metaphor for the removal of this middle ground. Ends are ludicrously out of proportion, and out of gear, with their beginnings, in the projects at Lagado. Language loses its function, of separating things by communicating between them, and idea and object are allowed to crash together. Thus a metaphor turns literal when Gulliver is obliged to lick the dust before the footstool of the king of Luggnagg. To the theme of the abuse of language belong also the schemes for doing away with nouns in favour of things, for the absorption of knowledge in the form of wafers, and the device for the exhaustive re-arrangement of words on a language frame. The flying island, too, is for ever in danger of crashing down on the mainland through abuse of the force which separates them. The return to base, like Gulliver's final return home, is likely to be painful.

IV.   *Gulliver and Gulliver*

In the stern but aesthetically satisfying polarizations of Book IV, between Yahoos and Houyhnhnms, Gulliver is uncomfortably present, a human middle ground which does not fit the allegorical, or would-be allegorical, terms of the fiction. But in Laputa he 'in effect, vanishes'. In Laputa each structure that I have mentioned (voyage narrative, utopian society, language, and the figure of Gulliver) suffers an internal breakdown of the whole into its disastrously unrelated parts. The division of Gulliver, though engendered in Book III, cannot become properly evident before his 'reappearance' in Book IV. I have suggested, initially, that Gulliver separates into two. One Gulliver belongs to the internal narrative and the terms of fiction. He belongs to the tradition of the utopian philosopher/traveller and invites certain expectations which he may then seem to betray. He does have a degree of consistency and coherence, the formality of a fictional character, which may partly account for his inability to do very much in Book III. The other Gulliver, however, is a much more complex artefact, which must move in and out of the inner fiction. It (rather than 'he', perhaps) may at times be a mask of Swift himself, is inconsistent in both form and attitude, and is bound to confuse our expectations from the start (since in all but the earliest editions we read the prefatory letters before we come to the Voyage narrative and, as in the case of More's fiction, the purpose of such prefatory material is to increase confusion).

This Gulliver is also, however, the new, common, Everyman hero of the real modern world or, at his most literary, of the travel book, and is ill at ease in utopian fiction. He seeks, perhaps, to have form, but he is a creature of illusion; one of these illusions being his idea of his own progress and another being the reader's illusion that such a figure can represent any kind of wholeness and coherence and consistency. The model for the divided figure comes very probably from More's *Utopia*, as may be seen from the similarity in methods of presentation and from the ambiguities surrounding interpretations of the figures of Raphael Hythlodaye, the fictional 'More', and More the author.[38] The fragmentation of Gulliver is crucial to the whole of the *Travels* and it is the fragmented figure which belongs to the real world and which makes the ideal of Book IV so impossible and so fictionally pure. But the *Voyage to Laputa* was the last to be written and its theme of fragmentation means that it is not a collection of afterthoughts but Swift's way of tying the whole work together and of saying the most difficult things he needed to say about structure and illusions of structure. Without it the pure fable of inaccessible Houyhnhnmland would make very much less sense. Swift's final attack on human pride is directed at man's illusion that he has form and can recognize himself. Thus the last list in Gulliver's narrative is all about *forms*: 'a Lawyer, a Pick-pocket, a Colonel, a Fool, a Lord, a Gamester, a Politician, a Whoremunger, a Physician, an Evidence, a Suborner, an Attorney, a Traytor, or the like' (p. 296). *These* are indeed *forms*; they are never *men*. Men are, instead, describable only in terms of 'a Lump of Deformity, and Diseases both in Body and Mind'. As for consistency and coherence, how can we expect that of Gulliver, who is supposed to belong to the real world, when the modern world we are shown in the third Voyage is the setting appropriate to him, and one in which there is no logical sequence to events or connexion between features?

Gulliver, then, has form of a sort so long as he confines himself to the fiction; so long as the fiction is only *like* the real world; so long as metaphor does not *replace* reality. The Gulliver who travels in Lilliput and Brobdingnag has no real trouble with his identity. He has enough form to be recognized, in spite of discrepancies of size, as one of the same kind as the people among whom he moves.

---

[38]See Edward Surtz, S. J., Introduction to the Yale edition of *Utopia*, pp. cxxiv–cxliii; and John Traugott, 'A Voyage to Nowhere . . .'. Sutherland (cited above) discusses Gulliver as a divided or multiple character (pp. 49–52) but manages to tidy up inconsistencies because he sees Gulliver as progressing and developing through the 'novel'. Munro disagrees with Sutherland for reasons similar to my own. Most relevant on More is David M. Bevington's 'The Dialogue in *Utopia*: Two Sides to the Question', *SP*, 58 (1961), 496–509.

Recognition is a matter of establishing the proportions rather than the nature of his needs. In Lilliput it is a simple calculation to work out how much meat will feed him, how much material will serve him for a shirt. And in Brobdingnag Gulliver's mimickings of recognizable human behaviour enable him to be put on show as a miniature man. In Laputa, however, no one is really interested in 'recognizing' Gulliver except Lord Munodi, himself an outcast. And he has to warn Gulliver, in effect, that to show normal human attributes is shameful. He sends his guest quickly on to the Academy, where Gulliver is briefly popular as a potential victim of the bellows cure for colic, and then as one worthy of mention in a scholarly footnote on methods of codifying reality. The climax of the third Voyage is of course the point at which Gulliver makes his greatest mistake, in fusing the ideal and the actual, dreaming that he might be an immortal without grasping that his situation would be that of Tithonus. But however abstract Gulliver may seek to become in Book III, he has to remain human. And in Book IV he is at his most human of all, which is why the fable must obviously reject him. In Book IV, for the first time, Gulliver cannot be identified as one of the same kind with his hosts or their servants (Swift makes his reader work hard at discounting any such possibility). It is no longer the proportion of his needs, but their nature, which has to be discovered with some pains. He eats like neither Houyhnhnm nor Yahoo. His clothing is studied not because it is something apparently unfamiliar which will become familiar as soon as the scale registers, but because clothing itself is unfamiliar. Gulliver is examined, prodded, and wondered over by the Houyhnhnms as never before—and then claimed by Yahoos, whom *he* did not recognize.

Who, then, is the Gulliver outside the narrative? He introduces himself as a Yahoo, a term which means nothing to us but which picks up disagreeable connotations. Gulliver himself is disagreeable and splenetic; he also contradicts himself on more or less every point he raises in complaint. Richard Sympson, on the other hand, gives his cousin the most sober and respectable of references. The effect is to confuse the reader and to make him suspend judgement. Only a reader familiar with the utopian tradition and with More's *Utopia* (More's own letter about his lack of time and skill for literary pursuits, and his friends' letters on the veracity of the fiction), able to make an ultra-rapid association between the two fictions, might take both figures and both presentations with a pinch of salt and consider the claims made on either hand as comments on fictional persuasion and the sale of illusion. Normally, however, the reader begins the narrative in a state of mind already disorientated sufficiently to be obliged to take Gulliver as he comes: he is simply not in a position to judge. He is, of course, wooed by the 'plain and simple' style and the sober pace which leads him from suspension of judgement to suspension of disbelief, totally preoccupied with details of sensuous experiences up to the beginning of the satire in Chapter 3. The satire, from here on, *can* be read as Gulliver's own, since we have knowledge of a mature and disillusioned author outside the narrative. But then how does one take the 'naive' Gulliver who praises his 'dear native land' and its customs from time to time? This, assuming that Gulliver is the author of the book, means that he is capable of satiric attacks upon his own younger self, and might therefore be capable in addition of satire against the splenetic image we have just been relying on as 'Gulliver the satirist'. In which case we must then trust ourselves to Richard Sympson's presentation as being that of the true Gulliver: we have come full circle to see that behind the plain man is a satirist and behind the satirist is another plain man.

However, we know in fact that Swift, and not Gulliver, is the author. So behind the second plain man is a second satirist (and behind the second satirist, of course, a third plain man, and behind him a third satirist mocking the plain man who is 'the real Swift'?). It might seem that we should be able to keep all these separate people clear in our heads, and thus work out what kind of an artefact the inconsistent Gulliver really is. But if anything is to be grasped from Swift's devious games it is that all these levels are equally present all the time, and that it is only Gulliver's illusion that they take over and cancel each other out in some sort of sequential progress towards maturity, or perfection. The task, then, is to find the line that divides Gulliver from Swift. For the primary plain man is someone who fails to learn from experience and the primary satirist thinks he had nothing to learn because he knew it all from the beginning and was never under any kind of illusion. Evidently the final level of Gulliver, as distinct from Swift, must be that of the splenetic letter-writer, whose satire is itself the product of illusion. Behind him is the real author who, in order to make a satire out of this kind of illusioned man, must surely himself be at base (if one can ever be sure that one has reached base) a straight man without illusions.

That Gulliver's illusioned state is the final one is confirmed by the fact that the tone of the last stage of the narrative, in the concluding paragraphs of Book IV, is exactly the same as that of the letter to Sympson. The features of the illusion and its tone of expression are absolutism in ideals and demands, matched in the same person by equally absolute rejection and defeatism. This figure is one who puts his faith in time and in progress ('it must be owned, that seven Months were a sufficient Time to correct every Vice and Folly to which *Yahoos* are subject') and in the same breath has no hope of improvement in a permanent situation ('if their Natures had been capable of the least Disposition to Virtue or Wisdom') (p. 7).[39] 'I wrote for their Amendment ', but 'I have now done with all such visionary Schemes for ever' (p. 8). Above all, however, it was the fresh *corruption* by contact with fellow Yahoos which made Gulliver seek to reform the Yahoo race (and further degrees of corruption still which made him then give up the idea as impossible?). Gulliver's illusion is to see time as sequential and linear, each moment cut off from the last. In the same way each level of himself is cut off from the others. An example of this (recognizable as one of those points at which the reader has to decide how far he has felt *with* Gulliver and how far he may dissociate himself *from* Gulliver) occurs at the beginning of Chapter 11

[39]Compare Gulliver's attitudes here with those of Thomas More, as narrator emerging from fiction to fact, at the end of *Utopia.*

of the *Voyage to Laputa*. For Gulliver is not always waiting in the wings, in Book
III, and in the episodes at Luggnagg and among Struldbruggs he is more than
usually central to the action. Gulliver's involvement, on both occasions, shows
him what happens when something essentially unreal (a figure of speech, or
immortal life), becomes real. Immediately after an episode where Gulliver has
been at his most vulnerable, deeply disturbed by the encounter with the
Struldbruggs and the shock of learning that distinction between dream and reality which is an essential lesson in all utopian fiction (a lesson he forgets in
Houyhnhnmland just *because* his responses are so rarely determined by memory
of past experience), comes this passage:

> I thought this Account of the *Struldbruggs* might be some Entertainment to the Reader,
> because it seems to be a little out of the common Way; at least, I do not remember to
> have met the like in any Book of Travels that hath come to my Hands: And if I am
> deceived, my Excuse must be, that it is necessary for Travellers, who describe the same
> Country, very often to agree in dwelling on the same Particulars, without deserving the
> Censure of having borrowed or transcribed from those who wrote before them. (p. 215)[40]

All Gulliver is doing, quite independently of Swift, is making that rapid switch
from character to author, from experiencing self to editing self, which he is entitled to, in the circumstances. But his coolness and distance are unsettling. It is as
though Gulliver himself is not conscious of his separate selves and does not feel
the relationship between them; as though there is no whole to contain and organize the parts. The fragmentation of Gulliver, and our dissatisfaction with it,
shows up the strength and general desire that he *should* have consistent form,
that the accumulation of experience *should* express its meaning in some organized structure or pattern, in life as in fiction. The fragmentation of the *Voyage
to Laputa* is in some ways very rightly discussed in terms of the real world
instead of those of literature. As the rest of *Gulliver's Travels* provides a context
for it, and *is* a whole containing and ordering its parts, so the third Voyage also
'contains' the rest and is a context for the fiction. It was written last and then
placed before the utopia of Book IV. In the same way, Thomas More wrote his
utopian vision before coming home to fill in the real-life background out of
which that vision arose. In both works the utopian vision is experienced by an
idealist, Hythlodaye or Gulliver, who is not the author, and who has not come to
terms with the distinction between ideal and actual, time and the timeless.

In so far as Houyhnhnmland is Gulliver's utopia, then, it can never accommodate him. In so far as it is Swift's it keeps its validity by rejecting Gulliver and
remaining fabulous and unreal. But Swift is part Gulliver, as More is part
Hythlodaye. There is an inevitable mixture of admiration and scorn in the rejection by the author of his fictional character. Or is it really rejection? It may be
that we are failing Swift when we try to separate Gulliver from him and ourselves from Gulliver. Perhaps we have no right to do so, and perhaps this fact is

---

[40]Swift is presumably making a joking reference here to his own sources in, for instance, Lucian
and Rabelais, to the common mockery of travellers' tales, and to his own use of Gulliver.

a source of our discomfort. Are we really entitled to laugh so easily at Gulliver's 'strange Tone in speaking, which resembled the Neighing of a Horse', or to condemn the inhumanity with which he avoids his wife and finds solace in the stable? The sobriety required, if we are to refrain from laughing, is not that of 'there, but for the grace of God . . .', but of a recognition that somewhere beneath the surface of this ridiculous figure is another, whose preoccupations are almost identical, and who deserves nothing less than serious admiration.[41]

> The man whose mind is truly fixed on eternal realities has no leisure to turn his eyes downward upon the petty affairs of men, and so engaging in strife with them to be filled with envy and hate, but he fixes his gaze upon the things of the eternal and unchanging order, and seeing that they neither wrong nor are wronged by one another, but all abide in harmony as reason bids, he will endeavour to imitate them and, as far as may be, to fashion himself in their likeness and assimilate himself to them. Or do you think it possible not to imitate the things to which anyone attaches himself with admiration? (*Republic,* VI. 500)

---

[41]See Reichert, pp. 188–90, and Malcolm M. Kelsall, '*Iterum* Houyhnhnm: Swift's Sextumvirate and the Horses', *Essays in Criticism,* 19 (1969), 35–45, on Houyhnhnm life as a serious ideal and on the ambiguous nature of Gulliver's madness.

Gulliver Among the Horses

A. D. Nuttall

Gulliver, newly landed on unknown soil, some leagues south of Nuyts Land, sees in a field a group of repulsive animals. Revolted by the sight he eagerly pursues his way along the beaten road, hoping to find some human habitation. But, almost at once, he meets with one of the unpleasant creatures, full in his path:

> The ugly Monster, when he saw me, distorted several Ways every Feature of his Visage, and stared as at an Object he had never seen before; then approaching nearer, lifted up his fore Paw, whether out of Curiosity or Mischief, I could not tell: But I drew my Hanger, and gave him a good Blow with the flat Side of it; for I durst not strike him with the Edge, fearing the Inhabitants might be provoked against me, if they should come to know, that I had killed or maimed any of their Cattle. (*Gulliver's Travels*, Part IV, Chapter 1 (p. 224))[1]

This is how Swift begins his narrative of Gulliver's sojourn among the Houyhnhnms, or rational horses. The creatures he saw, first in the field and then in the road, are of course not Houyhnhnms but Yahoos. Only gradually does it become clear, to Gulliver and to the first-time reader, that the bestial Yahoos are in fact human beings (that the horses are rational is revealed much more rapidly). The writing, as usual, is spare and colourless. But this does not so much preclude as enhance a certain dream-like intensity. When I say 'dream-like' I mean just that: like a dream—*not* like most literary versions of dreams. The resemblance has something to do with a combination of distinctness and paucity of information and also with the way the horrible animals are first seen at a safe distance in an ordinary field and then, without transition or preparation, one suddenly appears in the human territory of the road. Childhood memories of some huge cow or bull, dung-encrusted, encountered unexpectedly in a lane may play their part. But what Gulliver sees is, of course, much worse.

From *Yearbook of English Studies*, 18 (1988), 51–67. Reprinted by permission of the author, the editor and the Modern Humanities Research Association. (This essay also reprinted in A. D. Nuttall, *The Stoic in Love: Selected Essays on Literature and Ideas* [New York and London: Harvester-Wheatsheaf, 1989], 100-116).

[1]*Gulliver's Travels* is quoted from *The Prose Writings of Jonathan Swift*, edited by Herbert Davis and others, 16 vols (Oxford 1939–74), XI (revised 1959). Other references to this edition of the prose writings (*Works*) are indicated by volume and page numbers in parentheses.

Such is the immediate impression made by the passage: an absolute, undoubted nastiness (not an evil; we need the more childish word) threatening the person with whom we are for the moment entirely identified, occurring in an almost blank environment. The elementary impression of something utterly and manifestly revolting is, and remains, the most important feature of the passage, but other things are happening. Even a first-time reader is caught for a moment in a faint counter-identification with, of all things, the Yahoo. The dry prose finds space to make us aware that, just as Gulliver is seeing something he cannot name, so the creature before him is staring 'as at an Object he had never seen before'. Thus even within this narrative of primary, utterly objective, repulsion there is a moment of implied reciprocity, or relativism. The first-time reader may even wonder, 'When the other raised his fore-paw, was he perhaps making a gesture of friendship, as it were, offering to shake hands?'. The complex distortion of the visage carries, moreover, an implicit suggestion of human facial expression, so much richer and more various than anything we see in brutes. Even if the thought is not there when we first read the passage, it can gradually enter our sense of what must have happened as we read on and become aware that the Yahoos are human.

But in that case Gulliver is wildly astray; he would, but for a ludicrously-misconceived apprehension, have killed without provocation an unarmed fellow human being who had done no more than extend his hand. The other may even have been smiling.

The passage, with its strong and its weak signals, is doubly disorientating. Gulliver is of course immediately surrounded by the Yahoos, who attack him by dropping excrement on him from the branches above his head. But Gulliver, the intruder in Utopia, is the aggressor. The Yahoos, themselves no party to the happiness of Houyhnhnms Land, attack (ineffectively) with excrement. Later the Houyhnhnms themselves will repel Gulliver's intrusion in an opposite manner; as they deal with diseases by 'a great *Evacuation*' (IV. 6 (p. 253)) so they will deal with this unwanted invasion of the body politic by a simple act of extrusion.

What I have called 'the weak signals' in the present passage are, as it turns out, immediately congenial to the prejudices of the twentieth century. If we try to write 'Gulliver' in the 'little language' of the *Journal to Stella* we get 'Gullible' and this, it might be said, is the key. There is, however, a snag. *Gullible* is not known to the *Oxford English Dictionary* before the nineteenth century, though the puzzling word *cullible* (having the same meaning) appears to have been in use in Swift's time (see, for example, Swift's letter to Pope of 16 July 1728).[2] Meanwhile the verb, *to gull*, was of course common currency. Certainly Gulliver is from the first entirely deceived by appearances. The reader quickly intuits that the horses Gulliver admires so fervently are cold, passionless, and, at the last, cruel. This impression, faint at first, is overwhelming by the end of the book, when Gulliver shrinks from the obviously virtuous Portuguese captain and

---

[2] *The Correspondence of Jonathan Swift*, edited by Harold Williams, 5 vols (Oxford, 1963–65), III (1963), 294.

prefers the society of his horses to that of his wife and children. No one, at the end of Gulliver's last voyage, can doubt, it is said, that the hero is mad.

Such is the critical orthodoxy of the twentieth century, though it is true that since the beginning of the 1960s various powerful voices have been raised in dissent.[3] There is moreover one forceful technical argument which supports this orthodoxy. Gulliver's fourth voyage is, quite clearly, a comic extravaganza. If there is one observation which applies as plainly to the first readers of *Gulliver's Travels* as it does to the most recent, it is that this book astonishes by reversing the ordinary disposition of characters; it turns human beings into dumb animals and it makes horses into grave sages. The logical implication of this is simple and unavoidable; in ordinary life it *must* be the other way round: horses must be dumb animals and such sagacity as is available must be gleaned from human beings. Were it otherwise the book would not be extravagant, would not be comic. Where did Swift find the characteristics, the thoughts, the behaviour of the Houyhnhnms, unless from human beings in their graver moments (especially, say, from certain Stoics of antiquity)?

The argument cuts cleanly but every good Swiftian will wish to resist it. The Dean would never have wasted time on the vacuous irony of mere reversal. He will always wish to fold into the most extravagant image, the most preposterous invention, an element of nagging likeness, or even of mere truth. The argument from comic extravagance needs to be put, however, because its failure is instructive. We begin to realize in consequence that all the great ironists, since Socrates said that he knew he knew nothing, have at some level always meant the thing they said in jest. Even tragic irony (a different but related thing) actually works most potently through an unlooked-for coincidence with truth rather than by any pleasure we may take in the manifest error; when Oedipus says he will track down the murderer of Laius he errs in supposing the culprit to be someone other than himself, but the force of the tragic irony lies in the fact that he will, in due course, carry out his promise to the letter. Swift, we know in our bones, will want us to think, if only at moments and against the odds, 'What are we but Yahoos?'.

[3]The satirist satirized view is most ably argued, perhaps, by Robert C. Elliott in his *The Power of Satire: Magic, Ritual, Art* (Princeton, New Jersey 1960), especially pp. 211–21. W. B. Carnochan, 'The Complexity of Swift: Gulliver's Fourth Voyage', *SP*, 60 (1963), 23–44 (p. 23), provides a useful summary of criticisms pursuing the view that in the fourth book it is Gulliver and the horses who are satirized, rather than the human race. R. S. Crane, 'The Houyhnhnms, the Yahoos and the History of Ideas', in *Reason and Imagination: Studies in the History of Ideas, 1600–1800*, edited by J. A. Mazzeo (New York, 1962), 231–53, gives a similar but shorter list (pp. 231–32). Carnochan and Crane are themselves both 'dissenting voices' as are (to varying degrees) J. Traugott, 'A Voyage to Nowhere with Thomas More and Jonathan Swift: *Utopia* and the Voyage to the Houyhnhnms', *Sewanee Review*, 69 (1961), 534–65; I. Ehrenpreis, 'The Meaning of Gulliver's Last Voyage', *Review of English Literature*, 3 (1962), 18–38; James L. Clifford, 'Gulliver's Fourth Voyage: Hard and Soft Schools of Interpretation', in *Quick Springs of Sense: Studies in the Eighteenth Century*, edited by L. S. Champion (Athens, Georgia, 1974), 133–51; Donald Keesey, 'The Distorted Image: Swift's Yahoos and the Critics', *Papers on Language and Literature*, 15 (1979), 320–32; and C. J. Rawson, 'Gulliver and the Gentle Reader', in *Imagined Worlds: Essays on Some English Novels and Novelists in Honour of John Butt*, edited by Maynard Mack and Ian Gregor (London, 1968), 51–90. This last is reprinted, with some changes, in C. J. Rawson's book, *Gulliver and the Gentle Reader* (London and Boston, Massachusetts, 1973), 1–32.

Certainly it is not enough to point to the coldness of the Houyhnhnms, as if the manifest repulsiveness of frigid rationality will settle the case outright. That Swift might have preferred coldness to warmth is not just conceivable, it is probable. Moreover, the implication of this preference, that intense love is ruled out, is precisely the kind of unwelcome corollary he would delight in adducing. He may even have seen himself at such moments less as the English Rabelais than as the successor of that Siger of Paris whom Dante describes: 'leggendo nel vico delli strami | sillogizzo invidiosi veri' (*Paradiso*, x. 137; 'Lecturing in Straw street, he set forth in syllogisms truths his hearers hated').

That Gulliver's misanthropy is to some extent shared by Swift was the common presumption until the present century. William Warburton spoke for many when he accused Swift of *degrading his species* and carrying satire to the point of mere destruction: 'And now the Fig-leaf is so cleanly plucked off, what remains but bravely to strike away the rotten Staff, that yet keeps our doting Parents on their last legs.'[4] One half suspects the presence of a Freudian equivocation in 'the rotten Staff' immediately following the removal of the fig leaf, as if Warburton with some part of his mind perceived that Swift's real motive was a hatred of sexuality, so that he sought not only to degrade but also to emasculate mankind. Moreover, Swift, notoriously, accepted the charge of misanthropy. 'I hate and detest that animal called man', he told Pope, 'although I heartily love John, Peter, Thomas and so forth', and added, 'Upon this great foundation of Misanthropy (though not Timons manner) The whole building of my Travells is erected' (*Correspondence*, III, 103). Writing to Charles Ford on 19 January 1723/4 he affirms that he hates Yahoos of both sexes: even Stella and Madame de Villette are 'onely tolerable at best, for want of [the society of] Houyhnhnms' (*Correspondence*, III, 4). On 11 September 1725 he wrote to Thomas Sheridan: 'You will every day find my Description of Yahoes more resembling' (*Correspondence*, III, 94). To be sure, the tone is jesting, especially in the second of these. But (once more) few Swiftians will suppose that the irony is of the kind which simply cancels the apparent assertion. As the *Examiner* (7 June 1711), Swift wrote: 'Nothing can well be more mortifying, than to reflect, that I am of the same Species with Creatures capable of uttering so much Scurrility, Dulness, Falshood and Impertinence, to the Scandal and Disgrace of Human Nature' (*Works*, III, 171–72). The piece was anonymous but the voice is Swift's own.

Yet the peculiar frisson at one's biological kinship with the most odious of all creatures is precisely what is to charge the most powerful moment in *Gulliver's Travels*: Gulliver goes swimming on a hot day and a certain female Yahoo, seeing him, makes amorous advances. It is then that he knows, by a test used to this day by working scientists, that he is of the same species as the Yahoos, though of course the biologist requires, as Swift does not, that the union be fertile. Odysseus, the first traveller in European literature, wanted above all to go home. Gulliver's

[4]*A Critical and Philosophic Enquiry into the Causes of Prodigies and Miracles* (London, 1727), in *Swift: The Critical Heritage*, edited by Kathleen Williams (London, 1970), pp. 71–72.

'poor Wife' (IV. 1 (p. 221)) seems to have been quite as faithful as Penelope, but she and his home are alike odious to him after he has been permitted to kiss the hoof of the Houyhnhnm. The horror of wife, family, and home is, at its root, identical with the horror of biological kinship. Yet here, in the extremity of his madness, Gulliver can speak with what is recognizably the voice of Swift:

> My Reconcilement to the *Yahoo*-kind in general might not be so difficult, if they would be content with those Vices and Follies only which Nature hath entitled them to. . . . This is all according to the due Course of Things: But, when I behold a Lump of Deformity, and Diseases both in Body and Mind, smitten with *Pride*, it immediately breaks all the Measures of my Patience. (IV. 12 (p. 296))

Quite clearly the same savage indignation tore at Swift's heart: Patrick Delany tells how Swift asked a friend whether 'the corruptions and villainies of men in power did not eat his flesh and exhaust his spirits?'. When his friend answered that they did not, Swift cried out in a fury: 'Why, why, how can you help it, how can you avoid it?'[5] Of the two reactions Gulliver's is the more temperate.

W. B. Carnochan, reviewing these materials, concedes that at the end of the book Gulliver, like Timon or Molière's Alceste, is himself satirized. But, he adds, the joke is a painful one; he endorses the view of John F. Ross that it is 'at the expense of a very important part of himself'.[6] Claude Rawson, similarly, finds a certain doubleness in the final Timonian misanthropy of Gulliver. Plainly, he says, Gulliver is insane, but his reclusiveness and ranting stand for a position which is seriously asserted by Swift; meanwhile, however, the ranting, the *manner*, is Gulliver's, not Swift's. In this way Swift can distance himself from the charge of extremism while contriving to press his own central accusation against the human race.[7] This is criticism at its best, lucid, discriminating, and sensitive, but I am not quite persuaded that it is right. Carnochan suggests a simple clash of sympathies: Swift both despises and sympathizes with the misanthropy of Gulliver. Rawson suggests a more organized tension: both Swift and Gulliver despise the human race but Swift implicitly dissociates himself from *extreme* misanthropy. I would prefer to say that Swift simultaneously asserts both the full, extreme misanthropy of Gulliver and its human absurdity, knowing that the two are, at root, not opposed but logically interlocked.

Everyone knows, in a primary, perhaps a biologically primary, fashion that to be repelled by one's wife and child merely on account of their humanity is a kind of madness. Swift, who, to put it mildly, was no fool, certainly knew this. At the same time, if human kind stinks, then Gulliver is absolutely right. Here also the thought burns in Swift's mind with a primal force, rooted in infantile responses, growing powerfully from an instinctive to a fully ethical revulsion. By their dung

---

[5]Cited by W. B. Carnochan ('The Complexity of Swift', pp. 37–38) from Delany's *Observations upon Lord Orrery's Remarks on the Life and Writings of Jonathan Swift* (London, 1754), pp. 148–49.

[6]Carnochan, 'The Complexity of Swift', p. 32; John F. Ross, 'The Final Comedy of Lemuel Gulliver', *Studies in the Comic*, University of California Publications in English, 8 (1941), pp. 175–96 (p. 196).

[7]'Gulliver and the Gentle Reader', *Imagined Worlds*, p. 79.

ye shall know them: the human variety is so much more offensive than the equine. The horse is a comelier, more fragrant thing than this beast which, alone among animals, maims and tortures its own kind.

It may be that the point at issue between myself and Rawson is a vanishing one, for in the essay I have cited he immediately qualifies the opposition I described by adding: 'But his [Gulliver's] are the final words which produce the taste Swift chose to leave behind: it is no great comfort or compliment to the reader to be assaulted with a mean hysteria that he cannot shrug off because, when all is said, it tells what the whole volume has insisted to be the truth' (p. 73). These words close the gap I would have closed. Indeed it was shut fast from the beginning by the latent logic of the narrative. The effect of this is to expose an anomaly in ethics; moral discourse is sometimes species-based in a radical manner, sometimes not. Species-based morality makes love of mankind primary; to desire the destruction of the human race is, in this scheme, *axiomatically* wicked and no moral defence of such a desire is even conceivable. Non-species-based morality, on the other hand, recognizes no such practical axiom (it is, in G. E. Moore's terms, more clearly 'non-naturalistic').[8] It permits one to step back, even from one's own species, and to form an ethical judgement on it. Within this morality it is perfectly possible to argue, for example, that the human race taken as a whole is more bad than good, so that a collective suicide of the species is in truth our ultimate duty. Because the structure of species-based morality is simultaneously in force, this proposition immediately registers as both wicked and lunatic. But, because the non-species-based morality also figures powerfully in our conceptual scheme, the proposition 'man is vile' can be cogent. In *Gulliver's Travels* Swift, working simultaneously from a wicked humour and a black conviction of depravity, chose to cross the lines of nature and convention in a manner calculated to create the maximum disturbance.

The newly fashionable cultural relativisim of the Enlightenment, which led even the staid Locke to write with a kind of glee about the Christian Mengrelians who bury their children alive, gave Swift the opportunity for the necessary initial disorientation: what is bad here may be good there.[9] But then he switches from relativisim to an absolutism so stark as to be shocking. Lawrence Manley observes that Swift satirizes the very relativism of the travel writers when he shows that the apparent differences between civilizations are in fact real differences, 'so that the Lilliputian disgust with Gulliver and Gulliver's disgust with the Brobdingnagians are a function of their real degree of magnitude and magnanimity'.[10] When we come to the rational horses this strategy under-

---

[8]Naturalistic morality permits sentences containing the term 'ought' to be translated, without logical remainder, into ordinary indicative sentences or else to be derived from such sentences. For G. E. Moore on naturalism, see his *Principia Ethica* (Cambridge, the 1962 reprint of the first edition of 1903), especially pp. 39–41, 58, 59. See also John Hospers, *An Introduction to Philosophical Analysis* (London, 1956), pp. 568–74.

[9]*An Essay Concerning Human Understanding* (1689), 1.3.8; edited by Peter Nidditch (London, 1975), p. 71.

[10]*Convention, 1500–1750* (Cambridge, Massachusetts, 1980), p. 330.

goes a further, brilliant, transformation. For the unnaturally sagacious horses are themselves (in what anyone but the almost cultureless Gulliver will perceive to be a Stoic mode) followers of Nature: their own morality can be construed as thoroughly species-based, and at this level it simply mirrors the species-based presumptions of human beings. Thus far, Swift has shown us a novel figure in the dance of cultural relativism. If this were all, the Houyhnhnms would be subject to the same satiric scourge as mankind, in a precisely parallel manner. But in Houyhnhnm society we are gradually made to suspect that, after all, no fissure can ever be made to appear (as it can in our world) between the species-based and the absolute ethic. *Their* species really is superior. It follows that in their more or less Stoic philosophy reason will be in accord with this condition of nature and will in consequence exhibit no problems: 'Their grand maxim is, to cultivate *Reason*, and to be wholly governed by it. Neither is *Reason* among them a Point problematical as with us, where Men can argue with Plausibility on both Sides of a Question' (IV. 8 (p. 267)).

Thus, while human Stoics were constantly exercised by the transition from descript to prescript, no such difficulty arises for the Houyhnhnms. The Stoics affirmed that man was a rational animal and thereafter urged strenuously that he labour to become so. 'You are rational' was habitually followed not by 'Therefore relax' but by the (in the circumstances wholly irrational) 'Therefore subdue your passions'. We have moved, by implication, from 'You are rational' to 'You are, properly, rational', or 'You are basically/originally/at your best rational'. But the Houyhnhnms, unlike the ancient human Stoics, have no vast body of literature on the subjection of passion because they actually are as they say they are (there is indeed a mild inconsistency in Swift's having them continually dwelling in their poems on instances of benevolence (IV. 9 (p. 274)), since there can be no reason to praise that which is merely given by nature). The Stoic conception of man, it might be said, is noble and therefore the opposite of misanthropic. But because Stoics were in practice everywhere assailed by the rampant irrationality of real human beings, misanthropy seems to have come easily to them: 'One is sometimes seized', says Seneca, 'with hatred of the whole human race.'[11] It is as if the old Pindaric tag, 'Become what you are' (*Pythian Odes*, II. 72) came, with the rise of Stoicism, increasingly to express a state of disquieting tension. Indeed this slippage to the Stoic perception of human nature almost becomes a synchronic equivalent of the Christian conception of the fall of man.

The definition 'Man is a rational animal' reminds one that the fourth book of *Gulliver's Travels*, with its parade of inverse definitions ('The horse is a rational animal', 'Man is beast'), is parodically linked with logic manuals of the later seventeenth century. R. S. Crane was the first to point out that men and horses provide the running example of rationality and its converse in the treatises of Franco Burgersdijck, Narcissus Marsh (Swift's despised 'Primate Marsh'), and

[11]*De Tranquillitate Animi, Moral Essays*, edited with an English translation by J. W. Basore, 3 vols (Cambridge, Massachusetts, 1935), III, 273.

others.[12] Indeed the connexion with *Gulliver's Travels* may be more intricate even than Crane saw. Narcissus Marsh, in his manual designed 'for the use of the young academicians of Dublin', has a way of generating (*per accidens*) distinctions and paradoxes which can appear essentially Swiftian.[13] One of the simpler comic mechanisms in *Gulliver's Travels* works through the ambiguity of 'animal' in English. Because we commonly use this word to mean 'non-human' or 'beast' the phrase 'Man is a rational animal' carries a whiff of paradox from the start. But the Latin *animal* has the same ambiguity, and Marsh, in his plodding progress, makes sure that we are aware of the fact. In the very preface of his book he offers the following syllogism:

> *Nullum animal est homo.*
> *Omne rationale est homo.* Ergo
> *Nullum rationale est animal.*
> No animal is a man. Every rational being is a man. Therefore,
> no rational being is an animal.
>
> (*Protheoria Syllogistica*, Q.6)

After which (still in the 'Preface') horses and apes come crowding in (it will be said that there are no apes in the fourth book of *Gulliver's Travels*, but it is hard to avoid the sense that the Yahoos are, in a way which Swift cannot acknowledge, partly based on a simian original).

> *Si Simia non sit irrationalis, est homo*
> *Sed Simia non est homo.* Ergo,
> *Est irrationalis.*
> If an ape be not irrational, it is a man.
> But an ape is not a man. Therefore
> it is irrational.
>
> (Q.8)

All of this of course is also sober sense, though when we come to the section on the Individual we may wonder a little at Marsh's obvious partiality for *horses*:

> [Individuum incertum] exprimitur per Nomen commune et Pronomen
> particulare: ut, *Aliquis homo. Quidam equus.*
> We express the indeterminate individual by means of the
> common noun and the particularising pronoun, *Some man.*
> A certain horse.
>
> (pp. 9–10)[14]

But it is when we come to the examples of bad syllogisms that we really strike pay-dirt. On page 144 he offers the wholly witless:

---

[12]Crane, 'The Houyhnhnms, the Yahoos and the History of Ideas'. See also C. T. Probyn, 'Swift and the Human Predicament', in *The Art of Jonathan Swift,* edited by C. T. Probyn (London 1978), pp. 57–80.

[13]*Institutiones Logicae in usum Juventatis Academicae Dublinensis* (Dublin, 1681).

[14]*Aliquis* and *quidam* in Latin, unlike 'a certain' in English, can figure as pronouns.

Nullus homo est brutum.
Nullus equus est homo. Ergo,
Nullus equus est brutum.
No man is a brute. No horse is a man.
Therefore *no horse is a brute.*)

On pages 149 and 153 we have the following standard Undistributed Middles:

Omne brutum est animal,
Omnis homo est animal. Ergo,
Omnis brutum est homo.
Every brute is an animal.
Every man is an animal. Therefore,
every brute is a man.
Omnis homo est animal
Omnis equus est animal. Ergo,
Omnis equus est homo.
Every man is an animal. Every
horse is an animal. Therefore
every horse is a man.

And so the rattling mechanism of Marsh's pedagogy goes on its way. On page 167 the eye is caught by *Homo est brutum*, 'Man is a brute' and a page later by *Homo est Bucephelus*, 'Bucephelus [Alexander's famous horse] is a man'. There can be no doubt that all this had its effect on Swift. When he wrote his parodic syllogism on the Aeolists in *A Tale of a Tub* he followed the typographic habit of Marsh, italicizing the terms but leaving 'Ergo' in Roman: '*Words are but Wind; and Learning is nothing but words*; Ergo *Learning is nothing but wind.*'[15] It is easy to see in what spirit the young Swift would have read the *Institutiones Logicae*, making it a point of honour to believe the syllogisms laboriously offered as errors by his master and to disbelieve the rest. All this, note, was long before Locke attacked Stillingfleet's views on the nature of man. On this side we have clever undergraduate humour; on that, springing from and then freezing the game, a queerly absolute judgement *a priori*, a judgement fenced with every sort of irony yet inescapably asserted.

So far I have argued in terms of commonplaces of the age: reason, temperance, benevolence, and nature provide the framework. But if the effect of this is, as it were, to flatten Swift, to merge him with his background, then once again one is probably going wrong. For Swift's brand of misanthropy (and I mean Swift's, not Gulliver's) has its own note of hysteria, its own special extremism. Setting aside the precise medical character of Swift's final illness, we may still be struck with the way contemporaries and near contemporaries of Swift doubted his sanity while admiring his intellect. I will say nothing here of the obsession with excrement. Suppose instead that we add to the materials assembled by Carnochan and others the following passage from Swift's 'Letter to a Young

[15]Edited by A. C. Guthkelch and D. Nichol Smith (Oxford, 1958), p. 153.

Lady on her Marriage' (1723): 'Besides, yours was a Match of Prudence, and common Good-liking, without any Mixture of that ridiculous Passion which hath no Being, but in Play-Books and Romances' (*Works*, IX, 89). This corresponds with the dispassionately eugenic marriages of the Houyhnhnms so much admired by Gulliver (IV. 8 (p. 268)), and yet once more it is Swift, not Gulliver, who is speaking.

I have, however, another reason for singling out this passage. It is marked by a special tremor of the intellect which perhaps betrays much. For Swift congratulates Deborah Staunton on the absence of something which (he says it himself) does not exist outside the pages of books. We may seek to expunge the absurdity by saying that Swift obviously means to congratulate the young lady on being free of the *delusion* of supposing herself in love, since love outside play books and romances is always a mere tissue of illusions. But this rescue operation is not altogether comfortable or convincing; a sufficiently vivid delusion of being in love might surely constitute *real* 'passion'; it is, after all, passion that Swift hates and it is surely wonderful if humankind is wholly free of it, so that it lingers only in works of fiction. The almost unbearable, icy, patronizing blandness of this letter, with its deliberately-unlovable combination of stylistic majesty with personal intimacy is, at this point, disturbed by something which even Swift, perhaps, did not fully understand. It seems to be *fear* which, for the length of a sentence, here outruns the intelligence. The same fear shows in the 'Resolutions when I come to be Old' which Swift set down more than twenty years before he began to write *Gulliver's Travels*: 'Not to marry a young Woman. . . . Not to be fond of Children, or let them come near me hardly' (*Works*, I, xxxvii).

Johnson in his 'Life of Swift' makes his distaste for Swift's inhuman and obsessive rationality very clear. He is horrified by the way Swift lent to the poor, fixing a date for repayment and suing defaulters.[16] He describes Swift's private rule of giving one coin at a time when tipping and of always storing 'his pocket with coins of different value' (p. 58). Johnson's celebrated observation of Swift's 'inverted hypocrisy' is offered not in admiration but with some dismay (p. 54). Already one smells what the twentieth century has learned to call schizophrenia. The impression grows stronger when Johnson allows himself a freer rein with anecdotes of personal eccentricity, such as Pope's wonderful account of the occasion when he and Gay called on Swift: Swift asked if they had eaten and, on learning that they had, became very agitated by the thought that he would otherwise have had to give them lobsters, tarts, and a bottle of wine, at a cost of 2s. 6d. each; he was unable to rest until he had persuaded each of them to accept half-a-crown (pp. 58–59). I suspect that Johnson's obvious hostility springs in part from his recognition of obsessional tendencies within himself; certainly *he* dealt with them differently. His pausing to tell us how Swift continually washed his face forms part of the same general picture (p. 55). It is as if Johnson can more easily forgive Kit Smart for not changing his shirt than he can forgive Swift

[16]*Lives of the English Poets*, edited by George Birkbeck Hill, 3 vols (Oxford, 1905), III, 57.

for his cleanliness.[17] Meanwhile, however, one cannot feel that Johnson's anxieties are wholly misplaced.

The Portuguese sea captain is the strongest evidence in the fourth book for Swift's essential sanity, or so we are told. He is manifestly generous and Gulliver, conversely, is manifestly unbalanced in his response to that generosity. When I considered the behaviour of Gulliver on being reunited with his wife and family, I insisted on listening to the voice which said 'And the heart of the jest is that Gulliver is right, because human beings stink and horses are better than men'. Against all the odds (which is exactly how Swift loved to write) the same voice may even be heard here, if we care to listen. R. S. Crane got it right when he said that if Swift was to convey the full force of his indictment and shock the reader from his or her anthropocentric complacency it was necessary to include in the now-extended ranks of the Yahoos a person who would seem to most of us, in our innocent arrogance, virtuous and admirable. Or, as John Traugott put it more succinctly, 'Even good Yahoos are Yahoos'.[18] Your ordinary racist hates Jews because he believes that they poison wells or (in more recent times) destroy the economy. Your fundamental racist hates Jews because they are Jews and for no other reason. Among friends he will take pleasure in affirming that a good Jew is still a Jew, since in this way he can isolate the element of pure contempt. So with Swift. There is a part of his mind which has attained (so to speak) pure misanthropy, untainted by ordinary human reasons. This then obliges him to bring Gulliver face to face with the best of human kind—and then have his hero shrink in disgust. Of course he knows that the reader will laugh at the folly of Gulliver, but that is now an essential part of Swift's increasingly private joke. For what is the reader but another Yahoo? In the last resort Yahoos will stick together. Even now the joke is not quite over, for what is Swift himself?

If this really is the inner logic of the Don Pedro episode then it must be said that it carries a hint of insanity. If a Yahoo cannot be admired for his decent benevolence, then neither can a Houyhnhnm. Non-species-based (absolute) morality allowed Swift to accuse mankind as a whole of cruelty, mendacity, and pride. In this way he could establish a misanthropic base. Then the system gives a shake and, lo, we are presented with an inverse species-based morality. Instead of 'even a bad man is still a fellow human being' we have 'even a good man is still, ugh!, a man'. It may be thought that in contriving this mirror effect Swift's design was to satirize further the species-based morality which he earlier threw off, but this is one subtlety which I believe we must deny him. The writing is too dark and hot, the links with words uttered *in propria persona* are of the wrong kind.

When Gulliver catches sight of his face in a pool (IV. 10 (p. 278)) his reaction is the opposite of Narcissus's in the myth. Gulliver hates what he sees. In Ovid

[17]See Boswell, *Life of Johnson*, edited by George Birkbeck Hill, 6 vols (Oxford, 1887), I, 397 (24 May 1763).

[18]Crane, 'The Houyhnhnms, The Yahoos and the History of Ideas', p. 35; Traugott, 'A Voyage to Nowhere', p. 562.

(*Metamorphoses*, III. 339–510) Narcissus is an innocent and lives in the childhood of what is to become our own world. He has never seen his face before and as soon as he sees it he loves it. Indeed, even the shaggy Cyclops likes his face when he first sees it reflected (*Metamorphoses*, XII. 842–43). Gulliver, who saw his face many times in the world of men, finds himself translated to a counterworld in which innocence and truth are in a manner recoverable. Once again his reaction can be seen comoedically as part of the relativist game (what is fair here is foul there and vice versa). But at another level (and that the more important) it is as if the effect of his sojourn among the horses is to make the scales fall from his eyes. He can now see truly, but, although he has somehow strayed into Arcadia, what he sees is corruption.

In emphasizing an element of authentically Swiftian misanthropy I have perhaps privileged the tormented ego of the author above his more liberal and free-ranging imagination. Another way to express the antithesis is to say that the book is an altogether richer thing than its proudly invidious thesis. There is a sense in which simple imaginative postulates, such as 'Let us imagine people six inches high', can generate an increasingly rich variety of situations, almost of themselves. 'Let the horses be rational and the men brutes' is such a postulate. Admit to the scheme a rational man and the possibilities are richer still. Ancient structures of the imagination, ideal Commonwealths, Utopias, transposed pastorals, Paradises penetrated and overthrown begin to figure in the picture. It is as if a monomaniac central impulse is made to work within a polymaniac field of reference.

I have resisted the notion that the coldness of the horses implicitly condemns them. If, however, we substitute 'negative' or even 'stupid' for 'cold' the case is somewhat altered. The horses live by *reason* but they have no skill or facility in *ratiocination*. They are sages who never philosophize. The most frequent locution applied to them is that beginning 'They have no conception of . . .': 'Power, Government, War, Law, Punishment, and a Thousand other Things had no Terms, wherein that Language could express them' (IV. 4 (p. 244)); 'The Inhabitants have not the least Idea of Books or Literature' (IV. 3 (p. 235)); 'they have no Word in their Language to express Lying or Falshood' (IV. 3 (p. 235)); 'when I asserted that the *Yahoos* were the only governing Animals in my Country . . . my Master said [it] was altogether past his Conception' (IV. 4 (p. 240)). In addition they have no conception of the use of money (IV. 6 (p. 251)) or of what a ship is (IV. 3 (p. 235)), only an imperfect conception of illness (IV. 6 (p. 253)), and no conception, of course, of the various vices described by Gulliver (IV. 4 (p. 244)); *love* has 'no Place in their Thoughts' (IV. 8 (p. 269)), and the Sorrel Nag 'had no Conception of any Country beside his own' (IV. 10 (p. 281)).

This is in part an effect of genre. 'They have no word for "lie"' is a recurrent topos of travel literature and early anthropology. But in Swift the topos is immensely extended, and all the odder, it might seem, when we are dealing with paragons of rationality. More importantly we need to remember how rationality is treated by Stoic thinkers. The basic generative sentence of *Gulliver's Travels*,

Part IV, 'Man is a rational animal', is not, as is commonly supposed, an Aristotelian commonplace, but is largely the property of the Stoics. 'Man is a political animal', on the other hand, is the key sentence of Shakespeare's *Timon of Athens* and is a genuinely Aristotelian tag.[19] Aristotle is certainly keenly interested in man as an animal capable of acquiring knowledge, but this, as I shall argue, is too dynamic a conception for either the Stoics or Swift.[20] Similarly, Aristotle is willing to describe man as the only animal capable of deliberation.[21] The nearest he comes to the stock phrase of the logic books is perhaps in the *Politics* when he says (at 1332 b 3) that the rational principle is not found in brute animals. The central phrase, 'rational animal' (*zōon logikon*), occurs as far as I can discover only once, and in a most dubious manner. In a fragment of Aristotle which we owe to the Pythagorean Platonist Iamblichus (fourth century A.D.) we are told that among the secret doctrines of the Pythagoreans was one which ran, 'There are three kinds of rational animal: gods, men and beings like Pythagoras'.[22] It is hard to be sure, but it looks very like a joke. With the Stoics the phrase comes into its own. Chrysippus leads the way, using it in a work revealingly entitled *On the Failure to Lead a Consistent Life*.[23]

It is clear that Aristotle is interested in activity, in the things human beings do with their intelligence. What the Stoics are interested in is, despite the rhetorical ordonnance of the Senecan style, rather less perspicuous. Important in the scheme is a notional fusion of 'follow nature' with 'follow reason'. It is commonly said that in the technical philosophy of the seventeenth and eighteenth centuries reason is increasingly restricted to the deductive faculty, with a corresponding shift away from the traditional cognitive conception (reason as a just perception and moral appraisal of what is really the case). 'The traditional conception' appears to owe far more to Stoicism than to Aristotle. A powerful moral stress on cognitive reason can lead to the terminal notion of an inert conformity with nature (where 'nature' means not 'the green world' but That Which Is, considered as a divinely ordered whole). Seneca, in his *Moral Epistle* 'On the God within Us', explains the matter with an almost Chadbandian vacuousness:

> Praise in him that which can neither be torn from him nor given to him, that which is the Property of Man. You ask, what may that be? It is soul, and reason perfected in the Soul. For man is a rational animal. And so the highest good is accomplished if he has filled the role for which he was born. And what is it that is demanded from him by

[19] In referring to Aristotle I use the standard Bekker numbers. These are given in all good editions including English versions, for example, Sir David Ross, *The Works of Aristotle translated into English*, 12 vols (Oxford, 1926–52). See *Nicomachean Ethics*, 1097 b 11, 1162 a 17, 1169 b 18; *Eudemian Ethics*, 1242 a 22–27, 1245 a 11–27; *Politics*, 1253 a 2, 30, 1278 b 20.

[20] *Topics*, 130 b 8, 132 a 20, 133 a 21, 134 a 15, 140 a 36.

[21] *De Anima*, 433 a 12; *Historia Animalium*, 488 b 24; *De Partibus Animalium*, 641 b 8; *Politics*, 1332 b 5; *Rhetorica ad Alexandrum*, 1421 a 11.

[22] Fragment 187 (Rose's numbering), in Ross, XII, 137.

[23] Quoted by Plutarch, *On Moral Virtue*, 450 D, in Plutarch's *Moralia*, with an English translation by W. C. Helmbold, Loeb Classical Library, 15 vols (London, 1927–69), VI, 72.

this 'reason' of which I speak? The easiest thing of all, to live in accord with his own nature.[24]

There, to be sure, he ends, trapped in a subjective circle: 'Your nature is rational, what is reason? This life in accordance with your own nature; what is your own nature? Why, to be rational.' Elsewhere the circle is broken and he says, simply, 'Follow nature', the practice being firmly associated with the possession of a sane unclouded mind.[25]

The Stoic assimilation of reason to both internal and external nature is accomplished through a covert act of prescription. Man's *real* nature is rational (the 'honorific' use of *real*). The prescriptive identification was followed by the usual long rebellion of the *de facto* against the *de jure*. When the Stoics affirmed the rationality of following nature they intended 'nature in the sense opposed to 'convention' (*physis/nomos*): 'Scorn luxury and wild opinion, attend to what is truly noble.' But even in antiquity *nature* was also opposed by *art*, and it is this second opposition which lies behind all pastoral writing and will ultimately yield the 'green' nature of Romanticism. Meanwhile, what is the opposite of reason? In stoicism it is passion. But by the pastoral opposition it is the passions which seem most obviously natural, while reason belongs with art (we may remember at this point that *nomos*, which is the Greek for 'convention', also means 'law').

We may now be in a better position to understand the Houyhnhnms. Their minds and values, being perfectly adjusted to nature, need never stir from the consequent sleep: until, that is, they are visited by one whose rationality is of the dangerous, dynamic, *ratiocinative* kind. Until Gulliver occasioned the first debate in Houyhnhnms Land, these were sages who never once disputed any question. Is it not possible that Gulliver's sessions with his Master Horse are really (though Gulliver would be profoundly shocked at the description) strange tutorials in which Gulliver (not the Horse) is the teacher? The Yahoos are described as unteachable (IV. 8 (p. 266), 9 (p. 271)) but if we look for the opposite character we shall find it, not in the incurious Houyhnhnms but in *homo sapiens* as described by Gulliver. The Master Horse is obviously quite unable to account for the malignity implicit in Gulliver's very cleverness; reason ought to be a point in his favour yet it seems to be working the other way. A little desperately he suggests that it is because man has been given only a 'pittance' of reason, which is somehow susceptible of misuse, that he goes wrong (IV. 7 (p. 259)), as if a larger ration of the same would somehow have been all right.

Gulliver's description of the ship is a nice specimen of Enlightenment 'defamiliarization': 'I came over the Sea, from a far Place, with many others of my own Kind, in a great hollow Vessel made of the Bodies of Trees' (IV. 3 (p. 235)). He has learned to speak as if to a child. The Master Horse's response is touched

---

[24]*Epistulae Morales*, 41.8–9, in *Ad Lucilium Epistulae Morales*, with an English translation by R. M. Gummere, Loeb Classical Library, 3 vols (London, 1917–25), I, 276–78. The translation is mine.
    [25]*On the Happy Life*, 3.3, in *Moral Essays*, with an English translation by J. W. Basore, Loeb Classical Library, 3 vols (London, 1927–35), II, 106.

with inadvertent pathos: 'He was sure no *Houyhnhnm* alive could make such a Vessel, or would trust *Yahoos* to manage it.'

The truth is that the Houyhnhnms are just not very clever. Not only do they abstain from disputes, but they have no technology. When Gulliver makes two chairs, using his knife, the Sorrel Nag, for all his undoubted membership of the Master Race, is, comfortably and without comment, assigned the simpler and more laborious tasks (IV. 10 (p. 276)). When, later, Gulliver goes Crusoe-like to work on his ingenious 'Canoo' the Sorrel Nag once more plays the part of Man Friday, performing 'the Parts that required most Labour' (IV. 10 (p. 281)).

The Stoics were driven to philosophize, to engage in pursuasive discourse, only because man was not in practice invariably rational in the way he was expected to be: the active rationality of Seneca, such as it is, can live and breathe only in the space afforded by the failure of that primal definition. But the horses really are thus and, as the gap is closed, we realize that we are indeed confronted by a species of rationality which has no tincture of the ratiocinative. Such rationality is indeed not so much the correct appraisal of nature as a mere identity with nature, a surrender of thought. We are very close to saying that Swift might, with greater consistency, have used perfectly ordinary well-adjusted horses, without entangling himself in the treacherous business of anthropomorphism; how could he think that he could dignify a noble horse by making him resemble the Yahoo Seneca?

The presentiment that Part IV might be, in some remote fashion, a transposed pastoral is not so wide of the mark. The pre-Argonautical Houyhnhnms, like the men of Virgil's Golden Age, know not the use of iron (*Georgics* I. 143; *Gulliver's Travels*, IV. 9 (p. 274)).[26] Their use of sledges (IV. 2 (p. 231)), IV. 9 (p. 275)) suggests that they may not even have invented the wheel, though 'carriages' are mentioned at IV. 9 (p. 274). Their world is indeed a green one. I have asked, in effect, when Gulliver converses with the Master Horse which is the teacher, which the taught? There is an obvious sense in which Gulliver's pride in mechanical contrivance is exposed by the horse, but this also conforms to the pastoral pattern. Gulliver encounters not the authority of intellect but the authority of innocence. Spenser's Sir Calidore, who with all his civil courtesy brings change and death to a pastoral society, is similarly wrong-footed by innocent wisdom: he makes the mistake of offering money to the aged shepherd Melibee (*Faerie Queene*, IV. 9. 32–33). One lesson, we find, the Master Horse is capable of learning; when Gulliver first explains how horses were castrated in his own country the Master is shocked, chiefly no doubt because the operation is performed on horses (IV. 4 (pp. 241–42)). Later the Master proudly announces how it is possible to learn from the lower animals, and that rebellious Yahoos might be rendered more tractable by castration (IV. 9 (pp. 272–73)). This time it is we who are shocked, chiefly no doubt because the operation is to be performed on men.

[26]See Margaret Anne Doody, '*Gulliver's Travels* and Virgil's *Georgics*', in *Augustan Studies and Essays in Honour of Irvin Ehrenpreis*, edited by Douglas Lane Patey and Timothy Keegan (Newark, Delaware, London, and Toronto, 1985), 145–74, especially p. 171.

Like Milton's Satan, Gulliver brings with him dynamism and change, transforming the world of unfallen Stoics. He shows how any world in which the intelligence will function as a live thing will contain evil as well as good. Unlike Satan, however, he is no rebel but, had they only known it, their first and only perfect pupil. For Gulliver's abject submission was wholly unfeigned. He swallowed everything, the Spartan (Hitler Youth) exercises, the pride of caste (like Nietzsche's archaic Greeks in *The Genealogy of Morals,* who draw their terms of disapproval from synonyms of 'slave', the horses derive theirs variously from the word *Yahoo*), the moral platitudes, the equine Pindaric odes on athletic victories—the lot.[27] But they decided he was a potential revolutionary and therefore expelled him (IV. 10 (p. 279)). It may be said that they were wise, since Gulliver, whatever his intentions, carried the corrupting taint of the civilized Yahoo which would in due course have had its effect. At that level, however, it is likely that the subtle damage was already done. What the Houyhnhnms actually suggest is that Gulliver would have led the local Yahoos in revolt, and it is difficult to resist the conclusion that the Assembly, with its habitual stupidity, simply got it wrong. Gulliver himself, whose attitude to the Assembly is a little like that of George Herbert towards God, makes no complaint.

There was one Houyhnhnm, however, who got it right. Near the end of the story Gulliver tells how he put out to sea in his makeshift boat, watched by the Master Horse and some friends. When he was almost out of sight, he says, 'I often heard the Sorrel Nag (who always loved me) crying out, *Hnuy illa nyha maiah Yahoo,* Take Care of thy self, gentle *Yahoo*' (IV. 11 (p. 283)). Not 'seditious', notice, but 'gentle'. The parenthesis '(who always loved me)', after so many pages of rational benevolence and the perfunctory 'better feelings' of the Master (IV. 10 (p. 279)) has a sudden power. It is here rather than in the Don Pedro episode that the Swiftian fear of love is shaken. In the first ideal Commonwealth they expelled the poet. Swift himself with his breath-taking, ever-moving, intelligence would have been expelled from Houyhnhnms Land more rapidly, one surmises, than Gulliver. But to tell Swift this would be to tell him what he already knows, that he must include himself in his misanthropy.

It is always unwise to patronize good writers, but it is especially unwise in the case of Swift. We must allow him to say what he must say, however it offends us. Like the tree with which Stoic Aeneas is compared by Virgil, his roots are in hell (IV. 446). Even so, however, pious Aeneas is too high-minded a hero for our purpose. If Boswell is allowed to compare the mind of Dr Johnson to the Colosseum, perhaps we can say that the mind of Swift resembled the Augean Stable, remembering only that he was also his own Hercules, labouring within it.[28] But, if we remember the word *lacerare* from Swift's epitaph in St Patrick's cathedral, we may think of him as not a Luciferan but an ascetic Prometheus, tormented on his rock, yet able still to torment posterity.

[27]*The Genealogy of Morals,* I. 4 and 10, in *The Birth of Tragedy and the Genealogy of Morals,* translated by F. Golfing (New York, 1956), pp. 162, 171–72.
[28]Boswell, *Life of Johnson,* II, 106 (26 October 1769).

The Last Proposals

Oliver W. Ferguson

I

Swift was one of the few men writing on Irish affairs in 1729 who evaluated accurately the significance of the famine caused by three successive years of bad harvests. He was moved to fierce compassion by the spectacle of wholesale misery, but he realized that to regard the famine as the consequence merely of the scarcity of grain was a naïve oversimplification. In the *Proposal . . . [to] the Ladies*, he argued that "the three seasons wherein our corn hath miscarried, did no more contribute to our present misery, than one spoonful of water thrown upon a rat already drowned would contribute to his death," and in a letter to Pope he said that Ireland's sufferings came from deeper causes than the famine: "Imagine a nation the two thirds of whose revenues are spent out of it, and who are not permitted to trade with the other third, and where the pride of women will not suffer them to wear their own manufactures, even where they excel what come from abroad. This is the true state of Ireland in a very few words."[1]

This brief account of the true state of Ireland makes it clear that, in Swift's eyes, the guilt for the country's lamentable condition was shared by the English and the Irish alike. Swift certainly assigned the greater portion of blame to the English, and he was aware that Ireland's guilt was somewhat mitigated by the fact of generations of oppression. The Drapier had acknowledged that "A People long used to Hardships, lose by Degrees the very Notions of *Liberty*, they look upon themselves as Creatures at Mercy. . . . Hence proceeds that *Poverty* and *Lowness of Spirit*, to which a *Kingdom* may be subject as well as a *Particular Person*. And when *Esau came fainting from the Field at the Point to Die*, it is no wonder that he *Sold his Birth-Right for a Mess of Pottage*."[2] But Swift was realist enough to see that since no major change in England's Irish policy was possible, especially so long as it was directed by Walpole, the Irish should do what they could to help themselves; and he was moralist enough to believe that erring man had ultimately to be judged not as the helpless victim of his environment but as a free moral agent.

From Oliver W. Ferguson, *Jonathan Swift and Ireland* (Urbana: University of Illinois Press, 1962) 167–80. Reprinted by permission of the author and the University of Illinois Press.

[1] *Prose Works*, XII, 122; *Corr*, IV, 90.
[2] *Drapier's Letters*, p. 67. Cf. similar statements in *Corr*, IV, 328, and *Letters to Ford*, p. 86.

Liberty of the subject was a cardinal tenet of Swift's political philosophy, and the liberties of the Irish had been shamefully abrogated. This fact, however, only made the responsibility which the Irish owed to themselves and their country all the more obligatory. Swift shared Bishop Berkeley's opinion that liberty "is the greatest human blessing that a *virtuous* man can possess, and is very consistent with the duties of a good subject and a good Christian."[3] In his tracts to the people of Ireland, Swift constantly emphasized the duty of patriotism and equated it with virtue. In a sermon preached against Wood's halfpence, he told his congregation that the "love of our country, was in antient times properly known by the name of *Virtue*, because it was the greatest of all virtues, and was supposed to contain all virtues in it." In the first *Drapier's Letter* he told the people that it was their duty "next to your Duty to God, and the Care of your Salvation" to resist Wood's attempt on their liberty, and he appealed to them as "*Christians . . .* and as *Lovers of your Country.*" In another of his sermons, *Causes of the Wretched Condition of Ireland,* he granted that the people suffered from many disadvantages "not by our own faults," but he urged that they do what they could to remove "at least, some Part of these Evils."[4] The Irish were sorely tried, but this was no excuse for their own sins. The Injured Lady had been seduced, but she was no less a fallen woman.

In writing his various proposals and entreaties to the people of Ireland, Swift was fulfilling his own responsibility, the moral obligation of his calling: "The two principal Branches of Preaching, are first to tell the People what is their Duty; and then to convince them that it is so."[5] He wrote this statement in 1720, the year in which he first began telling the Irish people their duty. But even as he preached—in sermons and in pamphlets—the Irish persisted in the practices which had contributed to their ruin. The gentry continued to import luxuries and to neglect agriculture. The shopkeepers and common laborers continued in their knavish and slovenly ways. And at the very bottom of the economic scale, the beggars—more sinning than sinned against—continued to infest the country, their idleness and wretchedness representing in small the state of the whole nation: "As a great Part of our publick Miseries is originally owing to our own Faults . . . so I am confident, that among the meaner People, nineteen in twenty of those who are reduced to a starving Condition, did not become so by what Lawyers call the Work of God, either upon their Bodies or Goods; but meerly from their own Idleness, attended with all Manner of Vices, particularly Drunkenness, Thievery and Cheating."[6] Once—at the time of the halfpence crisis—the people had responded to the preacher's call; and if the victory which resulted was a limited one, it was at least a victory. But Wood and his bad copper had been a sudden and specific danger. Once the danger had passed, the coun-

---

[3]*The Works of George Berkeley,* VI, 70. The italics are mine.
[4]*Prose Works,* IX, 233; *Drapier's Letters,* p. 3; *Prose Works,* IX, 199 (for the probable date of the composition of this sermon, see p. 136).
[5]Ibid., IX, 70.
[6]Ibid., XIII, 135.

try lapsed into its old ways. The member of Parliament who had voted bold addresses to the Crown on the subject of the halfpence resumed his attitude of indifference to his country's good. The small tradesman who had signed a resolution refusing to accept Wood's coin in payments resumed his shabby dealings with his customers. The beggar who had helped burn Wood in effigy resumed his idle and unproductive way of life: "and so are all inevitably undone, which I have been telling them in print these ten years," Swift wrote to Pope in 1729, "to as little purpose as if it came from the pulpit."[7]

In the 1720 *Proposal*, Swift had asked, "Is there Vertue enough left in this deluded People to save them from the Brink of Ruin?"[8] By 1729 the people were indeed at the brink of ruin. "Melancholy Accounts" in the public prints told of "the greatest Extremities for want of Bread" which the northern farmers were suffering. Large numbers of unemployed weavers in Dublin were forced "to the Necessity of feeding on Grains, and Blood from the Slaughter-Houses," and they lived in such unsanitary conditions that the city feared an outbreak of plague. Tradesmen who had been men "of Repute and Credit" were now, with their wives and children, "a Curse to themselves and [a] heavy burthen to the Nation."[9] The author of *A Letter to the People of Ireland* (published in August, 1729) gave a moving account of the calamity which had crept on the people by degrees until it now affected even the middle classes: "We . . . see . . . our Publick Streets crowded with living Spectres, Bodys of our Species with half Life, rambling about for Sustenance, in the most miserable Condition human Nature can be reduc'd to. . . . Infinite are the numbers of these poor Wretches that . . . would be content with Death, as the only way to put an End to their Misery. . . . If they happen to hear of the Death of a Horse, they run to it as to a Feast."[10]

On October 23, 1729, the Irish Commons resolved itself into a committee of the whole to consider the state of the nation. Marmaduke Coghill was present, and he sent Secretary Southwell an account of the session. He noted particularly the speech made by Lt. Col. Alexander Montgomery, a member for County Donegal. It was an elaborate one, "of near an hour," on the causes of the present crisis. Montgomery discussed such topics as absenteeism, tillage, emigration, foreign imports (he made special mention of "the extravagance of the ladies"), and "our want of publick spirit." He enlarged on each of these heads, Coghill wrote, "but concluded without proposing any thing."[11]

It was in these circumstances, in the midst of superfluous reports and useless debates, that Swift offered the people of Ireland his *Modest Proposal*. On November 8, 1729, *The Dublin Intelligence* informed its readers that the "apparent spirit of patriotism . . . so abounding of late, has produced a new scheme, said in public to be written by D—— S——, wherein the author . . . advises that

[7]*Corr*, IV, 106.
[8]*Prose Works*, IX, 16–17.
[9]*The Monthly Chronicle*, pp. 2, 99; *The Dublin Intelligence*, April 29, 1729.
[10]*A Letter to the People of Ireland*, pp. 3–4. The tract is dated at the end, "Dublin, Aug. 28, 1729."
[11]Southwell Papers, B.M. Add. MSS 21, 122, fol. 88.

one fourth part of the infants under two years old, be forthwith fattened, brought to market and sold for food. . . ."[12] Swift had at last found a way to make applicable to Ireland the maxim that people are the riches of a nation.

A *Modest Proposal* grew out of a terrible anger, an anger of the kind one finds in Jeremiah: "Therefore I am full of the fury of the Lord; I am weary with holding in: I will pour it out upon the children abroad. . . ."; "And I will make this City desolate. . . . And I will cause them to eat the flesh of their sons and the flesh of their daughters." But if his anger is the same, Swift's tone in the *Modest Proposal* is not that of Jeremiah. Swift chose to speak in the voice, not of God's angry prophet, but of a well-meaning patriot who, like himself, had "been wearied out for many Years with offering vain, idle, visionary Thoughts" to the people of Ireland.[13] The "author" of the *Modest Proposal* is an economic projector who, after much study, has conceived of the perfect solution for Ireland's ills. Viewed from one angle, his plan was not altogether new; it was but the logical extension of a plea Swift had made unceasingly to the Irish since 1720: domestic consumption of domestic products.

In outlining, in the voice of his naïve persona, the advantages of this plan, Swift systematically condemned the landlords, the idle rich of both sexes, the Irish poor, Protestant dissenters, Papists, absentees, shopkeepers—in short, "the whole People of Ireland." The proposed commodity, the projector admits, will be "somewhat dear, and therefore very *proper for Landlords*; who, as they have already devoured most of the Parents, seem to have the best Title to the Children." But the benefits far outweigh the expense. Relations between the Squire and his tenants will improve enormously, since the Squire will be a regular customer and the tenants "will have something valuable of their own" with which to pay their rent.[14] The commodity will also be popular with the beau monde. The skins of the slaughtered infants will furnish elegant gloves for the ladies and boots for the gentlemen; and for all the gentlemen "who have any Refinement in Taste," a clever cook will be able to make the new delicacy "as expensive as they please." As for the ladies of fashion, although the projector is unwilling to adopt the "Refinement" on his scheme that the eligible age limit of the children be extended to fourteen, he confesses that Ireland would indeed benefit if it could thus destroy "several plump young girls in this Town, who . . . appear at the *Play-house*, and *Assemblies* in foreign Fineries, which they never will pay for."[15] Further, the scheme will decrease the number of Catholics in Ireland, thereby partially restoring the balance between Protestants and Catholics—a balance which was in danger of being upset by "so many good

---

[12]Ball (*Corr*, IV, 124, n. 3) and Davis (*Prose Works*, XII, xix) date the publication of *A Modest Proposal* in late October. This may be correct, but the advertisement in *The Dublin Intelligence* does not preclude the possibility of publication at any time during the first week in November. It was first reprinted in London on November 22 (see *The Monthly Chronicle*, p. 247).

[13]*Prose Works*, XII, 117. The substance of the following interpretation of *A Modest Proposal* first appeared in my article, "Swift's Saeva Indignatio and *A Modest Proposal*," *Philological Quarterly*, XXXVIII (1959), 473–479.

[14]*Prose Works*, XII, 112, 114–115.

[15]*Ibid.*, XII, 115, 114.

Protestants, who have chosen rather to leave their Country, than stay at home, and pay Tithes against their Conscience, to an idolatrous *Episcopal Curate.*"[16] And—as a peripheral benefit—the projector's proposal will have other than economic advantages for the Irish poor: it will teach them common humaneness. During his wife's pregnancy, a man will now curb his usual brutality for fear of causing a miscarriage, and the new economic value of children will decrease the number of abortions and infanticides—crimes committed "more to avoid the *Expense* than the *Shame.*"[17]

The projector's enumeration of the advantages of his plan is Swift's covert indictment of the Irish people. This indictment is made openly when the projector dismisses the "expedients" of other patriots. These expedients had been repeatedly urged by Swift and other writers. Like the proposal at hand, they were in Ireland's own power to implement. Not one of them even remotely applies to England's legislative or commercial tyranny in Ireland. The projector now refuses to regard them seriously, because the Irish people have always refused to do so. "Therefore," he exclaims, "let no man talk to me of other Expedients:

> *Of taxing our Absentees at five Shillings a Pound: Of using neither Cloaths, nor Houshold Furniture except what is of our own Growth and Manufacture: Of utterly rejecting the Materials and Instruments that promote foreign Luxury: Of curing the Expensiveness of Pride, Vanity, Idleness, and Gaming in our Women: Of introducing a Vein of Parsimony, Prudence and Temperance: Of Learning to love our Country, wherein we differ even from LAPLANDERS, and the Inhabitants of TOPINAMBOO: Of quitting our Animosities, and Factions; nor act any longer like the Jews, who were murdering one another at the very Moment their City was taken: Of being a little cautious not to sell our Country and Consciences for nothing: Of teaching Landlords to have, at least, one Degree of Mercy towards their Tenants. Lastly, Of putting a Spirit of Honesty, Industry, and Skill into our Shop-keepers; who, if a Resolution could now be taken to buy only our native Goods, would immediately unite to cheat and exact upon us in the Price, the Measure, and the Goodness; nor could ever yet be brought to make one fair Proposal of just Dealing, though often and earnestly invited to it.*
>
> THEREFORE I repeat, let no Man talk to me of these and the like Expedients; till he hath, at least, a Glimpse of Hope, that there will ever be some hearty and sincere Attempt to put *them in Practice.*[18]

Swift's use of what one scholar has called *le mythe animal*[19] in the *Modest Proposal* is more than an effective rhetorical device. It expresses a point of view

[16]*Ibid.,* XII, 114.

[17]*Ibid.,* XII, 110. Italics are mine.

[18]*Ibid.,* XII, 116–117. Swift's frustration at Ireland's rejection of these "expedients" is even more understandable when it is realized how long some of them had been urged. Unquestionably, Swift was recalling a passage from Sir William Temple's *Essay upon the Advancement of Trade in Ireland* (1673) at this point in *A Modest Proposal.* Temple wrote that for Ireland to preserve the little capital left in the country, it was essential "to introduce as far as can be, a vein of Parsimony throughout the Countrey in all things that are not perfectly the native growths and manufactures. . . . And . . . to force men to a degree of industry, by suffering none to hope that they shall be able to live by rapine or fraud" (p. 109).

[19]Emile Pons, *Swift: les années de jeunesse et le 'Conte du tonneau'* (Strasbourg, 1925), p. 395.

integral to Swift's judgment of Ireland. Swift is saying to the Irish, in effect, "You have acted like beasts; hence you no longer deserve the title of men." Some seven months before *A Modest Proposal* was published, this point of view was anticipated in Swift's *Letter to the Archbishop of Dublin*:

> I cannot reflect on the singular condition of this Country . . . without some Emotion, and without often examining as I pass the streets whether those animals which come in my way with two legs and human faces, clad, and erect, be of the same species with what I have seen very like them in England, as to the outward Shape, but differing in their notions, natures, and intellectualls more than any two kinds of Brutes in a forest, which any men of common prudence would immediately discover, by persuading them to define what they mean by Law, Liberty, Property, Courage, Reason, Loyalty or Religion.[20]

These animals the preacher had tried to show their duty; but their sloth and viciousness had defeated him. "I am . . . banished," he wrote to a friend in 1732, "to a country of slaves and beggars,—my blood soured, my spirits sunk, fighting with beasts like St. Paul, not at Ephesus, but in Ireland."[21]

It is *le mythe animal* that allows Swift to make the one proposal so singularly appropriate to this abandoned nation—cannibalism. The commodity is of "too tender a Consistence" to be exported to England; it is the Irish alone who are to commit the final barbarity, the last indignity to human reason. And the paradox of their position accounts for the ambivalence between pity and wrath which Swift shows in his pamphlet. The wretchedness that surrounds him *is* a "melancholly Object" to Swift—the strolling mothers with their children, the young laborers unable to find work, the aged dying "as fast as can be reasonably expected."[22] But the more melancholy the object, the greater his anger at the object itself. When he demonstrated in his proposal how children could be put to profitable use and when he explained that he would allow only one male for every four females of his livestock (because "these Children are seldom the Fruits of Marriage"[23]), he was merely showing the idle beggars of Ireland how to use their resources more efficiently than they were in fact already doing. "They exercise the greatest Barbarities upon Children," Dobbs wrote in his *Essay on Trade*, "either their own or those they pick up; by blinding them, or breaking and disjoynting their Limbs . . . to make them objects of compassion and charity. Not to mention their debauching the Girls when grown up; who go about Bigg-belly'd, pretending their Husbands are dead or sick, and they have them to maintain."[24] Swift saw the Irish people—whether impoverished or solvent—as at once victims and villains, devouring themselves by their own folly and selfishness.

---

[20]*Prose Works*, XII, 65.

[21]*Corr*, IV, 357.

[22]*Prose Works*, XII, 117, 109, 114.

[23]*Ibid.*, XII, 111. Swift's attack on the morals of the Irish poor is probably in reference to the marriages performed by "couple-beggars," Roman priests who officiated at clandestine—and from an Anglican point of view—illegal ceremonies. For an account of the practice, see Lecky, I, 382.

[24]Dobbs, pt. II, p. 45. There is no question of "influence" here. The second part of Dobbs's book was published in 1731.

That Swift adopted the technique of contemporary economists and "political arithmeticians" in *A Modest Proposal* should not obscure his intent.[25] He was not concerned with satirizing the proposals of other writers on Irish affairs. He was in general agreement with many of the suggestions of Molesworth, Prior, Dobbs, and Macaulay; and although he objected to specific projects of Maculla and Browne, he respected the authors' intentions. Whatever parody Swift employed in the *Modest Proposal* at the expense of such writers was to show their foolishness—like his own—in trying to help an indifferent Ireland. The rhetorical function of his ironic use of the economists' technique is to create a feeling of horror that will be commensurable with his terrible anger. Swift is not really so far removed from his ingenuous persona, for the projector's remedy for the Irish is a hyperbolic parallel to Swift's abandonment of them. In their conception of the Irish as beasts, Swift and the projector are one. The crucial difference is in their attitudes toward this conception: the projector's is economic; Swift's is moral. Consequently, Swift did not (as has been argued[26]) interrupt the projector in his own voice in the key "other Expedients" passage. The voice is the same, and the weary impatience with which these expedients are rejected is the same. And the one reference to England in the tract ("*I could name a Country, which would be glad to eat up our whole Nation*"[27]) is inconsistent not because Swift drowned out the projector's voice with his own, but because he momentarily diverted the direction of his attack.

In *A Modest Proposal*, ten years of warning and exhortation gave way to frustration and despair, and Swift directed the full weight of his wrath not against England, or callous economists, or visionary projectors, but against Ireland herself. Savage as this expression of his anger is, a passage in his *Answer to a Memorial* is even more terrible than any in *A Modest Proposal*:

> If so wretched a State of Things would allow it, methinks I could have a malicious Pleasure, after all the Warning I have in vain given the Publick . . . to see the Consequences and Events answering in every Particular. I pretend to no Sagacity: What I writ was little more than what I had discoursed to several Persons, who were generally of my Opinion: And it was obvious to every common Understanding, that such Effects must needs follow from such Causes. . . . *Wisdom crieth in the Streets; because I have called and ye refused; I have stretched out my Hand, and no Man regarded. But ye have set at nought all my Counsel, and would none of my Reproof. I also will laugh at your Calamity, and mock when your Fear cometh.*[28]

Here is the promise which Swift fulfilled in the day of Ireland's fear; and here, stripped of all irony and grounded in the authority of Scripture, is the moralist's judgment on the Irish people.

---

[25]Swift's awareness of the technique of "political arithmetic" is discussed in Louis Landa's "*A Modest Proposal* and Populousness," and in George Wittkowsky's "Swift's *Modest Proposal*: The Biography of an Early Georgian Pamphlet," *Journal of the History of Ideas*, IV (1943), 75–104.

[26]W. B. Ewald, *The Masks of Jonathan Swift* (Cambridge, Mass., 1954), pp. 171, 173.

[27]*Prose Works*, XII, 117.

[28]*Ibid.*, XII, 22–23.

II

In November, 1730, almost exactly a year after the publication of *A Modest Proposal,* Swift's economic projector was at work on another scheme. In revealing his newest project, Swift's persona is the same disinterested patriot, the same obtuse political arithmetician with a flair for statistics; and he still has his old fondness for the maxim that people are the riches of a nation. This time, however, his interest is not confined to the problems of Ireland's internal economy. He is by now sufficiently confident to discuss Anglo-Irish relations. While his earlier plan was offered for "the *publick Good*" of his country, this one is dedicated to the ideal of an Ireland living in perfect amity with England.[29] In showing the means to this "blessed End," the projector is again the unwitting instrument of Swift's satire. This time, the object of that satire is England.

The projector's renewed interest in public affairs was occasioned by an event that caused the administration in Ireland and the English government itself a great deal of embarrassment. Since the fall of Limerick, Irish soldiers had been leaving their country to serve in various armies on the Continent, especially in France and Spain. Over 12,000 of them had done so legally in 1691, under the military articles of the Treaty of Limerick. During the reign of Queen Anne, however, both the English and Irish Parliaments passed acts making it a capital crime to enlist in the service of a foreign prince, unless by special permission from the Crown. Despite this prohibition—and without the royal license—the "Wild Geese" continued to augment the armies of France and Spain throughout the first half of the eighteenth century.[30] In 1729, in response to repeated requests from the French government, George II promised the French ambassador to permit the recruiting of seven hundred and fifty Irishmen. According to an official letter sent to Lord Lieutenant Dorset, the King had acceded to the ambassador's request in the interest of "the strict alliance between the two Crowns."

George's promise caused much concern among the ministry. It was obvious that the authorized presence of French recruiting officers in Ireland would provoke a violent reaction both there and in England—in England, because the Tories and the antiministerial Whigs would label it as a particularly stupid piece of statecraft to augment the armies of Louis, strict alliances notwithstanding; in Ireland, because emigration was already a serious enough problem without this additional stimulus. George's advisers did the best they could in the face of these difficulties. Since the act of the Irish Parliament allowed foreign recruiting either under the royal sign manual or "under the hands of the Chief Governors of Ireland," Lord Chancellor Yorke advised that the King authorize the Irish lords justices to grant the license. Orders were accordingly sent to Dublin Castle, along with the superfluous suggestion that the recruiting be done as qui-

[29]*Ibid.,* XII, 118, 177.

[30]Williams, *The Whig Supremacy,* pp. 274–275; Lecky, I, 418–422; *The Statutes at Large* (Cambridge, 1765), 12 Anne 2, c. 11; and see the *Journals* of the Irish Commons for January 18, 1721.

etly as possible (without "Beat of Drum") and that the recruits be got out of Ireland before the English Parliament met. One of the letters to Dorset offered the feeble hope that since Ireland was losing so many Protestants through emigration, the recruiting scheme "might have the appearance of right policy, to diminish, on that account, the Number of the Popish Inhabitants."[31]

Colonel Hennecy, the French recruiting officer, arrived in Dublin on October 9, 1730. As Boulter and other Irish officials had feared, neither his presence nor the purpose of his visit could be kept quiet. Four days after the arrival of Hennecy and his staff, Faulkner's *Dublin Journal* reported that they had "dined last Sunday with his Excellency the Primate."[32] The recruiters behaved as discreetly as possible, but news of their mission made such "a great ferment" in Ireland and in England that Walpole, assuming the responsibility for George's blunder, admitted that the recruiting scheme had been a mistake. In December, Hennecy and his staff were recalled from Dublin.

The reaction to the affair had been much greater in England than in Ireland.[33] On November 7, *The Craftsman*, the opposition journal written by Pulteney and Bolingbroke, made a strong protest against the government's connivance in the scheme. One of the objections which the paper raised was that after the special license for this occasion had expired, the "poor, ignorant Wretches" in Ireland could be easily imposed upon in the future by unauthorized recruiting agents and thereby incur the penalties for high treason. This method of providing for the Irish Catholics, *The Craftsman* sardonically observed, "is indeed a little more charitable than a *late Project* for preventing *Irish Children* from being starv'd, by fatting them up, and selling them to the *Butcher*."[34] When Swift read this ironic acknowledgment from his friends, he decided to return the compliment in kind, by answering *The Craftsman* in the voice of his economic projector.

For all its importance as Swift's last major attack on England's treatment of Ireland, *The Answer to the Craftsman* seems to have been written for the private diversion of Swift and his friends in England. It was not published until 1758, but Faulkner (the first publisher) noted that the manuscript was sent to England "and handed about there."[35] It is possible that by the time Swift finished writing it, the French officers had been recalled and he therefore withheld publication, but this does not seem likely. *The Craftsman* had appeared on November 7, and Hennecy did not receive his orders to leave Dublin until late December.[36] The interval would have been time enough for Swift to write this relatively short piece. Swift was tired of fighting lost causes, but he could still divert himself with "follies, merely for amusement."[37]

[31]*S.P.D.* (P.R.O.) 63/391–393, *passim.*
[32]Boulter, II, 25; Faulkner's *Dublin Journal*, October 10–13, 1730.
[33]Boulter, II, 29–33, *passim.*
[34]*Prose Works*, XII, 317. This issue of *The Craftsman* is reprinted on pp. 311–321.
[35]*Ibid.*, XII, xxxi.
[36]Boulter, II, 32.
[37]*Corr*, IV, 194.

The Craftsman had attacked the "author" of *A Modest Proposal* at his most sensitive point: it had charged him with cruelty, and he prided himself upon his compassion. It is *The Craftsman*, and not himself, who shows a lack of charity—or rather, a lack of knowledge about conditions in Ireland—in opposing the plan to ship unwanted Irishmen out of the country: "PERHAPS Sir, You may not have heard of any Kingdom so unhappy as this, both in their Imports and Exports. . . . But now, when there is a most lucky Opportunity offered to begin a Trade, whereby this Nation will save many Thousand Pounds a Year, and *England* be a prodigious Gainer, you are pleased . . . to interpose with very frivolous Arguments." In the seventeenth century, England had forbidden Ireland to export live cattle, to the subsequent disadvantage of both kingdoms. Now *The Craftsman*, unwilling to learn from this past mistake, was urging a similar restraint on the export of live men.[38]

The projector (who boasts that he is a loyal Whig) makes it clear that he finds no fault with Ireland's legislative status. The English have every right to control Ireland's trade; and the Anglo-Irish "who conquered this Kingdom for them, ought, in Duty and Gratitude, to let them have the whole Benefit of that Conquest to themselves."[39] Any project, therefore, designed not only for England's benefit but for Ireland's as well, should win the approval of all loyal subjects. The benefits of the recruiting scheme are obvious. Ireland will be immediately relieved of a part of her manpower, her greatest liability. If foreign enlistments continue and if, as is likely, Spain should also request volunteers, Ireland might in time send off as many as six thousand natives annually—at a saving (based on the estimate that the maintenance of "a tall, hungry, Irish Man" comes to five pounds a year) of £30,000. And if France and Spain should ever some day be at war with each other, "what a Number of Friends would the Pretender lose, and what a Number of Popish Enemies all true Protestants get rid of." And as more and more Irishmen are transported to the Continent, more and more lands will be turned into pasture for the want of workers to till them, and England will thus get more of Ireland's wool and sell the Irish more grain.[40] The only weak point in this otherwise excellent scheme is that it does not go far enough or fast enough. The projector humbly offers a refinement. If the seventeen million acres of profitable land in Ireland were turned into pasture, it could be managed by sixty-seven thousand, two hundred graziers. Therefore, he proposes that *all* of Ireland he converted into one vast pasture, utterly depopulated except for an English army of occupation and the peasants needed to tend the livestock. The Irish will be forced to send their raw wool to England, and the English in turn will be *forced* to accept it "at their own Rates" and to supply Ireland with manufactured goods, again at their own rates. In this "new *Arcadia*," civil administration will be negligible, and in the place of money,

---

[38] *Prose Works*, XII, 173–174.
[39] *Ibid.*, XII, 177.
[40] *Ibid.*, XII, 174–175.

leather tokens (manufactured in England) will be used by the remaining inhabitants. Finally, the landlords will all be required to live in England, and as the native population of Shepherds increases annually, the surplus will be shipped "to whatever Prince will bear the Carriage," or be sent to the American colonies as a shield between the *English* settlers and the Indians.[41]

The Answer to the Craftsman was simply an ironic exaggeration of a suggestion made by Sir William Petty, the seventeenth-century statistician and economist. In his *Political Arithmetic* (which was in Swift's library[42]), Petty half seriously argued ("rather as a Dream or Resvery, than a rational Proposition") that England would become substantially richer and more powerful "if all the *moveables* and People of *Ireland* and of the Highlands of *Scotland*, were transported into the rest of *Great Brittain*."[43] *A Modest Proposal* had refuted, by ironic misapplication, the maxim that people are the riches of a nation. *The Answer to the Craftsman* refuted not only this maxim but four equally fundamental principles of economy: that a nation's exports should exceed its imports; that if goods had to be imported, they should be in raw condition, if at all possible; that a surplus of gold and silver should be maintained and increased; and that a country should promote sufficient tillage to answer its own needs. From an economic standpoint, *The Answer to the Craftsman* is really more shocking than *A Modest Proposal*, for it proposes not the slaughter of Irish children but the annihilation of Ireland herself. Together, the two proposals are Swift's final and most powerful condemnation of the English and the Irish for having created a nation in which such "Dreams or Resveries" seemed perfectly apposite.

[41]*Ibid.*, XII, 175–177, *passim.*

[42]It is item number 412 in Faulkner's catalog of Swift's library (see Harold Williams, *Dean Swift's Library* [Cambridge, 1932]).

[43]*The Economic Writings of Sir William Petty*, ed. Charles Henry Hull (Cambridge, 1899), I, 285–287. *Spectator* No. 200, an essay on the subject of "political arithmetic," refers to Petty's scheme.

Chronology of Important Dates

1660	Restoration of Charles II
1663–64	Samuel Butler, *Hudibras,* I and II
1667	Birth of Swift in Dublin on 30 November; birth of John Arbuthnot; Milton, *Paradise Lost* (1st edition); Thomas Sprat, *History of the Royal Society*
1670	Birth of William Congreve, (?) Bernard Mandeville
1671	Milton, *Paradise Regained, Samson Agonistes*
1672	Birth of Joseph Addison, Richard Steele; Buckingham and others, *Rehearsal*; Andrew Marvell, *Rehearsal Transpros'd* (Part II, 1673)
1673–82	Swift at school at Kilkenny
1674	Milton, *Paradise Lost* (2nd edition, in 12 books); death of Milton; Boileau, *Le Lutrin, L'Art Poétique.*
1675	William Wycherley, *The Country Wife*
1676	Thomas Shadwell, *The Virtuoso*
1678	John Bunyan, *Pilgrim's Progress*, I; Samuel Butler, *Hudibras,* III; Popish Plot; death of Andrew Marvell
1679	Birth of Thomas Parnell, poet and friend of Swift and Pope, and member of Scriblerus Club; death of Hobbes
1680	Death of Butler, Rochester, La Rochefoucauld; Sir Robert Filmer, *Patriarcha*; Rochester, *Poems*; Sir William Temple, *Miscellanea*, I
1681	Dryden, *Absalom and Achitophel*, I; John Oldham, *Satyrs upon the Jesuits*
1682–86	Swift attends Trinity College Dublin, B.A. *speciali gratia* 1686
1682	Dryden, *The Medall, Religio Laici, Mac Flecknoe, Absalom and Achitophel*, II; Sir William Petty, *Essay Concerning the Multiplication of Mankind; together with an Essay on Political Arithmetick* (see 1690)
1683	Rye House Plot; death of Oldham
1684	Bunyan, *Pilgrim's Progress*, II; Thomas Creech, trs Horace

1685	Death of Charles II, accession of James II; birth of John Gay and George Berkeley
1687	Newton, *Principia*; death of Buckingham, Waller
1688	Glorious Revolution: William of Orange invades England and ousts James II from throne; as civil war breaks out in Ireland, Swift leaves for England (perhaps early the following year); birth of Alexander Pope; death of Bunyan; Shadwell named Poet Laureate in succession to Dryden; Charles Perrault, *Parallèle des Anciens et des Modernes* (completed 1697)
1689	Swift given employment in Sir William Temple's household at Moor Park, near Farnham, Surrey; meets Esther Johnson (Stella), then eight years old; accession of William and Mary; John Locke, *First Letter on Toleration*; birth of Samuel Richardson
1690	James II defeated by William III in Ireland (Battle of the Boyne) and flees to France; Swift returns to Ireland in May; Temple, *Miscellanea,* II, includes "An Essay upon the Ancient and Modern Learning," which triggers Phalaris controversy (rev. 1692); Locke, *Two Treatises of Government, Essay Concerning Human Understanding* (enlarged 1694–1700); *Second Letter on Toleration*; Petty, *Political Arithmetick* (see 1682)
1691	Swift back in England in August, and returns to Moor Park
1692	Swift obtains M.A., Oxford; his first published work, "Ode to the Athenian Society"; Locke, *Third Letter on Toleration*; death of Shadwell
1693	Dryden, "Discourse Concerning Satire," prefixed to trs. of Juvenal and Persius; Locke, *Thoughts Concerning Education*
1694	Swift returns to Ireland, takes deacon's orders; William Wotton, *Reflections on Ancient and Modern Learning*; death of Mary II; founding of Bank of England; *Dictionary* of French Academy
1695	Swift ordained priest, becomes prebendary of Kilroot, near Belfast; Charles Boyle, ed., *Epistles of Phalaris*; Locke, *Reasonableness of Christianity, Vindication of the Reasonableness of Christianity* (second *Vindication*, 1697)
1696–99	Swift again at Moor Park, works on *A Tale of a Tub* and related works
1697	Richard Bentley, "Dissertation upon the *Epistles of Phalaris*" (in 2nd edn. of Wotton's *Reflections*, see 1694); birth of William Hogarth
1698	Boyle, *Dr. Bentley's Dissertations Examined*; Jeremy Collier, *Short View of the Immorality and Prophaneness of the English Stage* (controversy involving Congreve, Vanbrugh, Dryden and others continues for several years); William Molyneux, *The Case of Ireland . . . Stated*
1699	Swift returns to Ireland after Temple's death, becomes chaplain to Earl of Berkeley, Lord Justice of Ireland; Bentley, *Dissertation upon the Epistles of Phalaris, with an Answer to the Honourable Charles Boyle*; Sir Samuel Garth, *Dispensary*
1700	Swift becomes Vicar of Laracor, Co. Meath, and prebendary of St. Patrick's Cathedral, Dublin; death of Dryden; Temple, *Letters*, ed. Swift; Congreve, *Way of the World*

1701	Swift goes to England with Lord Berkeley; publishes *Contests and Dissensions in Athens and Rome*; Temple, *Miscellanea,* III, ed. Swift; death of James II
1702	Swift becomes D.D., Trinity College, Dublin; Defoe, *Shortest Way with the Dissenters*; death of William III, accession of Queen Anne
1703	Death of Samuel Pepys, Charles Perrault
1704	Swift, *Tale of a Tub, Battle of the Books,* and *Mechanical Operation of the Spirit*; Defoe, *Review,* started; battle of Blenheim; death of Locke
1705	Wotton, *Reflections upon Ancient and Modern Learning,* 3rd edn., with a *Defense of the Reflections* including "Observations upon *The Tale of a Tub*"; Mandeville, *The Grumbling Hive*
1706	Birth of Benjamin Franklin
1707	Union with Scotland; Swift writes "Story of the Injured Lady"; birth of Henry Fielding
1707–09	Swift in London on Church of Ireland business; meets Addision, Steele and other authors, writes tracts on political and ecclesiastical issues; begins friendship with Esther Vanhomrigh (Vanessa)
1708	Shaftesbury, *Letter Concerning Enthusiasm*
1708–09	Swift, *Bickerstaff Papers*
1709	Swift, *Project for the Advancement of Religion*; Pope, *Pastorals*; Temple, *Memoirs,* III, ed. Swift; Berkeley, *New Theory of Vision*; Steele starts *Tatler* with Swift's help and Swift's poem "A Description of the Morning" appears in No. 9; birth of Samuel Johnson
1710	Swift comes to London in September on behalf of Church of Ireland; meets Robert Harley, Tory head of government; appointed editor of pro-government paper, *The Examiner*; friends include Matthew Prior, John Arbuthnot and others; writes letters known as *Journal to Stella,* 1710–13; "A Description of a City Shower" appears in *Tatler,* No. 238; *Tale of a Tub,* 5th edn.; Berkeley, *Principles of Human Knowledge*
1710–14	Swift active as political journalist, writing for Tory government against Marlborough and Whig party; estrangement from Addison and Steele; friendship with Pope, Gay, Congreve, Arbuthnot, Parnell; close friendship with Vanessa
1711	Swift, *Miscellanies in Prose and Verse* (includes *Sentiments of a Church-of-England Man, Argument Against Abolishing Christianity*), *Conduct of the Allies*; Pope, *Essay on Criticism*; Addison and Steele start *Spectator,* to which Swift contributes; Shaftesbury, *Characteristics*; Harley becomes Earl of Oxford; birth of David Hume, death of Boileau
1712	Swift, *Proposal for Correcting the English Tongue*; Pope, *Rape of the Lock* (2-canto version); Arbuthnot, *History of John Bull*; Gay, *The Mohocks*
1713	Swift installed as Dean of St. Patrick's Cathedral, Dublin, and returns to London; founding of Scriblerus Club (including Swift, Pope, Arbuthnot, Gay,

Parnell, and Robert Harley, now Earl of Oxford); Swift, *Importance of the Guardian Considered*; Pope, *Windsor-Forest*; Gay, *Rural Sports*; Parnell, *Essay on the Different Styles of Poetry*; Addison, *Cato*; Steele, *Guardian, Englishman*; Anthony Collins, *Discourse of Free-Thinking*; Treaty of Utrecht ends War of Spanish Succession; birth of Sterne; death of Shaftesbury, Thomas Sprat

1714 Swift returns to Ireland after fall of Tory government and death of Queen Anne; Swift, *Mr. Collins's Discourse, Publick Spirit of the Whigs*; Pope, *Rape of the Lock* (5-canto version); Gay, *Shepherd's Week*; Mandeville, *Fable of the Bees* (expanded 1723); accession of George I

1715 First Jacobite Rebellion; impeachment of Earl of Oxford on charges of Jacobite intrigue; death of Louis XIV of France

1715–17 Walpole Chancellor of the Exchequer and "prime minister"

1715–20 Pope, trs. of *Iliad*, 6 vols.

1716 Gossip about possible secret marriage to Stella; Gay, *Trivia*; death of Wycherley

1717 Earl of Oxford released from impeachment on procedural grounds; Pope, *Works*; Gay, Pope and Arbuthnot, *Three Hours after Marriage*; Parnell, *Homer's Battle of the Frogs and Mice*

1718 Death of Parnell

1719 Defoe, *Robinson Crusoe*; death of Addison

1720 Swift, *Proposal for the Universal Use of Irish Manufacture; Letter to a Young Gentleman, Lately Entered into Holy Orders*; British House of Lords becomes ultimate court of appeal in Irish cases and British Parliament's right to legislate in Ireland asserted (Declaratory Act); South Sea Bubble

1721–42 Walpole prime minister

1721 Death of Matthew Prior

1722 Parnell, *Poems on Several Occasions*, ed. Pope; Defoe, *Journal of the Plague Year, Moll Flanders, Colonel Jack*

1723 Death of Vanessa

1724 Swift, *Drapier's Letters;* becomes known as Hibernian Patriot and government offers reward for "discovery" of Drapier; death of Earl of Oxford

1724–34 Gilbert Burnet, *History of My Own Times*

1725 Pope's edn. of Shakespeare (6 vols.)

1725–26 Pope's trs. of *Odyssey* (5 vols.)

1726 Swift travels to London for several months, stays with Pope, has unfruitful discussion of Irish affairs with Walpole; *Gulliver's Travels, Cadenus and Vanessa;* Lewis Theobald, *Shakespeare Restored; Craftsman* (opposition paper) started

1727 Swift's final visit to London; death of George I, accession of George II

1727–38 Gay, *Fables*

1728   Death of Stella, Swift writes "On the Death of Mrs. Johnson"; *Short View of the State of Ireland;* Swift and Thomas Sheridan, *Intelligencer;* Pope, *Dunciad* (3-book version), dedicated to Swift; Gay, *Beggar's Opera*

1728–37   Henry Fielding's career as playwright, over twenty plays acted and published

1729   Swift, *Modest Proposal;* Pope, *Dunciad Variorum;* death of Congreve, Steele

1730   Colley Cibber, Poet Laureate

1731   Swift writes *Verses on the Death of Dr. Swift* (published 1739) and several of the so-called "scatological poems"; Pope, *Epistle to Burlington;* death of Defoe

1732   Pope, *Epistle to Bathurst;* death of Gay

1733   Swift, *On Poetry: A Rapsody, Epistle to a Lady;* Pope, *Epistle to Cobham;* death of Mandeville

1733–34   Pope, *Essay on Man, First Satire of the Second Book of Horace, Imitated*

1735   Swift, *Works,* Dublin (4 volumes; volume 3 includes revised version of *Gulliver's Travels*); Pope, *Epistle to Dr. Arbuthnot, Epistle to a Lady;* death of Arbuthnot

1736   Swift, *The Legion Club,* attacking members of Irish Parliament

1737   Swift, *A Proposal for Giving Badges to the Beggars;* Stage Licensing Act

1738   Swift, *Complete Collection of Genteel and Ingenious Conversation;* Pope, *Epilogue to the Satires;* Samuel Johnson, *London*

1739   Swift, *Verses on the Death of Dr. Swift* published

1739–40   Hume, *Treatise of Human Nature*

1740   Richardson, *Pamela;* Colley Cibber, *Apology for his Life;* birth of James Boswell

1741   Arbuthnot, Pope and others, *Memoirs of Martinus Scriblerus;* Fielding, *Shamela*

1741–42   Hume, *Essays*

1742   Swift declared "of unsound mind and memory"; Pope, *New Dunciad* (Book IV of *Dunciad*); Fielding, *Joseph Andrews;* Walpole resigns all offices, is pensioned and created Earl of Orford

1743   Pope, *Dunciad* (4-book version, with Cibber replacing Theobald as hero); Fielding, *Miscellanies,* 3 vols. (includes *Jonathan Wild*)

1744   Death of Pope, Theobald

1745   Death of Swift, 19 October; Swift, *Directions to Servants;* death of Walpole

Notes on Contributors

ROBERT C. ELLIOTT taught at the University of California, San Diego. He is the author of *The Power of Satire* (1960), *The Shape of Utopia* (1970) and *The Literary Persona* (1982).

RICHARD FEINGOLD is Professor of English at the University of California, Berkeley. He is the author of *Nature and Society: Later Eighteenth-Century Uses of the Pastoral and Georgic* (1978) and *Moralized Song: The Character of Augustan Lyricism* (1989).

OLIVER FERGUSON is Professor Emeritus of English at Duke University. He compiled the entries on Swift in the *New Cambridge Bibliography of English Literature*, and is the author of *Jonathan Swift and Ireland* (1962), and of articles on Swift and other eighteenth-century authors.

IAN HIGGINS teaches English Literature at the Australian National University. He is the author of *Swift's Politics: A Study in Disaffection* (1994).

JOHN LAWLOR is Professor Emeritus of English at the University of Keele. His books include *The Tragic Sense in Shakespeare* (1960), *Piers Plowman* (1962) and *Chaucer* (1968). He is the editor of *Patterns of Love and Courtesy: Essays in Memory of C. S. Lewis* (1966).

MICHAEL MCKEON teaches English Literature at Rutgers University. He is the author of *Politics and Poetry in Restoration England* (1975) and *The Origins of the English Novel* (1987).

JENNY MEZCIEMS is a Senior Lecturer in English Literature at the University of Warwick. She is the author of numerous articles on Swift and the Utopian literary tradition, and is currently completing a study of *Gulliver's Travels* and a book on Swift.

A.D. NUTTALL is Professor of English at the University of Oxford and a Fellow of New College. His many books include *A New Mimesis* (1983), *Pope's Essay on Man* (1984), *The Stoic in Love: Selected Essays on Literature and Ideas* (1989), and *Openings: Narrative Beginnings from the Epic to the Novel* (1992).

DOUGLAS LANE PATEY is Professor of English at Smith College. He is the author of *Probability and Literary Form* (1984), and is now working on a study of disciplinary divisions among the arts and sciences in the eighteenth century.

CLAUDE RAWSON is the George M. Bodman Professor of English at Yale University and Chairman of the Yale Boswell Editions. His books include *Henry Fielding and the Augustan Ideal under Stress* (1972, 1991), *Gulliver and the Gentle Reader* (1973, 1991),

Order from Confusion Sprung: Studies in Eighteenth-Century Literature (1985, 1992), and *Satire and Sentiment 1660–1830* (1994).

CHRISTINE REES teaches English Literature at King's College, University of London. She is the author of *The Judgment of Marvell* (1989).

MICHAEL SEIDEL teaches at Columbia University. His books include *Satiric Inheritance: Rabelais to Sterne* (1979), and *Exile and the Narrative Imagination* (1986).

JOHN F. TINKLER teaches Rhetoric at the University of Virginia and has held several visiting positions at the University of California, Berkeley. He has published numerous articles on Renaissance humanism, rhetorical criticism and the history of rhetoric.

MARCUS WALSH is a Senior Lecturer in English at the University of Birmingham. He is editor, with Karina Williamson, of the *Poetical Works of Christopher Smart*, (1980–   ), and with Ian Small, of a collection of essays on *The Theory and Practice of Text-Editing* (1991), and author of articles on Swift, Johnson and Sterne, on the history and theory of editing and on eighteenth-century biblical scholarship.

PENELOPE WILSON is a Fellow and Senior Tutor at New Hall, Cambridge. She studied English and Greek at the Universities of Edinburgh and Oxford. She has published articles on Pindar, on eighteenth-century classical reading, and on Pope and other eighteenth-century authors, and is currently working on a book on poetic commentary.

Bibliography

Bibliographical Aids

Berwick, Donald M. *The Reputation of Jonathan Swift, 1781–1882.* 1941. Reprinted New York: Haskell, 1965.

Landa, Louis A., and Tobin, James Edward. *Jonathan Swift. A List of Critical Studies Published from 1895 to 1945.* 1945. Reprint. New York: Octagon Books, 1975.

Rodino, Richard H. *Swift Studies, 1965–1980. An Annotated Bibliography.* New York, Garland, 1984.

Stathis, James J. *A Bibliography of Swift Studies 1945–1965.* Nashville, Tenn.: Vanderbilt University Press, 1967.

Teerink, H., and Scouten, Arthur H. *A Bibliography of the Writings of Jonathan Swift.* 2d ed. Philadelphia: University of Pennsylvania Press, 1963.

Vieth, David M. *Swift's Poetry 1900–1980. An Annotated Bibliography of Studies.* New York: Garland, 1982.

Voigt, Milton. *Swift and the Twentieth Century.* Detroit, Mich.: Wayne State University Press, 1964.

Williams, Harold. *Dean Swift's Library.* Cambridge: Cambridge University Press, 1932.

Concordances

Shinagel, Michael. *A Concordance to the Poems of Jonathan Swift.* Ithaca, New York: Cornell University Press, 1972.

Kelling, Harold D., and Preston, Cathy Lynn. *A KWIC Concordance to Jonathan Swift's A Tale of a Tub, etc.* New York: Garland, 1984.

Modern Editions

Correspondence. Edited by Harold Williams. 5 vols. Oxford: Clarendon Press, 1963–65.

Poems. Edited by Harold Williams. 3 vols. 2d ed. Oxford: Clarendon Press, 1958; *Collected Poems* edited by Joseph Horrell, 2 vols. London: Routledge, 1958; *Poetical Works,* edited by Herbert Davis. Oxford Standard Authors. London: Oxford University Press, 1967; *Complete Poems,* edited by Pat Rogers. Harmondsworth: Penguin, and New Haven: Yale, 1983 (best annotated edition); *Selected Poems,* ed. Pat Rogers, Harmondsworth, 1992.

Prose Works. Edited by Herbert Davis et al. 16 vols. Oxford: Blackwell, 1939–74. Vol. 14,

Index by Irvin Ehrenpreis and others; vols. 15–16, *Journal to Stella*, ed. Harold Williams. Standard edn. Mainly unannotated. Important introductions.

The Writings of Jonathan Swift. Edited by Robert A. Greenberg and William Bowman Piper. Critical Edition Series. New York: Norton, 1973. Best one-volume selection.

Swift's Irish Pamphlets: An Introductory Selection. Ed. Joseph McMinn. Gerrards Cross: C. Smythe, 1991.

Individual Works

A Discourse of the Contests and Dissentions Between the Nobles and the Commons in Athens and Rome. Edited by Frank H. Ellis. Oxford: Clarendon Press, 1967. Annotated.

The Drapier's Letters. Edited by Herbert Davis. Oxford: Clarendon Press, 1935. Annotated.

An Enquiry into the Behaviour of the Queen's Last Ministry. Edited by Irvin Ehrenpreis. Bloomington: Indiana University Press, 1956. Annotated.

Gulliver's Travels. The Text of the First Edition. Edited by Harold Williams. London: First Edition Club, 1926.

Gulliver's Travels. Introduction by Michael Foot, edited by Peter Dixon and John Chalker. Harmondsworth: Penguin, 1967; edited by Robert A. Greenberg. Critical Edition Series (revised). New York: Norton, 1970; edited by Louis A. Landa. London: Methuen, 1965, reprint of the Riverside edition, Boston: Houghton Mifflin, 1960.

Gulliver's Travels. Edited by Paul Turner. London: Oxford University Press, 1971. Best annotated edition.

The Intelligencer, ed. James Woolley. Oxford: Clarendon Press, 1992.

Journal to Stella. Edited by Harold Williams. 2 vols. Oxford: Clarendon Press. Reprinted as vols. 15 and 16 of *Prose Works*, above.

Memoirs of Martinus Scriblerus (with Pope et al.). Edited by Charles Kerby-Miller. New Haven: Yale University Press, 1950. Annotated.

A Modest Proposal. Edited by Charles Beaumont. Merrill Literary Casebook. Columbus: Charles E. Merrill Publishing Company, 1969.

Polite Conversation. Edited by Eric Partridge. London: Deutsch, 1963. Annotated.

Swift vs. Mainwaring: The Examiner and the Medley. Edited by Frank H. Ellis. Oxford: Clarendon Press, 1985. Annotated.

A Tale of a Tub. Edited by A.C. Guthkelch and D. Nichol Smith. 2nd ed. Oxford: Clarendon Press, 1958. Annotated.

General Studies, Biographical and Critical

Brown, Norman O. "The Excremental Vision", *Life Against Death: The Psychoanalytical Meaning of History*, London: Routledge and Kegan Paul, 1959.

Bullitt, John M. *Jonathan Swift and the Anatomy of Satire: A Study of Satiric Technique*. Cambridge, MA: Harvard University Press, 1953.

Carnochan, W.B. *Confinement and Flight: An Essay on English Literature of the Eighteenth Century*. Berkeley: University of California Press, 1977.

Castle, Terry. "Why the Houyhnhnms Don't Write: Swift, Satire and the Fear of the Text", *Essays in Literature*, VII.1 (1980), 31–44.

Craik, Henry. *The Life of Jonathan Swift*. 2d ed. 2 vols. London, 1894.

Davis, Herbert. *Jonathan Swift. Essays on His Satire and Other Studies*. New York: Oxford University Press, 1964.

Donoghue, Denis. *Jonathan Swift. A Critical Introduction*. Cambridge: Cambridge University Press, 1969.

Ehrenpreis, Irvin. *Literary Meaning and Augustan Values*. Charlottesville: Univ. Press of Virginia, 1974.

Ehrenpreis, Irvin. *The Personality of Jonathan Swift*. London: Methuen, 1958.

Ehrenpreis Irvin. *Swift: The Man, His Works, and the Age*. Vol. 1: *Mr. Swift and His Contemporaries*. London: Methuen, 1962. Vol. 2: *Dr. Swift*. London: Methuen, 1967. Vol. 3: *Dean Swift*. London: Methuen, 1983.

Elliott, Robert C. *The Power of Satire*. Princeton, NJ: Princeton University Press, 1960.

Elliott, Robert C. *The Literary Persona*. Chicago: University of Chicago Press, 1982.

Fabricant, Carole. *Swift's Landscape*. Baltimore and London: Johns Hopkins University Press, 1982.

Flynn, Carol Houlihan. *The Body in Swift and Defoe*. Cambridge: Cambridge University Press, 1990.

Higgins, Ian. "Swift and Sparta: The Nostalgia of *Gulliver's Travels*", *Modern Language Review* 78 (1983), 513–31.

Johnson, Samuel. "Swift." In *Lives of the English Poets*.

Kelly, Ann Cline. *Swift and the English Language*. Philadephia: University of Pennsylvania Press, 1988.

Landa, Louis A. *Essays in Eighteenth-Century Literature*. Princeton, NJ: Princeton University Press, 1980.

Leavis, F.R. "The Irony of Swift." In *The Common Pursuit*. London: Chatto, 1952; Harmondsworth: Penguin, 1962. Essay frequently reprinted in collections of critical essays on Swift.

Levine, Joseph M. *The Battle of the Books: History and Literature in the Augustan Age*. Ithaca and London: Cornell University Press, 1991.

Levine, Joseph M. *Dr. Woodward's Shield: History, Science, and Satire in Augustan England*. Berkeley, Los Angeles and London: University of California Press, 1977.

Mack, Maynard. *"Collected in Himself": Essays, Critical, Biographical, and Bibliographical on Pope and Some of his Contemporaries*. Newark, DE: University of Delaware Press, 1982.

Paulson, Ronald. *The Fictions of Satire*. Baltimore, MD: Johns Hopkins Press, 1967.

Price, Martin. "Pope, Swift and the Past", *Studies in the Eighteenth Century* 5, ed. J.P. Hardy and J.C. Eade. Oxford: The Voltaire Foundation, 1983, pp. 19–31.

Price, Martin. "Swift in the Interpreter's House", *Satire in the 18th Century*, ed. J.D. Browning. New York: Garland, 1983, pp. 100–115.

Price, Martin. *Swift's Rhetorical Art*. New Haven: Yale University Press, 1953; Carbondale: Southern Illinois University Press Arcturus paperback, 1973.

Price, Martin. *To the Palace of Wisdom: Studies in Order and Energy from Dryden to Blake*. Garden City, NY: Doubleday, 1964.

Quintana, Ricardo. *The Mind and Art of Jonathan Swift*. 1936. Reprint, Gloucester, MA: Peter Smith, 1965.

Quintana, Ricardo. *Swift: An Introduction*. London: Oxford University Press, 1955. The best short introductory book, reliable and lively.

Quintana, Ricardo. *Two Augustans: John Locke, Jonathan Swift*. Madison: University of Wisconsin Press, 1978.

Rawson, Claude. "Cannibalism and Fiction: Reflections on Narrative Form and 'Extreme' Situations. Part I: Satire and the Novel (Swift, Flaubert and Others)". *Genre*, 10 (1977), 667–711.

Rawson, Claude. *Gulliver and the Gentle Reader: Studies in Swift and Our Time*. London: Routledge, 1973; paperback, Humanities Press: New Jersey and London, 1991.

Rawson, Claude. *Order from Confusion Sprung: Studies in Eighteenth-Century Literature from Swift to Cowper*. London: Allen and Unwin, 1985; paperback, New Jersey and London: Humanities Press, 1992.

Rawson, Claude. *Satire and Sentiment 1660–1830*. Cambridge: Cambridge University Press, 1994.

Rogers, Pat. *Grub Street. Studies in a Subculture*. London: Methuen, 1972; abridged as *Hacks and Dunces: Pope, Swift, and Grub Street*. London: Methuen, 1980.

Rosenheim, Edward W. *Swift and the Satirist's Art*. Chicago: University of Chicago Press, 1963.

Sams, Henry. "Swift's Satire of the Second Person". *ELH*, 26 (1959), 36–44.

Selby, Hopewell R. "The Cell and the Garret: Fictions of Confinement in Swift's Satires and Personal Writings". *Studies in Eighteenth-Century Culture*, 6 (1977), 133–56.

Selby, Hopewell R. " 'Never Finding Full Repast': Satire and Self-Extension in the Early Eighteenth Century", *Probability, Time, and Space in Eighteenth-Century Literature*, ed. Paula R. Backscheider. New York: AMS Press, 1979, pp. 217–47.

Steele, Peter. *Jonathan Swift, Preacher and Jester*. Oxford: Clarendon Press, 1978.

Strang, Barbara. "Swift and the English Language: A Study in Principles and Practice." In *To Honor Roman Jakobson*. The Hague and Paris: Mouton de Gruyter, 1967. III. 1947–59.

Thackeray, W.M. "Swift." In *English Humorists of the Eighteenth Century*. London, 1853. The best-known and most controversial nineteenth-century discussion.

Traugott, John. "Swift's Allegory: The Yahoo and the Man-of-Mode", *University of Toronto Quarterly*, 33 (1963), 1–18.

Ward, David. *Jonathan Swift: An Introductory Essay*. London: Methuen, 1973.

Williams, Kathleen. *Jonathan Swift and the Age of Compromise*. London: Constable, 1959.

Williams, Kathleen, ed. *Swift: The Critical Heritage*. London: Routledge, 1970. Collection of early criticism of Swift.

Wood, Nigel. *Swift*. Harvester New Readings. Brighton: Harvester, 1986.

Wyrick, Deborah B. *Jonathan Swift and the Vested Word*. Chapel Hill: University of North Carolina Press, 1988.

Zimmerman, Everett. *Swift's Narrative Satires: Author and Authority*. Ithaca: Cornell University Press, 1983.

Collections of Essays
(excluding volumes devoted to single works)

Donoghue, Denis, ed. *Jonathan Swift. A Critical Anthology*. Harmondsworth: Penguin, 1971. The best single collection of essays; includes an historical section with comments from Swift's time to 1934, followed by a section entitled "Modern Views," including

George Orwell, "Politics vs. Literature: An Examination of *Gulliver's Travels*," J.C. Beckett, "Swift as an Ecclesiastical Statesman," R.S. Crane, "The Houyhnhnms, the Yahoos, and the History of Ideas," and extended pieces by Louis A. Landa, Norman O. Brown, Irvin Ehrenpreis, Herbert Davis, Robert M. Adams, Ronald Paulson, Hugh Kenner, Geoffrey Hill, Denis Donoghue, A.E. Case, C.J. Rawson, Hugh Sykes Davies.

Jeffares, A. Norman, ed. *Swift: Modern Judgments*. London: Macmillan, 1968. Reprints F.R. Leavis's important essay, "The Irony of Swift," George Orwell's essay "Politics vs. Literature," Marjorie Nicolson and Nora M. Mohler's "The Scientific Background of Swift's 'Voyage to Laputa'," and other essays.

Jeffares, A. Norman, ed. *Fair Liberty Was All His Cry: A Tercentenary Tribute*. London: Macmillan, 1967. A larger book than the preceding one, reprinting many essays, notably Leavis's, Orwell's, and Nicolson's and Mohler's, as above; part of Yeats's introduction to his play about Swift, *The Words upon the Window-Pane*; and J.C. Beckett's important article of 1949, "Swift as an Ecclesiastical Statesman." There are also a survey by Ricardo Quintana and a checklist by Claire Lamont of writings about Swift from 1945 to 1965.

McHugh, Roger, and Edwards, Philip. *Jonathan Swift 1667–1967: A Dublin Tercentenary Tribute*, Dublin: Dolmen Press, and Oxford: Oxford University Press, 1967 (essays by Herbert Davis, Irvin Ehrenpreis, Louis A. Landa, Ricardo Quintana, Austin Clarke, George P. Mayhew and others; a little known book of exceptional interest).

Probyn, Clive T., ed. *The Art of Jonathan Swift*. London: Vision Press, 1978. A collection of new essays, including W.B. Carnochan, "The Consolations of Satire" (on the poems); essays by Angus Ross and J.A. Downie on the Irish and English political writings; David Woolley on the Armagh copy of *Gulliver's Travels*; Jenny Mezciems, "Gulliver and Other Heroes"; and essays by David Nokes, Clive T. Probyn, and Pat Rogers.

Rawson, Claude, ed. *The Character of Swift's Satire: A Revised Focus*. Newark, DE: University of Delaware Press, and London: Associated University Presses, 1983. Essays by John Traugott, F.P. Lock, J.C. Beckett, Richard Feingold, Pat Rogers, Jenny Mezciems, Ricardo Quintana, Ian Watt and Claude Rawson.

Rawson, Claude, ed. *English Satire and the Satiric Tradition*. Oxford: Blackwell, 1984: reprinted from *Yearbook of English Studies*, 14 (1984). Essays on *Gulliver's Travels* by John Traugott and William S. Anderson.

Rawson, Claude, and Mezciems, Jenny, eds. *Pope, Swift and their Circle*: Special Number, *Yearbook of English Studies*, 18 (1988); includes new essays on Swift by Denis Donoghue ("Swift and the Association of Ideas"), Daniel Eilon ("Swift's Satiric Logic"), Pat Rogers ("Swift's Poem on the Bubble"), A.D. Nuttall ("Gulliver Among the Horses"), Margaret Anne Doody ("Swift Among the Women"), Bertrand Goldgar ("Swift and the Later Fielding") , Brean S. Hammond ("Scriblerian Self-Fashioning").

Schakel, Peter J., ed. *Critical Approaches to Teaching Swift*. New York: AMS Press, 1992 (essays by Joseph McMinn, Frederik N. Smith, John Traugott, A.B. England, Deborah Baker Wyrick, Ellen Pollak, Michael DePorte, Edward W. Rosenheim, Claude Rawson and others).

Traugott, John, ed. *Discussions of Jonathan Swift*. Boston: D.C. Heath, 1962. Reprints extracts from Johnson's *Life*; Thackeray's *English Humorists*; W.B.C. Watkins's *Perilous Balance*; the whole of Leavis's and Orwell's essays; part of Yeats's introduction to *The Words upon the Window-Pane*; Norman O. Brown's important Freudian reading from his *Life Against Death*; J.C. Beckett's "Swift as an Ecclesiastical Statesman"; and useful discussions by A.E. Dyson, Martin Price, and A.E. Case. One of the best paperback collections.

Tuveson, Ernest, ed. *Swift: a Collection of Critical Essays*. Englewood Cliffs, NJ: Prentice-Hall, 1964. One of the best paperback collections, reprinting Leavis, Brown, and Joseph Horrell's "What Gulliver Knew," Ricardo Quintana's "Situational Satire," John Traugott on Swift and Thomas More, and good pieces by Maynard Mack, Ernest Tuveson, and others.

Vickers, Brian, ed. *The World of Jonathan Swift*. Oxford: Blackwell, 1968. An expensive hardback, mostly of new essays, but reprinting a 1967 essay on Swift's politics by W.A. Speck and a 1966 essay by Herbert Davis on Swift's irony. Important new pieces are Pat Rogers, "Swift and the Idea of Authority," essays on the poems by Roger Savage and Geoffrey Hill, and Brian Vickers on Swift and Thomas More.

A Tale of a Tub

Adams, Robert M. "The Mood of the Church and *A Tale of a Tub*." In *England in the Restoration and Early Eighteenth Century*, edited by H.T. Swedenberg, Jr. Berkeley and Los Angeles: University of California Press, 1972, pp. 71–99.

Clark, John R. *Form and Frenzy in Swift's "Tale of a Tub"*. Ithaca, NY: Cornell University Press, 1970.

Harth, Phillip. *Swift and Anglican Rationalism: The Religious Background of "A Tale of a Tub"*. Chicago: University of Chicago Press, 1961.

Josipovici, Gabriel. "A Tale of a Tub", *The World and the Book* (1971). St. Albans: Paladin, 1973, pp. 161–66.

Levine, Joseph M. *The Battle of the Books* (see General Studies).

Lund, Roger. "Strange Complicities: Atheism and Conspiracy in *A Tale of a Tub*". *Eighteenth Century Life*, 13.3 (1989), 34–58.

Kenner, Hugh. *The Stoic Comedians: Flaubert, Joyce, and Beckett*. Berkeley, Los Angeles and London: University of California Press, 1962.

Paulson, Ronald. *Theme and Structure in Swift's "Tale of a Tub"*. New Haven: Yale University Press, 1960.

Rogers, Pat. *Grub Street* (see General Studies).

Smith, Frederik N. *Language and Reality in Swift's "A Tale of a Tub"*. Columbus: Ohio State University Press, 1979.

Starkman, Miriam K. *Swift's Satire on Learning in "A Tale of a Tub"*. Princeton: Princeton University Press, 1950. Reprinted New York: Octagon Books, 1968.

Traugott, John. "*A Tale of a Tub*," *Focus: Swift*, ed. Claude Rawson. London: Sphere Books, 1971, rptd. in *The Character of Swift's Satire: A Revised Focus*, ed. Rawson (see Collections of Essays).

Politics and the Church in England and Ireland

Beckett, J.C. *Confrontations: Studies in Irish History*. London: Faber and Faber, 1972. Includes "Swift: The Priest in Politics" and some historical studies in Swift's period.

Beckett, J.C. "Swift and the Anglo-Irish Tradition", in *Focus: Swift*, ed. Claude Rawson. London: Sphere Books, 1971; rptd. in *The Character of Swift's Satire: A Revised Focus*, ed. Rawson (see Collections of Essays).

Beckett, J.C. "Swift as an Ecclesiastical Statesman." In *Essays in British and Irish History in Honour of James Eadie Todd*, edited by H.A. Cronne, T. W. Moody, and D.B. Quinn. London: Muller, 1949.

Cook, Richard I. *Jonathan Swift as a Tory Pamphleteer*. Seattle: University of Washington Press, 1967.

Downie, J.A. *Robert Harley and the Press: Propaganda and Public Opinion in the Age of Swift and Defoe*. Cambridge: Cambridge University Press, 1979.

Downie, J.A. *Jonathan Swift: Political Writer*. London: Routledge, 1984.

Ehrenpreis, Irvin. *Acts of Implication: Suggestion and Covert Meaning in the Works of Dryden, Swift, Pope, and Austen*. Berkeley: University of California Press, 1980. Essay on Swift deals with *Examiner* and *Drapier's Letters*.

Ferguson, Oliver W. *Jonathan Swift and Ireland*. Urbana: University of Illinois Press, 1962.

Foot, Michael. *The Pen and the Sword*. London: MacGibbon and Kee, 1957.

Goldgar, Bertrand A. *The Curse of Party: Swift's Relations with Addison and Steele*. Lincoln: University of Nebraska Press, 1961.

Goldgar, Bertrand A. *Walpole and the Wits: The Relation of Politics to Literature, 1722–1742*. Lincoln: University of Nebraska Press, 1976.

Higgins, Ian. *Swift's Politics: A Study in Disaffection*. Cambridge: Cambridge University Press, 1994.

Kramnick, Isaac. *Bolingbroke and His Circle: The Politics of Nostalgia in the Age of Walpole*. Cambridge, MA: Harvard University Press, 1968.

Landa, Louis A. *Swift and the Church of Ireland*. Oxford: Clarendon Press, 1954.

Lein, Clayton D. "Jonathan Swift and the Population of Ireland." *Eighteenth-Century Studies* 8 (1975): 431–53.

Lock, F.P. *Swift's Tory Politics*. London: Duckworth, and Newark: University of Delaware Press, 1983.

Molyneux, William. *The Case of Ireland Stated (1698)*. Introduction and afterword by J.G. Simms and Denis Donoghue. Dublin: Cadenus Press, 1977. Important source of Swift's thinking on the constitutional status of Ireland.

Moore, John Robert. "Was Jonathan Swift a Moderate?", *South Atlantic Quarterly*, 53 (1954), 260–67.

Rawson, Claude. " 'Indians' and Irish: Montaigne, Swift, and the Cannibal Question", *Modern Language Quarterly*, 53 (1992), 299–363.

Rawson, Claude. "The Injured Lady and the Drapier: A Reading of Swift's Irish Tracts," *Prose Studies* 3 (1980): 15–43.

Rawson Claude. "A Reading of *A Modest Proposal*." In *Augustan Worlds. Essays in Honour of A.R. Humphreys*, edited by J.C. Hilson, M.M.B. Jones and J.R. Watson. Leicester: Leicester University Press, 1978. Reprinted in *Order from Confusion Sprung* (see General Studies above).

Rogers, Pat. "Swift and Bolingbroke on Faction", *Journal of British Studies*, IX.2 (1970), 71–101.

Poems

Barnett, Louise K. *Swift's Poetic Worlds*. Newark: University of Delaware Press, 1982.

Brown, Norman O., "The Excremental Vision" (see General Studies).

England, A.B. *Energy and Order in the Poetry of Swift*. Lewisburg, PA: Bucknell University Press, 1980.

Fischer, John Irwin. *On Swift's Poetry*. Gainesville: University Presses of Florida, 1978.

Fischer, John Irwin, and Mell, Donald C., eds. *Contemporary Studies in Swift's Poetry*. Newark: University of Delaware Press, 1981.

Jaffe, Nora Crow. *The Poet Swift*. Hanover, NH: University Press of New England, 1977.

Johnson, Maurice. *The Sin of Wit: Jonathan Swift as a Poet*. Syracuse, NY: Syracuse University Press, 1950. Still the standard introduction.

Pollak, Ellen. *The Poetics of Sexual Myth: Gender and Ideology in the Verse of Swift and Pope*. Chicago: University of Chicago Press, 1983.

Rawson, Claude. " 'I the Lofty Stile Decline': Self-Apology and the 'Heroick Strain' in Some of Swift's Poems". In *The English Hero*, ed. Robert Folkenflik. Newark, DE: University of Delaware Press, 1982.

Rawson, Claude. "The Nightmares of Strephon: Nymphs of the City in the Poems of Swift, Baudelaire, Eliot." In *English Literature and the Age of Disguise*, edited by Maximillian E. Novak. Berkeley: University of California Press, 1977. Reprinted in *Order from Confusion Sprung* (see General Studies).

Rawson, Claude. "Rage and Raillery and Swift: The Case of *Cadenus and Vanessa*", *Connaissance et Création au Siècle des Lumières: Mélanges Michel Baridon*, ed. F. Ogée and others. Dijon: Editions Universitaires de Dijon, 1993, pp. 19–35 (special number of *Interfaces*).

Schakel, Peter J. *The Poetry of Jonathan Swift*. Madison: University of Wisconsin Press, 1978.

Scouten, Arthur H., and Hume, Robert D. "Pope and Swift: Text and Interpretation of Swift's Verses on His Death", *Philological Quarterly*, 52 (1973), 205–31.

Vieth, David M., ed. *Essential Articles for the Study of Swift's Poetry*. Hamden, CT: Archon, 1984.

Wimsatt, William K., "Rhetoric and Poems: The Example of Swift." In *The Author in His Work*, ed. Louis L. Martz and Aubrey Williams. New Haven: Yale University Press, 1978, pp. 229–44.

Woolley, James D. *Swift's Later Poems: Studies in Circumstances and Texts*, New York: Garland, 1988.

Gulliver's Travels

Brady, Frank, ed. *Twentieth-Century Interpretations of "Gulliver's Travels"*. Englewood Cliffs, NJ: Prentice-Hall, 1968. Mostly brief extracts rather than complete essays.

Carnochan, W.B. *Lemuel Gulliver's Mirror for Man*. Berkeley: University of California Press, 1968.

Case, Arthur E. *Four Essays on "Gulliver's Travels"*. Princeton: Princeton University Press, 1945.

Crane, R.S. "The Houyhnhnms, the Yahoos, and the History of Ideas." In *Reason and the Imagination: Studies in the History of Ideas, 1600–1800*, edited by J.A. Mazzeo. New York: Columbia University Press, 1962. Reprinted in Crane's *The Idea of the Humanities and Other Essays*. 2 vols. Chicago: University of Chicago Press, 1967. Contains important information crucial to a proper understanding of the Fourth Book.

Eddy, W.A. *"Gulliver's Travels": Critical Study*. Princeton: Princeton University Press, 1923. Despite its title, concerned mainly with sources.

Elliott, Robert C. *The Power of Satire: Magic, Ritual, Art*. Princeton: Princeton University Press, 1960. A brilliant book in general, with a very good study of *Gulliver* in particular.

Elliott, Robert C. *The Shape of Utopia*. Chicago: University of Chicago Press, 1970.

Erskine-Hill, Howard. *Gulliver's Travels*. Cambridge: Cambridge University Press, 1993.

Foster, Milton P., ed. *A Casebook on Gulliver among the Houyhnhnms*. New York: Crowell, 1961. An important collection of essays on the interpretation of the Fourth Book.

Goldgar, Bertrand A. *Walpole and the Wits: The Relation of Politics to Literature, 1722–1742*. Lincoln: University of Nebraska Press, 1976.

Gravil, Richard, ed. *"Gulliver's Travels": A Casebook*. London: Macmillan, 1974. Collection of essays that usefully supplements Milton P. Foster, 1961.

Hammond, Brean. *Gulliver's Travels*. Open Guides, Milton Keynes and Philadelphia, 1988.

Keener, Frederick M. *The Chain of Becoming: The Philosophical Tale, the Novel, and a Neglected Realism of the Enlightenment*. New York: Columbia University Press, 1983.

Kenner, Hugh. *The Counterfeiters: An Historical Comedy*. Baltimore and London: Johns Hopkins University Press, 1985 (first published 1968 by Indiana University Press).

Lock, F.P. *The Politics of "Gulliver's Travels"*. Oxford: Clarendon Press, 1980.

Mezciems, Jenny. "Gulliver and other Heroes", in *The Art of Jonathan Swift*, ed. Probyn (see Collections of Essays), pp. 189–208.

Mezciems, Jenny. "Swift's Praise of Gulliver: Some Renaissance Background to the *Travels*", in *The Character of Swift's Satire*, ed. Rawson (see Collections of Essays).

Mezciems, Jenny. " 'Tis not to divert the Reader': Moral and Literary Determinants in Some Early Travel Narratives." *Prose Studies* 5 (1982): 1–19; also in *The Art of Travel: Essays on Travel Writing*, edited by Philip Dodd. London: Frank Cass, 1982.

Mezciems, Jenny. "Utopia and 'the Thing which is not': More, Swift, and other Lying Idealists." *University of Toronto Quarterly* 52 (1982): 40–62.

Orwell, George. "Politics vs. Literature: An Examination of Gulliver's Travels (1946)." In *Collected Essays, Journalism, and Letters of George Orwell*, edited by Sonia Orwell and Ian Angus. Vol. 4, London: Secker and Warburg, 1968. Included in several collections of essays on Swift: see above.

Rawson, Claude. *Gulliver and the Gentle Reader* (see General Studies).

Rawson, Claude. "Gulliver, Marlow and the Flat-Nosed People: Colonial Oppression and Race in Satire and Fiction", in *Order from Confusion Sprung* (see General Studies).

Rawson, Claude. " 'Indians' and Irish" (see Politics and the Church).

Rielly, Edward J., ed. *Approaches to Teaching Gulliver's Travels*. New York: Modern Language Association of America, 1988.

Smith, Frederik N., ed. *The Genres of Gulliver's Travels*, Newark, DE: University of Delaware Press, and London: Associated University Presses, 1990 (includes essays by Paul K. Alkon, Louise K. Barnett, J. Paul Hunter, Maximillian E. Novak, William Bowman Piper, and others).

Tippett, Brian. *Gulliver's Travels*. The Critics Debate. Humanities Press. Atlantic Highlands, NJ, 1989.

Traugott, John. "A Voyage to Nowhere with Thomas More and Jonathan Swift: *Utopia* and *The Voyage to the Houyhnhnms*", *Sewanee Review*, 69 (1961), 534–65.
Traugott, John. "The Yahoo in the Doll's House: *Gulliver's Travels* the Children's Classic", in *English Satire and the Satiric Tradition*, ed. Rawson (see Collections of Essays).